How to Use the Internet

Eighth Edition

Rogers Cadenhead

201 W. 103rd Street
Indianapolis, Indiana 46290

How to Use the Internet

International Standard Book Number: 0-7897-2813-3

Library of Congress Catalog Card Number: 2002107980

Printed in the United States of America

First Printing: September 2002

05 04 03 02 4 3 2 1

Trademarks

All terms mentioned in this book that are known to be trademarks or service marks have been appropriately capitalized. Que cannot attest to the accuracy of this information. Use of a term in this book should not be regarded as affecting the validity of any trademark or service mark.

Warning and Disclaimer

Every effort has been made to make this book as complete and as accurate as possible, but no warranty or fitness is implied. The information provided is on an "as is" basis. The author and the publisher shall have neither liability nor responsibility to any person or entity with respect to any loss or damages arising from the information contained in this book.

Associate Publisher
Greg Wiegand

Acquisitions Editor
Stephanie J. McComb

Development Editor
Kate Shoup Welsh

Managing Editor
Thomas F. Hayes

Project Editor
Carol Bowers

Production Editor
Maribeth Echard

Indexer
Chris Barrick

Technical Editor
Jim Grey

Team Coordinator
Sharry Lee Gregory

Interior Designer
Anne Jones

Cover Designer
Anne Jones

Page Layout
Stacey Richwine-DeRome

Contents at a Glance

Contents

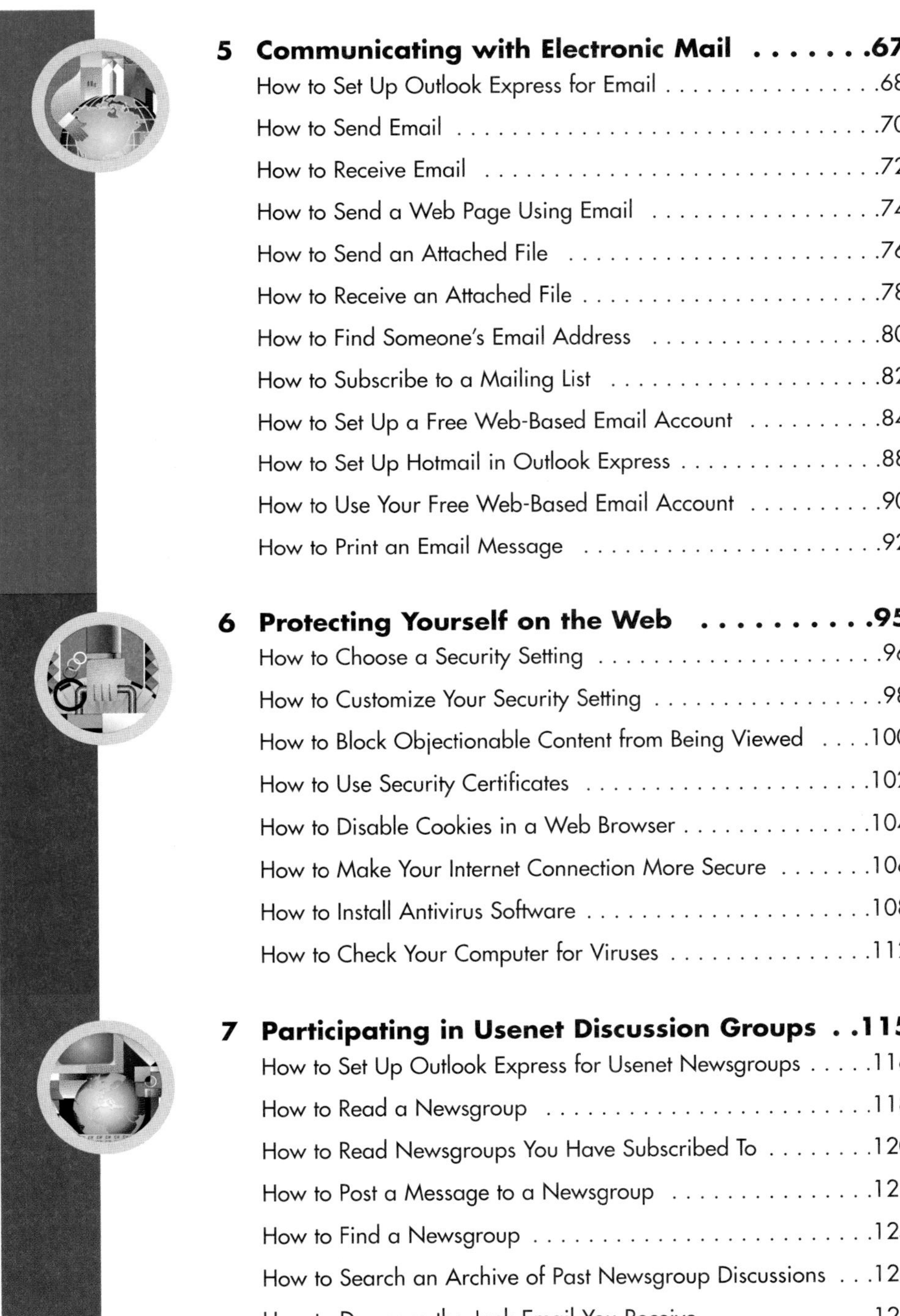

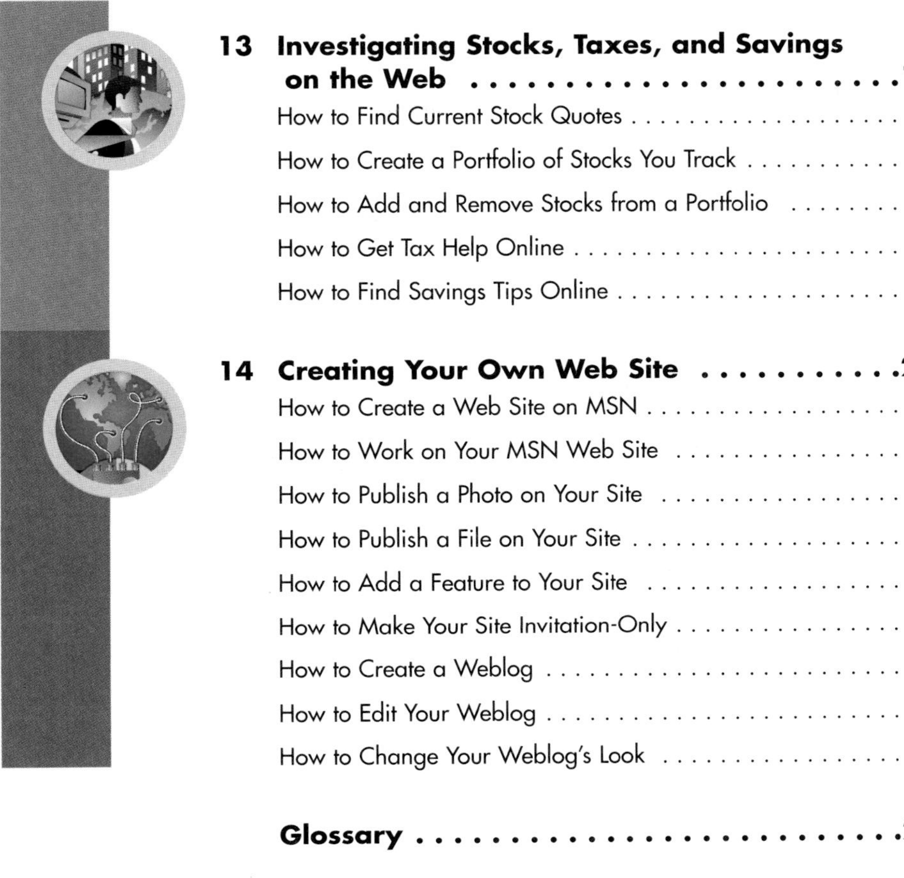

About the Author

Rogers Cadenhead is the author of 15 books on Internet-related topics, including *Sams Teach Yourself Java 2 in 21 Days, 3rd Edition* and *Sams Teach Yourself Microsoft FrontPage 2002 in 24 Hours*. He's also a Web publisher whose sites receive 7.3 million visits a year. To contact Cadenhead about this book, visit the World Wide Web site `http://www.cadenhead.info/internet2003/`.

Dedication

To Rita Craker (a.k.a. "Nana") and Mary Cadenhead (a.k.a. "Mimi"). Everyone should have grandmothers as loving, supportive, and fun to be around as these two. I love them dearly, even though they didn't get me the pony I really, really wanted when I was five. —Rogers

Acknowledgments

Thanks to the team at Que who made numerous contributions to this book while letting me hog the credit: Stephanie McComb, Sharry Lee Gregory, Carol Bowers, Diana Wodtke, Maribeth Echard, Jim Grey, and Kate Welsh.

Thanks to Neil Salkind and Jessica Richards at the Studio B agency, who worked hard on my behalf in regard to this title and many others.

Thanks to my wife, M.C., and my sons Max, Eli, and Sam—who make numerous contributions to my life.

And thanks to the Foo Fighters—who rock.

Tell Us What You Think!

As the reader of this book, *you* are our most important critic and commentator. We value your opinion and want to know what we're doing right, what we could do better, what areas you'd like to see us publish in, and any other words of wisdom you're willing to pass our way.

As an executive editor for Que, I welcome your comments. You can email or write me directly to let me know what you did or didn't like about this book—as well as what we can do to make our books better.

Please note that I cannot help you with technical problems related to the topic of this book. We do have a User Services group, however, where I will forward specific technical questions related to the book.

When you write, please be sure to include this book's title and author as well as your name, email address, and phone number. I will carefully review your comments and share them with the author and editors who worked on the book.

Email: `feedback@quepublishing.com`

Mail: Greg Wiegand
Executive Editor
Que
201 West 103rd Street
Indianapolis, IN 46290 USA

For more information about this book or another Que title, visit our Web site at `www.quepublishing.com`. Type the ISBN (excluding hyphens) or the title of a book in the Search field to find the page you're looking for.

The Complete Visual Reference

Each chapter of this book is made up of a series of short, instructional tasks, designed to help you understand all the information that you need to get the most out of your computer hardware and software.

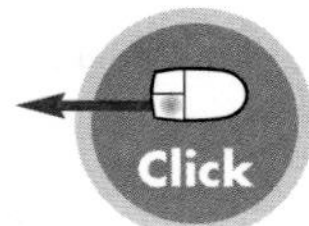

Click: Click the left mouse button once.

Double-click: Click the left mouse button twice in rapid succession.

Right-click: Click the right mouse button once.

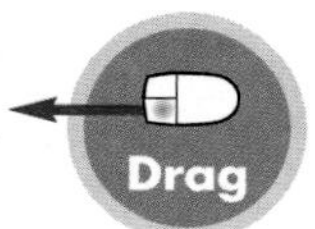

Drag: Click and hold the left mouse button, position the mouse pointer, and release.

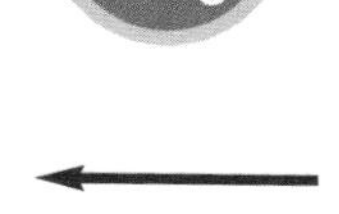

Pointer Arrow: Highlights an item on the screen you need to point to or focus on in the step or task.

Selection: Highlights the area onscreen discussed in the step or task.

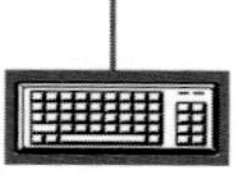

Type: Click once where indicated and begin typing to enter your text or data.

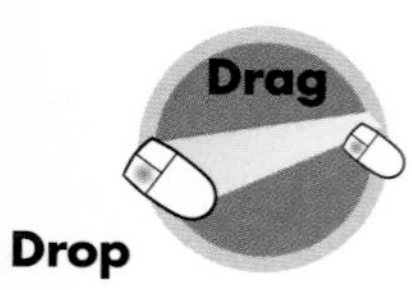

Drag and Drop: Point to the starting place or object. Hold down the mouse button (right or left per instructions), move the mouse to the new location, and then release the button.

Each task includes a series of easy-to-understand steps designed to guide you through the procedure.

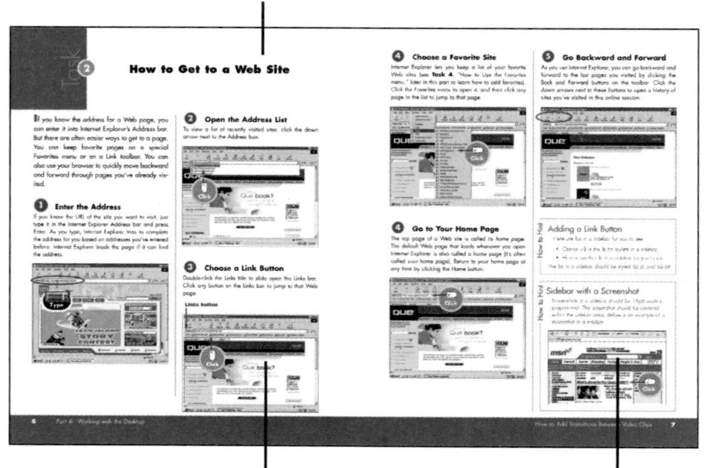

Each step is fully illustrated to show you how it looks onscreen.

Extra hints that tell you how to accomplish a goal are provided in most tasks.

Key icons: Clearly indicate which key combinations to use.

Menus and items you click are shown in **bold**. Words in *italic* are defined in more detail in the glossary. Information you type is in a `special font`.

Introduction

Even if you're not into computers, you have probably heard many great things about what the Internet can be used for, like these:

- Sending and receiving electronic mail (email)
- Surfing the World Wide Web
- Shopping online
- Talking in a chat room
- Sending instant messages
- Playing MP3 music

You have a computer that can handle each of these things and a thousand other useful and fun features of the Internet. What you don't have, though, is time to learn all this stuff. Reasons *not* to use the Internet easily come to mind:

Computers are complicated. Software takes hard work to figure out. No one can get hooked up to the Internet without years of diligent study or the help of a teenager. It's like the VCR clock problem all over again—wading through a confusing instruction manual is far worse than looking at a light that blinks `12:00` *over and over for the next 15–20 years.*

Right?

Put those thoughts out of your head. *How to Use the Internet* shows you how quickly you can get connected and make use of the Internet's most popular services. Whether you're a computer novice or a longtime veteran, the visual, step-by-step instructions in this book demonstrate exactly how to use the Internet on your computer.

The *How to Use* series of books is for people who want to accomplish specific things without spending time learning technical jargon and other computer gobbledygook.

You can read this book from cover to cover, or you can use it to look up something when you're ready to try out that aspect of the Internet. Want to buy a book or participate in an online auction? Turn to Part 12, "Shopping on the Internet." Ready to do a little job hunting in one of the Internet employment sites you heard about on the news? Turn to Part 4, Task 8, "How to Find a Job on the Web."

How to Use the Internet focuses on the information you need to get going. Most tasks are broken down into seven or fewer steps so that you can get something done right away. When you need to know a little extra, the How-To Hints provide tips that make your Internet experience more complete.

Most of the software you use in this book is on your computer already as part of your Windows operating system. Any other software you need can be set up at no cost using the Internet—we'll show you how to do that, too.

The only software you need to get started is one of the later versions of the Windows operating system (we're using the latest and greatest, Windows XP) and the World Wide Web browser that comes with the operating system, Internet Explorer 4 or higher. Featured in this book's figures is Internet Explorer 6.

This book is also suitable for readers using Windows 98, Windows Me, and Windows 2000. Although Windows XP looks different from any other version of Windows, the software you use in this book—such as Internet Explorer, Outlook Express, and AOL—works the same in each operating system.

How to Use the Internet is the instruction manual for everything you've wanted to do on the Internet. With this book at your side, you'll be coming up with reasons to use the Internet instead of convincing yourself that you can't surf the Web:

Computers aren't so complicated. Forget those years of study—I'd rather golf. Any teenager who owes me a favor can tend the garden—there are weeds out there big enough to have their own ZIP Codes!

As for your VCR clock, sorry. Ours has been blinking `12:00` since the Reagan years.

Task

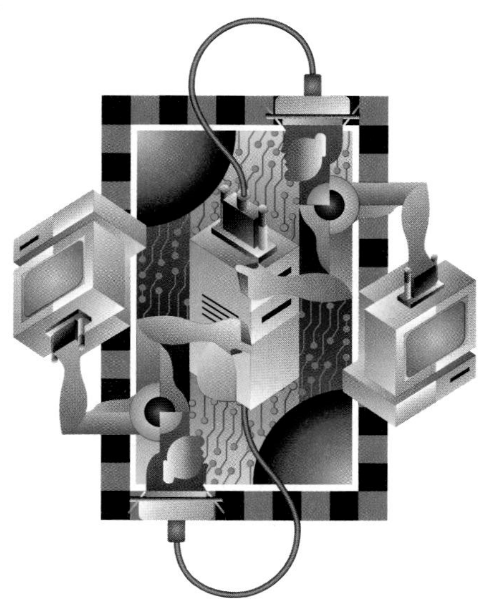

1

Getting Connected for the First Time

Every day, millions of people use a worldwide network of computers called the *Internet*. This network, once the province of scholars, students, and the military, has changed the way many of us communicate, shop, work, and play.

The Windows operating system includes software to connect to the Internet and its most popular services. One of these services is the *World Wide Web*. Exploring the Web requires software called a *Web browser*; one of the most popular browsers is installed along with Windows: Microsoft Internet Explorer.

Before you can use the Web or any other Internet service, you must establish a connection between your computer and the Internet. That connection will be used automatically by each program designed to send and receive information using the Internet.

How to Set Up an Internet Connection

Before you can connect to the Internet, you must have an account with an *Internet service provider* (also called an *ISP*). An ISP offers access to the Internet through your computer's modem. Most cities have local companies that offer Internet service. To find them, look in the Yellow Pages under "Internet" or "Internet Services." These companies often offer a local access number to call, meaning that when your computer dials in to the Internet, no long-distance fees apply. Windows also can help you find an ISP and set up a connection. To do this, skip ahead to Task 2, "How to Choose an Internet Service Provider."

1 Open the Control Panel

To begin setting up a new Internet connection, click the **Start** button and choose **Control Panel**. The **Control Panel** window opens.

2 Choose a Category

The **Control Panel** window displays a list of categories that can be used to set up your computer and change existing settings. Click the **Network and Internet Connections** link. The **Network and Internet Connections** window opens.

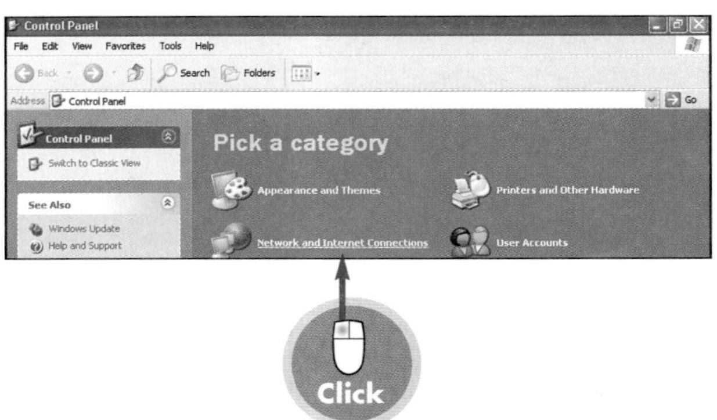

3 Begin a New Setup

To set up Internet service for the first time, click the **Set up or change your Internet connection** link. The **Internet Properties** dialog box opens.

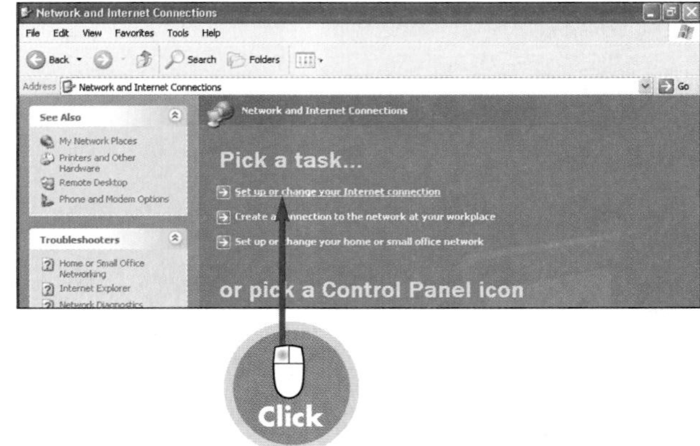

4 Set Up a Connection

When the **Internet Properties** dialog box opens, the **Connections** tab is displayed on top. To start a wizard that helps you create a new Internet connection, click the **Setup** button. The **New Connection Wizard** appears.

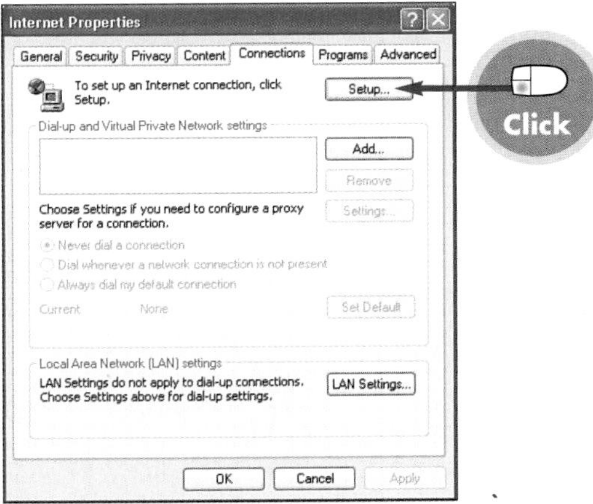

5 Start the Wizard

Wizards are programs that make complex tasks easier by breaking them down into a series of simple questions for which you select responses. The **New Connection Wizard** helps you connect to the Internet and other networks. Click **Next** to begin.

6 Choose a Connection Type

This wizard can be used for several kinds of network connections. For the Internet, choose the **Connect to the Internet** option and click **Next** to continue.

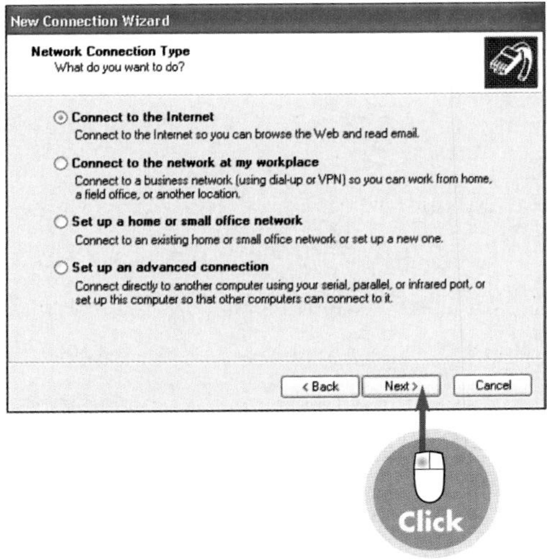

How to Hint

Choosing an ISP

In addition to the local companies listed in your Yellow Pages, there are several dozen national ISPs. Some of the most popular are America Online, AT&T WorldNet, BellSouth, and EarthLink. Using America Online as your Internet service provider is covered in Part 10, "Using America Online's Internet Capabilities." To find out how to join the others, call their customer-service numbers or use someone else's computer to visit their Web sites:

- **AT&T WorldNet**: Call (800) 967-5363 or visit `http://www.att.net`
- **BellSouth**: Call (800) 436-8638 or visit `http://www.bellsouth.net`
- **EarthLink**: Call (800) 395-8425 or visit `http://www.earthlink.net`

After you have subscribed to an ISP and received an access number, username, and password, you can begin this task and set up an Internet connection on your computer.

7 Choose a Provider

The wizard asks whether you need help choosing an ISP. Because you already have subscribed to one, choose the **Set up my connection manually** option and click **Next**.

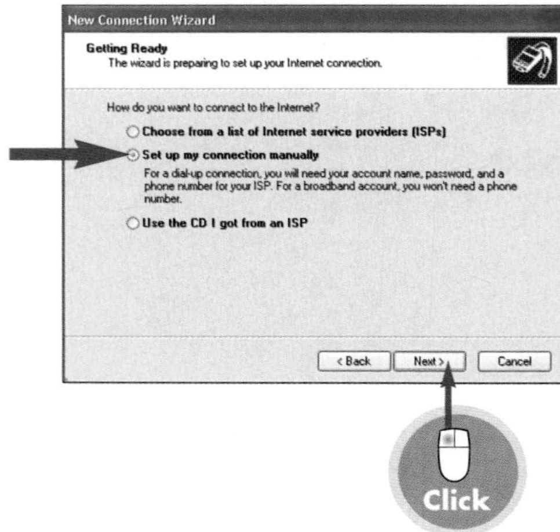

8 Choose a Connection Type

Choose the option that describes your Internet connection. If you don't know, you're probably using a *dial-up connection* and should choose **Connect using a dial-up modem**. After you choose the appropriate option for your computer, click **Next**.

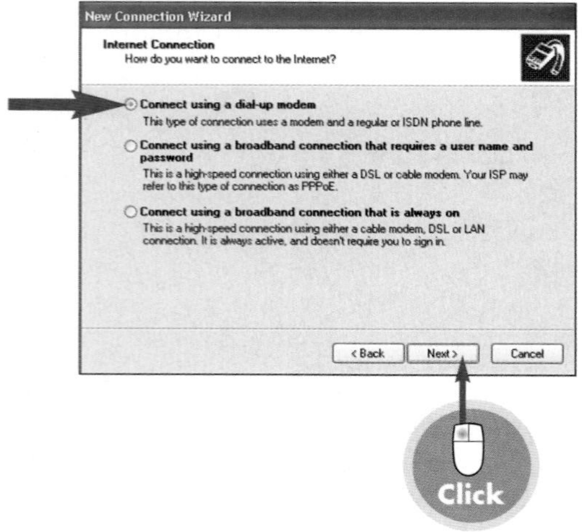

9 Name the Connection

Type the name of your ISP in the **ISP Name** text box (the name *BellSouth.Net* was used in this example) and click **Next** to continue.

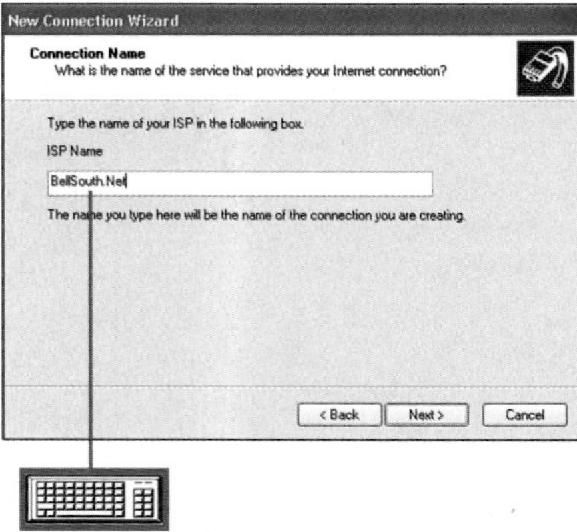

10 Enter Your Access Number

Your ISP should have provided the phone number you need to connect to the Internet. Type the access number in the **Phone number** text box, including an area code if it is required. If you have to dial long distance to connect (which can be extremely expensive), include a **1** before the access number. Click **Next** to continue.

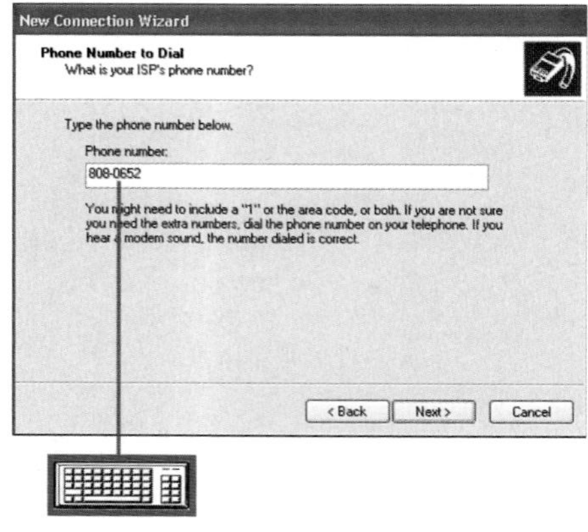

11 Connect to the Internet

Your ISP also should have provided a username and password for your account. Type your username in the **User name** text box and your password in the **Password** and **Confirm Password** boxes. If you are setting up your computer's main (or only) Internet connection, enable the **Make this the default Internet connection** check box. Don't click **Next** yet.

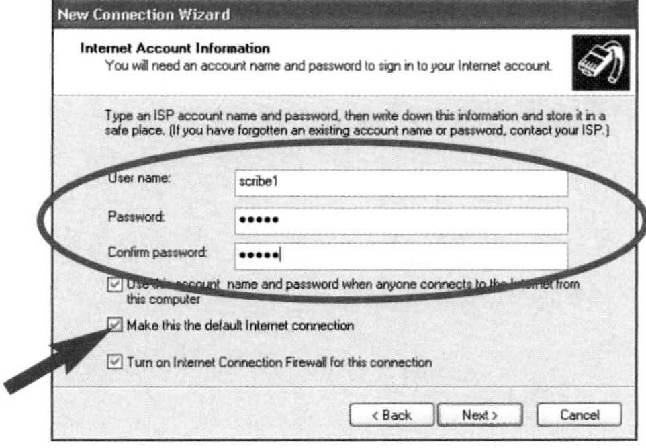

12 Enable a Firewall

Windows XP can make your Internet connection safer by using a *firewall*—a security measure described in detail in Part 6, Task 6, "How to Make Your Internet Connection More Secure." To turn this feature on, enable the **Turn on Internet Connection Firewall for this connection** check box. Click **Next** to continue.

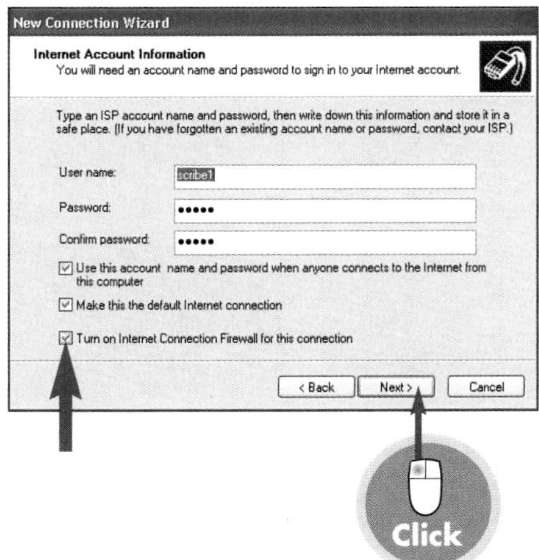

13 Finish the Wizard

The **New Connection Wizard** describes your new Internet connection; click **Finish** to set it up. You'll learn how to connect to the Internet and begin using it in Task 3, "How to Connect to the Internet."

How to Hint

Choosing an Internet Subscription

Most national Internet service providers offer two kinds of monthly subscriptions, depending on how much you want to use the service.

One subscription plan limits the number of hours you can use the service per month. If you exceed that number, you must pay an extra per-hour fee. For example, AT&T WorldNet currently offers 150 hours a month for $16.95 and 99 cents for each extra hour.

A more expensive subscription plan offers unlimited hours, so you never pay a per-hour cost. AT&T WorldNet's unlimited plan sells for $21.95 per month.

Although 150 hours is a lot—around five hours a day—it can be expensive to use an Internet service with per-hour charges if you forget about the limit.

Installing a Broadband Connection

A broadband Internet connection, which is generally 10–20 times faster than a dial-up connection, uses a cable modem or DSL modem. These high-speed connections usually require special installation—a service provided by an Internet service provider—and cost from $40 to $60 a month.

2 How to Choose an Internet Service Provider

Before you can connect to the Internet, you must obtain an account with an *Internet service provider* (ISP). Windows XP can help you set up an account with one of several national ISPs such as AT&T WorldNet, EarthLink, or Prodigy. To use this feature, you must live in an area where one of these providers offers service. Most cities, suburbs, and large towns fit this description. If you'd like to use an ISP that isn't offered in Windows XP, set up your Internet service using Task 1, "How to Set Up an Internet Connection."

1 Open the Control Panel

To begin choosing an Internet service provider, click the **Start** button and choose **Control Panel**. The **Control Panel** window opens.

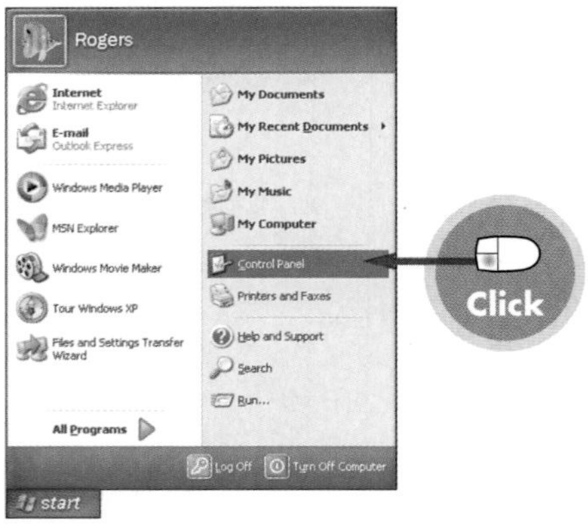

2 Choose a Category

The **Control Panel** window displays a list of categories that can be used to set up your computer and change existing settings. Click the **Network and Internet Connections** link. The **Network and Internet Connections** window opens.

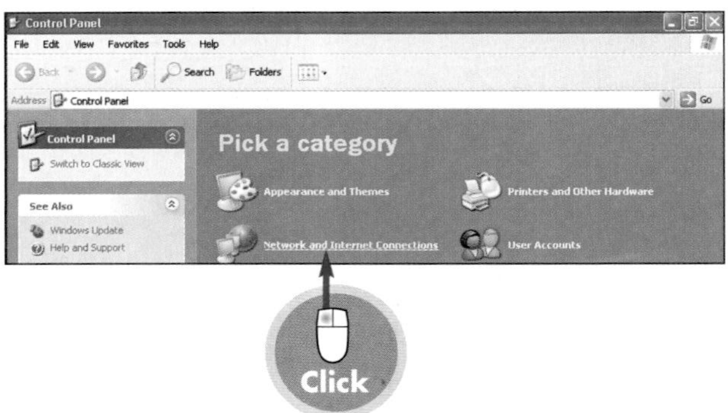

3 Begin a New Setup

To begin setting up Internet service, click the **Set up or change your Internet connection** link. The **Internet Properties** dialog box opens.

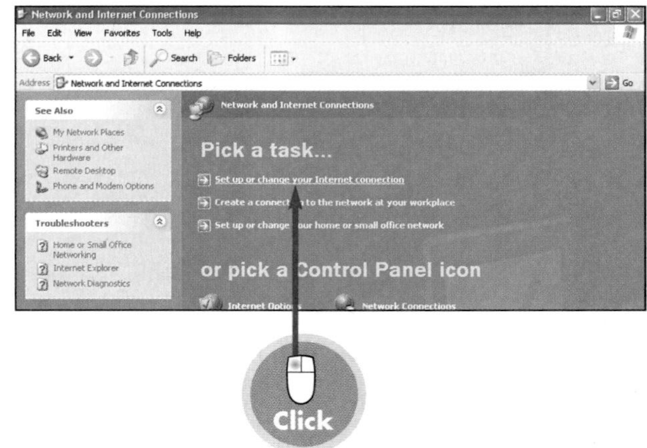

4 Set Up a Connection

The **Connections** tab is displayed on top of the **Internet Properties** dialog box. To start a wizard that helps you find an Internet service provider, click the **Setup** button. The **New Connection Wizard** appears.

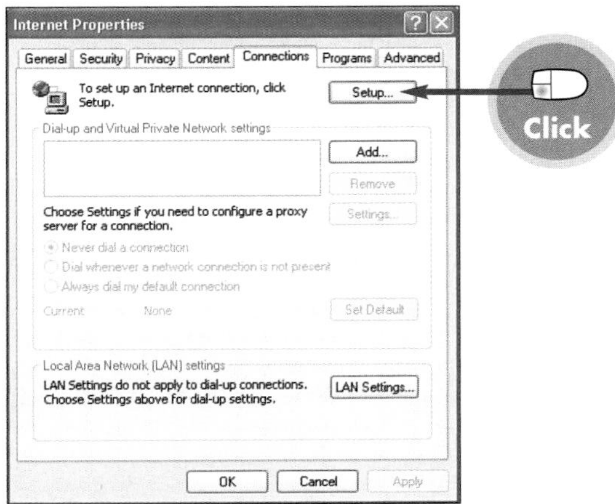

5 Start the Wizard

Wizards are programs that make complex tasks easier by dividing them into a series of simple questions, for which you select responses. The New Connection Wizard helps you connect to the Internet and other networks. Click **Next** to begin.

6 Choose a Connection Type

The New Connection Wizard can be used for several kinds of network connections. Choose the **Connect to the Internet** option and click **Next** to continue.

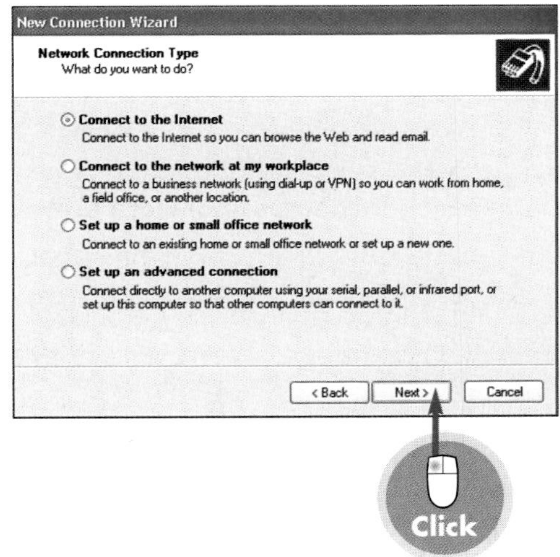

7 Find a Provider

The wizard asks how you want to connect to the Internet. Because you do not yet have an ISP, select the **Choose from a list of Internet service providers (ISPs)** option and click **Next**.

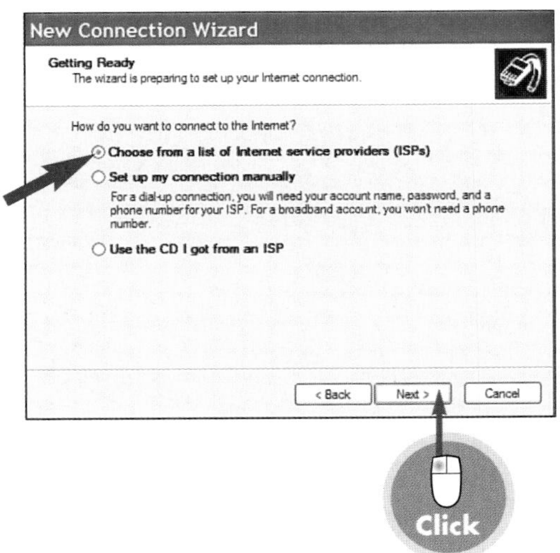

Continued 2

8 Close the Wizard

Because you don't have an account with an ISP at this point, the New Connection Wizard can't finish the job. Choose the **Select from a list of other ISPs** option and click **Finish**. The **Online Services** folder opens.

9 Look for an ISP

The **Online Services** folder enables you to set up an account with MSN or see what other ISPs are available. Double-click the **Refer me to more Internet Service Providers** icon. The Internet Connection Wizard starts.

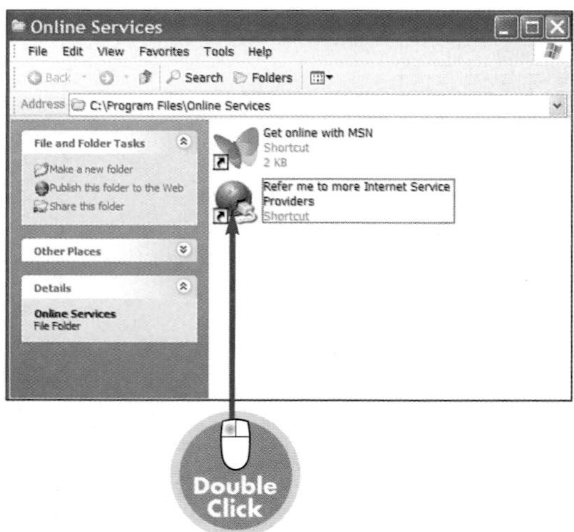

10 Choose an ISP

The Internet Connection Wizard dials a toll-free number to retrieve a list of ISPs you can join. When it's done, click a provider's name to find out more about it in the Provider information box. If you're ready to join one, select its name and click **Next**.

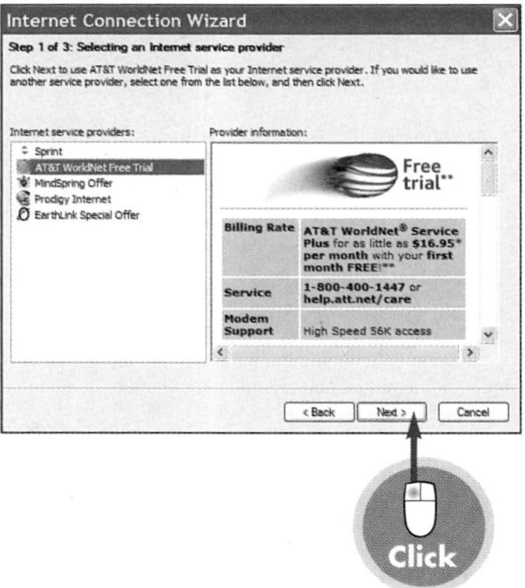

11 Identify Yourself

All ISPs require your name, mailing address, and phone number to join. Type these things in the text fields and click **Next**. The wizard may ask you to select a subscription plan. If so, choose one and click **Next** again.

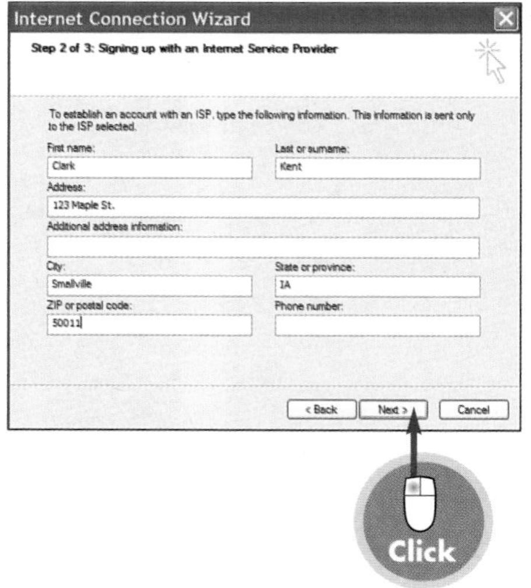

12 Pay the ISP

You must have a credit card to subscribe to an ISP. Type your credit-card information in the text fields and choose the card type in the **Select a method of payment** drop-down box. Click **Next** when you're finished.

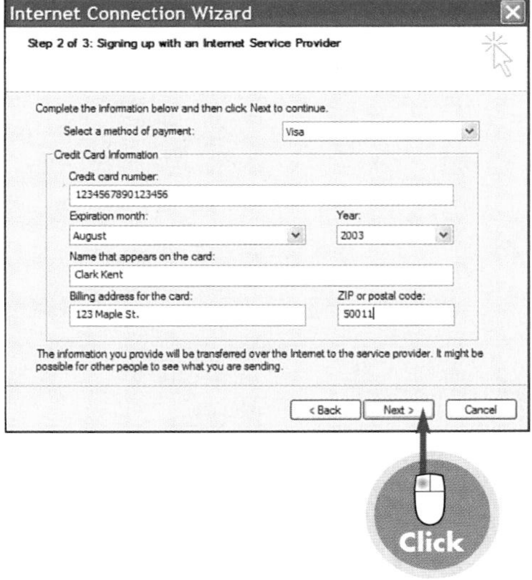

13 Pick a Service Number

In the drop-down box, pick the *access number* (the number your modem will dial to connect to the Internet) that's closest to you. Be warned that if the access number you pick is a long-distance call, you'll run up long-distance charges every time you connect to the Internet. Click **Next**.

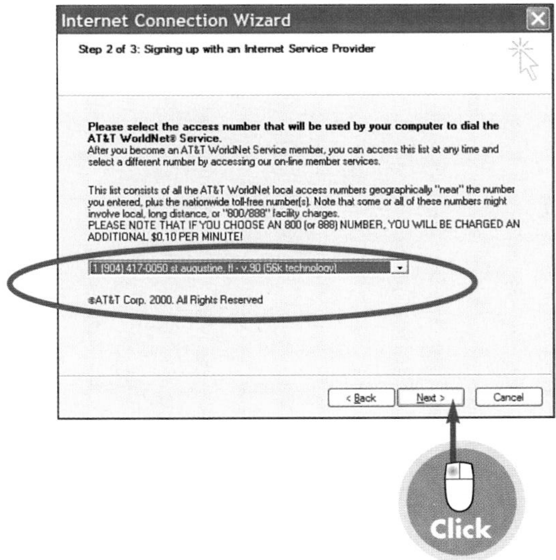

14 Choose an Address

The wizard suggests an email address for you. Use this or type your own in the **E-mail Address** field and click **Next**. If your preferred address is not available, you'll be asked to pick again; do so until you hit upon an available valid address. You will be shown the ISP's terms of service. If you agree to them, choose **I accept the agreement** and then click **Next**.

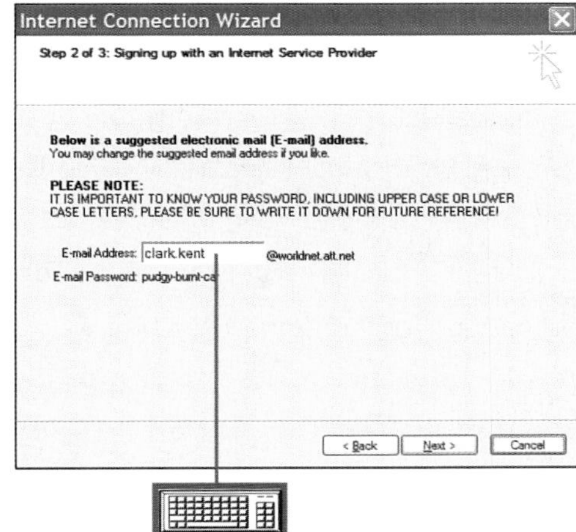

15 Finish the Wizard

After the terms of service, the wizard displays your email address and password. Write these down and click **Next**. Your Internet connection will be set up with your new username and password. You're done; click **Finish**. The next task covers how to begin using your new ISP subscription to access the Internet.

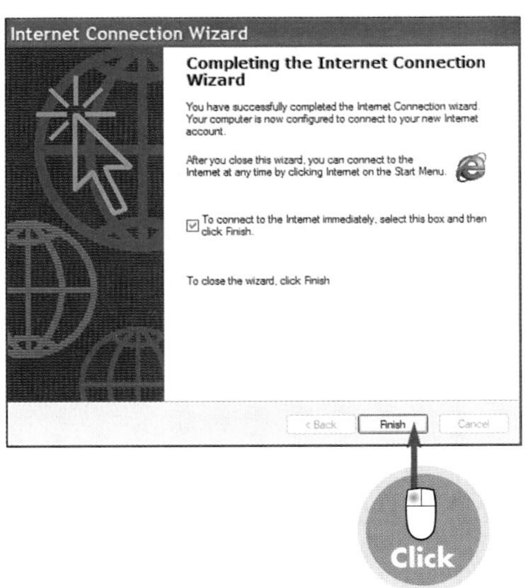

Task 3

How to Connect to the Internet

Before you can surf the World Wide Web, check your email, or do anything else involving the Internet, you must establish a connection between your computer and the Internet. Some programs such as Microsoft Internet Explorer will try to connect to the Internet when you begin using them. Other programs will display an error message if you haven't connected first. This task explains what to do when you see the instruction to "connect to the Internet."

1 List Your Internet Connections

To see what Internet connections are available on your computer, click the **Start** button, choose **Connect To**, and choose **Show all connections**. The **Network Connections** folder opens with the connections you can use.

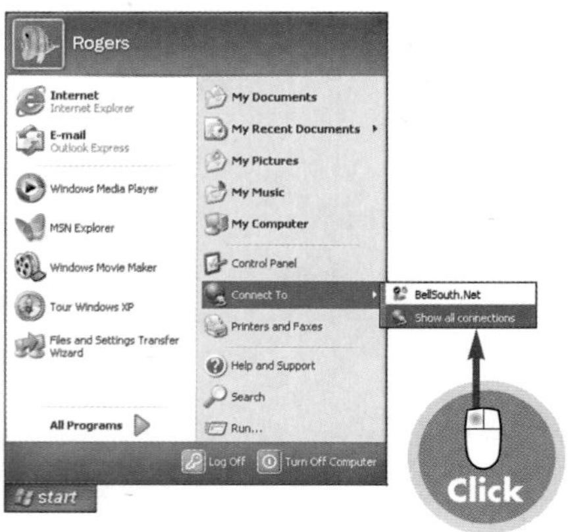

2 Dial Your Access Number

Double-click the icon that represents the Internet connection you want to use. The **Connect** dialog box opens.

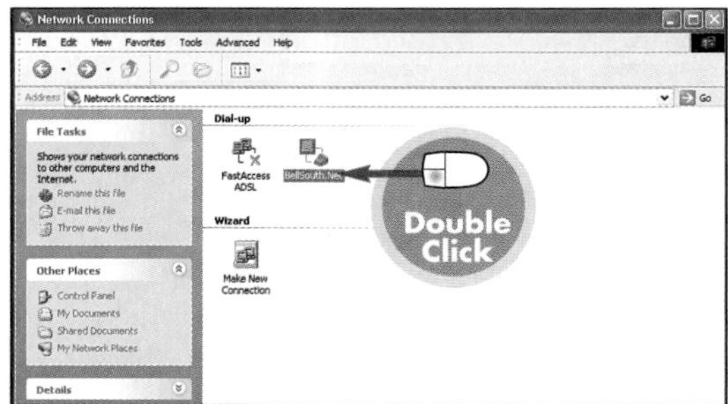

3 Review Your Settings

Make sure that your username and access number are correct, and then click the **Dial** button to make a connection. Note that if you are using a DSL connection, the procedure for connecting is exactly the same as that for a dial-up connection (except that the "access number" isn't really a phone number).

4 Connect to the Internet

If your computer can't connect because of a busy signal or another problem, you'll get the chance to try again or to adjust your Internet settings. When you successfully connect, the **Connecting** dialog box disappears.

5 Check Your Connection Speed

While you're connected, a connection icon appears on your Windows taskbar in the system tray (near the current time). Double-click this icon to open the **Status** dialog box to check the speed of your connection.

6 Stay Connected

In this example, the connection speed is 49.2Kbps. Even if you have a 56Kbps modem, you may connect at slower speeds such as 28Kbps or 35Kbps—the speed depends on phone line quality and other factors. To close the **Status** dialog box and remain connected to the Internet, click the **Close** button.

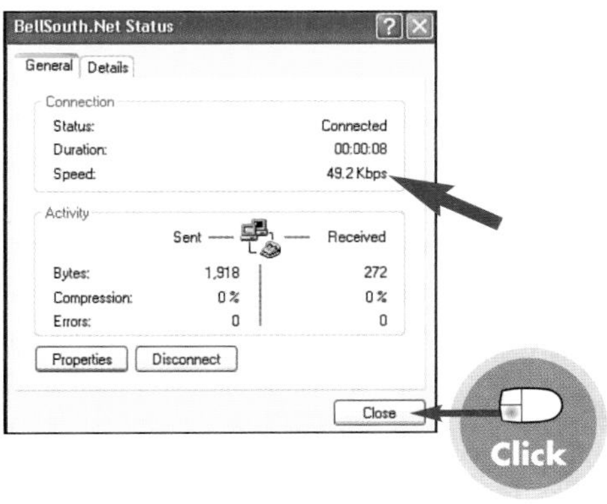

7 Disconnect from the Internet

When you're finished using the Internet and want to disconnect, double-click the connection icon in the system tray. Then, when the **Status** dialog box opens, click the **Disconnect** button.

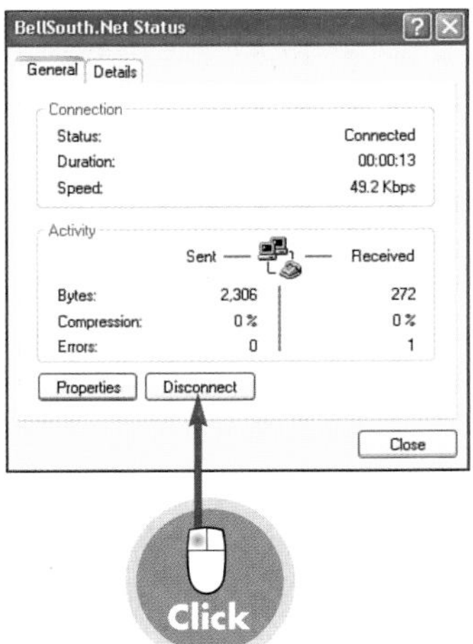

How to Connect to the Internet Through a Proxy Server

If you're using the Internet at work, you may not be able to connect directly to the Internet with your Web browser. For security reasons, a *proxy server* (or *firewall*) is sometimes used as an intermediary between your computer and the Internet. They make it much more difficult for outsiders to access your computer system or your company's files illegally over the Internet. You can set up Internet Explorer to connect through a proxy server when loading Web pages.

1 Start Internet Explorer

Before you can set up Internet Explorer to connect to the Internet through a proxy server, you must have the proxy server's address and port number (check with your network administrator). When you have that information, click the **Start** button and choose **Internet**. The **Internet Explorer** window opens and displays a default Web page.

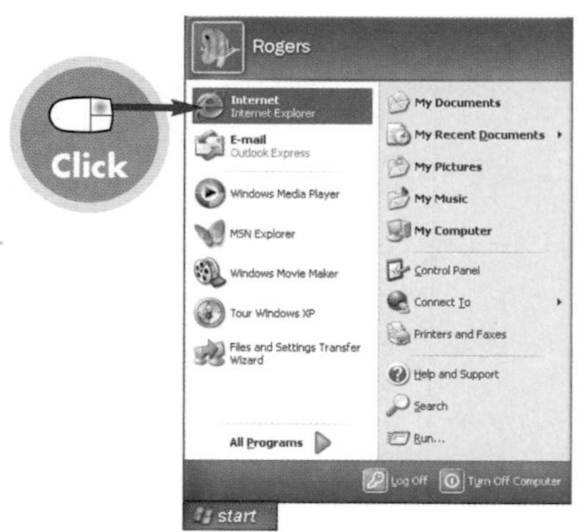

2 Set Your Internet Options

From the **Tools** menu at the top of the **Internet Explorer** window, choose **Internet Options**. The **Internet Options** dialog box opens; you can use this dialog box to customize Internet Explorer.

3 Configure Your Connection

Click the **Connections** tab to bring all the settings related to your Internet connection to the front. This window shows how your browser connects to the Internet.

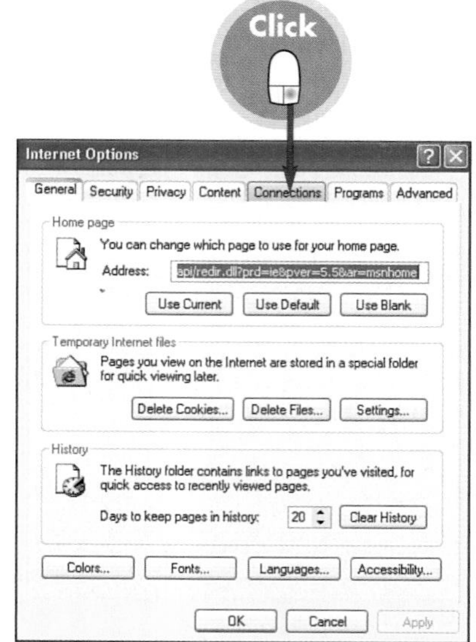

4 Change Dial-Up Settings

A proxy server is associated with a specific Internet connection. Choose the appropriate connection in the **Dial-up settings** list box and click the **Settings** button. The **Settings** dialog box opens.

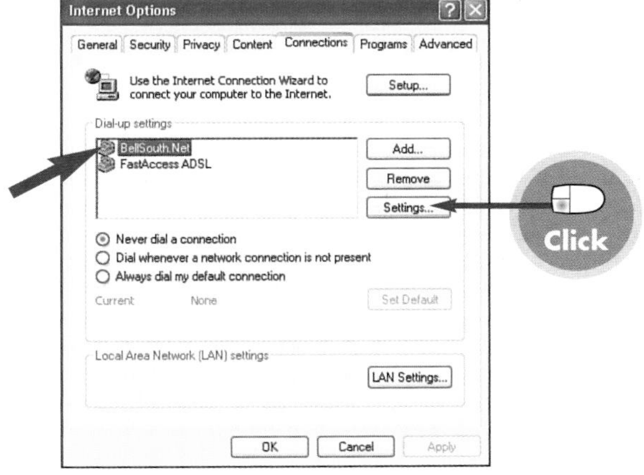

5 Set Up a Proxy Server

Enable the **Use a proxy server** check box and type the address and port number of the server in the **Address** and **Port** text boxes. (You can obtain this information from a computer administrator at the place where you're accessing the Internet.)

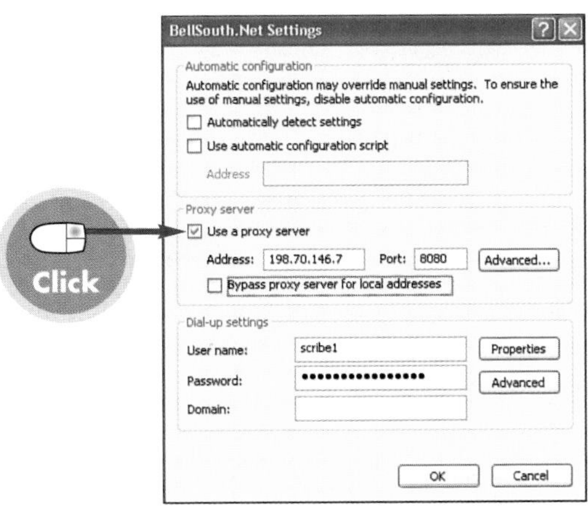

6 Save the New Settings

Click the **OK** button to save your new Internet Explorer settings and close the dialog box, and then click **OK** to close the **Internet Settings** dialog box. (The **Apply** button also saves your settings, but it doesn't close the dialog box.) After you save the settings, all attempts to connect to Web pages with your browser will now be routed through the proxy server.

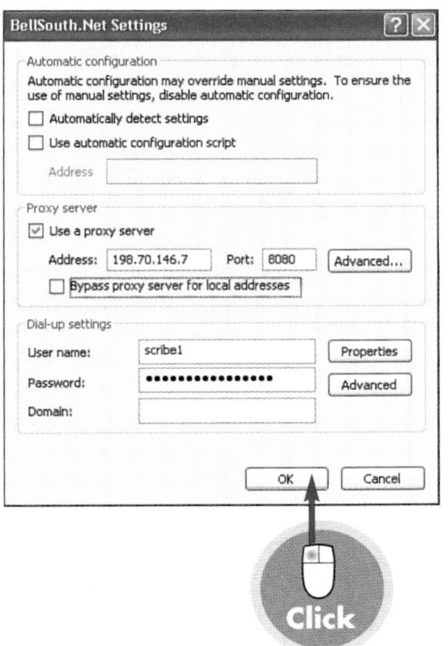

How to Hint

Bypassing the Proxy Server

If you're using a proxy server in a corporate setting, you might not need it when you're visiting Web pages on your company's intranet. If so, you can bypass the proxy server for those pages. In the **Settings** dialog box for the connection you're setting up (shown in Step 5 of this task), enable the **Bypass proxy server for local addresses** check box.

Task 5

How to Load a Web Page

After you connect to the Internet, you are ready to use Internet Explorer, the World Wide Web browsing software included with Windows. If you're not already connected to the Internet when you run Internet Explorer, Windows gives you the opportunity to establish a connection. You'll learn more about the Web in Part 2, "Browsing the World Wide Web."

1 Run Internet Explorer

To run Internet Explorer and open a Web page, click the **Start** button and choose **Internet**. The browser opens and displays a starting page. This page is called the browser's *home page*, and it can be set to any page on the Internet or your own computer.

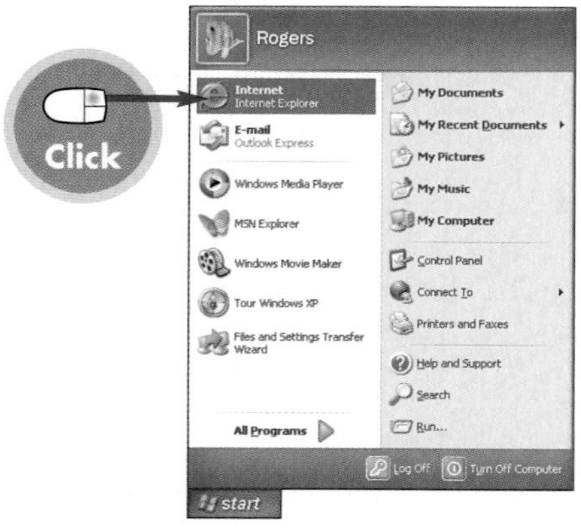

2 Explore the Browser

The Internet Explorer window includes a menu bar, toolbar buttons along the top edge of the window, and an Address bar. You'll use all three as you visit different World Wide Web sites. Click the **Search** button in the toolbar at the top of the screen to open a pane from which you can search the Web.

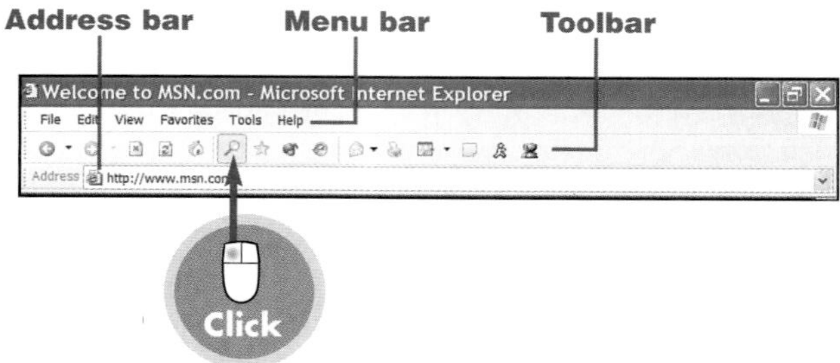

3 Search the Web

Internet Explorer works with MSN's *search engine*, a database containing the text of millions of Web pages. You use a search engine to find Web pages that contain text such as a phrase or company name. Type the text you want to look for and click the **Search** button.

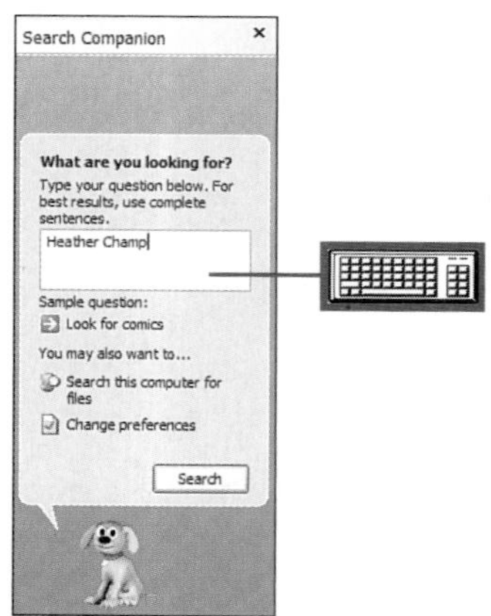

④ View Search Results

The results of your search are presented as a list of Web-page titles and descriptions on the right side of the window. Each of these results is a *hyperlink*—text or a graphic you can click to load a new page in your browser. Click one of these hyperlinks to open the linked page.

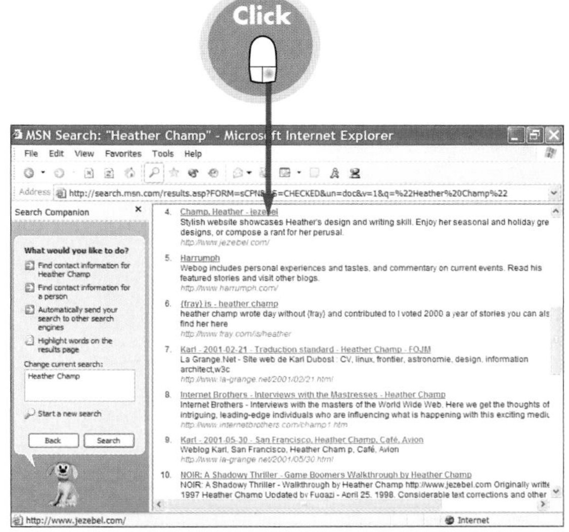

⑤ Load a Web Page

The Web page associated with the hyperlink is loaded in the window to the right of the search-results list. Click the **Search** button along the top of the Internet Explorer window to close the search pane so that the Web page you've loaded can take up the entire window.

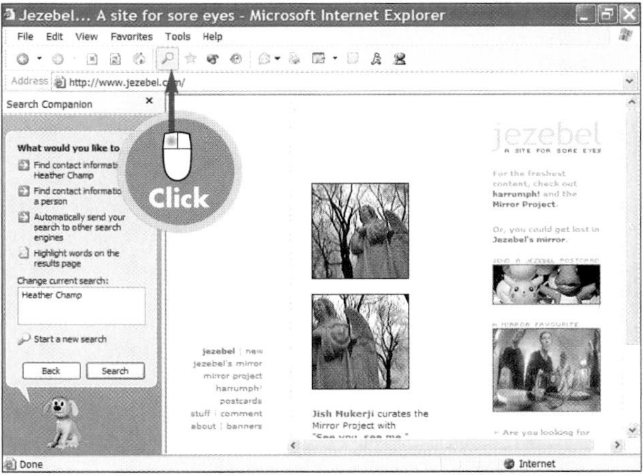

⑥ View a Page's Address

Every Web page has a unique address called a *uniform resource locator* (or *URL*), which is displayed in the Address bar at the top of the Internet Explorer window. You can type URLs into the Address bar to load pages in the browser. For example, type `http://www.yahoo.com` in the **Address bar** and press **Enter** to visit the Yahoo! Web site.

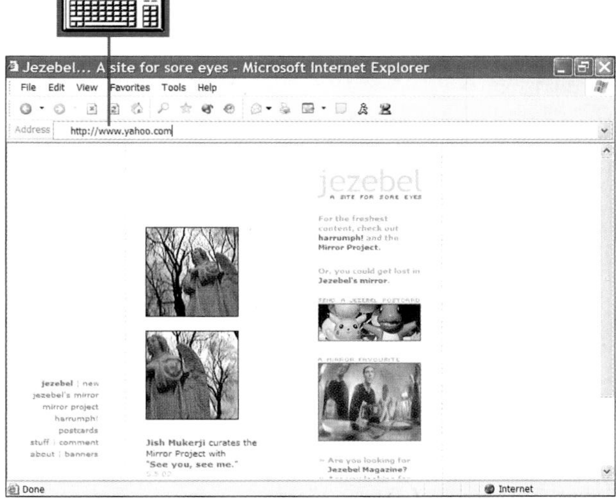

How to Hint

Returning to Your Home Page

The first page your Web browser displays when you open the program is its **home page**. Click the browser's **Home** button (in the toolbar at the top of the window) at any time to return to this page.

Visiting an Interesting Site

If you're curious about Heather Champ, the person I used MSN's search engine to find in this task, she's a talented Web designer and writer whose sites include Jezebel, Harrumph!, and the Mirror Project. To visit her personal Web site and see some of her work, type `http://www.jezebel.com` in Internet Explorer's **Address bar** and press **Enter**.

Task

2

Browsing the World Wide Web

Although the Internet dates back to 1969, for most of its existence the network had been used primarily by scholars, students, and the U.S. military.

This changed with the popularization of a new Internet information service: the World Wide Web. The Web, which was invented by Tim Berners-Lee of the European Laboratory for Particle Physics in 1989, was designed to be an easy way to publish and share information. It also became the simplest way for millions of people to receive information over the Internet.

The World Wide Web uses *hypertext*—a way of publishing information so that documents can be linked to relevant places in other documents. Everything that's on the Web can be connected together, creating the largest database of knowledge in human history.

A *Web browser* such as Internet Explorer enables you to visit sites on the Web.

How to Use a Web Site

The easiest way to navigate the World Wide Web is to use *hyperlinks*—text or images on a Web page that can be clicked to load another document in your browser. Hyperlinks can connect to anything on the Web, such as pages, graphics files, and programs you can download. Although Internet Explorer 6 has a toolbar with useful buttons that you can use as you're visiting Web pages, you'll likely use hyperlinks most often to move from one Web page to another.

1 Load Internet Explorer

To run Internet Explorer, click the **Start** button and choose **Internet**. When started, the first Web page that Internet Explorer loads is its *home page*—often a page on MSN or one hosted by your computer's manufacturer. Click the **Home** button in Internet Explorer to go to your browser's home page.

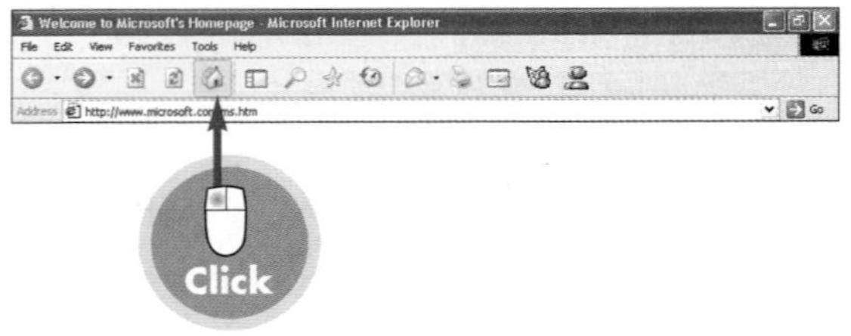

2 Click a Hyperlink

Web pages often contain hyperlinks that make it easy to visit other pages. Your mouse pointer changes to a hand when it's over a hyperlink. Click a hyperlink to load the Web page or other document associated with the link.

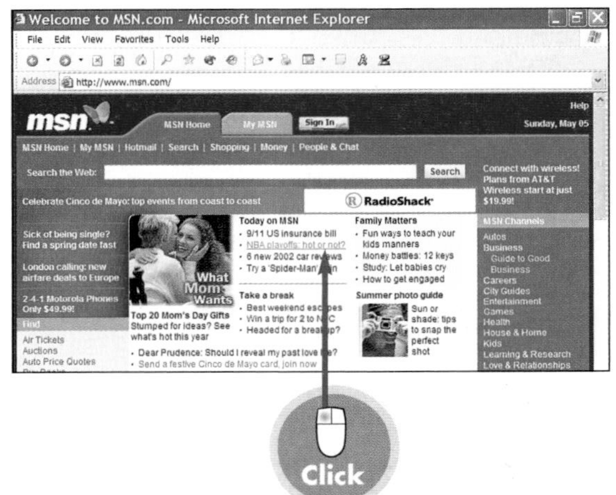

3 Go Back to the Last Page

If you have viewed multiple Web pages, you can click the **Back** button on the Internet Explorer toolbar to return to the previous page that was displayed in your browser.

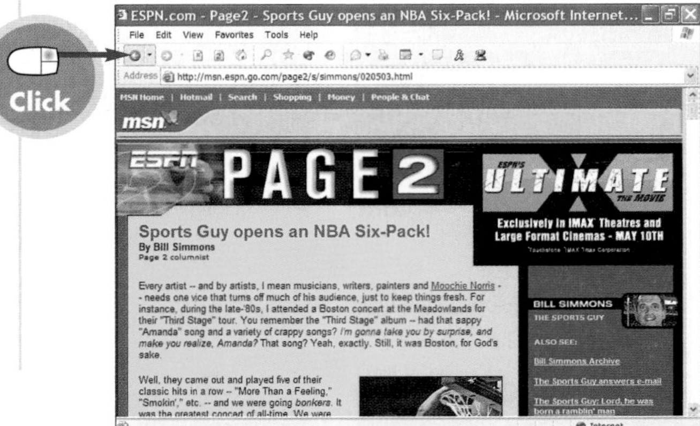

4 Move Forward Again

After you have clicked the Back button, you can click the **Forward** button on the toolbar to see the page you displayed before clicking **Back**. Click the **Back** and **Forward** buttons to cycle through all the pages you've looked at while Internet Explorer has been running.

5 Reload the Current Page

Click the **Refresh** button on the toolbar to reload the current page. When Web pages are updated frequently, you can click **Refresh** to make sure that you are viewing the most current version of a page. This is especially useful on news and financial sites, which are often updated several times an hour.

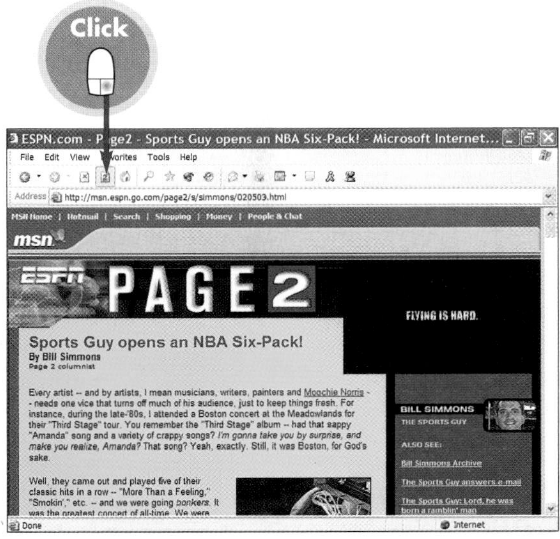

6 Stop Loading a Page

If you decide not to wait for a Web page to finish loading, click the **Stop** button. Your Web browser displays everything that was loaded up to that point, as if it were the entire document.

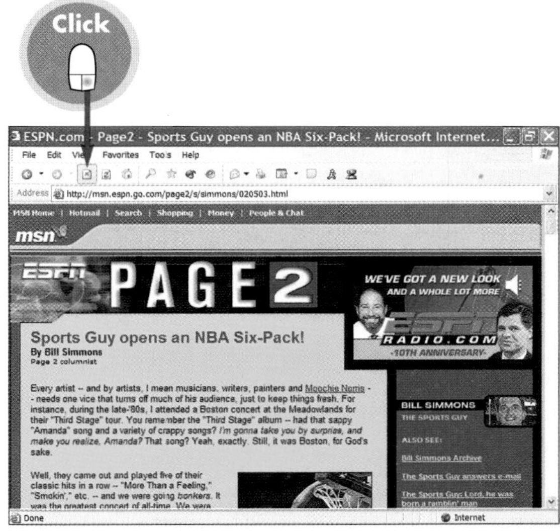

How to Hint

Opening Pages in a New Window

You can instruct Internet Explorer to open Web pages in a new window, leaving the current page on display. To do so, hold the **Shift** key down and click a hyperlink to open the linked page in a new window.

Closing a Pop-Up Window

Some Web sites open additional pages in their own browser windows. These are called *pop-ups* because they pop up on the screen in front of other pages, usually to display advertising.

Often, pop-up windows do not include a title bar, so you can't close them by clicking the **X** button found on that bar. To close one, press **Ctrl+W** on your keyboard.

How to Visit a Web Site When You Know Its Address

Every page you can view on the World Wide Web has a unique address called a *uniform resource locator* (*URL*). Internet Explorer 6's **Address bar** normally shows the URL of the document currently being displayed (some Web sites, however, display their main URLs even if you load a different page on the site). If you know a Web page's URL, you can view it without using hyperlinks.

1 Enter a URL

To go directly to a Web page, type its URL in the **Address bar** and press **Enter**. Internet Explorer attempts to load the document associated with that URL, if one exists. Try this: type `http://www.yahoo.com` in the **Address bar** and press **Enter**.

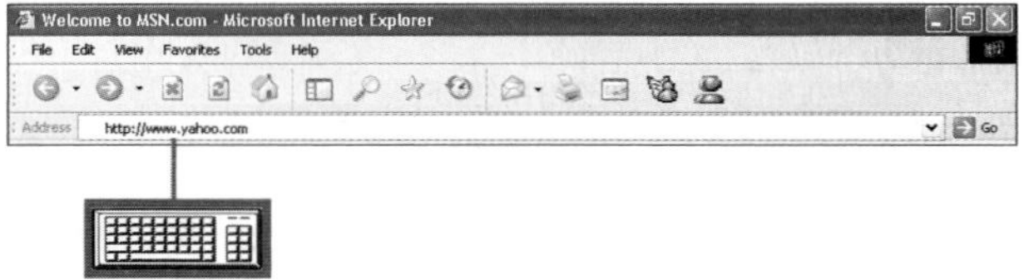

2 Use a Shortcut

Internet Explorer can find many popular Web sites even if you only know a site's name or its subject matter. To see this feature in action, type `Excel` in the **Address bar** and press **Enter**. The browser's Autosearch feature loads Microsoft's official Excel site, the best match for the topic keyword *Excel*.

3 Find the Best Sites

If Autosearch cannot match a URL, Internet Explorer loads a Web page on the MSN Web site that lists popular sites matching the topic. Use the scrollbar to view the list of sites and click a hyperlink to visit that site. Here you see the results of a search for the word `Journalism`.

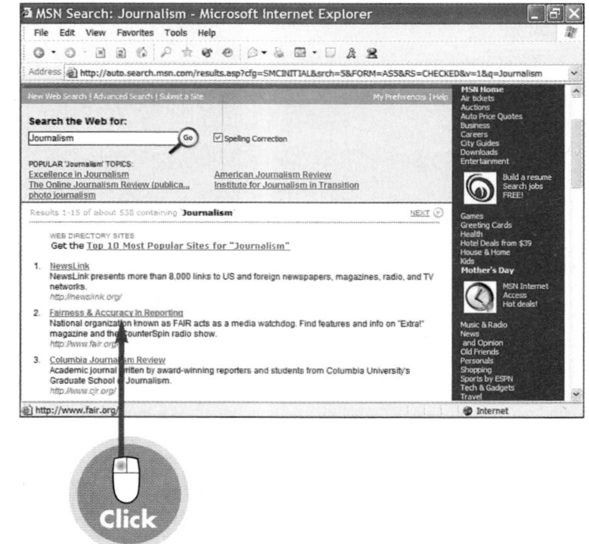

4 Select an Address Again

Click the arrow next to the **Address bar** to see a list of entries you have recently typed into the bar, including URLs and Autosearch shortcuts. Click an item in the list to load that page again.

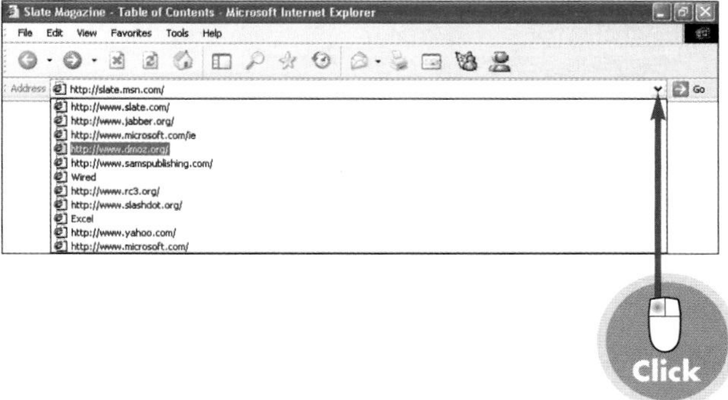

5 Remove Address Bar Requests

Internet Explorer automatically deletes past **Address bar** requests after a designated number of days. You also can delete all the entries manually. Open the **Tools** menu and choose **Internet Options**. The **Internet Options** dialog box opens.

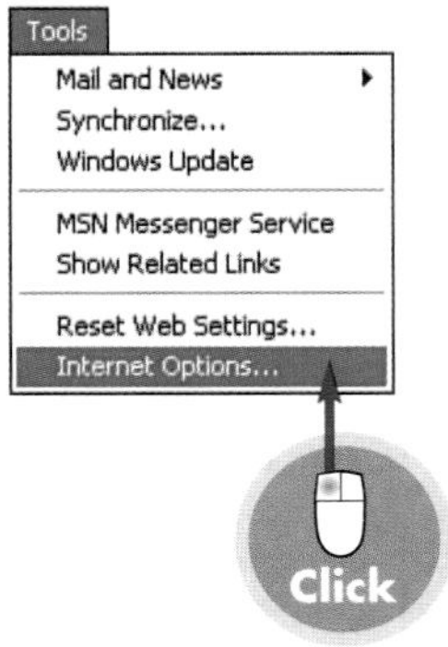

6 Clear the History Folder

Internet Explorer saves all **Address bar** requests you make in a **History** folder. Click the **Clear History** button in the **Internet Options** dialog box to delete all the entries from the **History** folder *and* from the **Address bar** drop-down list.

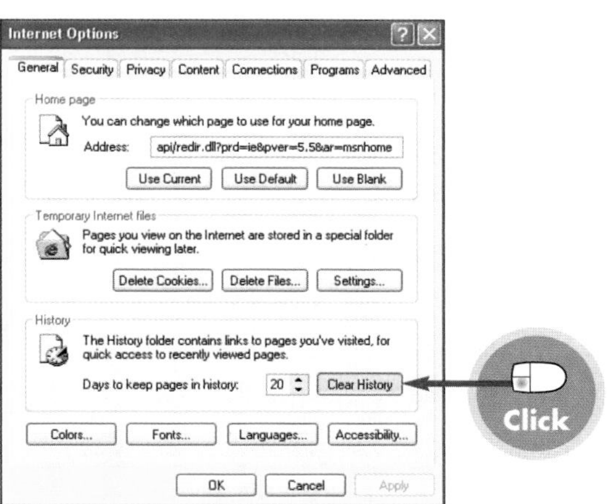

How to Hint: Displaying the Address Bar

If the **Address bar** is not visible, choose **View, Toolbars, Address Bar**. The Internet Explorer toolbar expands to show an **Address** combo box.

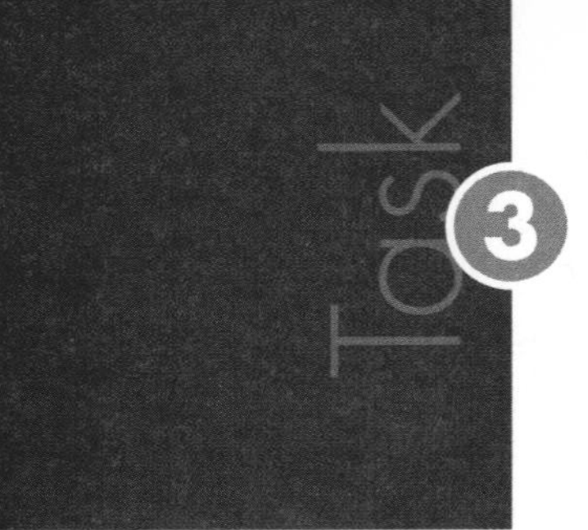

How to Revisit Your Favorite Web Pages

One of the biggest timesavers Internet Explorer 6 provides is the **Favorites** list, which can be used to hold shortcuts to Web pages you visit frequently. (In contrast, the **History** list simply tracks the last sites you've visited, whether you liked them or not.) Internet Explorer comes with a default list of favorites when it is installed, which may have been customized by your computer manufacturer. You can easily edit the **Favorites** list by adding your own shortcuts and removing any you don't want.

1 Visit Your Favorite Sites

In Internet Explorer, click the **Favorites** button to open the **Favorites** list along the left side of the browser window. The list is organized like a file folder, and it can contain both Internet shortcuts and subfolders. (Note that you don't have to be connected to the Internet to edit your list of favorites.)

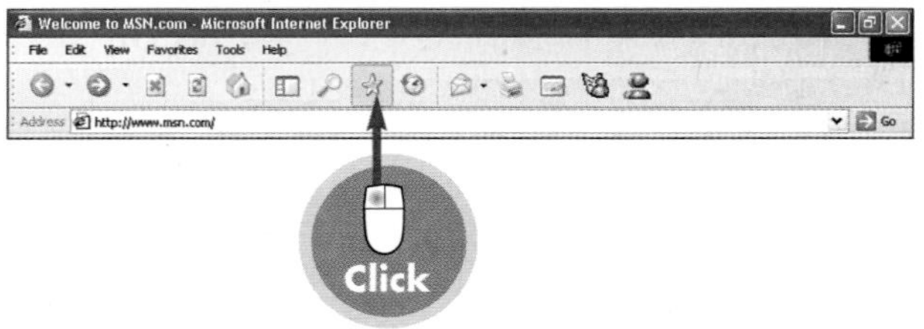

2 Select an Internet Shortcut

To load a Web page from the **Favorites** list, click its Internet shortcut (the entries in the **Favorites** list are really just links to Web pages). If you are not connected to the Internet, a dialog box opens that enables you to establish an Internet connection.

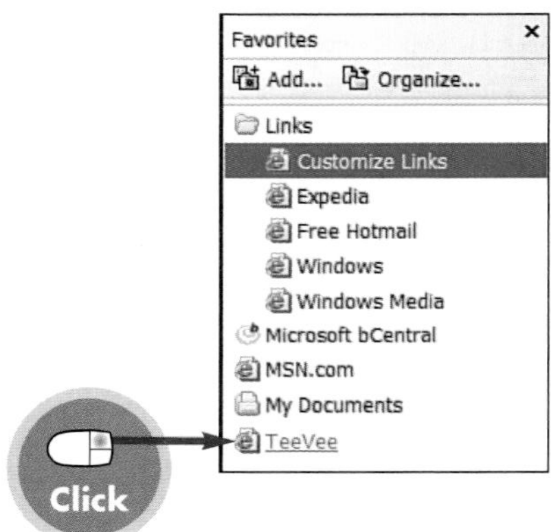

3 Add the Current Site to the List

If you'd like to add the currently displayed Web document to your **Favorites** list, click the **Add** button. The **Add Favorite** dialog box opens.

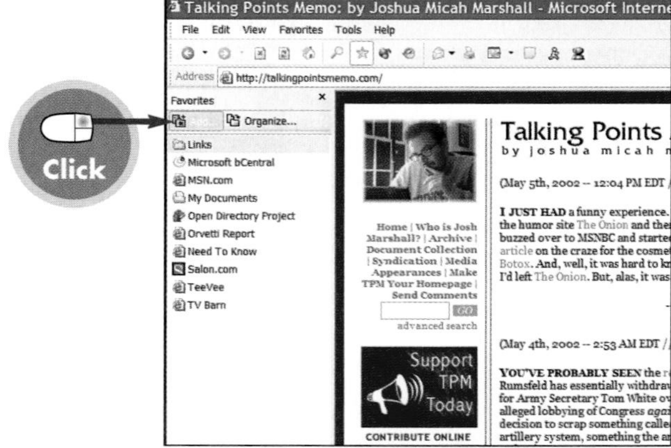

4 Save Your New Favorite

The **Add Favorite** dialog box displays a name for the site in the **Name** text box. You can use this name or change it—the name will appear in your **Favorites** list. Click **OK** to continue.

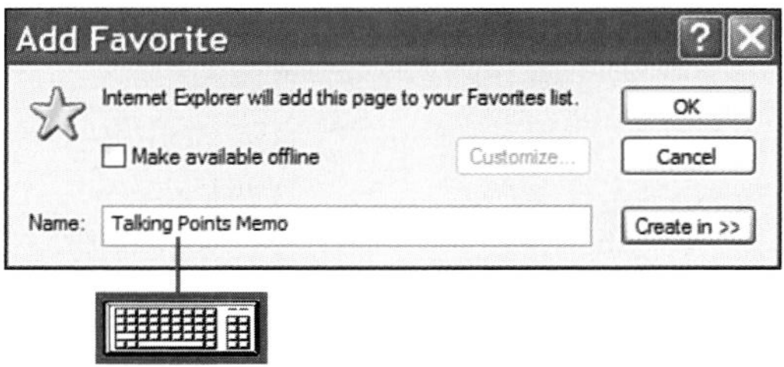

5 Delete a Site from the List

You might want to delete entries from your **Favorites** list if your interests change or if the link to the site breaks. To remove a shortcut from the **Favorites** list, right-click the entry and select **Delete** from the shortcut menu that appears.

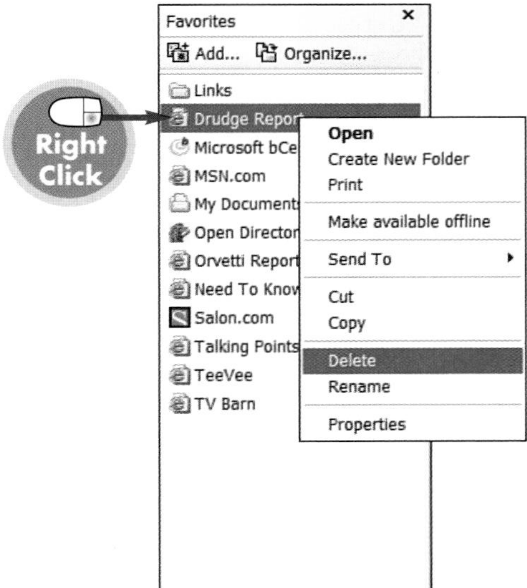

6 Move a Site to a New Folder

You can move shortcuts to different folders in the **Favorites** list. You might want to do this to group your favorites in a more logical manner. Drag the shortcut from its present location to a new folder; release the mouse button to make the change.

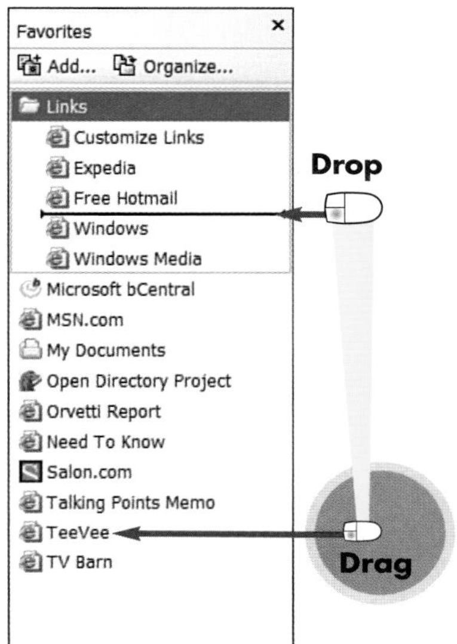

How to Hint

Renaming an Internet Shortcut

You can change the name of any shortcut in your **Favorites** list. To do so, right-click the shortcut, select the **Rename** command from the shortcut menu, type the new name, and press **Enter**.

Adding New Favorites Quickly

You can add favorites in Internet Explorer even if the **Favorites** list is not visible. With the Web page you want to add displayed in the browser, open the **Favorites** menu and choose the **Add to Favorites** command to open the **Add Favorite** dialog box described in Step 4. The **Favorites** menu also contains all the shortcuts in your **Favorites** list, so you can access your favorite Web pages without devoting a portion of the screen to the **Favorites** list pane.

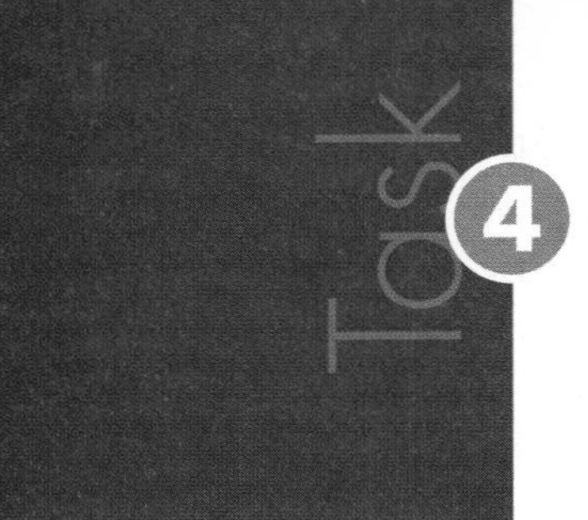

How to Load a Web Page for Faster Viewing

Internet Explorer 6 can speed up your use of the World Wide Web by downloading your favorite sites ahead of time—especially if you use a dial-up connection. These sites can then be viewed while you're *offline*—that is, disconnected from the Internet. Because the files have already been downloaded to your computer, they load more quickly into your browser. You can set up a Web page for offline viewing as you're adding it to your **Favorites** list. You view the page by clicking its link in the list.

1 Select Offline Browsing

To select a page for offline browsing, you must first add it to your **Favorites** list. With the page open in your browser, open the **Favorites** menu and choose **Add to Favorites**. In the **Add Favorite** dialog box that appears, choose the folder in which you want to store your new favorite and select the **Make available offline** option. Don't click the **OK** button yet.

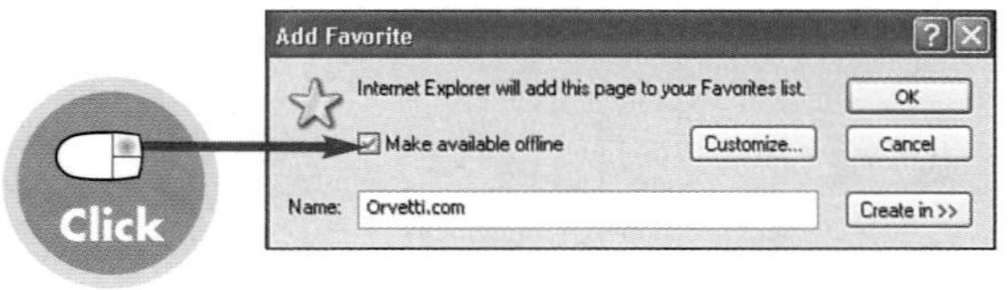

2 Use the Offline Wizard

Click the **Customize** button. The **Offline Favorite Wizard** opens with an explanation of what the wizard does. Click **Next** to continue.

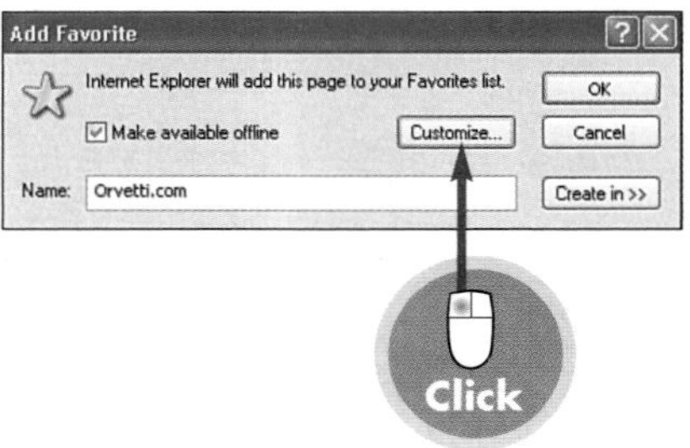

3 Save Linked Pages

You can retrieve pages that are linked to your new favorite, even if they're not part of the same Web site. To save linked pages, click the **Yes** radio button.

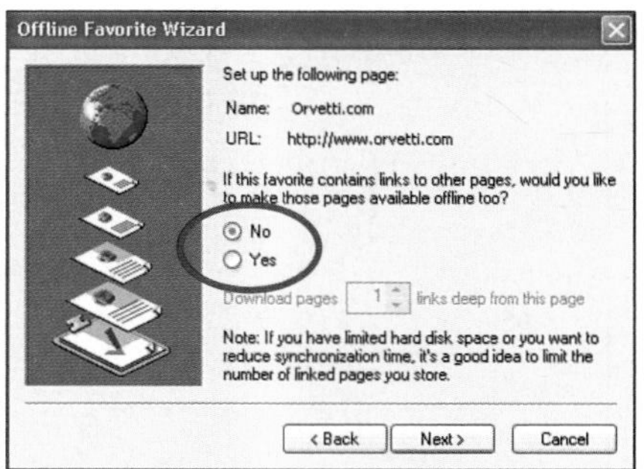

4 Choose How Much to Retrieve

If you clicked **Yes** in step 3, use the **Download pages** text box to specify how many links Internet Explorer should follow as it retrieves documents. Higher values save more pages for offline browsing, but they also take more time and disk space—3 is probably as high as you need. Click the **Next** button to continue.

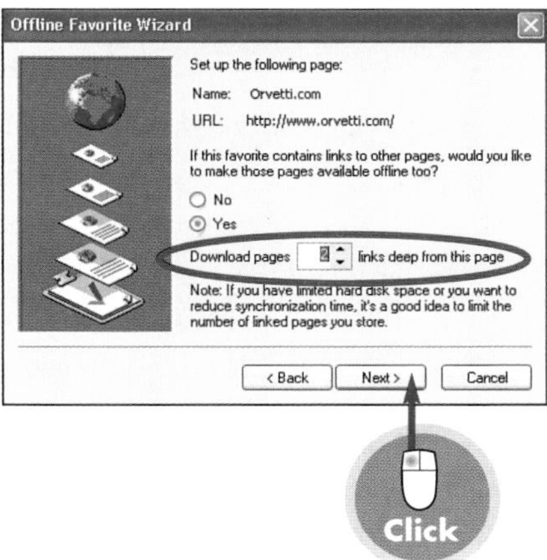

5 Choose When to Retrieve Pages

You can retrieve a favorite for offline viewing in two ways: manually or at a scheduled time each day. For the latter approach, click the **I would like to create a new schedule** radio button. Then, click the **Next** button to continue.

6 Set Up a Schedule

Choose the time and days on which pages should be retrieved. There's also an option to connect to the Internet automatically at the scheduled time, in case you're not already connected. Click the **Next** button, answer the wizard's remaining questions, and click the **Finish** button to add this new shortcut to the Favorites list. Click **OK** to close the **Add Favorite** dialog box.

7 Download Offline Pages Manually

To immediately retrieve all pages set up for offline browsing without waiting for a scheduled time, open the **Tools** menu and choose the **Synchronize** command. To view a page after it has been retrieved, click its link in your **Favorites** list.

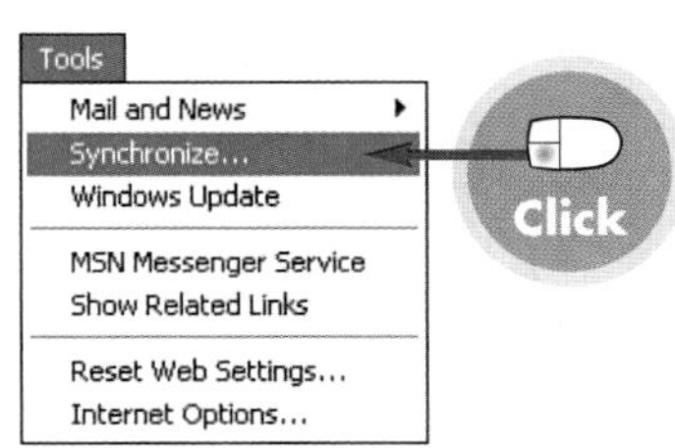

How to Pick a New Home Page for Your Browser

A term you'll see often on the World Wide Web is *home page*—the main page of a Web site. There's another kind of home page: the one loaded by a Web browser when it first starts. Internet Explorer 6 includes a **Home** button on its main toolbar, which you can click to quickly return to the browser's home page. The browser's default home page is usually MSN, although some computer manufacturers change this setting. You may, however, prefer to use a home page of your own choosing.

1 Set Up a New Home Page

Your Internet Explorer home page can be any page on the World Wide Web or even a page stored on your own system. When you have found a page you want to use as the browser's home page, load it into your browser.

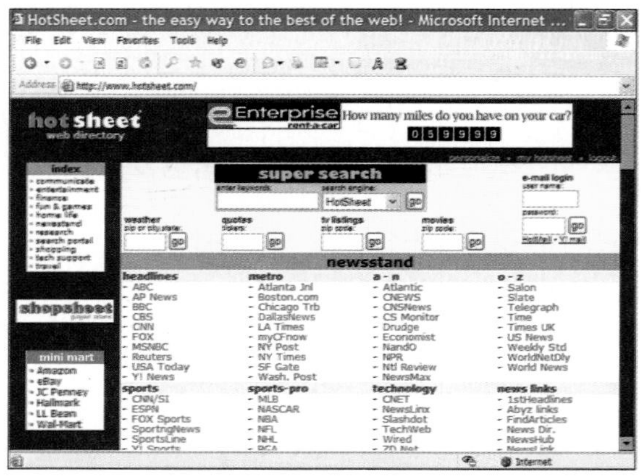

2 Adjust Your Browser Settings

With your prospective home page loaded, open the **Tools** menu and choose **Internet Options**. The **Internet Options** dialog box opens. (You were introduced to this dialog box in Task 2, "How to Visit a Site When You Know Its Address," when you cleared the **History** folder.)

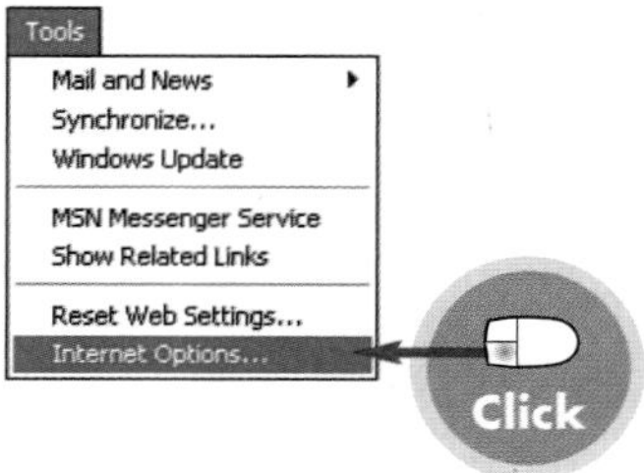

3 Display the General Settings

The **Internet Options** dialog box has seven tabs that display different settings you can adjust. If the **General** tab is hidden behind another tab, click the **General** tab to bring it to the front.

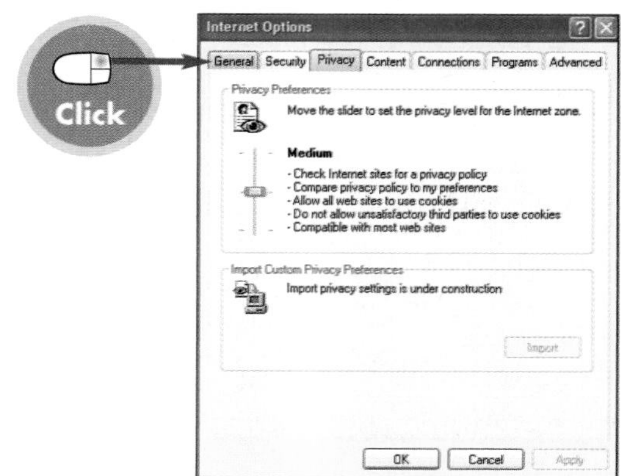

Change Your Home Page

4 The Address text box identifies your browser's home page. Click the **Use Current** button to change your browser's home page to the page currently displayed in the browser. If you decide to restore Internet Explorer's original home page, click the **Use Default** button. To save any changes you've made and close the dialog box, click the **OK** button.

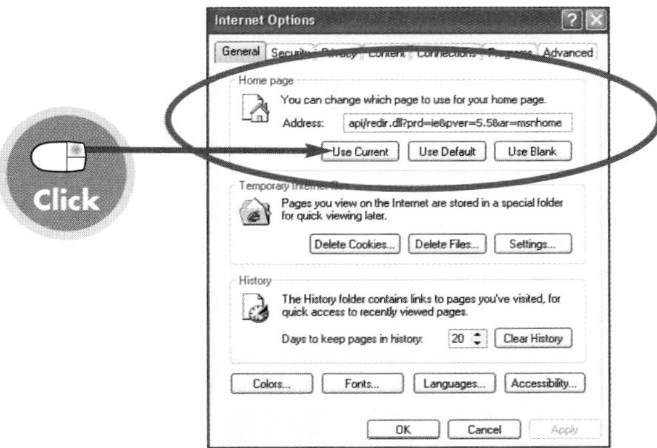

5 Load Your Home Page

Click the **Home** button in the browser's toolbar to return to your browser's home page at any time. When the home page loads in the browser, it will be the page you specified in Step 4.

How to Hint

Using a Blank Home Page

You can make your Internet Explorer home page an empty one that loads faster than the other alternatives. To set this up, choose **Tools**, **Internet Options**; click the **General** tab in the **Internet Options** dialog box; and then click the **Use Blank** button. Click **OK** to exit the dialog box.

Using a Page Stored on Your Computer

Any page that Internet Explorer can display is suitable for use as the browser's home page. To open a Web page stored on your computer, choose **File**, **Open**; in the **Open** dialog box, click the **Browse** button. Browse to find any document on your system and click **OK** to open that document in the browser. The document then can be set as your home page using Steps 2–5 of this task.

Choosing a Useful Home Page

The MSN homepage contains interesting content from Microsoft Web sites but doesn't offer much from other publishers. HotSheet.com, the site shown in this task, contains links to more than 150 sites in categories such as news, finance, travel, shopping, and tech support. To visit the site, type **`http://www.hotsheet.com`** in the **Address bar** and press **Enter**.

How to Change Internet Explorer's Settings

While using Internet Explorer 6, you can customize the way the browser looks, displays information, and operates. You've already used some of the software's customization features to set up a new home page and clear out past Address bar requests. There are more than 100 other settings you can adjust with the **Internet Options** dialog box, which is accessible from the **Tools** menu.

1 Configure Your Browser

You can change Internet Explorer's settings whether you're online or offline. To get started, open the **Tools** menu and choose the **Internet Options** command. The **Internet Options** dialog box opens.

2 Set Your Internet Options

To see groups of related settings, click the tabs along the top edge of the **Internet Options** dialog box. For example, click the **General** tab to display some of the browser's main settings.

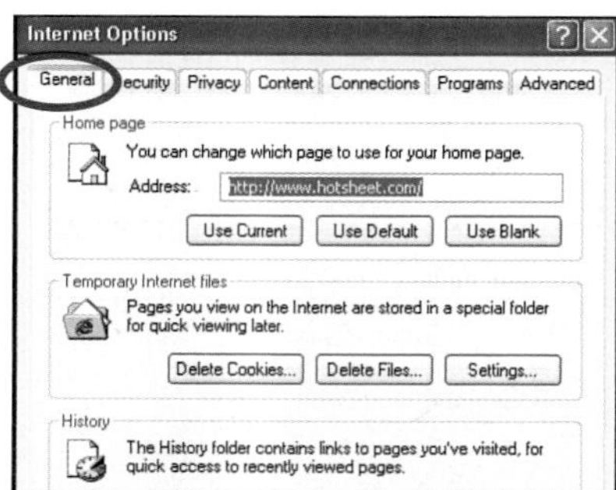

3 Clean Out Temporary Files

As you use Internet Explorer, Web pages you view are saved along with graphics and other files included on these pages. Your browser eventually deletes these files, but you can do so immediately to make room on your hard disk; simply click the **Delete Files** button in the **General** tab. You'll be asked to confirm by clicking **OK** before any files are deleted.

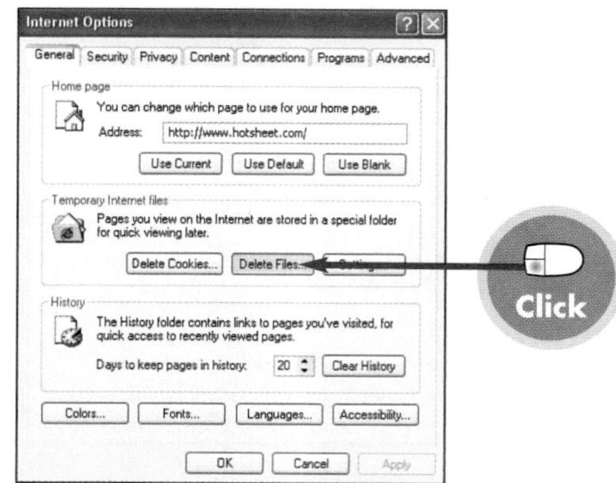

4 Resize the Temporary Folder

Internet Explorer deletes temporary files when the folder they are stored in exceeds a maximum size. To increase this maximum (which enables more to be stored in your **History** folder), click the **Settings** button on the **General** tab to open the **Settings** dialog box. Drag the **Amount of disk space to use** slider, releasing it where you want the new maximum to be. Click **OK**.

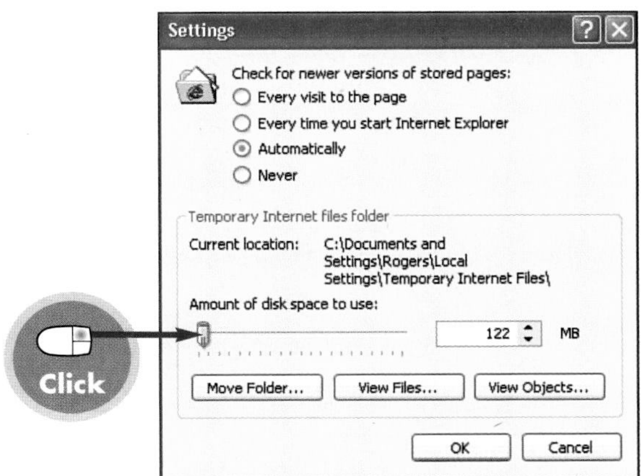

5 Change the Default Font

You can make many Web pages more readable by choosing different fonts for the text they display. Click the **Fonts** button on the **General** tab to open the **Fonts** dialog box. Select a default font for Web pages and a default font for plain text. Click **OK** to save your changes.

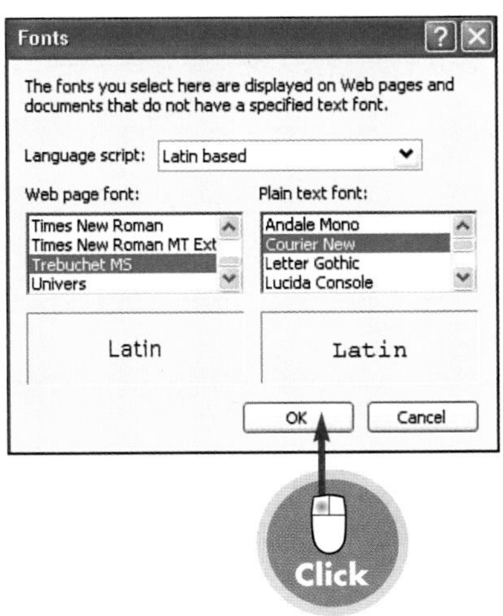

6 Close the Dialog Box

When you have finished changing the settings in the **Internet Options** dialog box, click **OK** to save your settings and close the dialog box. The next time you start your browser, all your new settings will be active.

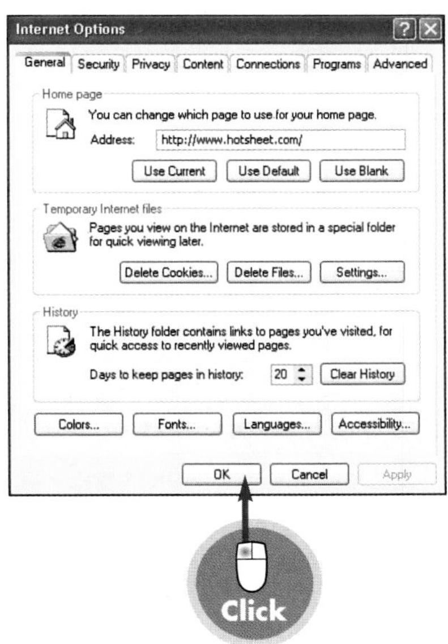

How to Hint

Making Your Font Selections Take Precedence

Normally, if a Web page is designed to use a specific font, that font is used for text instead of the one you specified for the browser in Step 5. You can change this functionality in the **Internet Options** dialog box: On the **General** tab, click the **Accessibility** button, and then select the **Ignore font styles specified on Web pages** option. This may make some pages look terrible, but it's useful if you want to make text larger or improve readability by using your own chosen font.

How to Print a Web Page

Internet Explorer 6, like many Windows programs, offers the capability to print documents. You can print the current Web page as it appears in the browser, print all the hyperlinks on the page, and even follow those hyperlinks and print every one of those pages at the same time. Web pages can be sent to a printer, sent out using a fax modem, and saved as a disk file optimized for printing.

1 Choose the Print Command

To print the Web page that's currently displayed in the browser window, open the **File** menu and choose the **Print** command. The **Print** dialog box opens.

2 Choose a Printer

You can send Web pages to any printer that has been installed on your system. To print the page, choose a printer from the **Select Printer** pane and click **Print**.

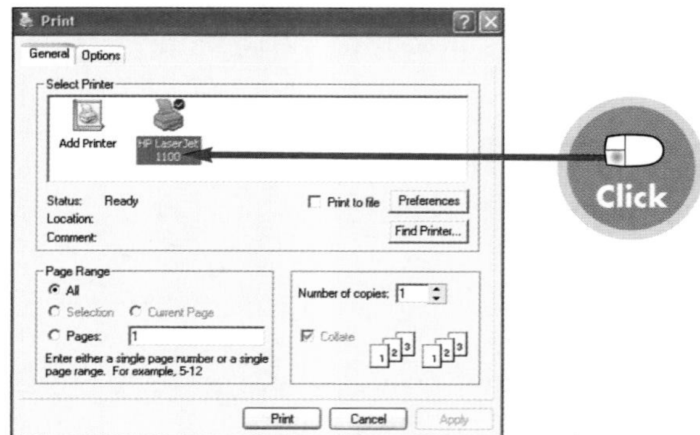

3 Customize How a Page Is Printed

You can make changes to how Internet Explorer 6 prints hyperlinks and *frames*—separate sections of a Web page that can have their own scrollbars and borders. To determine how these elements of a Web page will be printed, start by opening the **Print** dialog box and clicking the **Options** tab to bring it to the front.

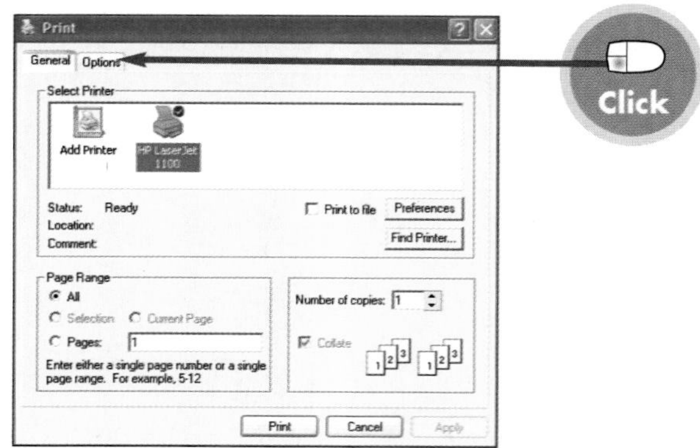

4 Print Associated Web Pages

Internet Explorer can look at all the hyperlinks on the current page and print the pages associated with those links, enabling you to print related pages on a Web site. Select the **Print all linked documents** option to print these linked pages.

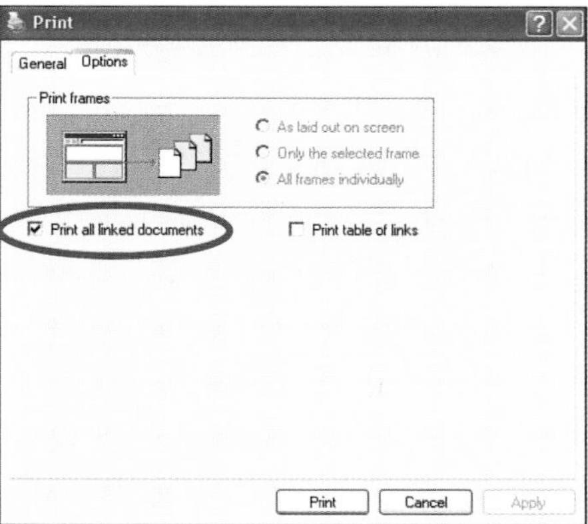

5 Print a Framed Web Page

Some World Wide Web sites divide the browser window into frames. You have three options when printing a page that uses frames: Print each frame individually, print the page as it looks in the browser, or print only the selected frame. To select a frame, click your mouse in that section of the Web page before printing the page and then select the **Only the selected frame** option.

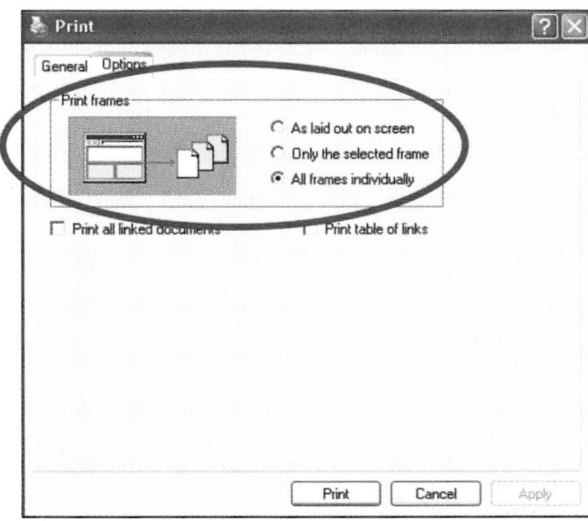

6 Print the Selected Frame

Click the **Print** button to print the Web page according to the options you have selected. A dialog box appears briefly as the page is sent to the printer. You should soon hear the printer working on the page.

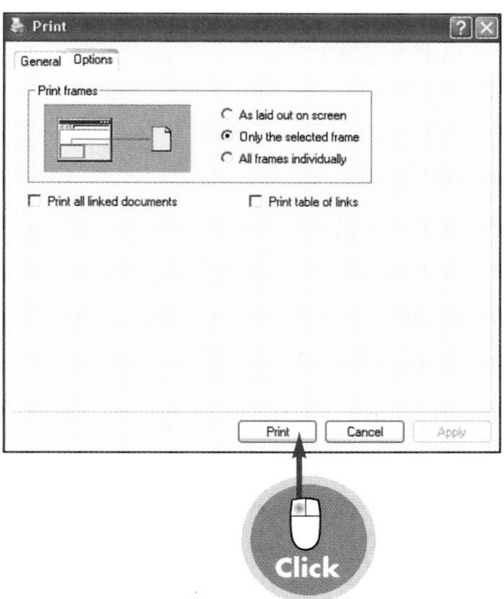

How to Hint

Printing News and Magazine Articles

When you print a Web page, you sometimes end up with a lot of stuff you don't need, such as large advertisements and a menu of other parts of the site. Some newspaper and magazine sites offer a different version of an article that's simplified for printing. Look for a **Print Page** link, **Printer-Friendly** link, or **Printer** icon at the top or bottom of the article. Two media sites that offer this feature are *Slate* at the address `http://www.slate.com` and the *International Herald Tribune* at the address `http://www.iht.com`.

How to Save a Web Page to Your Computer

One of the ways the World Wide Web is different from other media is in how quickly it changes. Sites are updated constantly, new sites appear, and old sites disappear. If you see a page on the Web you'd like to keep around for a while, no matter what happens to the company or individual hosting it, you can save it to your computer. Internet Explorer 6 can save the text of the page or save everything on a page in a single file, including the graphics and other content. You can later open the file in Internet Explorer, even if you are not connected to the Internet.

1 Save a Page

To save the Web page that's currently open in Internet Explorer, open the **File** menu and choose the **Save As** command. The **Save Web Page** dialog box opens.

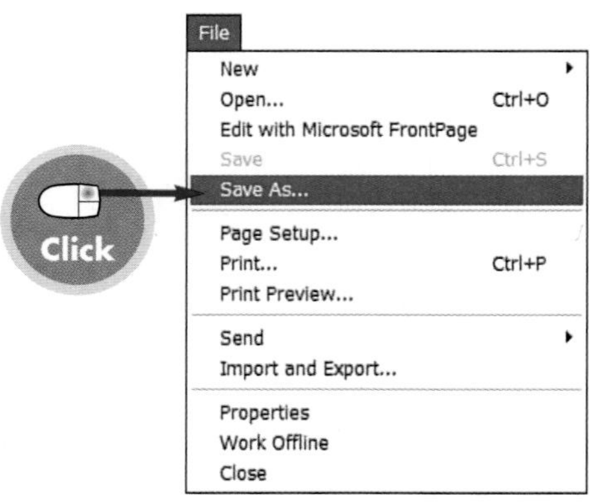

2 Choose the Format

Use the **Save Web Page** dialog box to choose a folder where the page will be saved. Type a name for the file in the **File name** text field, click the arrow next to the **Save as type** list box, and then choose **Web Archive single file (*.mht)**.

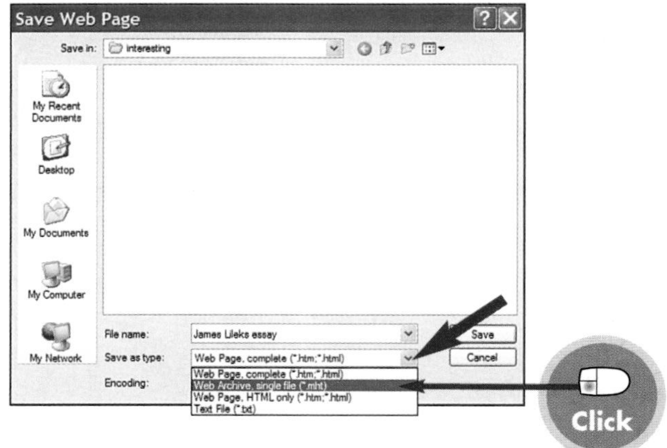

3 Store the Page

Click the **Save** button to save the page. If you chose the Web Archive format, the page and all its contents will be saved as a single file with the name you specified followed by **.mht**.

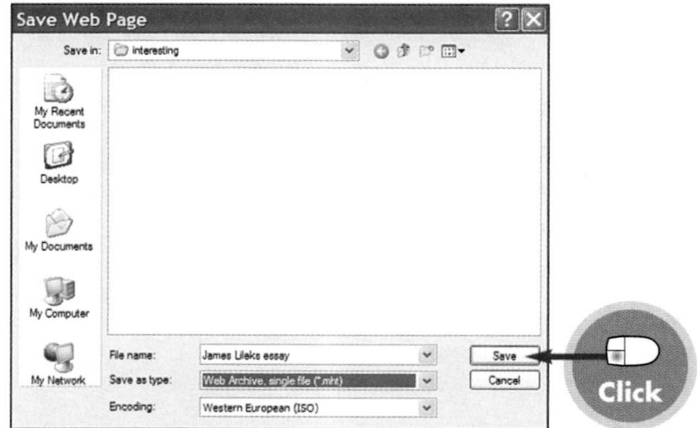

4 Open a Page

After you have saved a page, you can open it at any time with Internet Explorer, whether or not you are connected to the Internet. Open the **File** menu and choose the **Open** command. The Open dialog box opens.

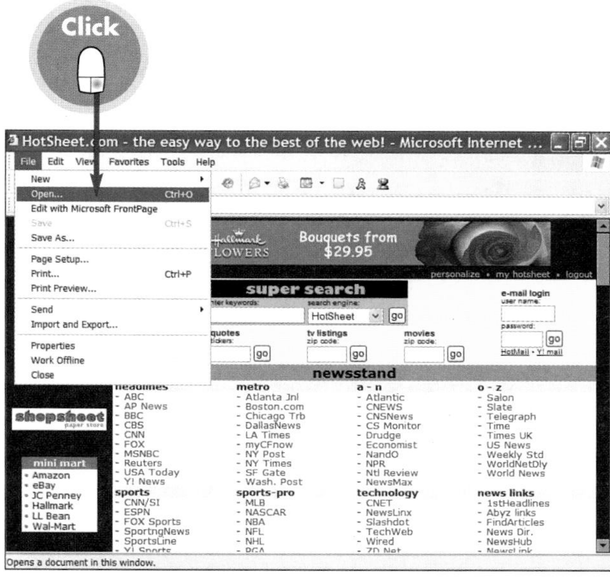

5 Find the Page

Click the **Browse** button in the **Open** dialog box. The Microsoft Internet Explorer dialog box opens.

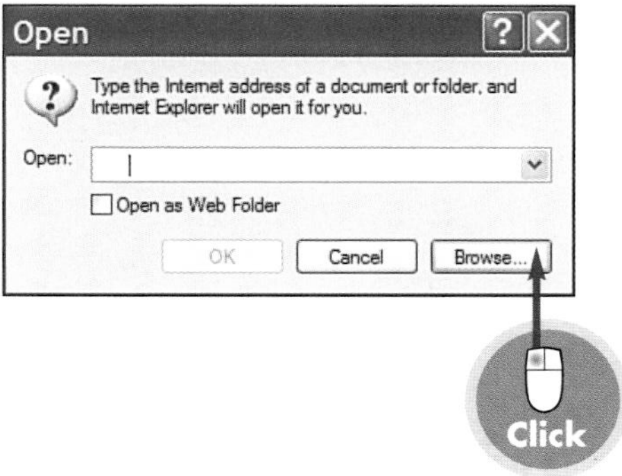

6 Choose the File

Use the Microsoft Internet Explorer dialog box to find the page you saved. It will have the **.mht** extension if it was stored in Web Archive format. Choose the file and click **Open**. The **Open** dialog box reappears.

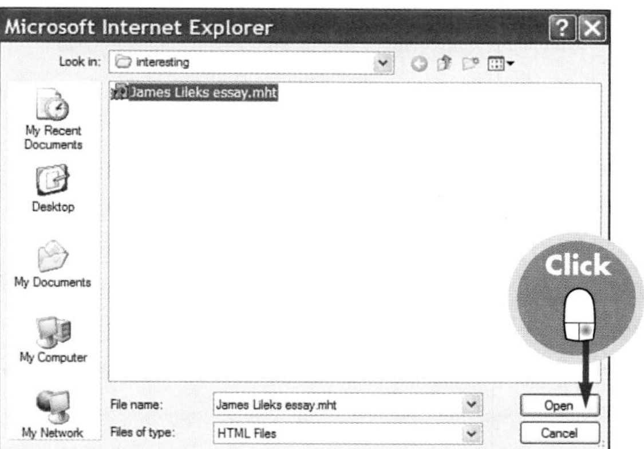

7 Open the Page

Click the **OK** button. The page opens in Internet Explorer and can be used like any other page you view in the browser.

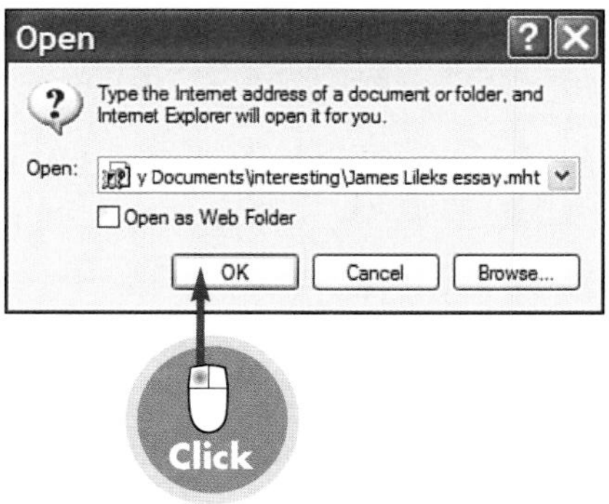

Task

3

Visiting a Portal Web Site

When someone uses the World Wide Web for the first time, one thing he or she may find surprising is the lack of an official place to start. You can begin exploring the Web at any page, end at any page, and visit any place you like in between. Although this lack of structure is often considered to be one of the Web's strong suits, some of the most popular Web sites are designed to be great starting places for your online explorations. These sites are called *portals* because they're intended to be gateways to the huge amount of information that has been amassed on the Web.

Popular portals include Yahoo!, Excite, Netscape, Lycos, and MSN. The core offering of these portals is a way to find Web sites on specific topics. When you enter keywords to search for particular information, the portal returns a list of relevant categories and Web sites. Portals also offer numerous services to keep you from leaving the site at all—news, sports scores, stock tickers, free email, and dozens of other attractions. In addition, every one of the major portals offers a way to customize its site to emphasize the topics that interest you most.

How to Set Up an Account on a Portal

For many Internet users, the first World Wide Web site they used as a portal was Yahoo!, a directory of hand-picked Web sites that launched in 1994. This directory, one of the first of its kind, has been one of the Internet's most popular sites for years, attracting millions of visitors each day. Today, the Yahoo! directory of sites is only one of the services it offers. There are also local phone listings, stock prices, free email accounts, and several dozen other features. Yahoo! offers free accounts through the My Yahoo! service.

1 Visit the Portal

Each Web portal has a different procedure for setting up an account, although most require the same things: your name, address, email address, and demographic information such as your profession and household income. To begin setting up a free My Yahoo! account, type `http://edit.yahoo.com` into your browser's **Address bar** and press **Enter**.

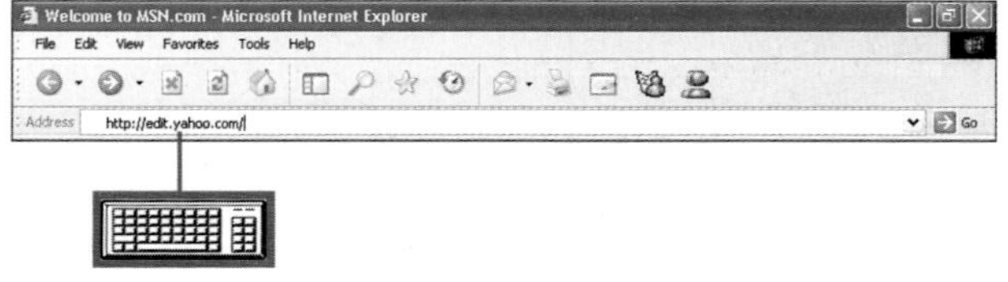

2 Request an Account

If you do not have an account, each portal will offer links you can use to request one. On Yahoo!, there's a `Sign up now` hyperlink. Click this link to request an account.

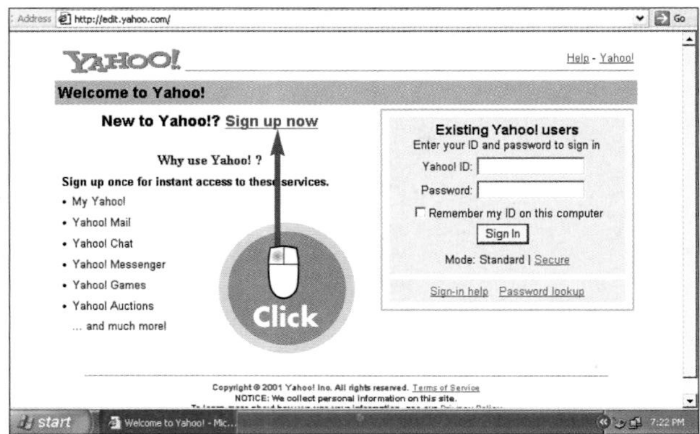

3 Choose a Unique ID

Each portal asks you to choose a unique username, which identifies you throughout the site and forms part of your free email address. In the **Yahoo! ID** text box, type your desired username. Your username can contain a combination of letters, numbers, and underscore characters (_).

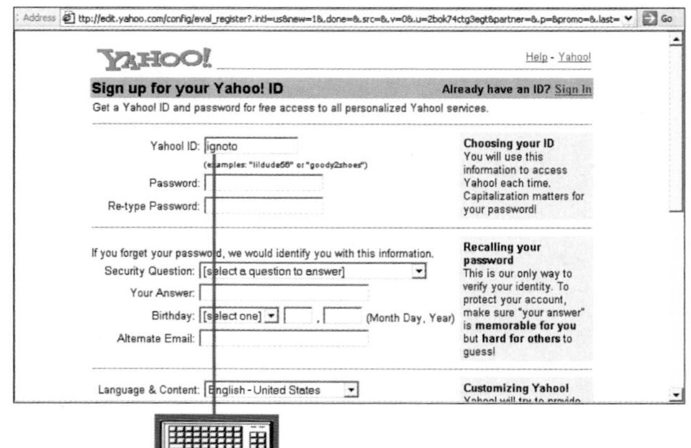

Choose a Password

Type the password you want to use in the **Password** and **Re-Type Password** text boxes. Choose a security question and type its answer in the appropriate boxes—Yahoo! uses these to verify your identity if you forget your password. Next, use the **Birthday** boxes to provide this information—Yahoo! requires this also.

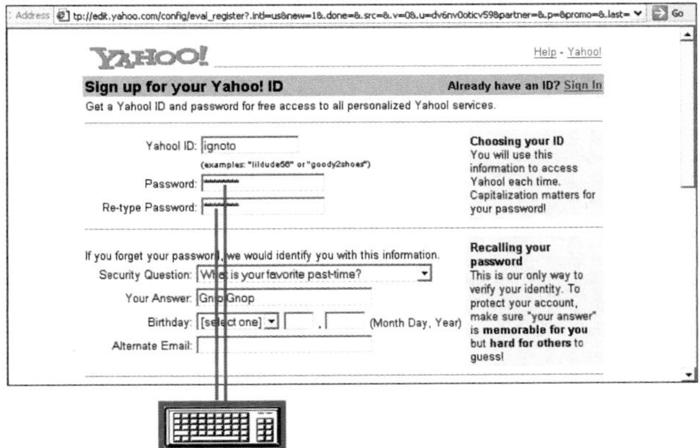

5 Enter Your Email Address

You must have an existing email address to join Yahoo!, such as the one provided by your Internet service provider. Type this address into the **Alternate Email** text box.

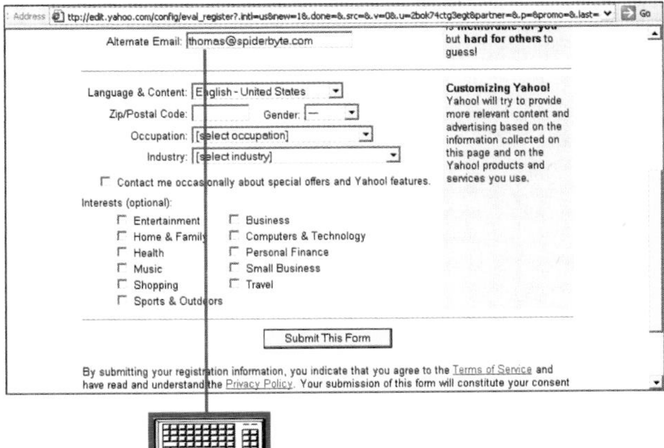

6 Complete the Sign-Up Form

When signing up for a portal, you may be asked several optional questions about your job, interests, and other information. After you've answered all mandatory questions and provided whatever optional information you desire, click the **Submit This Form** button.

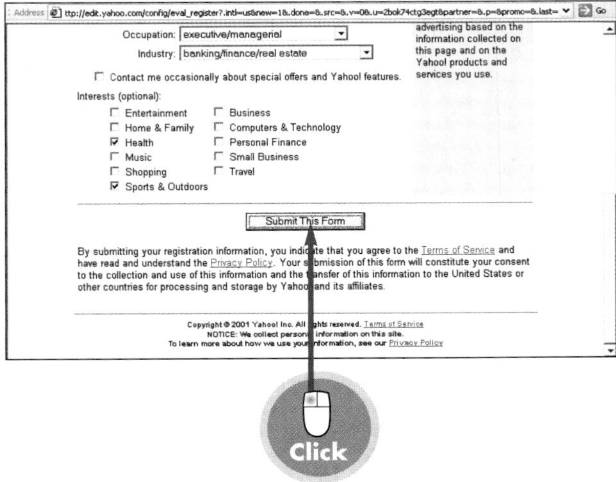

How to Hint

Choosing a Username

In most cases, your first choice for a portal username will already be in use by someone else. After all, thousands of people signed up before you did, leaving few common words, names, or surnames up for grabs. Yahoo! suggests a few alternatives to your first choice, or you can try other usernames until you find one that isn't taken.

Trying Other Portal Sites

Other large portal sites have offerings comparable to Yahoo!'s, so you may want to sign up for several. Visit the following Web sites to set up accounts:

- **Excite:** `http://www.excite.com`
- **My Lycos:** `http://my.lycos.com`
- **My Netscape:** `http://my.netscape.com`

To create an account you can use on MSN, Microsoft's Web portal, read Task 4 in this part, "How to Set Up a Microsoft Passport Account."

Task 2

How to Personalize a Web Portal

After you have established an account on a portal such as Yahoo!, you can personalize the site to focus on the news, information, and services in which you are most interested. For each selected topic, current headlines will be displayed on a page created for your account. You can also add hyperlinks, check local weather and travel information, read your email, and search for Web sites.

1 Load Your Portal Home Page

Yahoo! stores your username and other settings in a *cookie*—a special browser file stored on your computer. A sites can read a cookie that it has created, which enables a service such as My Yahoo! to recognize who you are when you enter `http://my.yahoo.com` in your browser's **Address bar**.

2 Edit a Subject Area

My Yahoo! groups information into topics such as health, weather, and technology. Many subjects have an **Edit** button next to the topic heading. Click a topic's **Edit** button to customize how it is presented, such as one next to **Portfolios** to track stocks.

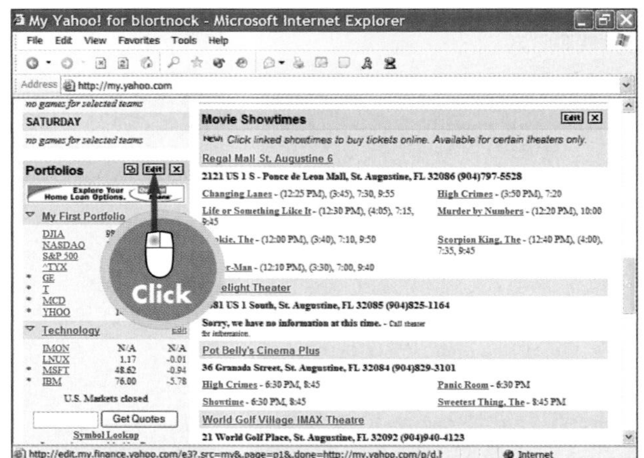

3 Customize a Topic

You can customize My Yahoo!'s **Portfolios** category to track any stocks you want. Click the **Create New Portfolio** hyperlink. The **Edit Portfolios** page opens.

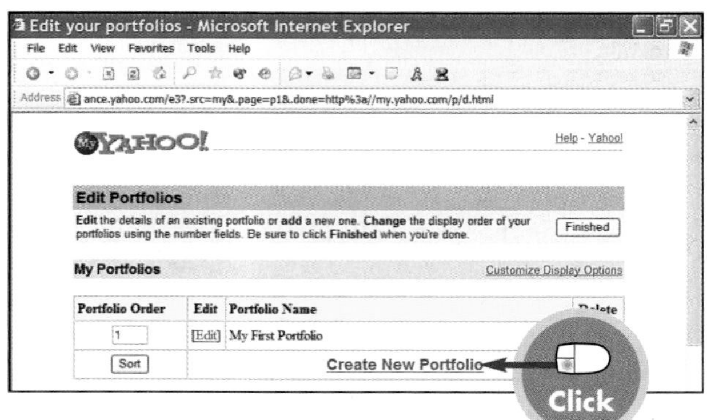

4 Make Your Changes Permanent

Type a name for your portfolio in the **Portfolio Name** text box. In the **Symbols** text box, type the ticker symbols of each stock you want to track, putting a space between each symbol. Click the **Finished** button to save the changes you've made. Your portal opens using your personalized settings.

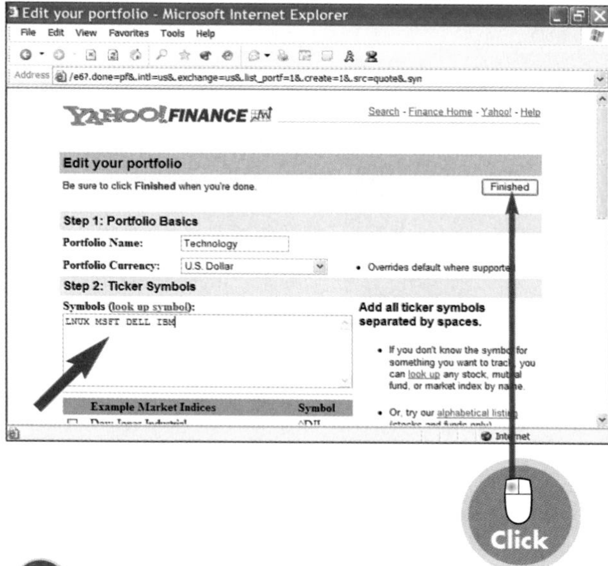

5 Delete a Subject

If you're not interested in a topic on your My Yahoo! page, click the **x** button adjacent to the topic heading to delete it. A dialog box opens; click the **OK** button to confirm the deletion.

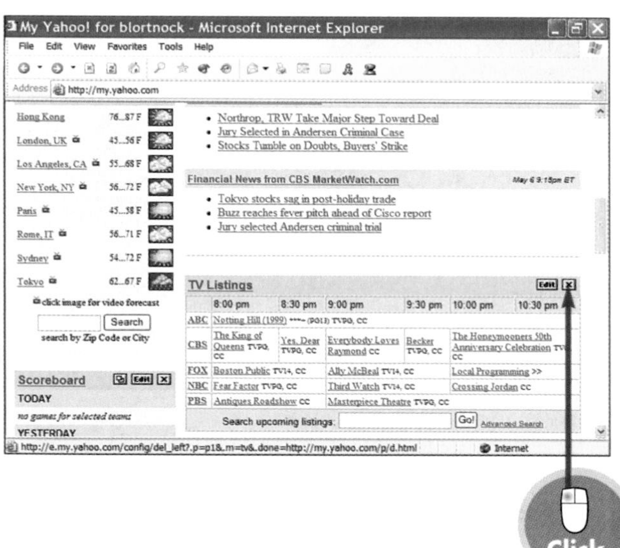

6 Add a Subject

To add subjects to My Yahoo!, scroll down to the bottom of the page. Open the left or right drop-down menu and scroll to the subject you want to add, select it, and then click the corresponding **Add** button.

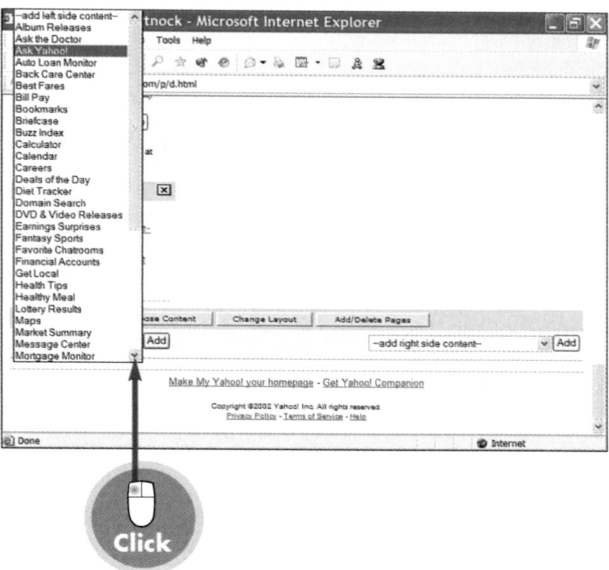

7 Choose New Content

To add or remove multiple topics, click the **Choose Content** button to see a checklist of all available topics. Enable the check box next to each topic you want to add, and disable the check boxes of all the topics you want to omit. Click the **Finished** button when you're finished.

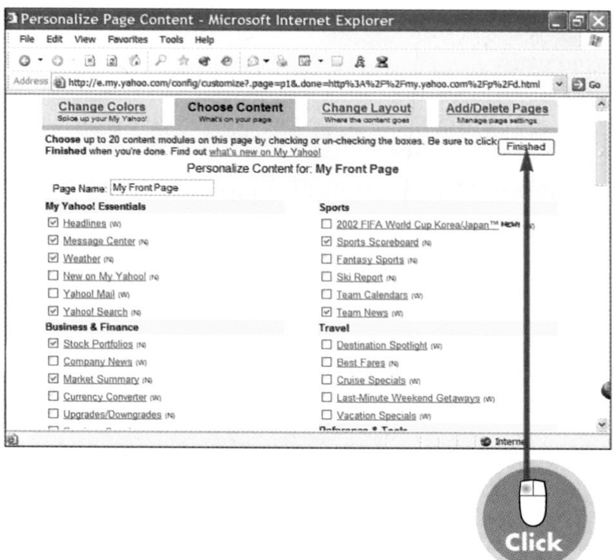

Task 3

How to Make a Portal Your Browser's Home Page

Task 5 in Part 2, "Browsing the World Wide Web," described how to turn any Web page into Internet Explorer 6's home page. The browser's home page appears when the browser is first run and whenever you click the **Home** button in the browser's toolbar. The home page is a useful starting point for your Web explorations. If you have personalized a Web portal using a service such as My Yahoo!, you might consider making this page your browser's home page.

1 Visit Your Portal

To get started, load your portal's customized page with your Web browser. For My Yahoo!, type `http://my.yahoo.com` into your **Address bar** and press **Enter**.

2 Sign In to Your Portal

If you have not signed in to your portal account, type your username and password, and click the associated button to submit the information (on My Yahoo!, click the **Sign in** button).

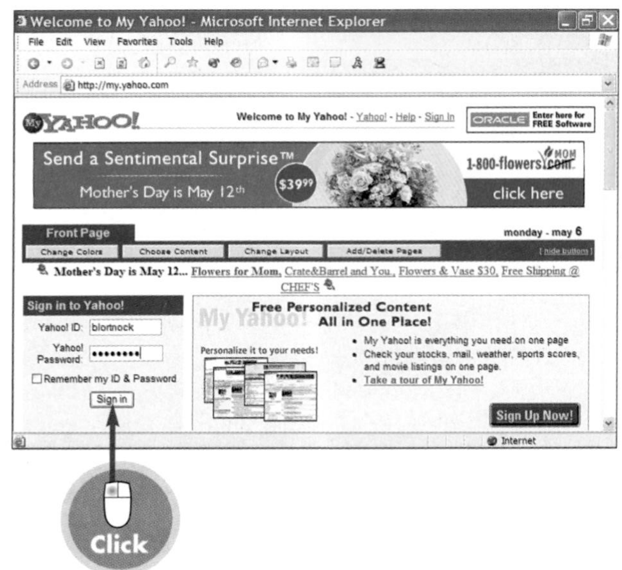

3 Adjust Your Browser Settings

After the page, has loaded, open the **Tools** menu on the Internet Explorer toolbar and choose the **Internet Options** command to adjust the Internet settings of the browser. The **Internet Options** dialog box opens.

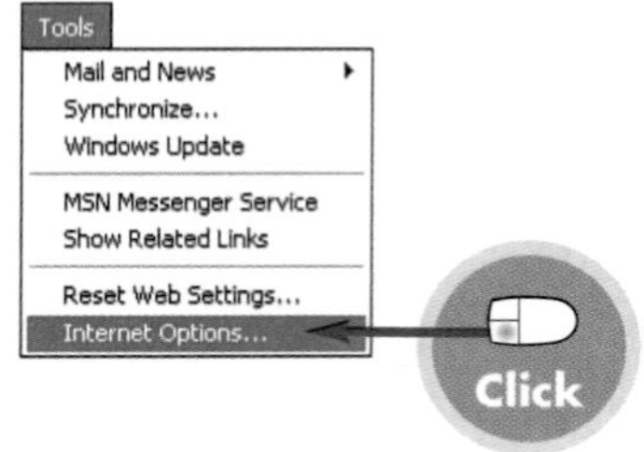

4 Display the General Settings

The seven tabs on the **Internet Options** dialog box display different settings you can adjust. Click the **General** tab to bring its settings to the front.

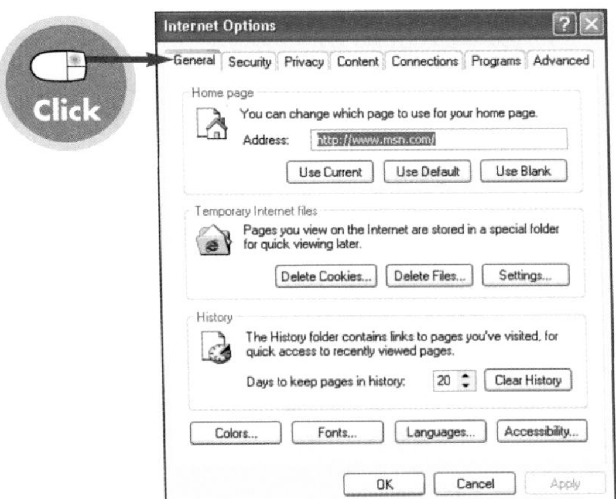

5 Make Your Portal the Home Page

The current home page used by your browser is displayed in the **Address** text box. Click the **Use Current** button to change this field to the customized portal page, and then click the **OK** button to save the change and close the **Internet Options** dialog box.

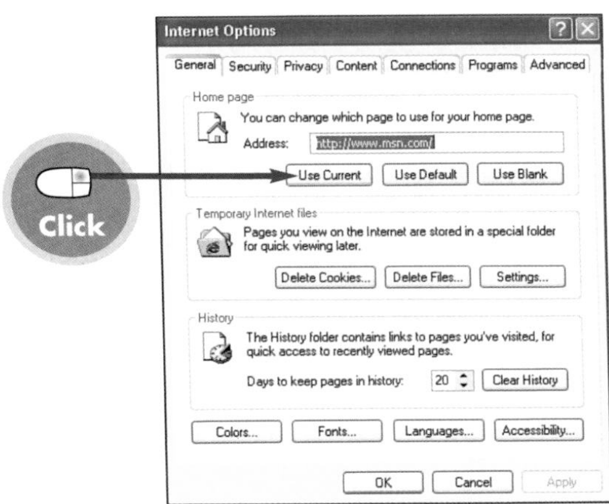

6 Load Your New Home Page

Click the **Home** button in the Internet Explorer toolbar at any time to return to your customized portal page.

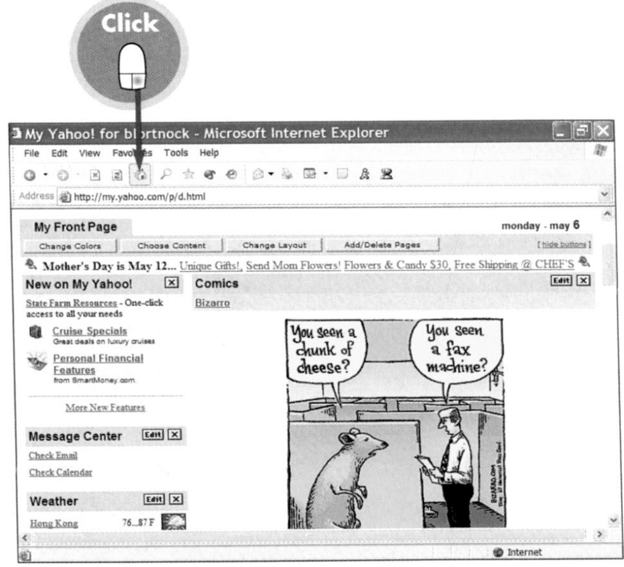

7 Restore the Original

If you change your mind and want to return to Internet Explorer's original home page, open the **Internet Options** dialog box, click the **Use Default** button, and then click the **OK** button.

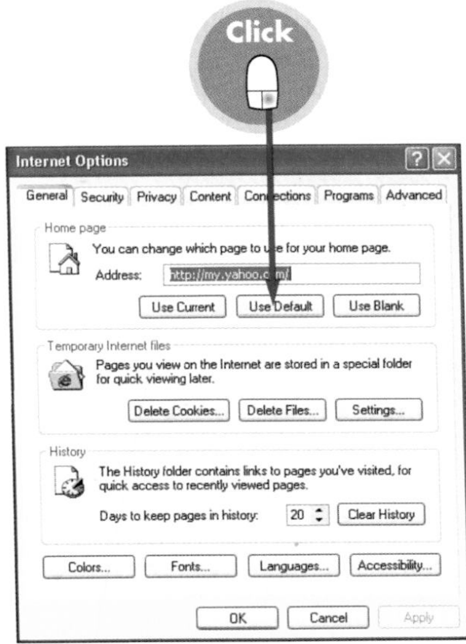

Task 4

How to Set Up a Microsoft Passport Account

One of the drawbacks of using numerous different Web sites is keeping track of all the different usernames and passwords you'll accumulate. Microsoft, which offers its own MSN portal, is trying to solve that problem with Microsoft Passport, an account you can use on all of Microsoft's Web sites as well as on more than 125 other sites, including 1-800-Flowers.Com, Buy.Com, eBay, RadioShack.com, and StarBucks. Passport keeps track of all your usernames, passwords, mailing and billing addresses, and other information to make your Internet surfing and shopping experience simpler.

1 Open the Control Panel

Windows XP includes built-in support for Microsoft Passport. To set up a Passport account, click the **Start** button and choose **Control Panel**. The **Control Panel** dialog box opens. (If you're not using Windows XP, you set up a Passport in your browser. To begin, type `http://www.passport.com` in the **Address bar** and press **Enter**.)

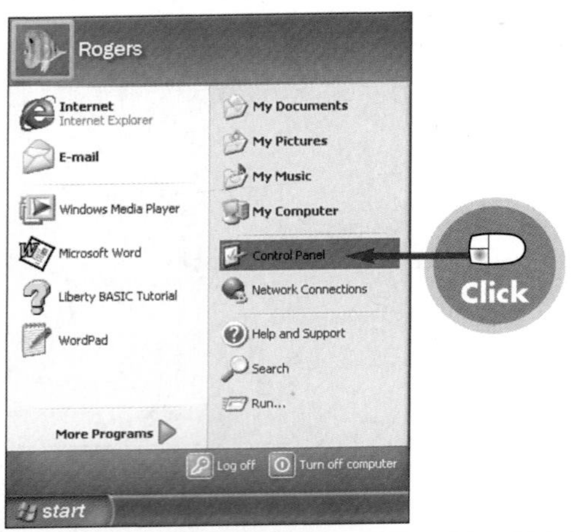

2 View Your User Accounts

Passport accounts are associated with the user account you have on Windows XP. Click the **User Accounts** link and then click the account for which you want to create a new Passport.

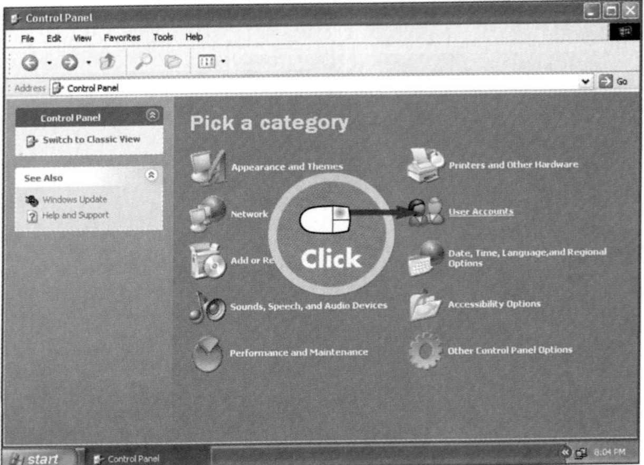

3 Connect to the Internet

To set up a Passport, you must be connected to the Internet. Make sure that a connection to your Internet service provider is open and then click the **Set up my Account to Use a .NET Passport** link.

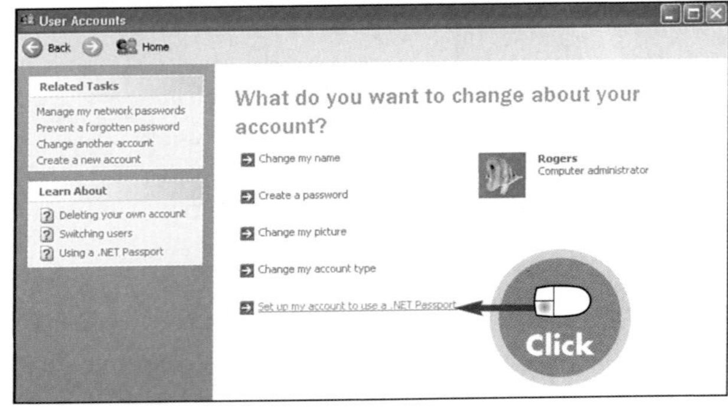

4 Set Up a Passport

The **Passport Wizard** asks a series of questions to which you must respond to set up a new Passport account. To associate a Passport with your email address, choose the **Yes, use an existing email account** radio button and click **Next**.

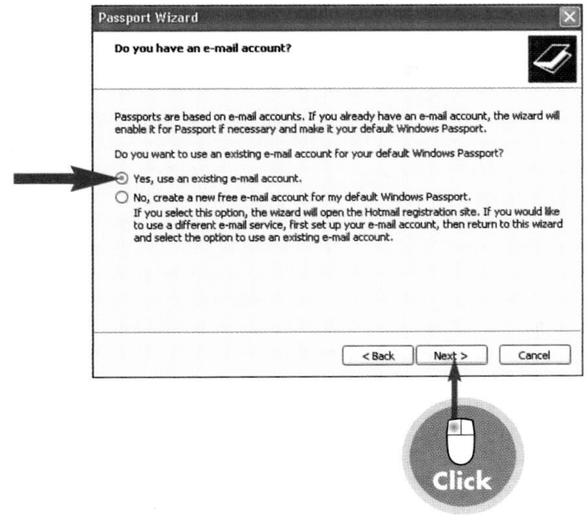

5 Enter Your Email Address

Although Microsoft recommends that your Passport be associated with a Hotmail or MSN address, you can set up the Passport using any email account. Type your email address in the **Email address or Passport** text box and click **Next**.

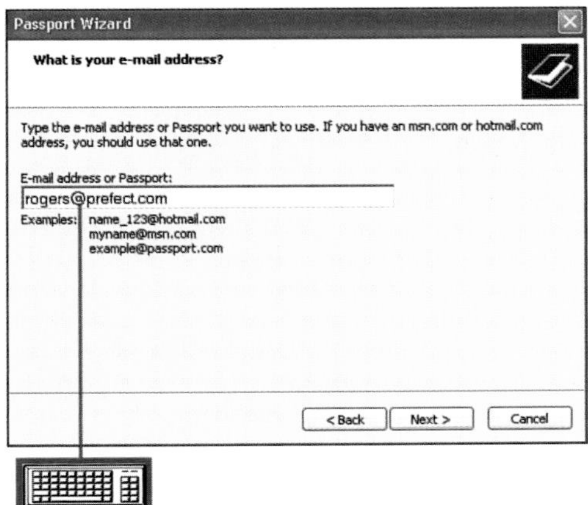

6 Choose a Password

To keep others from using your account, choose a password and type it in the **Password** and **Confirm Password** fields. You won't see the characters you are typing—asterisks will be displayed instead. Click **Next** to continue.

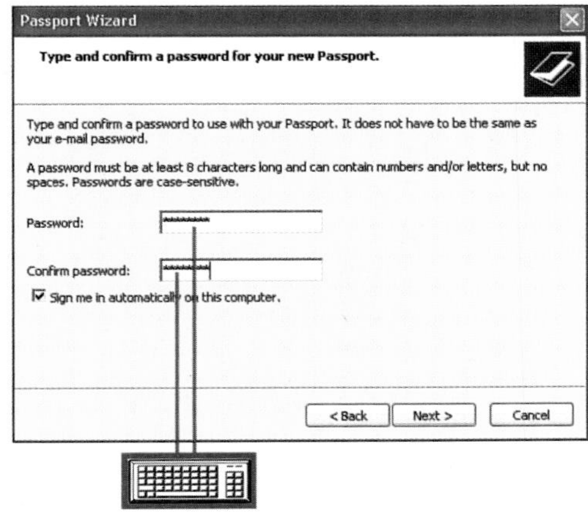

7 Create Your New Passport

After answering the wizard's remaining questions, click **Next**. On the final page of the wizard, click **Finish** to create your new Passport account. To find sites where you can use it, visit the Web site `http://www.passport.com`.

Task

4

Searching the World Wide Web

The World Wide Web has an unbelievable amount of useful information, whether you're using the Web as a student, shopper, worker, researcher, or job seeker.

You can search the World Wide Web in two ways: by exploring Web directories and by using search engines.

Directories such as Yahoo! and the Open Directory Project attempt to impose some order on the chaos of the Web, recruiting editors to prepare lists of related sites in a very structured manner.

Search engines are massive databases that attempt to index the entire Web. You can use these search engines to search for text on millions of Web pages at once, relying on the search engine to find the most appropriate pages.

How to Find a Site When You Don't Know Its Address

Every document on the World Wide Web has a unique address called a *URL*, which is short for *uniform resource locator*. A site's address can take many forms, but most of the largest Web sites have similar-looking and simple URLs, such as `http://www.yahoo.com`, `http://www.microsoft.com`, `http://www.internic.net`, `http://www.slashdot.org`, `http://www.nasa.gov`, and `http://www.unt.edu`. By learning a few things about these addresses, you can make an educated guess about the addresses of some of the Web sites you're looking for. Subsequent tasks cover how to use search engines and directories to find a site.

1 Look for a Company's Address

The most popular ending used in a Web address is `.com`. If you know the name of a company or publication, you can try to find its Web site by typing `http://www.companyname.com` in the **Address bar**, where `companyname` is the name of the company. Press **Enter** to see whether the browser can find a site at that address. One example: Dell Computer Corporation's URL is `http://www.dell.com`.

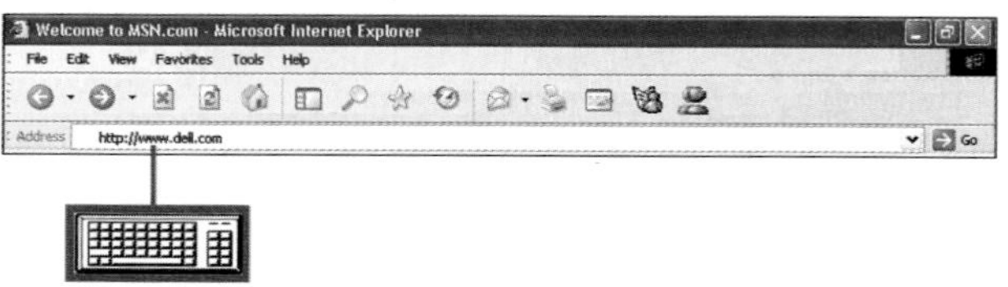

2 Try a Shorter Address

Some sites with addresses ending in `.com` don't start with the `www.` prefix. You can also look for a company or publication's address by typing the company's name followed by `.com` in the **Address bar** and then pressing **Enter**. One example: `http://monster.com`.

3 Look for an Organization

Many Web addresses that end in `.org` are for not-for-profit organizations (although this is not a requirement). Look for an organization by typing `http://www.organizationname.org` in the **Address bar**, where `organizationname` is the name of the organization. Press **Enter** after typing the full address. One example is `http://www.unicef.org`.

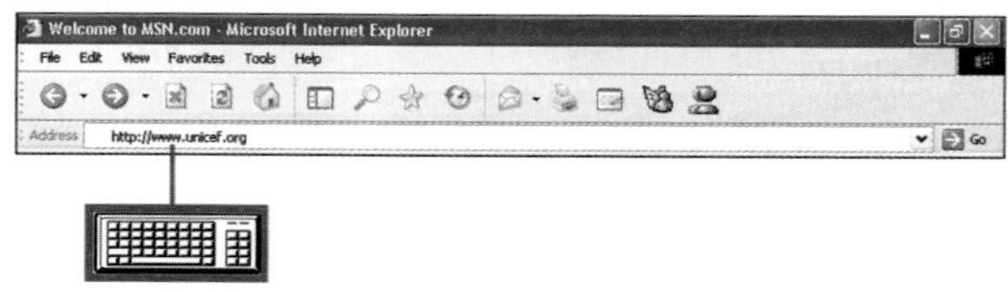

Look for a Government Site

All Web addresses that end in **.gov** are affiliated with the United States government. One of the most popular is **http://www.whitehouse.gov**, the White House site. To look for a government agency or similar entity, type **http://www.groupname.gov** in the **Address bar** (where **groupname** is the name of the government entity), and press **Enter**.

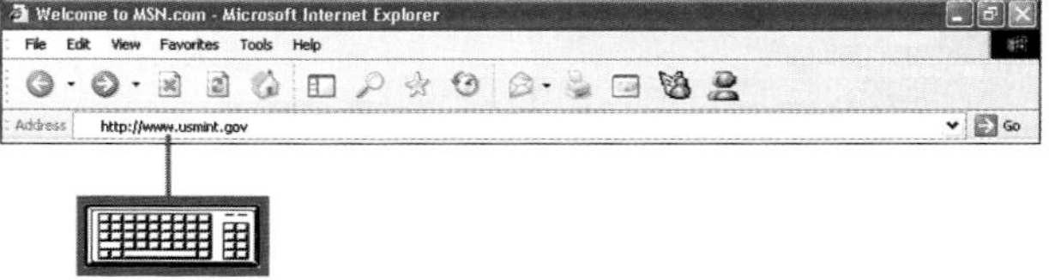

Search for the Name

Internet Explorer 6 has an Autosearch feature that searches the World Wide Web for pages containing keywords you type in the **Address bar**. Type the name of the entity you're looking for in the **Address bar**. As you are typing, a text box appears below the **Address bar**, describing what you are looking for. Press **Enter** to begin the search.

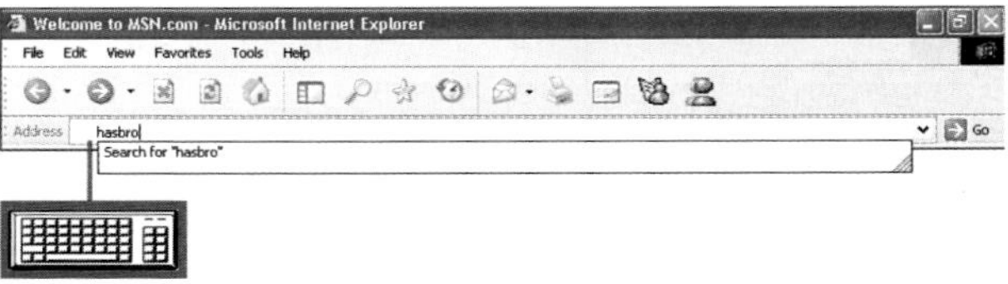

How to Hint

Finding Universities and Colleges

Using another type of Web address can help you locate the sites of colleges, universities, and advanced research institutions. These institutions almost always have Web sites with URLs that end with **.edu**; in the **Address bar**, type **http://www.institutionname.edu** (where **institutionname** is the name of the institution), and press **Enter**. For example, **http://www.unt.edu** is the home page of the University of North Texas.

Shortening Web Addresses

The URL associated with a Web page is usually prefaced with **http://** (which indicates the protocol used to send the page to your browser). Another common prefix is **ftp://**. The current crop of browsers (including Internet Explorer 6) will add **http://** automatically if you forget to include **http://** or **ftp://** in a URL. For this reason, you can type a shorter version of a site's URL, such as **www.dell.com** instead of **http://www.dell.com**.

Getting Your Own Address

Anyone can buy an address on the Web; it isn't restricted to companies, schools, and other large organizations. You can use your personalized address, which is called a *domain name*, in email, on your own World Wide Web site, and with instant messaging.

To find out how to register and purchase a domain name, visit the InterNIC Web site: Type **http://www.internic.net** into your browser's Address bar and press **Enter**. The site's Registrar Directory lists dozens of companies that sell domains, usually for about $15 to $25 per year.

How to See Pages You Have Recently Visited

Internet Explorer 6 can keep track of the sites you've visited in recent days. This information is stored in the **History** list, which is presented in a manner similar to the browser's Favorites list. By default, Internet Explorer keeps track of all the sites visited in the past 20 days. If you're searching for something you have recently viewed, the place to start looking for it is your browser's **History** list.

1 Open the History List

Click the **History** button in the browser's toolbar to open a window containing the **History** list.

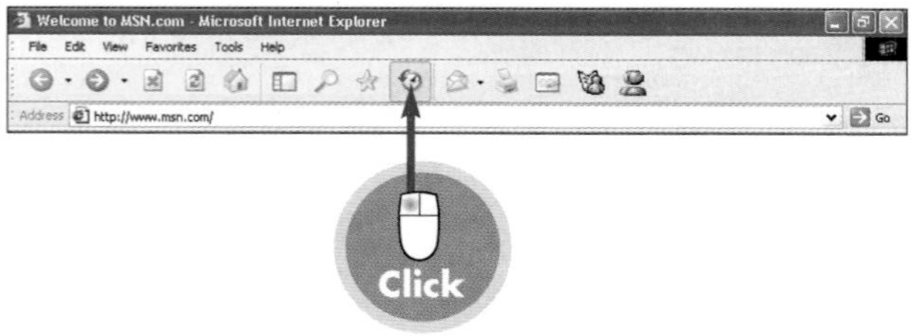

2 Open a Site's Hyperlinks

Each folder in the **History** list is devoted to a Web site you visited on a specific day or week. Open a folder by clicking it. You'll see Internet shortcuts for every page on that site you visited at that time.

3 Revisit a Web Site

To revisit a Web page, double-click its Internet shortcut in the **History** list. The page is loaded in a browser window.

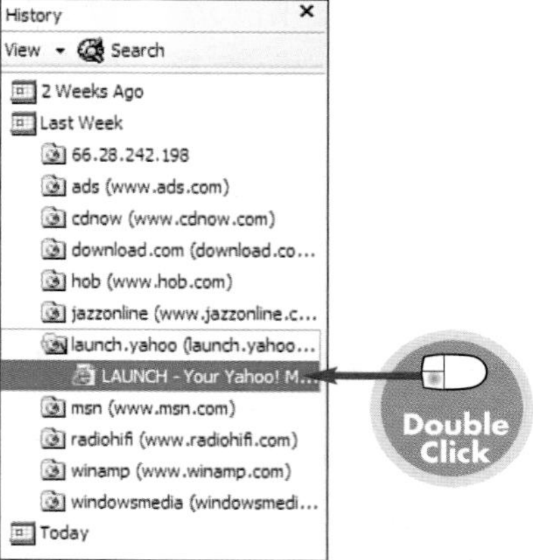

4 Search for a Shortcut

Looking through the **History** list by hand can be time consuming if you have visited a large number of Web sites. To search through the entire list, click the **Search** button in the bar above the **History** list.

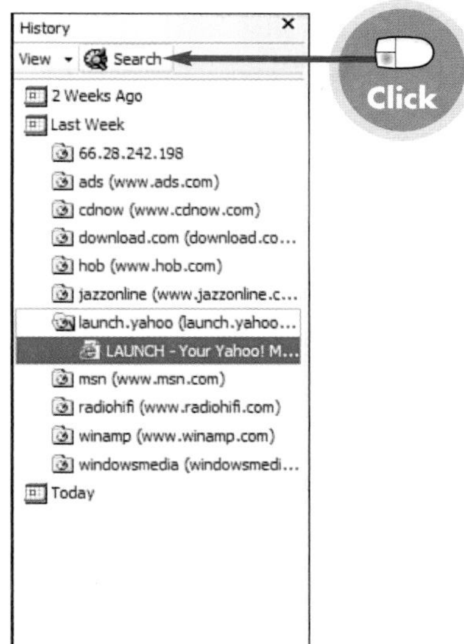

5 Conduct the Search

Type the text you're looking for in the **Search for** box and click the **Search Now** button. All items in the **History** list that match the search text will be displayed.

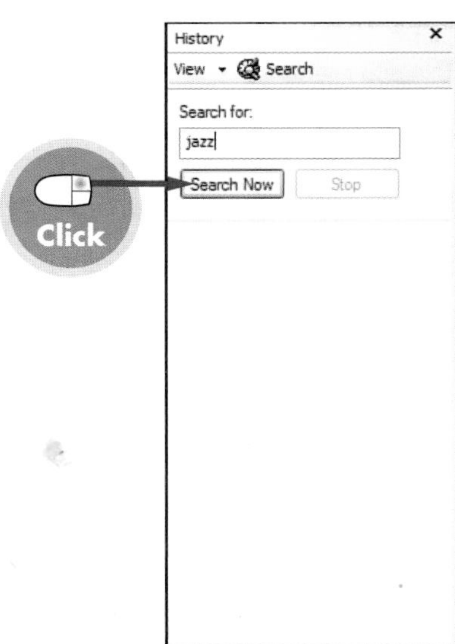

6 Delete History Items

To remove a folder or shortcut from the **History** list, right-click the item and choose **Delete** from the pop-up menu. (You also can delete all shortcuts in the entire **History** list: Pull down the **Tools** menu, choose **Internet Options**, and click the **Clear History** button to delete them.)

7 Rearrange History Items

Normally, items in the **History** list are organized by date. To arrange the list according to how often you visit pages, click the **View** button in the bar above the **History** list and choose the **By Most Visited** command.

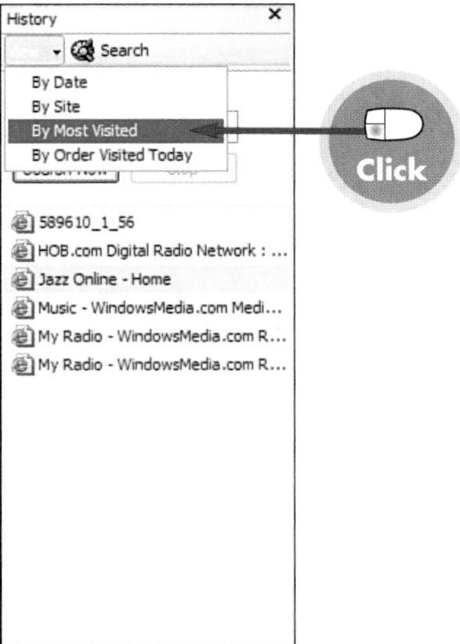

Task 3

How to Search for a Specific Topic on the Web

There are several ways to search for sites related to a specific topic on the World Wide Web. Task 2, "How to Visit a Web Site When You Know Its Address," in Part 2, "Browsing the World Wide Web," describes how to use Internet Explorer 6's **Autosearch** feature to search for sites by entering a topic in the browser's **Address bar**. Another way to search by topic is to use the World Wide Web directories published by Yahoo!, Excite, the Open Directory Project, and others.

1 Visit a Directory

Most Web directories function in a similar manner. The Open Directory Project is a volunteer effort coordinated by AOL that organizes more than 3.4-million sites into categories. To visit the site, type **`http://www.dmoz.org`** into Internet Explorer's **Address bar** and press **Enter**.

2 Search for a Topic

Type the topic you're looking for in the site's search box and click the **Search** button.

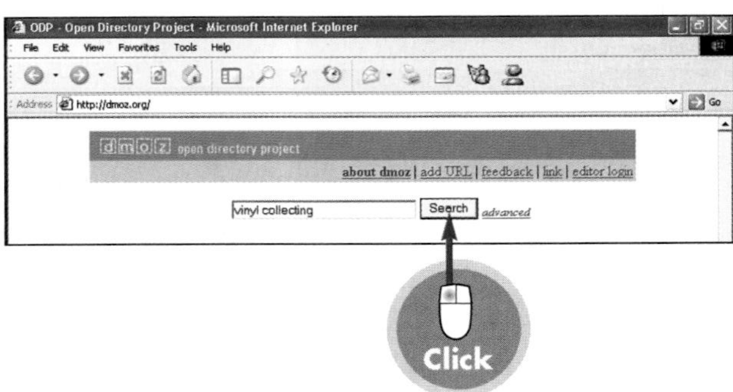

3 View the Results

Web directories are organized into categories—pages that contain Web sites and links to subcategories. Categories that match your topic are listed first in the search-results page and are usually the best place to find what you're looking for. To view a category, click its hyperlink in the results page.

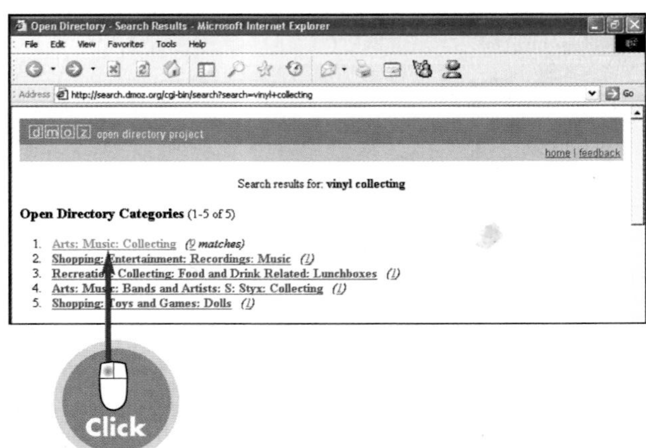

4 Scan a Category

Category pages display all subcategories and Web sites that match a given topic. Click a hyperlink to visit the associated site.

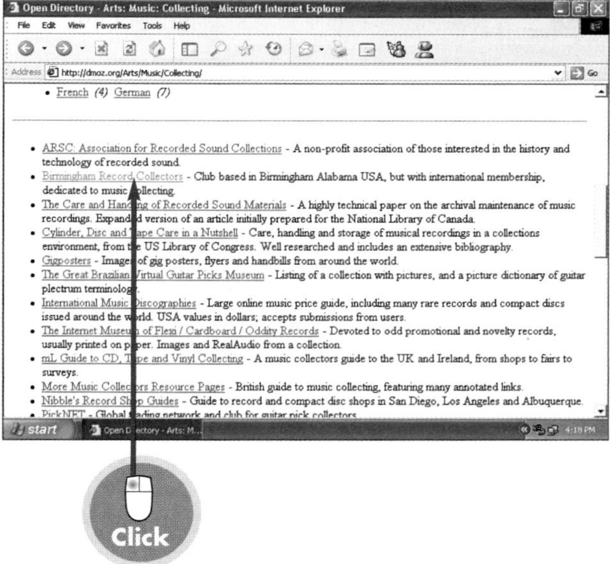

5 Search Within a Category

When you're viewing a page, you can conduct a new search that is confined to the portion of the directory related to the category. Type a topic in the search box, click the down-arrow button to the right of the drop-down menu, and select the **only in *category*** option, where ***category*** is the name of the category you're searching in; then click the **Search** button.

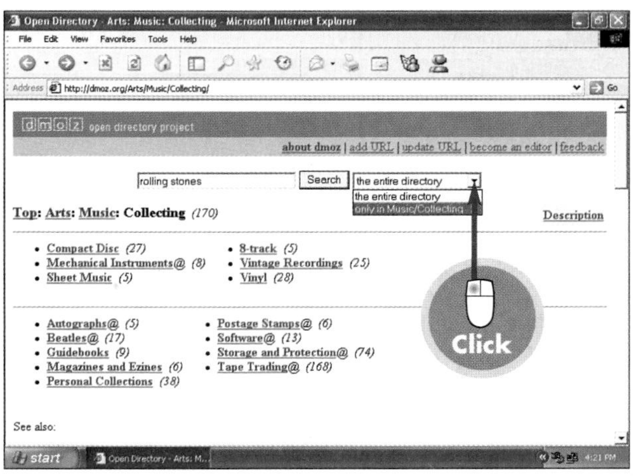

6 Begin a New Search

To begin a new search on the Open Directory Project home page, click the **dmoz** graphic ("DMoz" is short for "Directory Mozilla," an early name for the project).

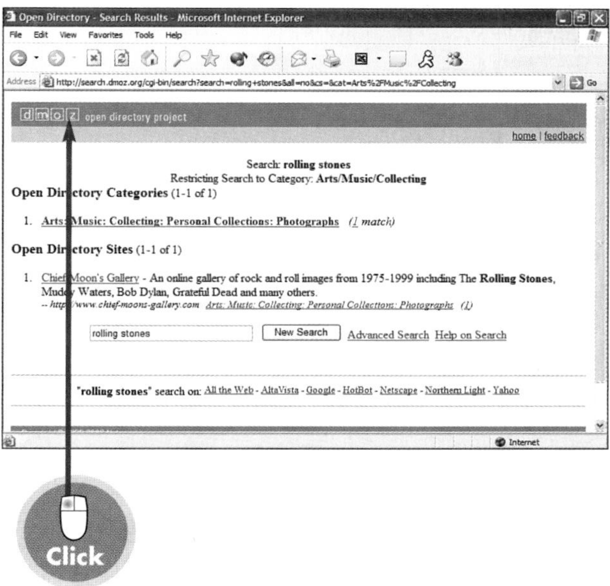

How to Hint

Using Other Web Directories

Each Web directory includes a different selection of Web sites, so you may want to try several directories in your search. Use the following URLs to visit some of the other popular services:

- **Yahoo!**: `http://www.yahoo.com`
- **Google Directory**: `http://directory.google.com`
- **Excite**: `http://www.excite.com`

Broadening Your Search

In the Open Directory Project and other directories, every category name includes hyperlinks to broader categories with which it is associated. For example, the `Top:Arts:Music:Collecting` category is a subcategory of the more general `Top:Arts:Music` category. Use these links to make your search *less* specific.

How to Search Through Millions of Web Pages

The World Wide Web grows at a speed much faster than any human-compiled directory can possibly match. To find sites the directories overlook, you can search through millions of machine-compiled pages by visiting a *search engine*. Search engines are massive databases containing the text of documents available on the Web. These engines continuously traverse links on the World Wide Web, adding new documents and deleting those that have been taken offline. Some of the most popular search engines are AltaVista, HotBot, Northern Light, and Google.

1 Visit a Search Engine

Currently, the most popular search engine is Google. To visit this engine, type `http://www.google.com` into the **Address bar** and press **Enter**.

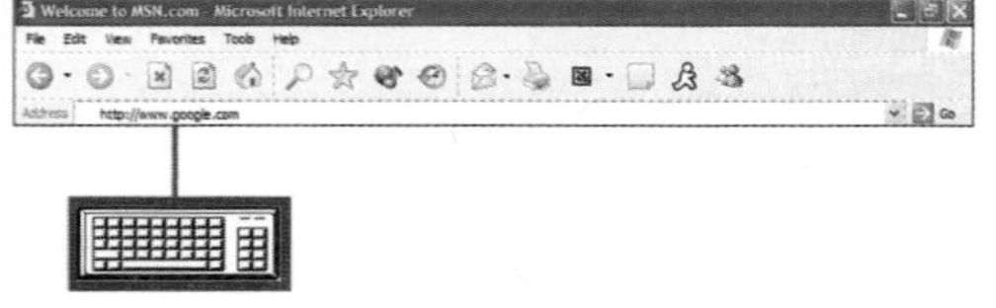

2 Conduct a Search

To search Google, type a keyword, question, sentence, or phrase describing what you're looking for into the search box. Be as specific as possible. Click the **Google Search** button to begin looking.

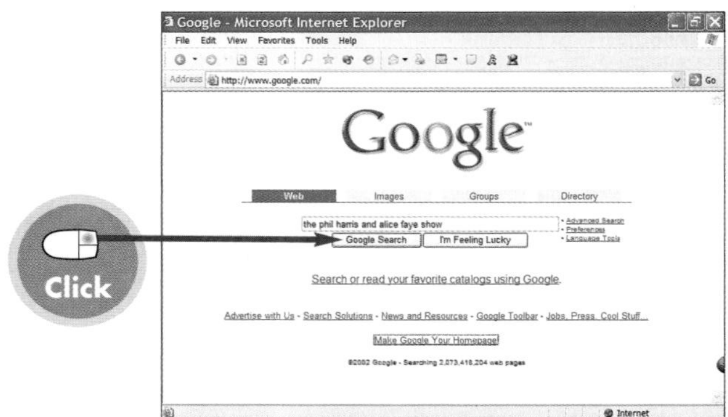

3 View the Search Results

Search engines rank the best-matching pages first. The engine ignores all common words you use (such as *the* or *and*) and ranks pages according to the number of other search words that were found. You can use the **Next** hyperlink at the bottom of a page to view more results. Click a page's title to visit that page.

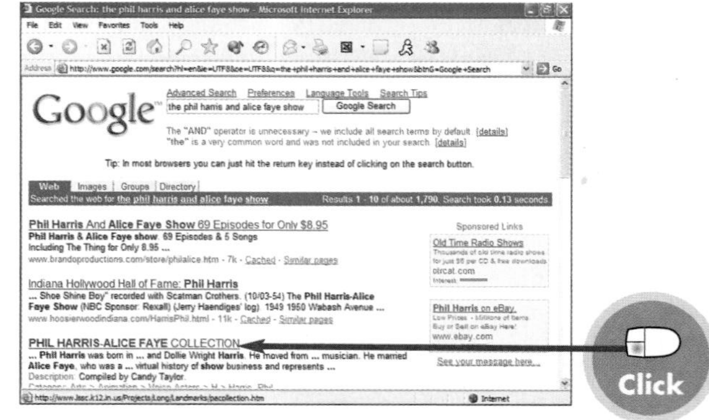

4 Conduct an Advanced Search

Google puts its advanced search features on a separate page. Click the **Advanced Search** hyperlink on the site's home page to conduct more complex searches.

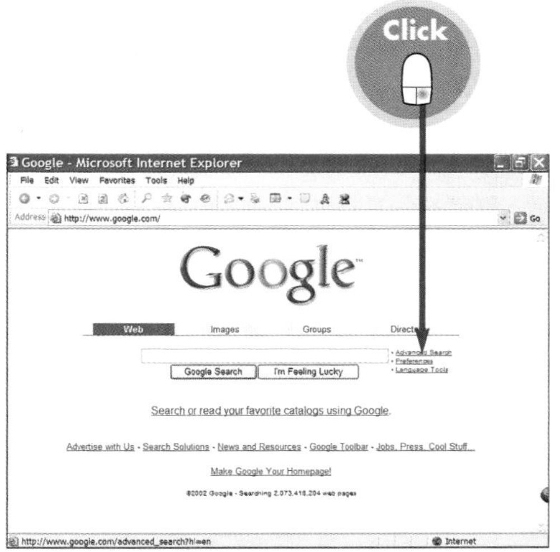

5 Search for a Specific Phrase

To look for a specific phrase, type it in the **exact phrase** box and then click the **Google Search** button. The search results include only those pages that contain this exact phrase.

6 Search for Text in a Page Title

A Web page's title often contains a succinct description of its contents. To search through page titles, in the **exact phrase** box type the text you're looking for and then choose **in the title of the page** from the **Occurrences** drop-down list. Click the **Google Search** button to view results.

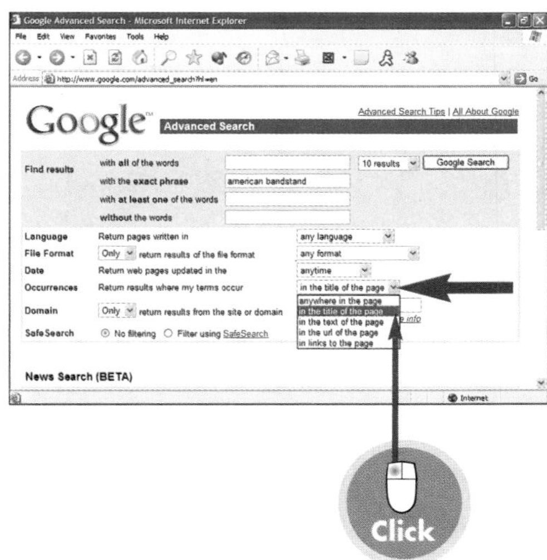

How to Hint

Visiting Other Search Engines

Even the best search engines can't keep up with how fast the World Wide Web is growing. For this reason, you may need to use more than one search engine to find Web pages with the information you need. Here are a few other search engines you can use:

- **HotBot**: `http://hotbot.lycos.com`
- **Google**: `http://www.google.com`
- **Northern Light**: `http://www.northernlight.com`
- **MetaCrawler**: `http://www.metacrawler.com`
- **WebCrawler**: `http://www.webcrawler.com`
- **Lycos**: `www.lycos.com`

Task

5 How to Find Software on the Web

As you might expect, many World Wide Web users do their computer-software shopping online. You can use the Web to purchase software, receive and install demo versions of software, and choose from thousands of useful free computer programs. One site that offers each of these services is Download.com. The name comes from the term *download*, which means to transmit a file from another network to your system.

1 Visit the Site

To get started, type **`http://www.download.com`** in Internet Explorer 6's **Address bar** and press **Enter**. The Download.com home page opens in your browser window.

2 Search for Software

Programs you can try before you buy are called *shareware*, and Download.com offers thousands of shareware items you can download. To search for a program, type its name in the **Search** box, choose **In Downloads** from the drop-down list, and click the **Go!** button.

3 Explore Search Results

Download.com lists all programs that match the name you entered. To find out more about a specific program, click its hyperlink.

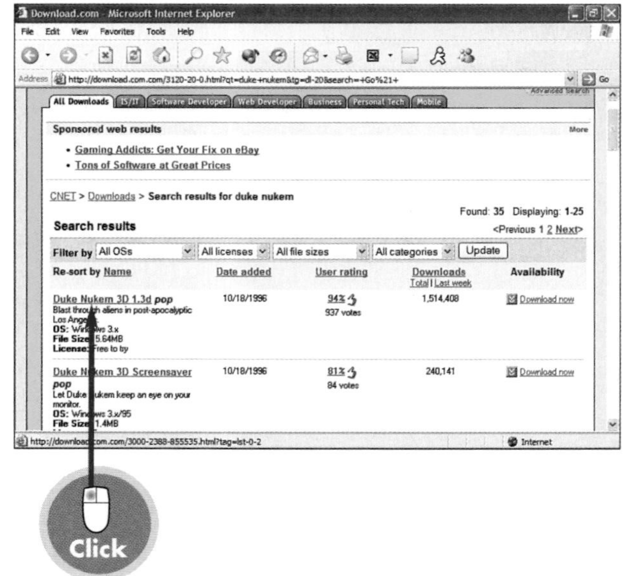

4 Download a Program

If you decide that you want to download the program whose description you have been reading, click the **Download Now** hyperlink. The **File Download** dialog box opens.

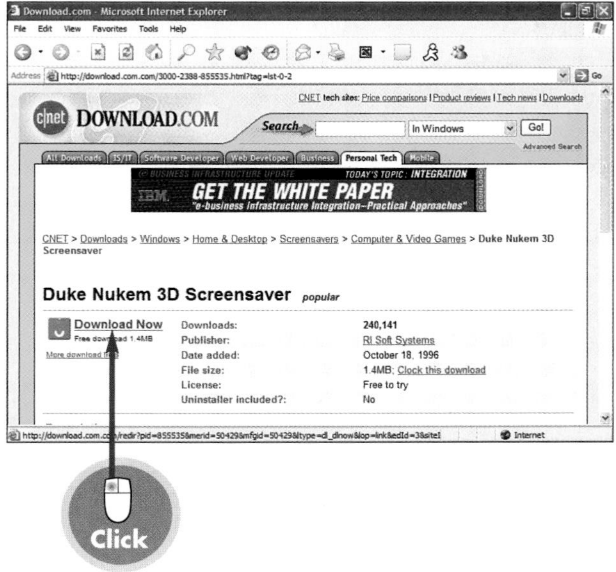

5 Choose a Download Method

Click the **Save** button to save the program in a folder on your system or the **Open** button to install the program immediately. If you save a program to a folder on your system, wait for the download to finish, then open the folder and double-click the program's icon to install it. After installation, use the **Start** menu to find and run the program.

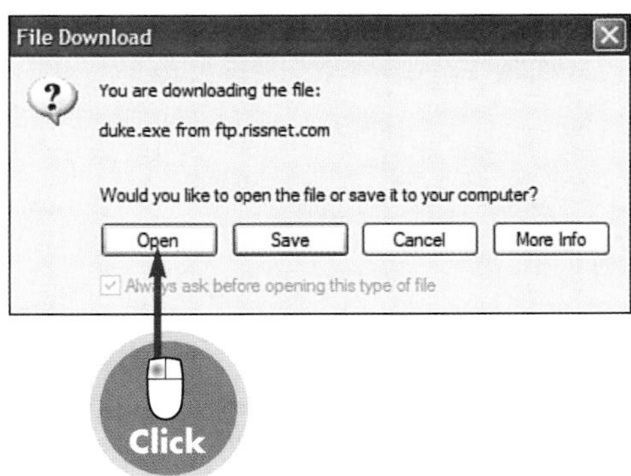

6 Look for Retail Software

To find commercial software—such as the software sold at computer superstores—click the **Price comparisons** hyperlink on the Download.com menu at the top of the home page.

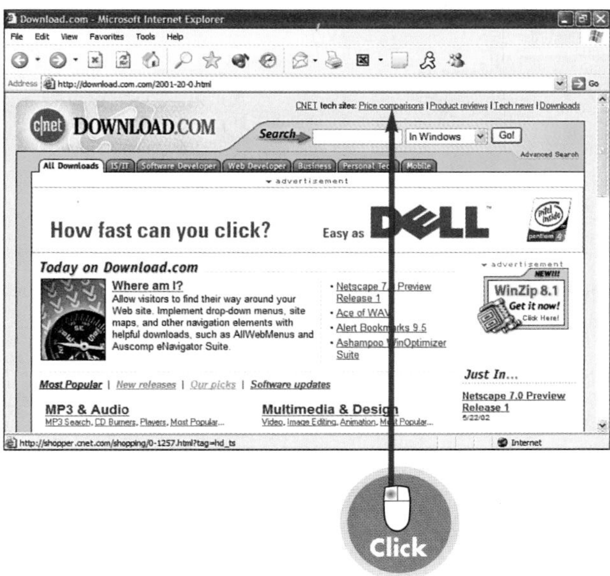

7 Begin a Search

Type the name of the software in which you're interested in the **Find Pricing and Availability** box, choose **In Shopping** from the drop-down list, and click the **Go!** button. Download.com will compare prices on that commercial-software product at several different online software stores, displaying the results in tabular form on a new Web page.

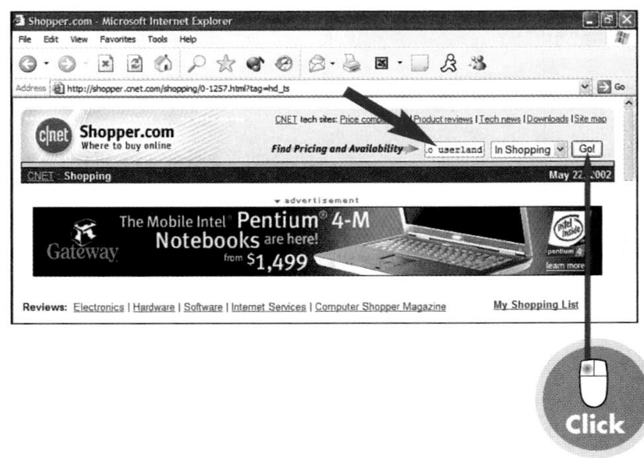

How to Find a Company on the Web

Most companies that do business on a national or international scale have a World Wide Web site. Thousands of smaller local companies also are online, making the Web a great place to look up companies, buy their products, and seek customer support. You can find a company using the techniques introduced in Task 1, "How to Find a Site When You Don't Know Its Address," earlier in this part. There are, however, a few ways to speed up your search, as discussed here.

1 Use Autosearch

As you learned in Task 1, Internet Explorer 6's **Autosearch** feature can direct you to many sites. Type the company's name in the **Address bar** and press **Enter**.

2 Find the Company Site

If Autosearch recognizes the company name, its home page opens. Otherwise, a page opens on MSN containing a list of possible sites that match the text you typed. Click a hyperlink to load that site.

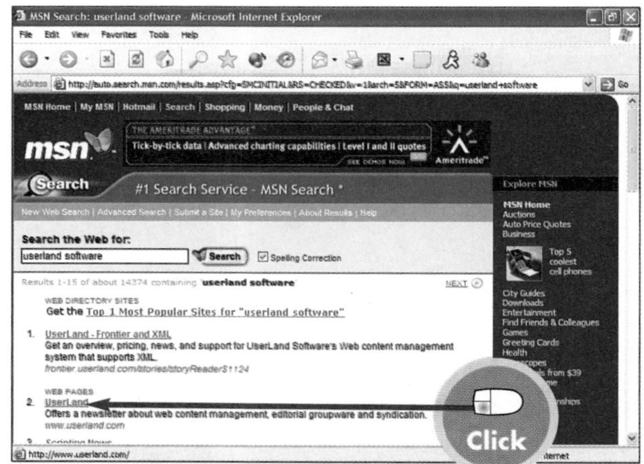

3 Search Yahoo!

Another good source for company sites is Yahoo!. Type `http://www.yahoo.com` in the browser's **Address bar** and press **Enter**. When the home page opens, type the name of the company you are looking for in the search box and click the **Search** button.

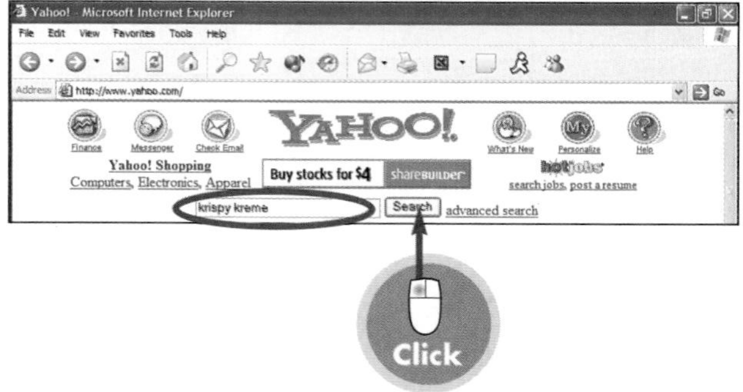

4 View Yahoo! Results

Yahoo! lists all categories and Web sites that match the name you typed, with the best matches displayed first. Click a hyperlink to visit the associated Web site.

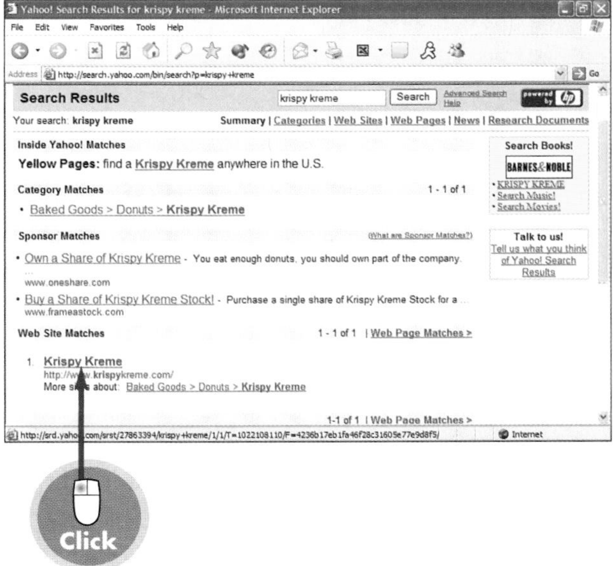

5 Use Google

The Google search engine is useful for company searches because of the unusual way it ranks Web sites. Type `http://www.google.com` in the **Address bar** and press **Enter** to go to the Google home page. When you're there, type the company name in the search box and click the **Google Search** button.

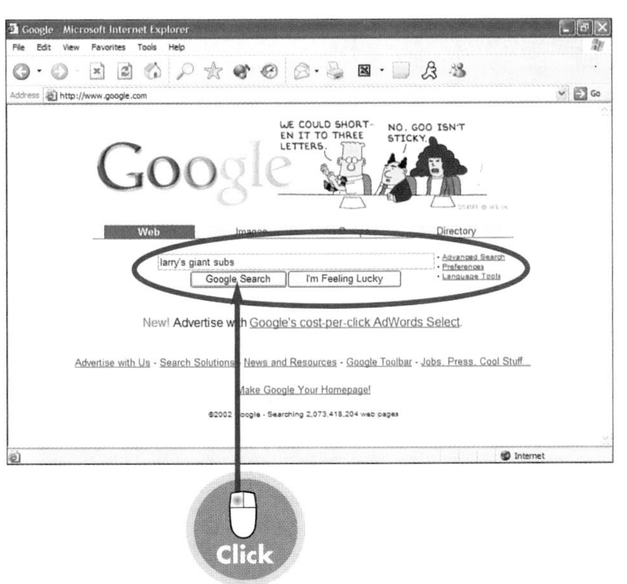

6 Visit a Site

When you use Google to search for a company, the first item listed on the search-results page is often a hyperlink to the company's official Web site. Click the link to visit that site.

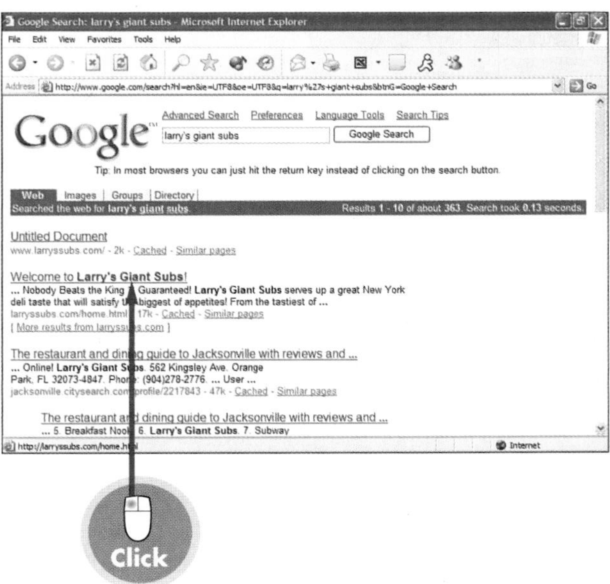

How to Hint

Getting Lucky on a Google Search

Because Google is so good at finding the best-matching Web sites in a search, it offers a feature to automatically look for the best possible match and load it. To use this feature, type a company's name in the search box and click the **I'm Feeling Lucky** button.

Using a Business Search Engine

Another useful resource when looking for a company is Business.com, a directory, search engine, and news site for employers and employment-related information. To visit the site, type the URL **`http://www.business.com`** in your browser's **Address bar** and press **Enter**.

How to Find a Person on the Web

You can search for people just as you do any other subject on the World Wide Web: using Web directories such as Yahoo! and search engines such as AltaVista and Google. A more focused search is available using directories such as Yahoo! People Search, a mailing address and email directory. People Search scans a collection of public databases for matching names and can be narrowed to specific states or provinces. People Search also links to other public directories, such as 1800USSearch.com.

1 Visit Yahoo!

Most of the special features on Yahoo! have a short, easy-to-remember address. To visit Yahoo! People Search, type `http://people.yahoo.com` in your browser's **Address bar** and press **Enter**.

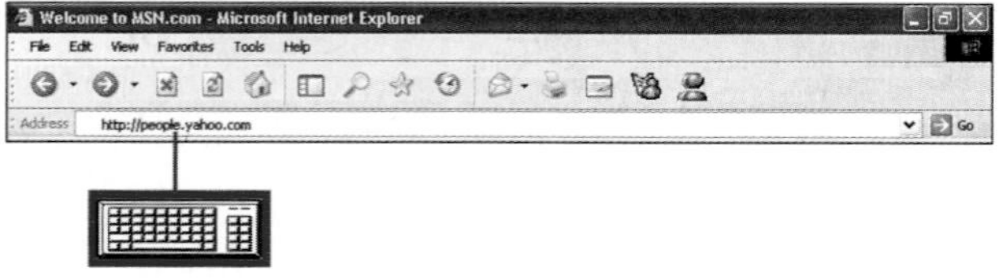

2 Search for a Phone Number

To search the entire database for someone's phone number, type the person's first and last names in the **Telephone Search** boxes and then click the **Search** button. You can omit the first name to see all matches for a surname. (Note that only publicly accessible phone numbers are returned by this search; private numbers are not returned.)

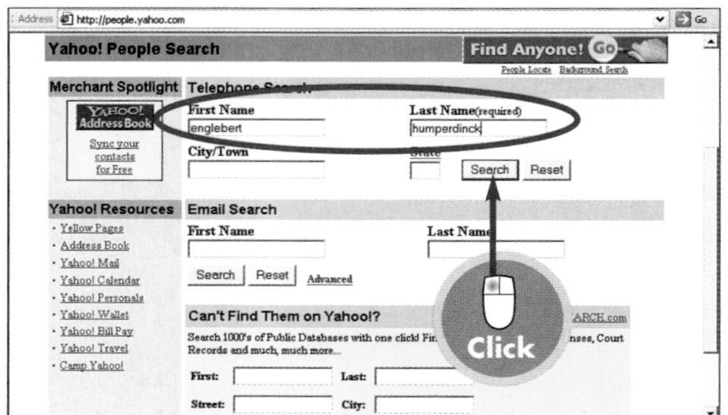

3 Narrow Your Search

If you want to narrow your search to a single state, type the state's postal abbreviation in the **State** box. Click **Search** to look for a match.

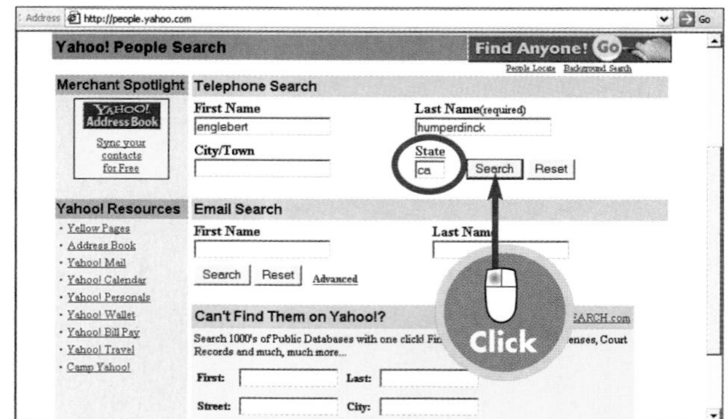

4 Search for an Email Address

To look for someone's email address, type the person's first and last names in the **Email Search** boxes and then click the adjacent **Search** button. Some of the addresses that are found are likely to be outdated, especially if the person has changed email addresses frequently.

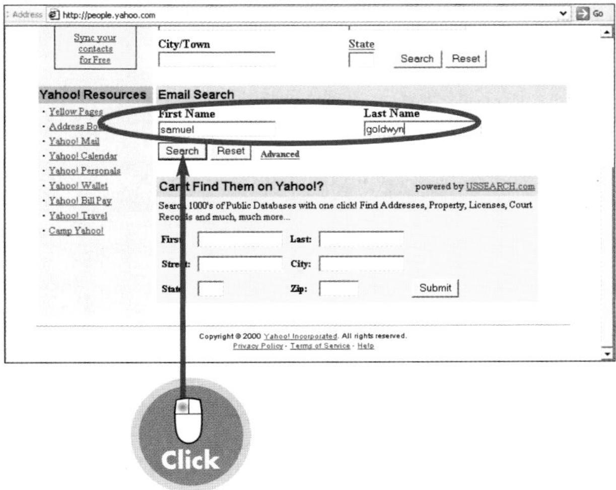

5 Make an Advanced Email Search

Yahoo! People Search offers even more options for email searches. If necessary, click the **Back** button in your browser's toolbar to return to the original search page. Then click the **Advanced** hyperlink to load the more sophisticated search page.

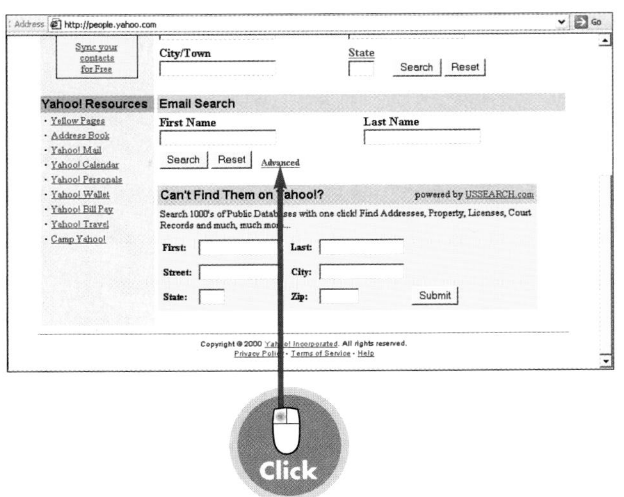

6 Fill Out the Search Form

Most fields in the **Advanced Search** page can be used to narrow a search. You can specify the state or province, country, former email address, and organization type. Enable the **SmartNames** check box to treat related first names (such as *Bill*, *Billy*, and *William*) as the same name. Click the **Search** button when you're ready to search.

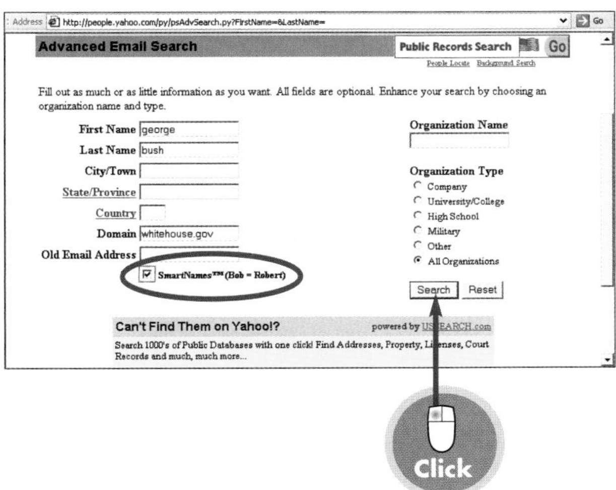

How to Hint

Finding Email Addresses on Usenet

Usenet (a collection of discussion forums on more than 20,000 topics) attracts thousands of Internet users who post messages that contain their email addresses. You can search Google Groups, an archive of Usenet messages, for a specific person. To visit the database, type `http://groups.google.com` into your browser's **Address bar** and press **Enter**. You learn more about searching this archive in Part 7, Task 6, "How to Search an Archive of Past Newsgroup Discussions."

Task 8

How to Find a Job on the Web

The World Wide Web has hundreds of different resources for job seekers. One of the most popular is CareerBuilder, a database of help-wanted classified ads compiled from hundreds of newspapers, Web sites, and employment services. CareerBuilder, formerly known as CareerPath.com, also offers a place to post your résumé, save job searches you conduct frequently, and receive help-wanted ads by email.

1 Visit the Site

Visit Career Builder by typing `http://www.headhunter.net` in your browser's **Address bar** and pressing **Enter**. When the site loads, click the **Advanced Job Search!** link. A job-search page opens.

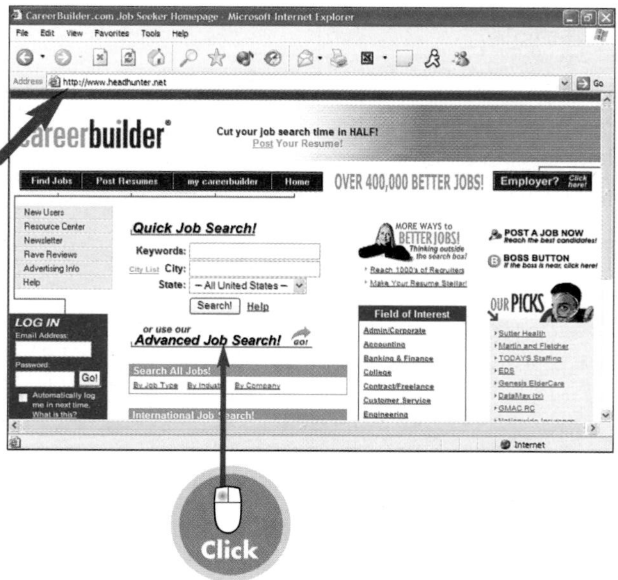

2 Narrow Your Job Search

If you are looking for specific words in job postings, type them in the **Keywords** text box. Choose the type of search you want to conduct in the **Using** drop-down list.

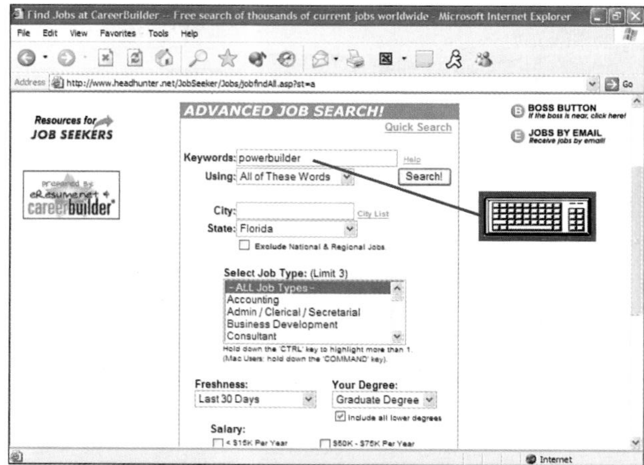

3 Select an Industry

You can narrow your search to a specific industry, or you can search all industry categories. From the **Select Job Type** list box, select the industry you're interested in.

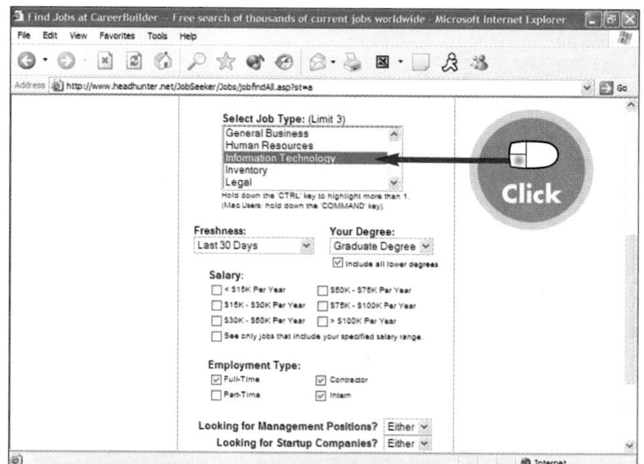

4 Indicate Your Degree

You can exclude postings based on your level of education. Select it in the **Degree** drop-down list and enable the **Include all lower degrees** check box if you want to include jobs looking for other levels of education.

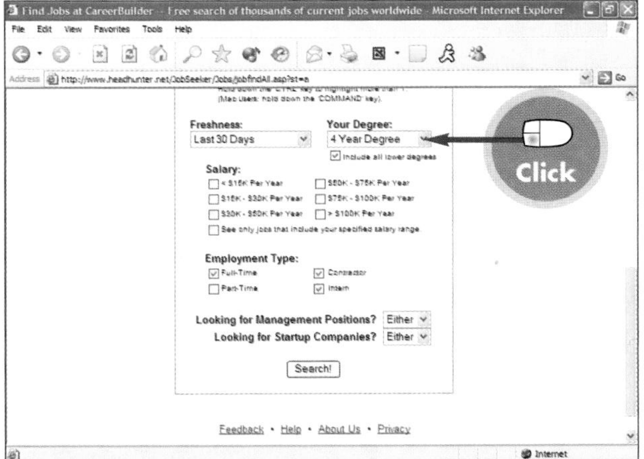

5 Indicate Your Desired Salary

You can exclude postings that don't meet your minimum-salary requirements by enabling one of the salary check boxes in the **Salary** section.

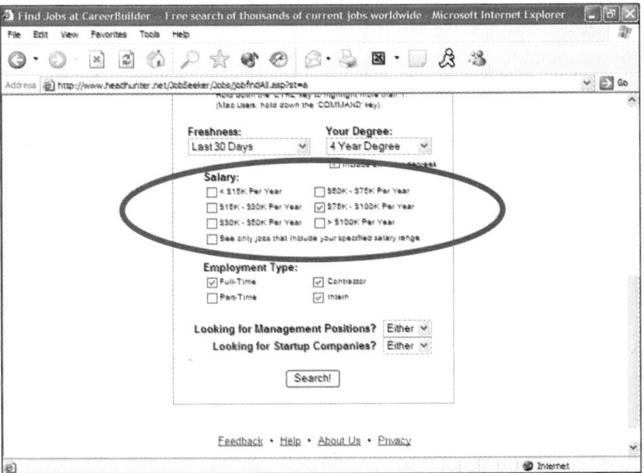

6 Search for a Job

After choosing one of the **Employment Type** check boxes, click **Search!**.

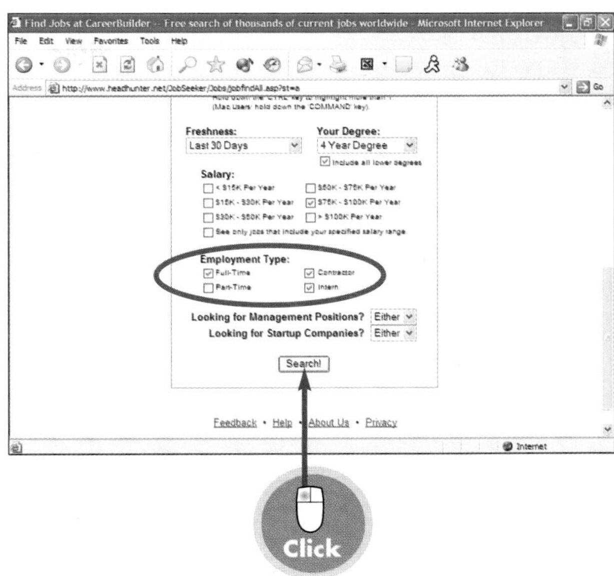

7 Read a Listing

CareerBuilder displays all the help-wanted ads matching your criteria. To read a job listing, click its entry in the **Title** column. If you're interested in a job, you can apply for it on the site.

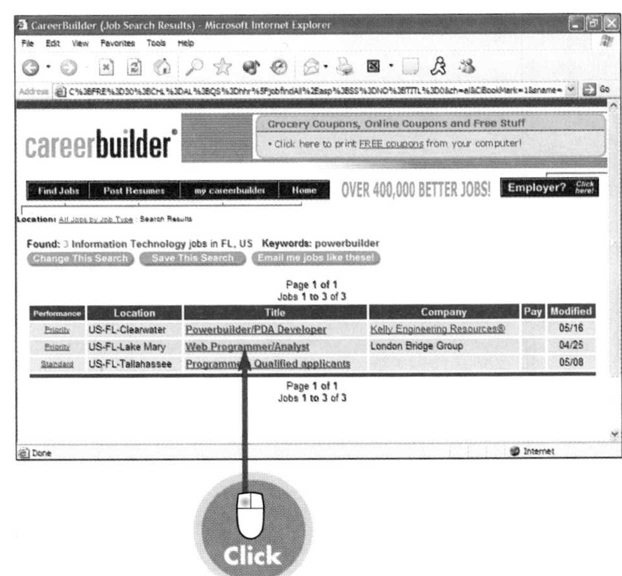

9 How to Find Your Ancestors on the Web

The World Wide Web has become a boon for people conducting genealogy research. Before the Web, genealogy research took place mostly through visits to libraries and cemeteries or personal contact with distant relatives. Today, on the RootsWeb site, genealogists can pore over databases containing 200 million ancestor names, view the work of more than 225,000 other genealogists, and exchange information on thousands of mailing lists and message boards. Many of these services are free, although you also can buy some information from a related site, Ancestry.com.

1 Visit the Site

Visit RootsWeb: Type `http://www.rootsweb.com` in your browser's **Address bar** and press **Enter**.

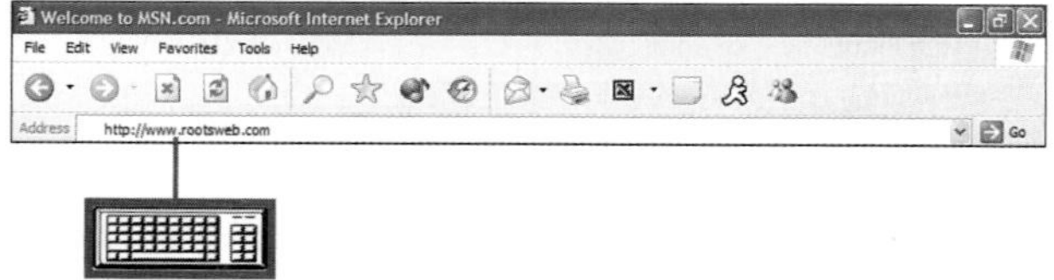

2 Look for a Name

In the **Search RootsWeb.com** section, type the name of an ancestor in the **First Name** and **Last Name** boxes and click the **Search** button.

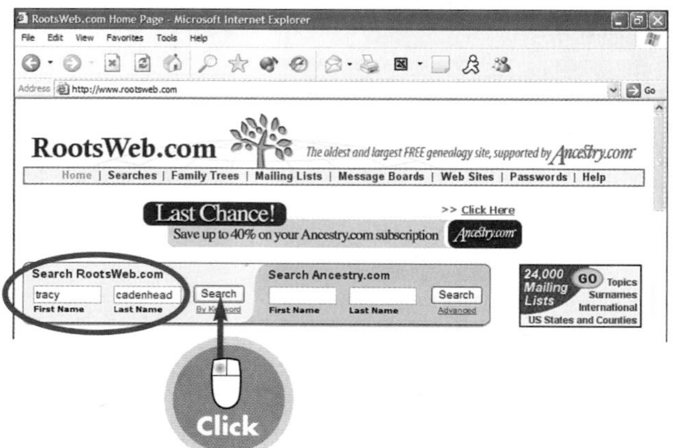

3 Choose a Database

RootsWeb searches 43 databases for your ancestor's name and displays a list of places where it was found. To view a database, click its name.

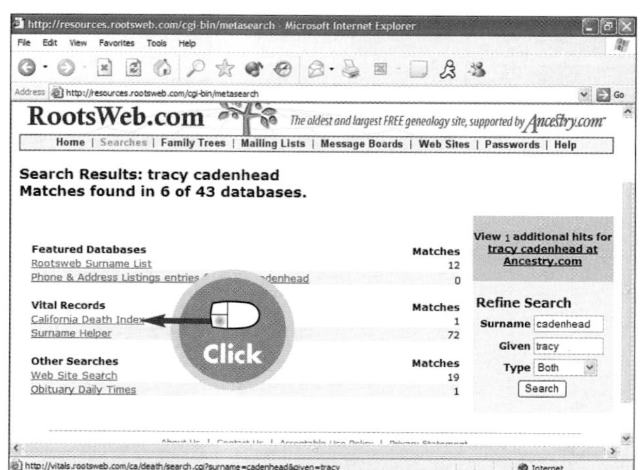

4 Exit the Database

When you're finished viewing the data, click your browser's **Back** button to return to the list of databases.

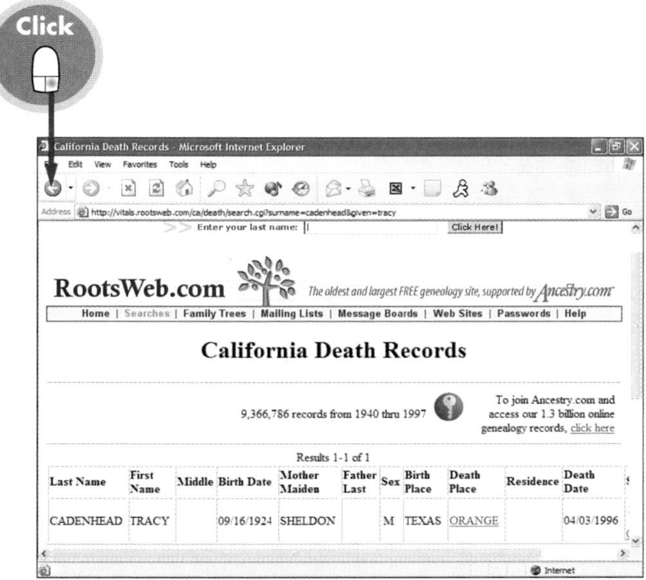

5 Search the Site

One of the databases you can search is the RootsWeb site, which contains pages submitted by thousands of genealogists. To see this data, click the **Web Site Search** link.

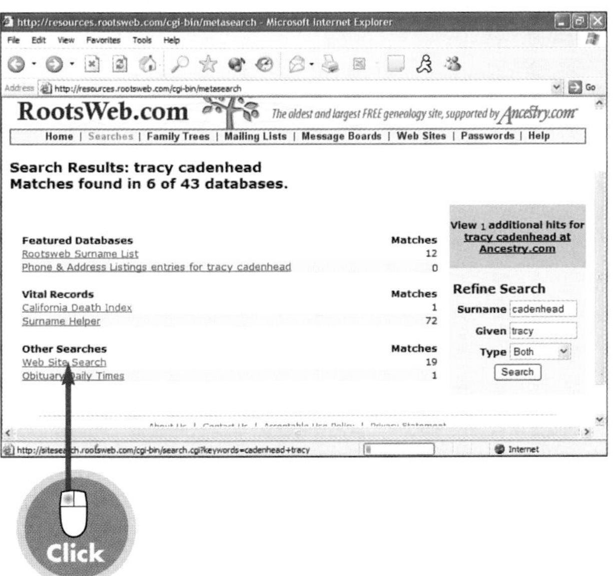

6 View a Page

The pages that come up in a search are published by RootsWeb members. To view a page, click its title.

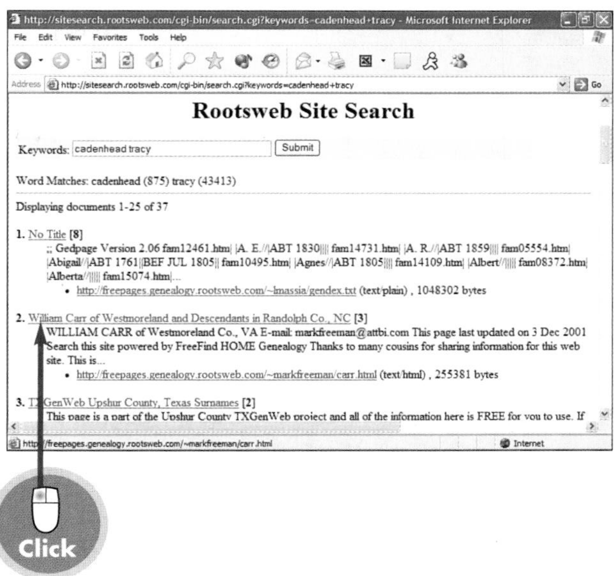

7 Try Ancestry.com

There may be records matching your ancestor's name on Ancestry.com, which charges for access. To see what's available before making a purchase, click the **Ancestry.com** link.

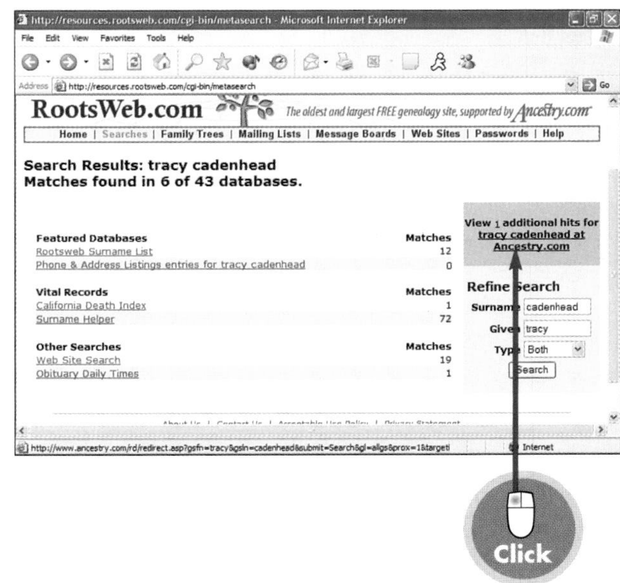

Task

5

Communicating with Electronic Mail

Electronic mail, more commonly called *email*, enables you to send messages to anyone who has an Internet email address. These messages, which are free to send and to receive, usually arrive within minutes of being sent.

Using email, you can communicate directly with friends, family members, and colleagues. You can send messages to your elected leaders, request customer support from a business, and exchange pictures with friends and family. You also can receive advertisements, although unfortunately many of these arrive unsolicited—a type of Internet marketing called *spam*.

Most Internet service providers offer an email account as part of your subscription. (One of the things you must obtain from your provider is the information necessary to use your new email account: your username and password, the name of your provider's mail servers, and other setup details.) In addition, many Web sites offer free lifetime email accounts, such as Microsoft Hotmail and Prontomail.

How to Set Up Outlook Express for Email

Windows XP includes Microsoft Outlook Express, a popular email program that can send and deliver email and manage an email address book. Before you can set up Outlook Express, you must have the following information from your Internet service provider: your username and password, the incoming mail server's name, the outgoing mail server's name, and the type of incoming mail server you'll be accessing (POP3, IMAP, or HTTP). Most incoming servers use a protocol called *POP3*.

1 Run Outlook Express

To begin, click the **Start** menu and choose **Email**. Alternatively, there may be an **Outlook Express** icon on your desktop; if there is, double-click this icon to start Outlook Express.

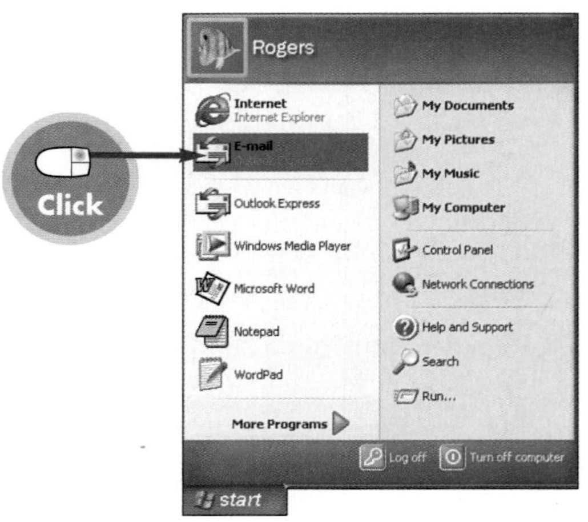

2 Identify Yourself

If Outlook Express has not been set up already, the **Internet Connection Wizard** opens. In the **Display name** text box, type a name (also called a *handle*) that will identify you on all outgoing mail. This name is displayed in addition to your email address on all email that you send. Most people use their full name. Click **Next** to continue.

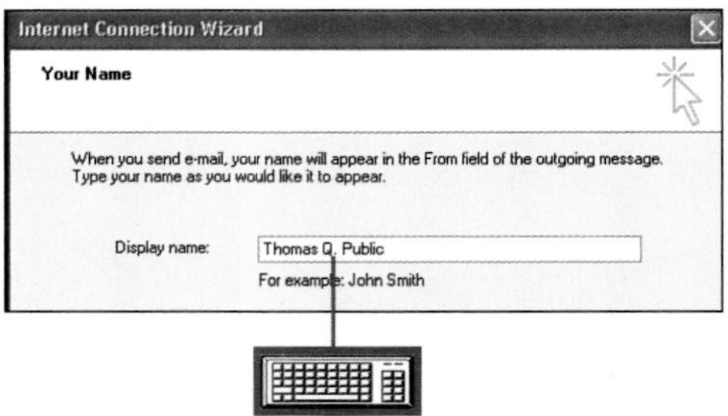

3 Set Up an Email Address

If you have a new email address provided by your Internet service (or an existing email address you'd like to continue using), type it into the **Email address** text box and click the **Next** button.

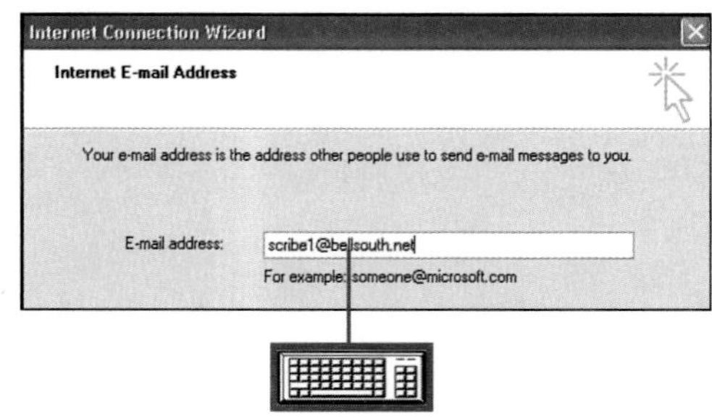

4 Identify Your Servers

If your Internet service provider supports email, you should have been given the names of its mail servers when you joined the service. Type the names of its mail servers in the **Incoming mail** and **Outgoing mail** text boxes. Use the drop-down list to indicate the kind of incoming server being used (most services use POP3). Click **Next** to continue.

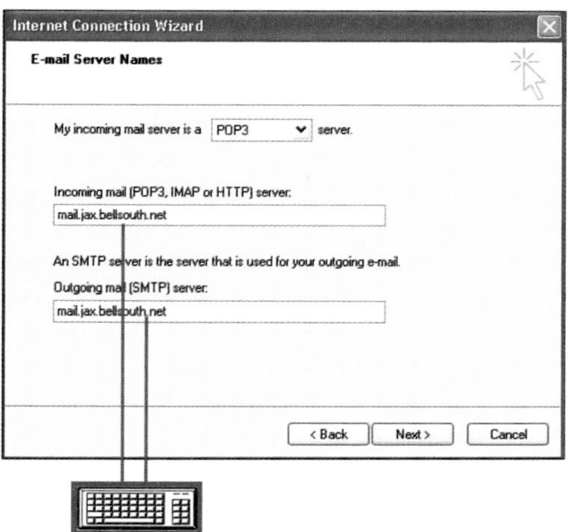

5 Enter Your Account Info

You must have a username and password to make use of Internet email servers. (You get this information from your Internet service provider.) Type these into the **Account name** and **Password** text boxes, checking the **Remember password** box if you want Outlook Express to log into your account automatically.

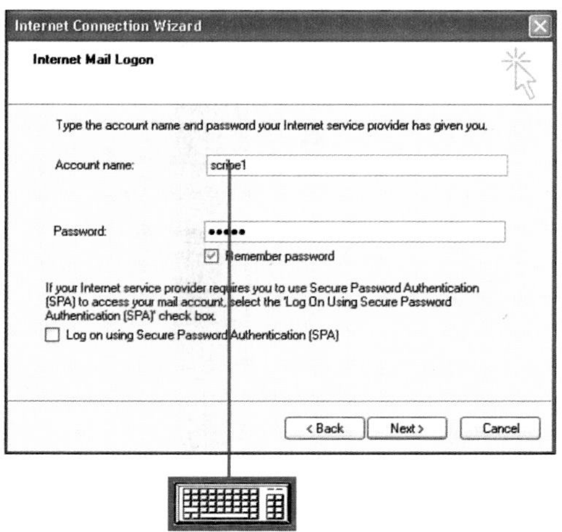

6 Set Up Authentication

If your Internet service requires it, check the **Log on using Secure Password Authentication (SPA)** option. To finish setting up Outlook Express to work with your email address, click the **Next** button and then click the **Finish** button.

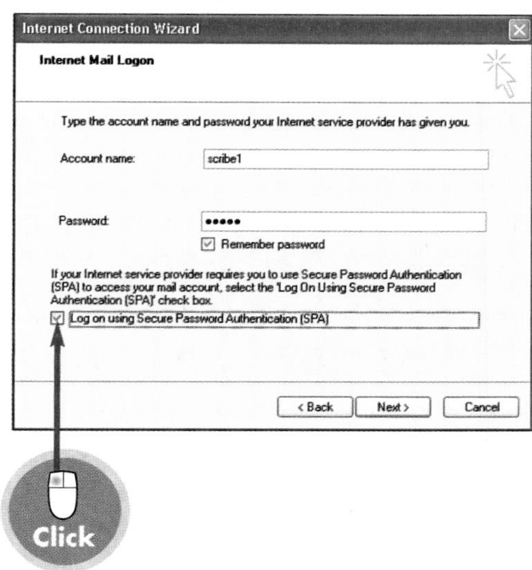

How to Hint

Using Different Versions of Outlook

The Microsoft Office software suite includes an expanded version of Outlook Express called *Outlook 2002*. Outlook 2002 can be used for other things in addition to email. For example, there's a task-management feature for keeping a to-do list, a calendar, a contact book, and a place to keep notes. For more information, visit Microsoft's Outlook Web site: Type the URL `http://www.microsoft.com/office/outlook` in Internet Explorer's Address bar and press **Enter**.

Task 2

How to Send Email

Writing a message in Outlook Express is similar to creating a document in a word processor such as Microsoft Word. You type the text of your message and apply formatting with familiar toolbar buttons such as Bold and Italic. Outlook Express normally composes email with HTML so that your messages can contain fonts, graphics, and formatting just like World Wide Web pages. Because your recipient must be able to read HTML mail to see all these features, you also can turn off HTML and send a message as text without any formatting.

1 Create a New Message

Click the **Start** menu and choose **Email** to launch Outlook Express. To begin writing a new message, click the **new Mail message** hyperlink. (If you don't see this link, click the **Outlook Express** icon in the **Folders** pane.) The **New Message** window opens.

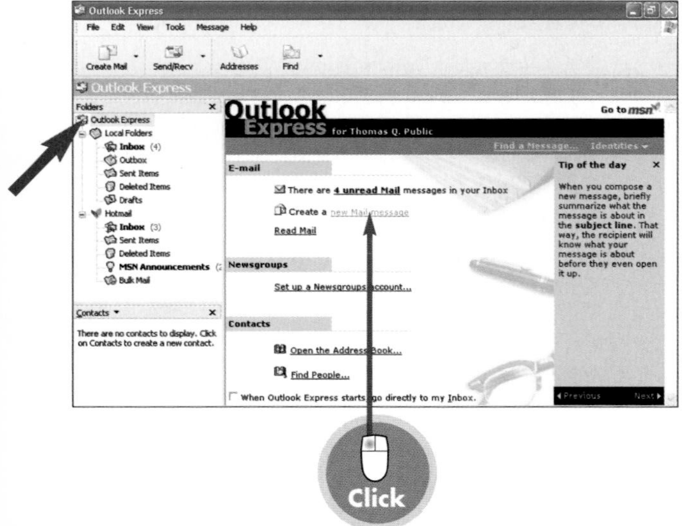

2 Address the Message

Type the email address of the message's recipient in the **To** text box. If you're sending a copy of this message to another email address, type that address in the **Cc** text box. Finish addressing the message by typing a short title for the message in the **Subject** box. The window's title bar changes to match the text you type in the **Subject** box.

3 Write the Message

Type the text of your message in the edit pane. If you're sending a message that should not contain any HTML formatting, pull down the **Format** menu (located at the top of the message window) and choose the **Plain Text** option.

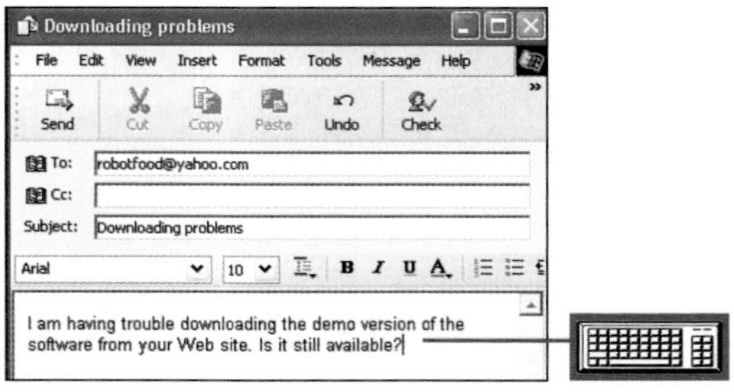

4 Format the Message

Messages you send with HTML formatting can contain different fonts, bold text, a graphical background, and other visual touches. These features are available on the toolbar above the edit pane. To make text bold, for example, select the text by dragging your mouse over it and then click the **Bold** button in the toolbar.

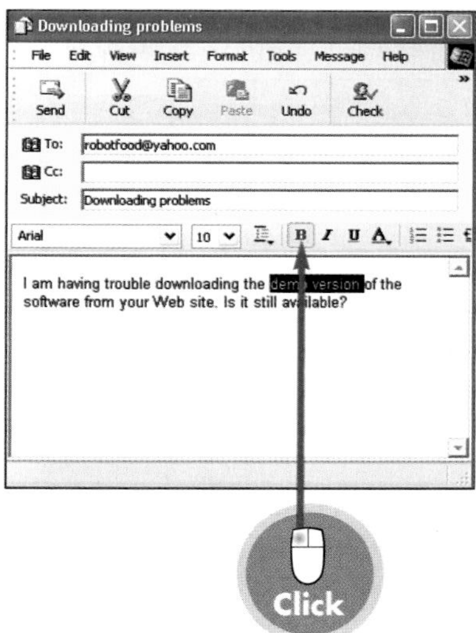

5 Set a Priority

To assign a priority to your message, choose **Message**, **Set Priority**, and then choose **High**, **Normal**, or **Low**. The priority setting does not cause the message to be delivered any differently, but the priority rating may be noted by the recipient's email program when the message is displayed in his or her inbox.

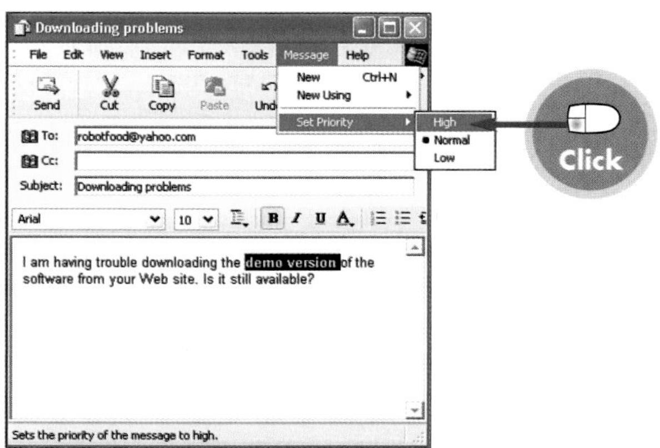

6 Send the Message

When your message has been addressed, typed, and formatted the way you want it, connect to the Internet and click the **Send** button to deliver the email message. A copy of the message is stored in the **Sent Items** folder of Outlook Express. (If you aren't connected, a copy is saved in the Outbox folder until it can be delivered.)

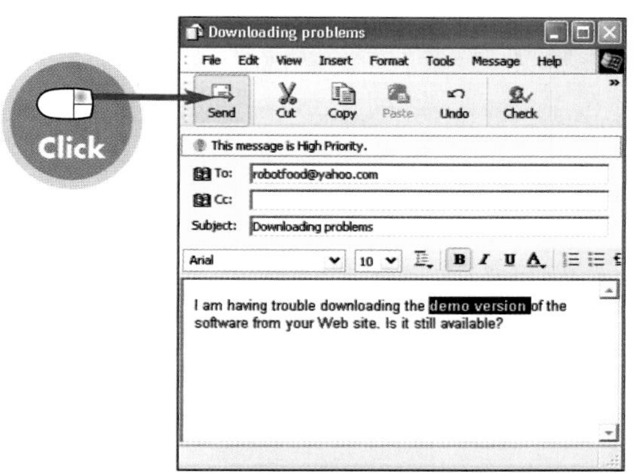

How to Hint

Applying HTML Formatting

Outlook Express, Hotmail, and other email services support email that contains HTML—the same kind of formatting used to create Web pages. To add images, colors, or sound to the background of your email message in Outlook Express, choose **Format**, **Background**, and select the **Picture**, **Color**, or **Sound** command. This special formatting, however, may make your message unreadable if your recipient's email program can't handle HTML-formatted email. For this reason, use special formatting only if you know that the recipient's email program supports it.

Task 3

How to Receive Email

Outlook Express is organized like a file folder, and it contains subfolders for **Inbox**, **Outbox**, **Sent Items**, **Deleted Items**, and **Drafts**. New messages are placed in your **Inbox**, where they stay until you move them to a new folder or delete them. If you are also using Hotmail, an extra set of folders exists for mail received with that service. (You learn more about Hotmail in Task 9, "How to Set Up a Free Web-Based Email Account.")

1 Read Unread Mail

Click the **Start** menu and choose **Email** to launch Outlook Express. If any new email has been received, click the **unread Mail** hyperlink to see the messages you have. Alternatively, you can click the **Inbox** icon in the **Local Folders** list to see your new messages as well as any messages you have read previously.

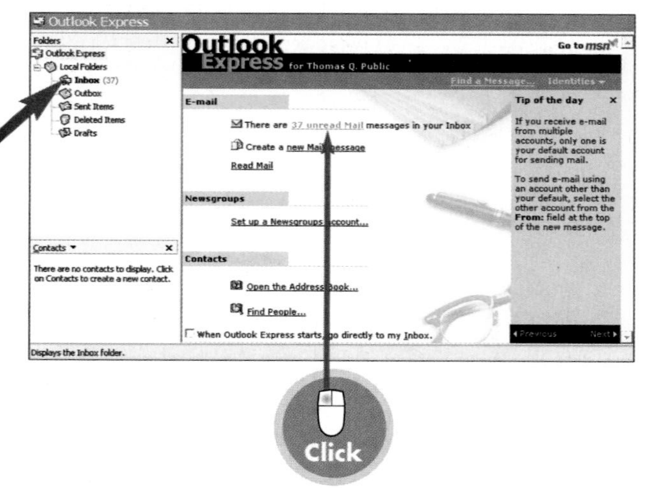

2 View Messages

The top-right pane of the **Inbox** window lists all the messages in the folder—new unread messages, and messages you've read previously. Use the scrollbar to move through this list. Click a message's icon to view the contents of that message in the bottom-right pane. To delete a message, click its icon in the top-right pane and then click the **Delete** button.

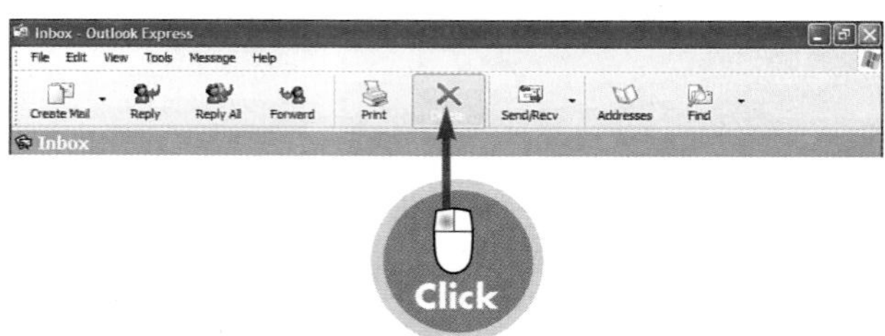

3 View a Message in a New Window

The bottom-right pane of the **Inbox** window doesn't have a lot of room to display a message. To view a message in a larger window, double-click the message's icon in the top-right pane of the **Inbox** window. A new window appears, with the selected message displayed.

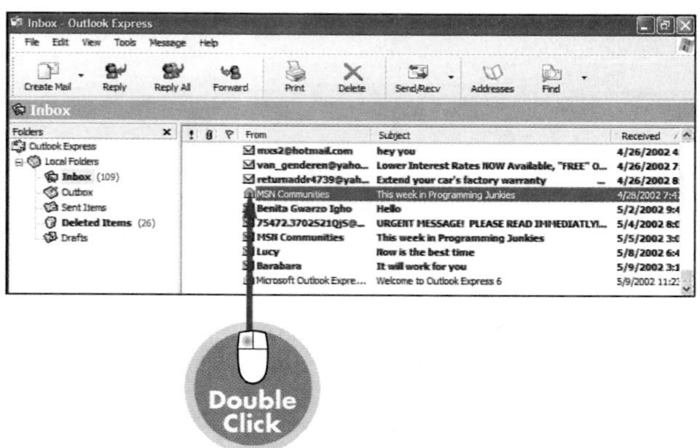

4 View Other Messages

As you're viewing a message in its own window, you can use the **Previous** and **Next** buttons in the toolbar at the top of the window to see other messages in the same folder. Click the **Next** button to view the next message in your Outlook Express Inbox window.

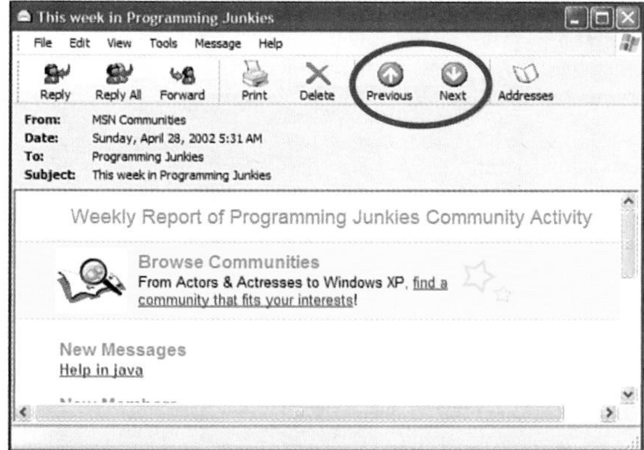

5 Reply to a Message

To reply to the message you're reading, click the **Reply** button. The **New Message** window opens with the text of the original message in the edit pane. If the message was sent to multiple addresses (as listed in the **To** and **Cc** text boxes), you can send your reply to all the addressees by clicking **Reply All** instead. Type your reply to the original message and click **Send**.

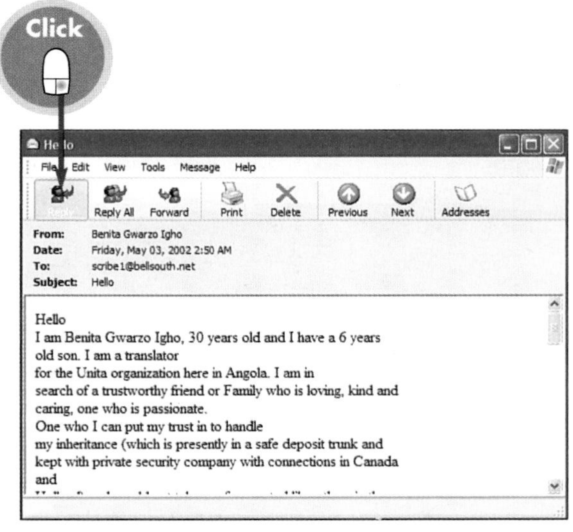

6 Forward a Message

To send a copy of a message to another email address, click the **Forward** button. You can send the forwarded message without changes, or you can add your own comments to it. (You also can forward a message while viewing your **Inbox** list: Click the message and then click the **Forward** button.) Type any additional comments you want to make to the message you're forwarding and click **Send**.

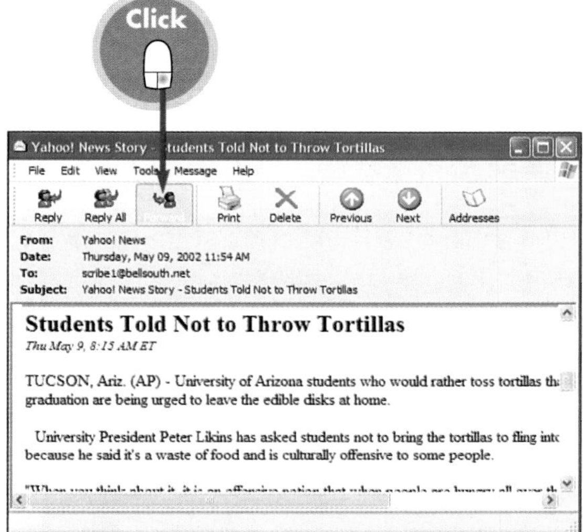

How-to Hint

Choosing Between Forward and Reply

Because the **Forward** and **Reply** features both open a **New Message** window, you may be confused about the difference between the two features. **Reply** is used to respond directly to the person who sent you an email message. **Forward** is used to send a copy of an email message to someone who hasn't seen it—thousands of jokes, inspirational sayings, and safety warnings are forwarded around the Internet each day because people receive email messages, like them, and send them to friends and relatives.

How to Send a Web Page Using Email

As you're visiting sites on the World Wide Web, you may run across something that's worth telling a friend or colleague about. Internet Explorer 6 can send hyperlinks and full Web pages using your preferred email program. When you first set up the IE browser, it is configured to work with Outlook Express. This is easy to change if you use Eudora, Hotmail, or another popular email service. (One program you *can't* use is America Online—its email program is incompatible with this browser feature.)

1 Choose a Hyperlink

To mail a hyperlink to someone from within Internet Explorer, load the page you want to recommend to someone else and choose File, Send, Link by Email. A new message is opened in your preferred email program.

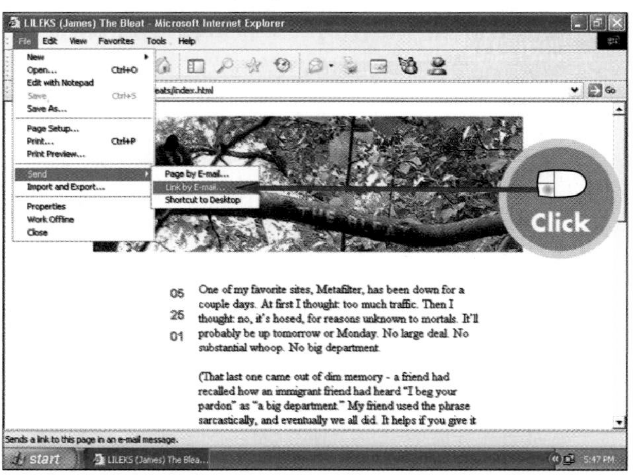

2 Write the Email

The new email message includes the hyperlink to the current page in Internet Explorer. You can add comments of your own to go with it. Type the email address of the recipient in the To text box and a subject in the Subject box, and any comments you want to send.

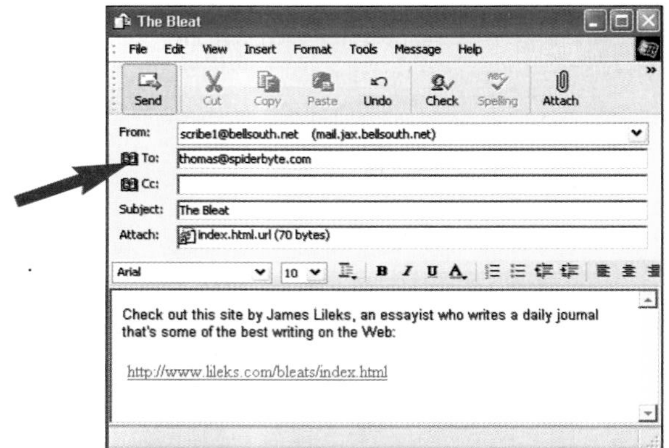

3 Send the Link

When you're ready to send the link and its accompanying message, click the Send button. If the recipient's email program supports hyperlinks, the recipient can click the link in your message to visit the page.

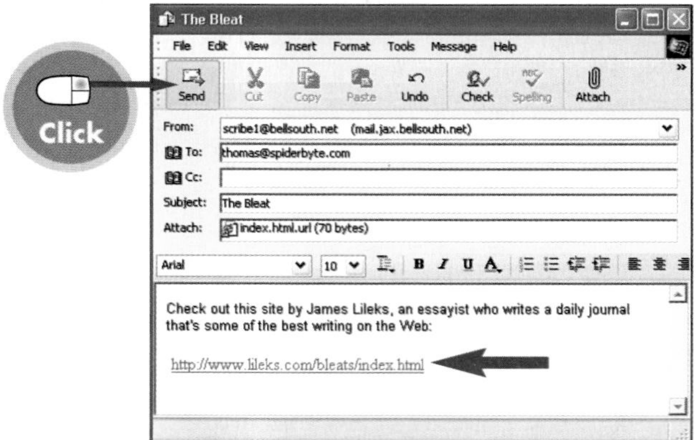

4 Choose a Page

To send an entire Web page using email, open the page in Internet Explorer and then choose File, Send, Page by Email. A new message is opened in your preferred email program containing a copy of the entire Web page.

5 Write the Email

You can make changes to the copy of the Web page in the edit pane before sending it. When you're done, type the recipient's address in the To text box and a subject in the Subject text box.

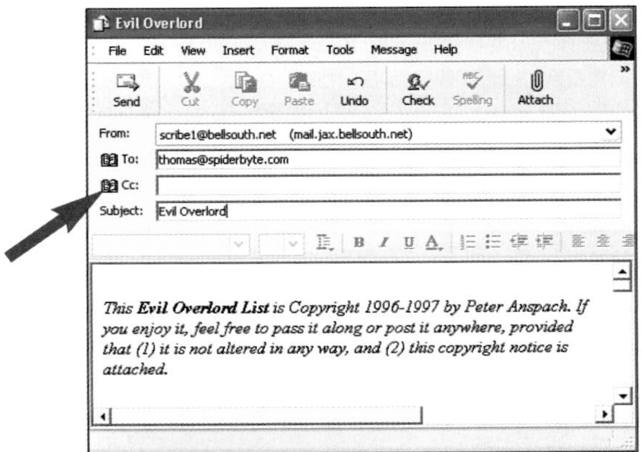

6 Send the Page

To send the page with any changes you made, click the Send button. If the recipient is using an email program that can display Web pages, the page will be displayed by the email program's built-in browser.

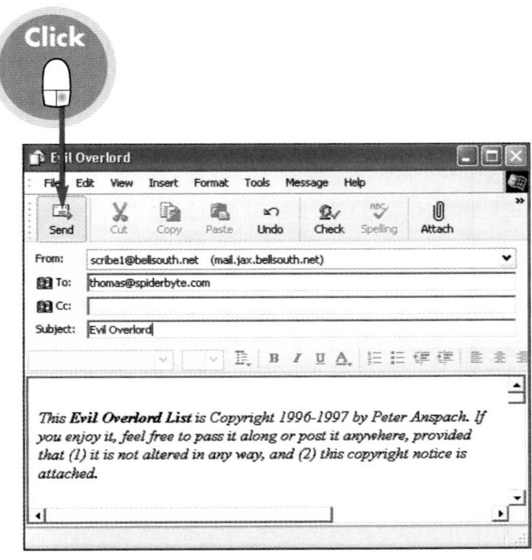

How to Hint

Sending a Link to Your Desktop

As you know, you can send to a friend the hyperlink to a particular Web page. You can also place a shortcut icon on your desktop that acts as a hyperlink to the Web page: Choose **File**, **Send**, **Shortcut to Desktop**. An Internet shortcut to the current Web page appears on your desktop. Connect to the Internet and double-click the shortcut to load the page in Internet Explorer.

How to Send an Attached File

Any file that's stored on your computer can be sent through email. Before the file can be opened by the recipient, however, it must be *downloaded*—transferred from the mail server to the recipient's computer. The amount of time this takes depends on the Internet connection speed and the file's size. A 200KB file takes more than five minutes to download at the most common Internet speed (56Kbps) and usually prevents the recipient from receiving other mail during the transfer. For this reason, you should send large files only to people who are expecting them.

1 Start Outlook Express

You send a file by attaching it to any email message you're sending out. Open Outlook Express (click the **Start** button and choose **Email**). Click the **new Mail message** hyperlink to begin writing a new message.

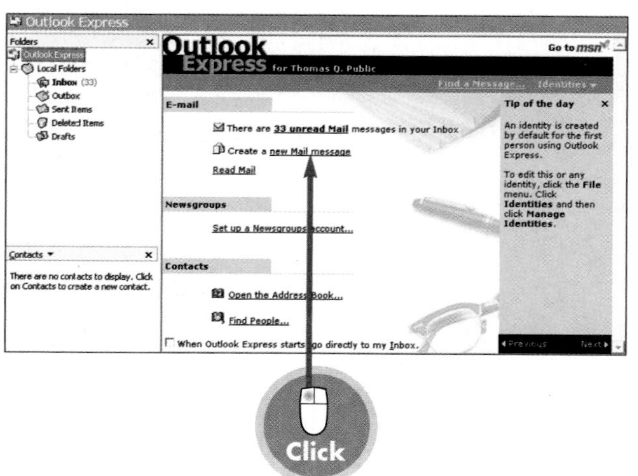

2 Attach a File

After writing and addressing the message, click the **Attach** button in the toolbar at the top of the window. The **Insert Attachment** dialog box opens; you use this dialog box to locate the file you want to attach to the message.

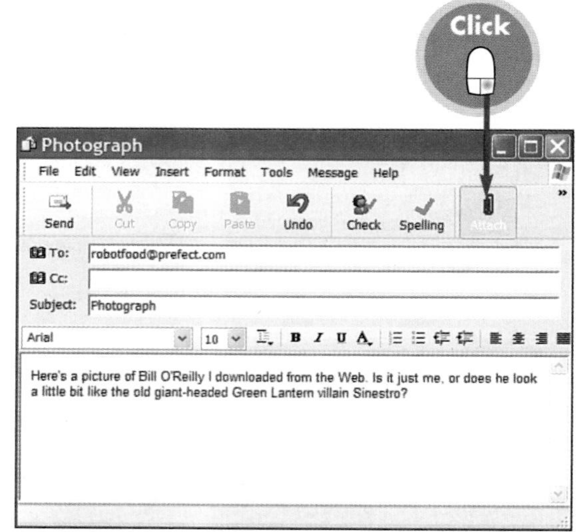

3 Choose the File

Use the **Insert Attachment** dialog box to find and open the folder that contains the file you want to send. Select the filename and then click the **Attach** button.

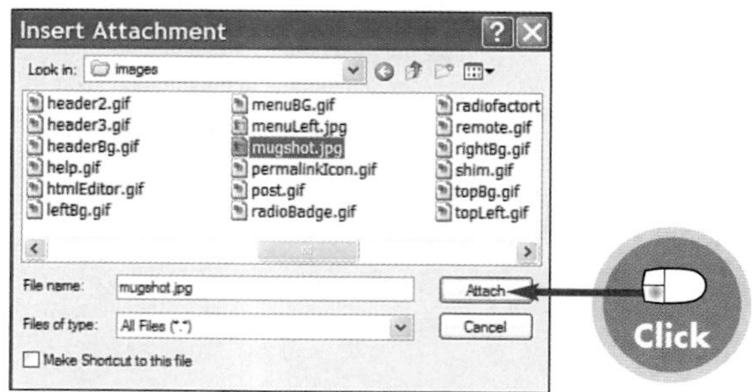

4 Send the Email and Its Attachment

The name of the file you've chosen is displayed in the **Attach** text box at the top of the message window. Click the **Send** button to deliver the message and its attached file. The file is uploaded to your mail server, so the time it takes to send the message depends on the speed of your Internet connection and the size of the file.

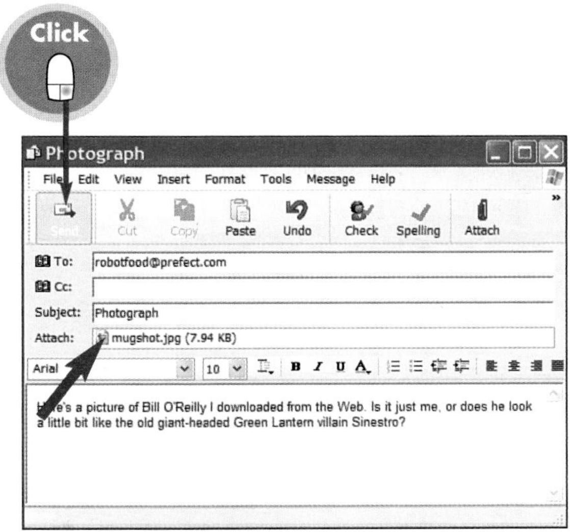

5 Choose Multiple Files

You can attach more than one file to a single email message. In the message window, click the **Attach** button to open the **Insert Attachment** dialog box. Hold down the **Ctrl** key as you click to select individual files. When all the desired files are highlighted, click the **Attach** button.

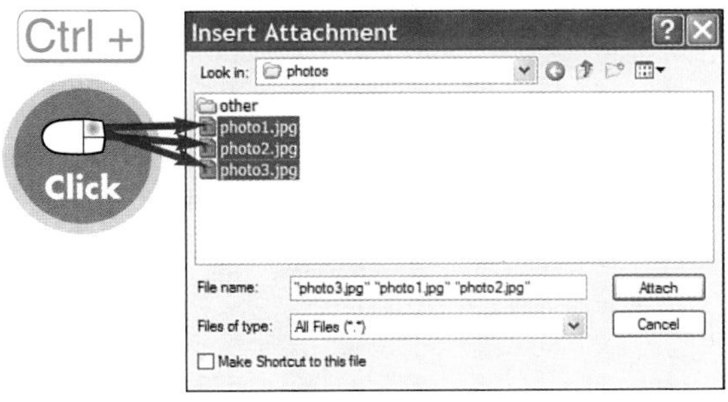

6 Send the Files

The name of each attached file appears in the **Attach** text box of the message window. Click the **Attach** button again if you want to choose another file to attach to the message. Click **Send** to send the message and its attached files.

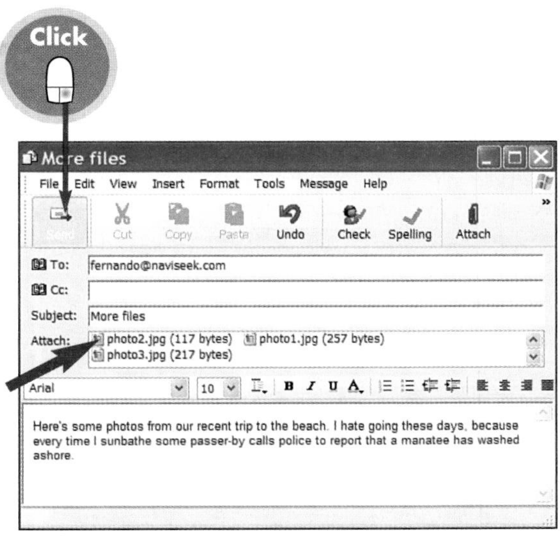

How to Hint

Sending a Shortcut Instead of a File

If you are sending an attached file to someone on the same *intranet*—computers networked together at a business, school, or other institution—you may be able to send a shortcut instead of the entire file. If the file you are sending is in a public folder on your intranet, open the **Insert Attachment** window, pick the file, and enable the **Make Shortcut to this file** check box before clicking the **Attach** button.

Task 6

How to Receive an Attached File

You deliver files through Internet email by attaching them to normal email messages. To receive an attached file in Outlook Express, you must first open the message associated with the file. You can open files directly from Outlook Express or save them to a folder on your system. Be aware, however, that attached files can contain viruses that execute damaging code on your computer—even in documents created with Microsoft Word. Although some antivirus programs can scan incoming files as they are received through email, you should be cautious before opening files sent to you.

1 Read Your Mail

Open Outlook Express (click the **Start** button and choose **Email**). If you have new mail, click the **unread Mail** hyperlink to open your Outlook Express **Inbox**.

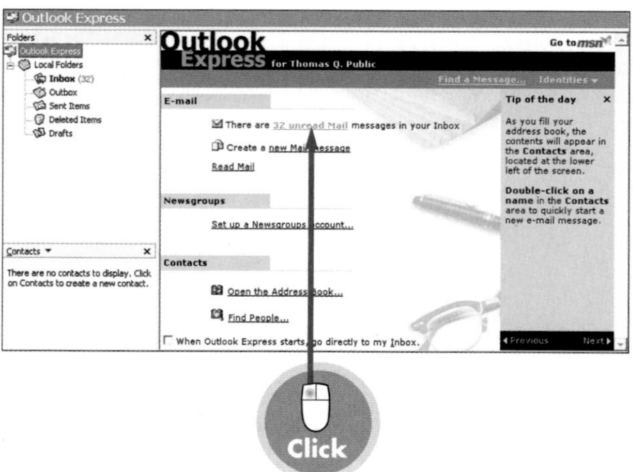

2 Check for Attachments

Mail that has attached files is displayed with a paper clip icon. Open the mail message (click the message in the top-right pane to view it in the bottom-right pane). To open the file attached to the mail message, click the paper clip button and select the name of the file attached to the mail message.

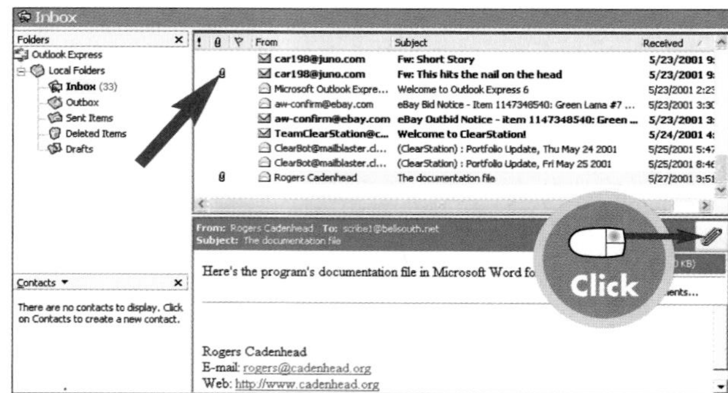

3 Open the File

Outlook Express might warn you before opening an attached file. If you decide to open the file in Outlook Express, click the **Open it** radio button in the **Open Attachment Warning** dialog box, and then click **OK**. The file is opened by the program associated with it (if there is one). If no program is associated with the file type, you'll be asked to pick one.

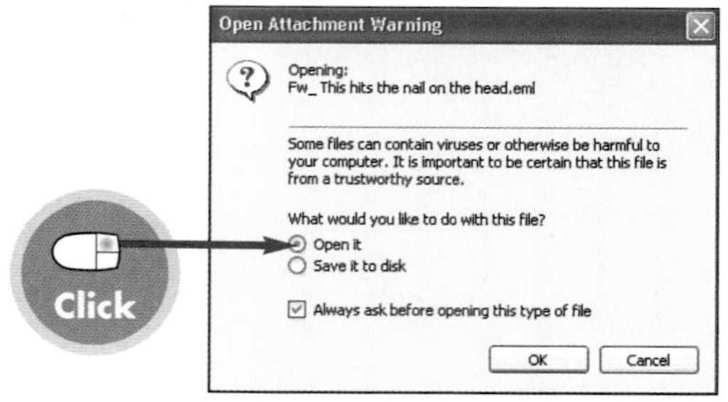

4 Save an Attachment

To save attached files to your system's hard drive instead of opening them in Outlook Express, click the paper clip button in the message window and choose **Save Attachments**. The **Save Attachments** dialog box opens.

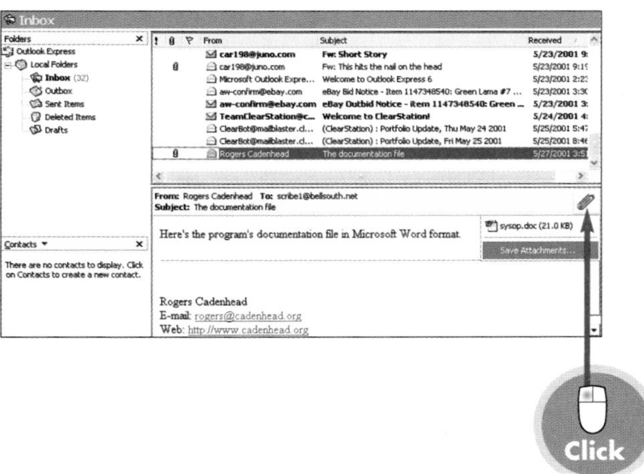

5 Choose a Location

Click the **Browse** button next to the **Save To** text box to choose the folder in which you want to save the attached file. Then click the **Save** button.

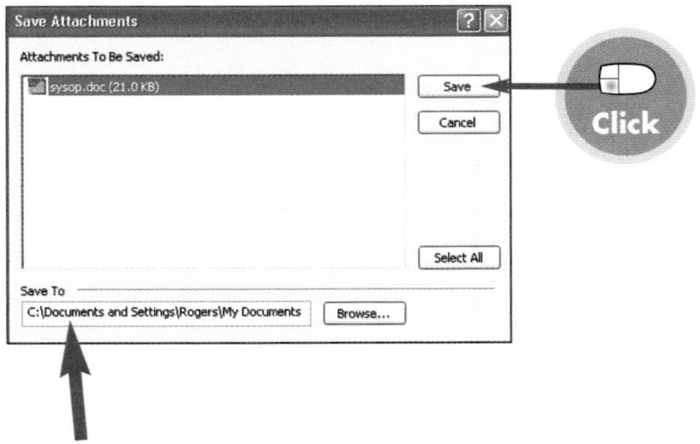

6 View Attachments

When you're reading mail in a separate window, Outlook Express does not display a paper clip icon. Instead, the name of the attached file is displayed in the **Attach** text box at the top of the window. Double-click the filename to see the **Open Attachment** dialog box, which you can use to open or save the attached file.

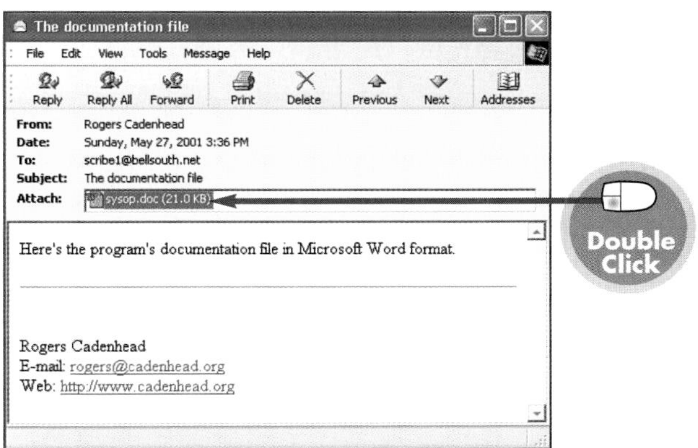

How to Hint: Protecting Yourself from Damaging Email

File attachments are a major source of computer viruses. If you open an attached file that contains a virus, the virus will run and could damage files on your computer. For this reason, you should not open an attached file unless you know who sent the file and are sure of its authenticity. If you run antivirus programs on your computer and keep them up to date, you should save attached files to disk and run a virus check on them before opening the files. (Some antivirus programs check incoming mail automatically.) You can also block some attachments in Outlook Express: Choose **Tools**, **Options** from the menu, click the **Security** tab, select the **Do not allow attachments to be saved or opened that could potentially be a virus** check box, and click **OK**.

How to Find Someone's Email Address

Several sites on the World Wide Web (including Bigfoot and InfoSpace) offer huge directories of email addresses. If you want to contact a person, company, or other organization but don't know the contact's email address, you can use Outlook Express to search through each of these directories. You can use these same steps to quickly search your own *address book* (a personal database of your email correspondents you can create in Outlook Express).

1 Find People

To begin looking for the email address of a person or company in Outlook Express, click the arrow next to the **Find** button and select the **People** option. The **Find People** dialog box opens.

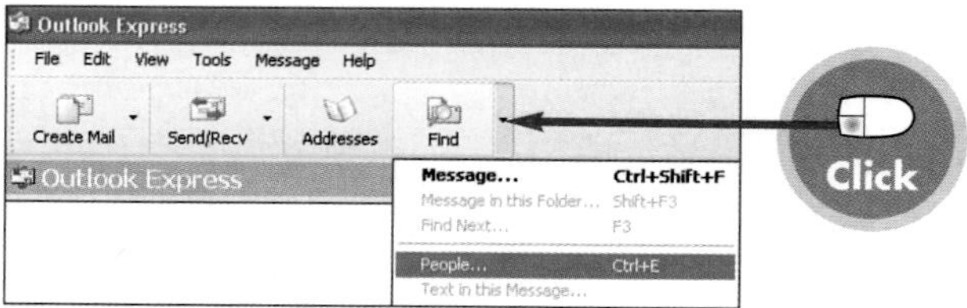

2 Search Your Address Book

To search through your personal address book in Outlook Express, choose **Address Book** from the **Look in** drop-down list at the top of the dialog box. Type information about the person you're looking for in at least one of the text boxes—**Name**, **Email**, **Address**, **Phone**, or **Other**. Click the **Find Now** button to start the search.

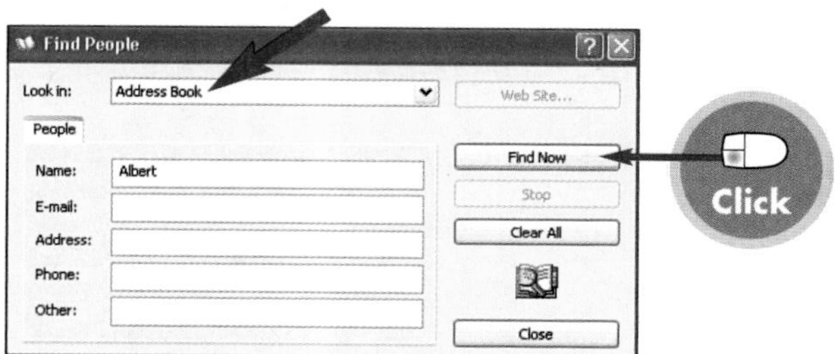

3 Send Someone a Message

The **Find People** dialog box expands to display the results of the search. To begin a new email message addressed to one of the people you find, right-click the name and choose **Action**, **Send Mail** from the pop-up menus that appear.

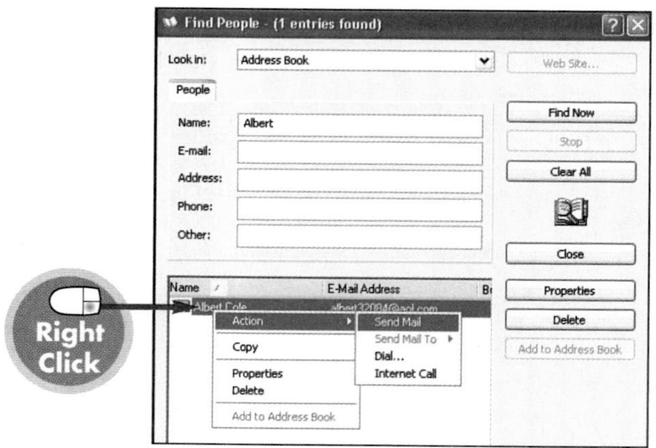

4 Search a Web Directory

You also can look for email addresses in several Web directories. In the **Find People** dialog box, in the **Look in** drop-down list, choose one of the directory services (for example, choose **Bigfoot** or **InfoSpace**). Type the name you want to look for in the **Name** text box and click the **Find Now** button.

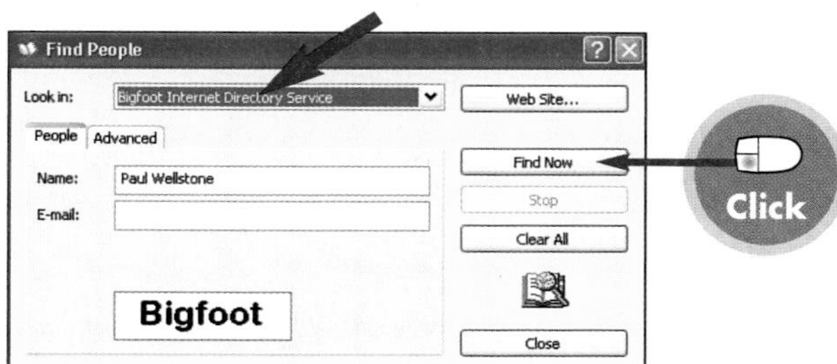

5 Add to Your Address Book

If you find the person or company you are looking for, you can copy the information from the Web directory to your personal address book. Click the name in the results pane and then click the **Add to Address Book** button.

6 Visit a Directory Site

Each of the address directories that you can access from Outlook Express has a related Web site that offers additional features and more sophisticated search tools. From the **Look in** list box, select the name of the directory you want to use and then click the **Web Site** button to visit that directory's site with your Web browser.

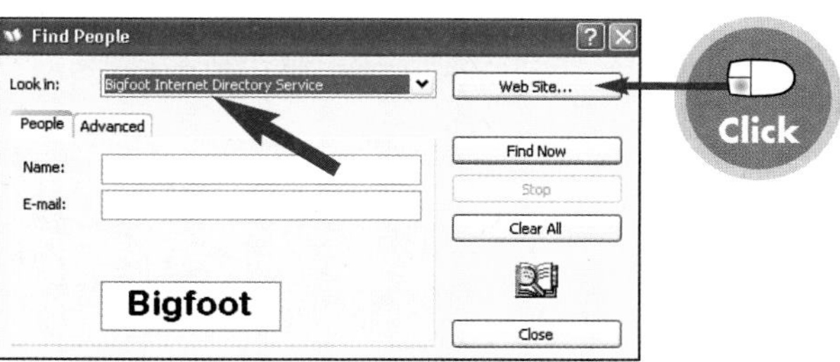

How to Hint

Adding Someone to Your Address Book

You can add a person to your Outlook Express address book as you are reading a message from him or her in its own window. Double-click the name or email address you want to add, and then click the **Add to Address Book** button.

Task

8 How to Subscribe to a Mailing List

A popular way to use email is to communicate with a group of people on a shared topic of interest. You can do this by joining an *electronic mailing list*, a discussion that takes place entirely with email. Lists are categorized by topic; people who are interested in a list's topic send an email message to subscribe. If the list allows public participation (as many do), you can use a special email address to send a message to all members of the list. Any message sent by another member of the list of subscribers winds up in your Inbox.

1 Run Outlook Express

To begin, click the **Start** menu and choose **Email**. Alternatively, there may be an **Outlook Express** icon on your desktop; if there is, double-click this icon to start Outlook Express.

2 Create a New Message

Before you can subscribe to a mailing list, you must know its subscription address and the command used to subscribe (see the "How-To Hints" section on the next page for information about finding mailing lists). When you have that information, begin a new email message in Outlook Express by clicking the **new Mail message** hyperlink.

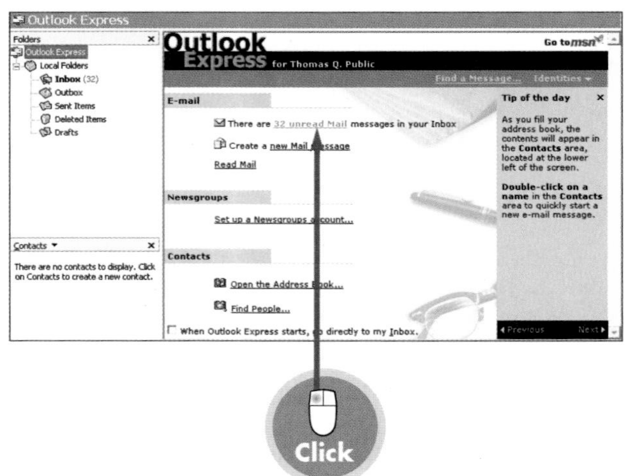

3 Subscribe to a List

Address the message by typing the list's subscription address in the **To** text box. Type the subscription command in the body of the message or in the **Subject** text box—whichever the mailing list requires you to do.

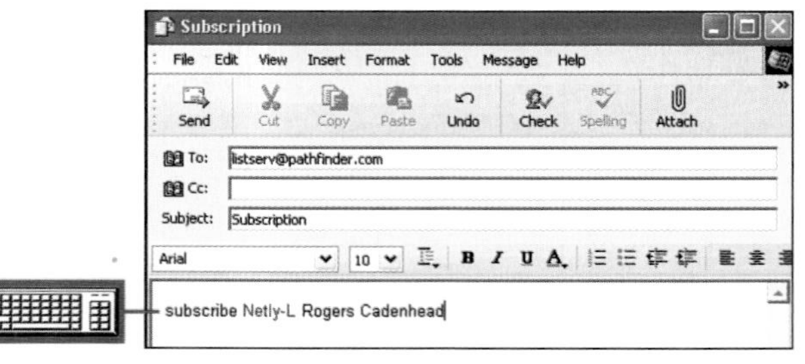

4 Send the Message

Click the **Send** button to deliver your subscription request. You'll receive a confirmation message when you have been added to the mailing list; the confirmation message usually contains helpful information about how to use the list.

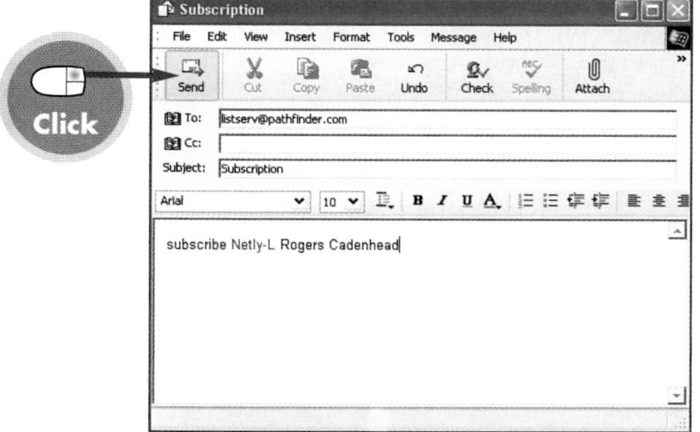

5 Contribute to the List

If the mailing list allows public participation, you can send a message to all list members using a special email address—probably not the same as the one you used to subscribe to the list. Usually, this address includes the name of the list—see your confirmation message for more information. Click **Send** to deliver the message.

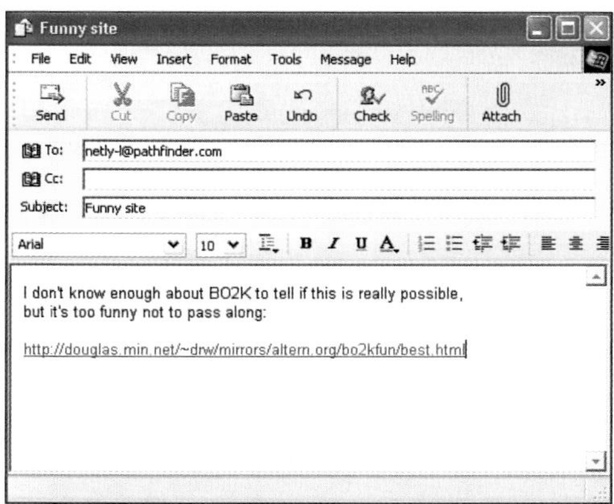

6 Unsubscribe from a List

When you subscribe to a mailing list, you should save the confirmation message you received. This message usually contains instructions on how to quit the list. The address to which you mail your request to be removed from the list is often the same as the one you used to subscribe, but the command will be slightly different. Click **Send** to deliver the request.

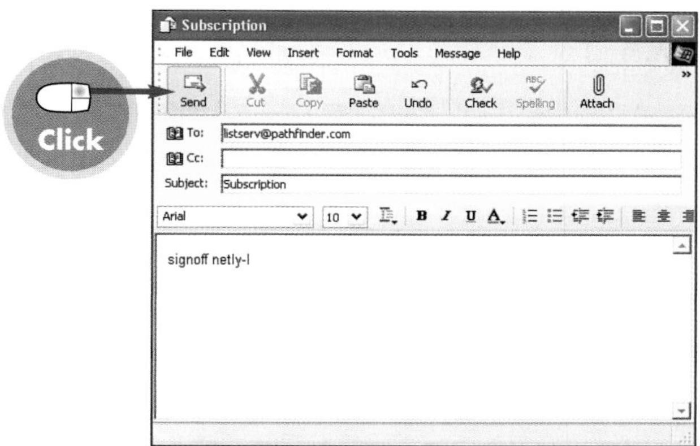

How to Hint

Finding Mailing Lists on Any Topic

There are thousands of mailing lists on topics related to technology, entertainment, hobbies, and more. To search a database of lists you can join, visit the Topica World Wide Web site at **`http://www.topica.com`**.

Joining the Netly-L Mailing List

One longtime general-interest mailing list is Netly-L, a place to discuss the Internet, online media, and technology. To subscribe, send an email message to **`listserv@pathfinder.com`**. In the body of the message, type **`subscribe Netly-L`** followed by your name (for example, if your name is Ulysses S Grant, type **`subscribe Netly-L Ulysses S Grant`** in the body of the message).

How to Set Up a Free Web-Based Email Account

Although you receive an email account when you subscribe to most Internet service providers, you may want to set up an account with a World Wide Web site that provides free lifetime email. These sites normally offer mail you can access by visiting the site with your Web browser. However, some services can work in conjunction with Outlook Express and other mail software. In this task, you set up Microsoft Hotmail, a free email service you can use in your browser or in Outlook Express.

1 Run Your Browser

You set up Microsoft Hotmail by visiting the service's Web site. Click the **Start** button and choose **Internet**. Internet Explorer opens and displays your home page.

2 Visit Hotmail

To visit Hotmail, type the URL `http://www.hotmail.com` in the browser's **Address bar** and press **Enter**. The main page of the Hotmail service loads.

3 Begin Signing Up

Hotmail email accounts are completely free. To join, click the **Sign Up** hyperlink. A page opens with a form asking for information about you.

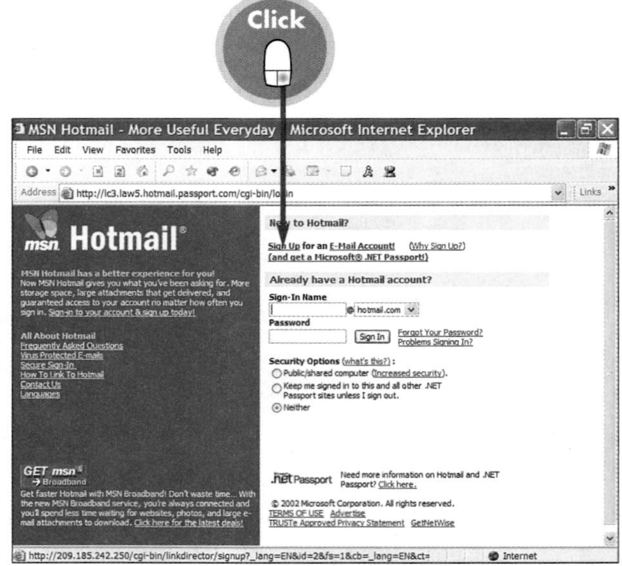

4 Identify Yourself

Type your name in the **First Name** and **Last Name** text boxes and fill out the rest of the fields in the **Profile Information** section. Your name will appear on all mail you send using Hotmail. Scroll down the page when you're done.

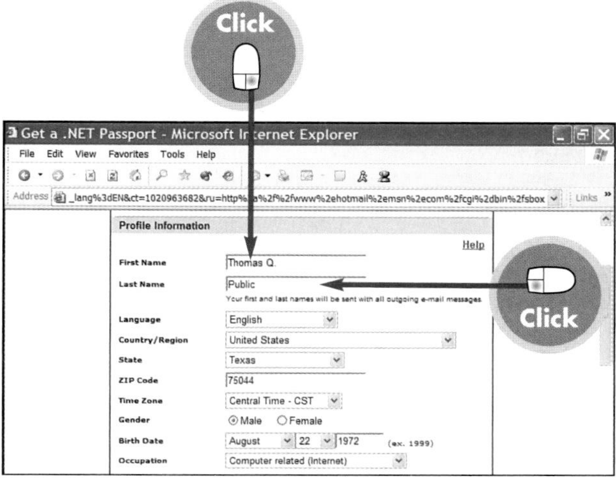

5 Choose an Address

Type the username you want to use in the **Email Address** text box and the password you want to use in the **Password** and **Retype Password** text boxes. Your email address will be your username followed by **@hotmail.com**. Your username must begin with a letter and contain only letters, numbers, or underscore characters (_).

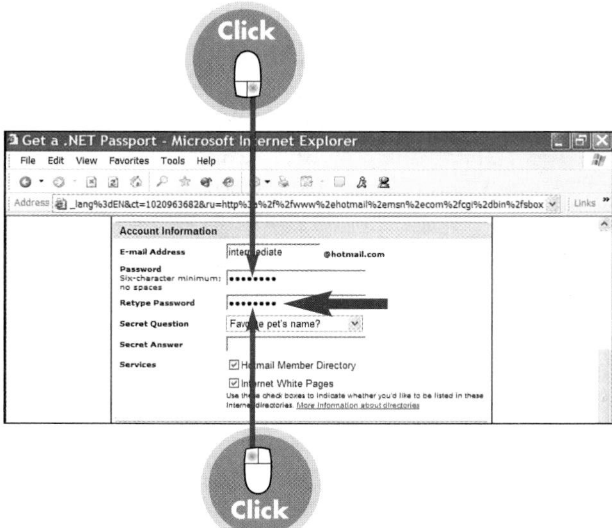

6 Pick a Secret Question

Choose a question in the **Secret Question** box and type an answer in the **Secret Answer** box. Only you should know the answer—Hotmail will ask the question if you forget your password and want to set up a new one.

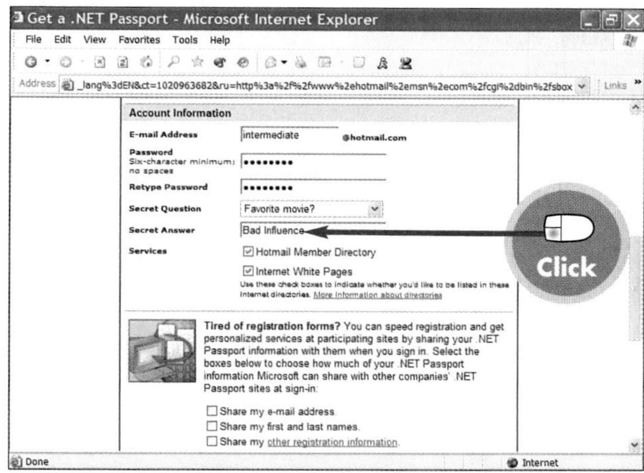

7 Go Public or Private

By default, Hotmail adds your name and email address to its public member directory and the Internet White Pages. To stay out of these directories, click to disable the check boxes next to the directory names.

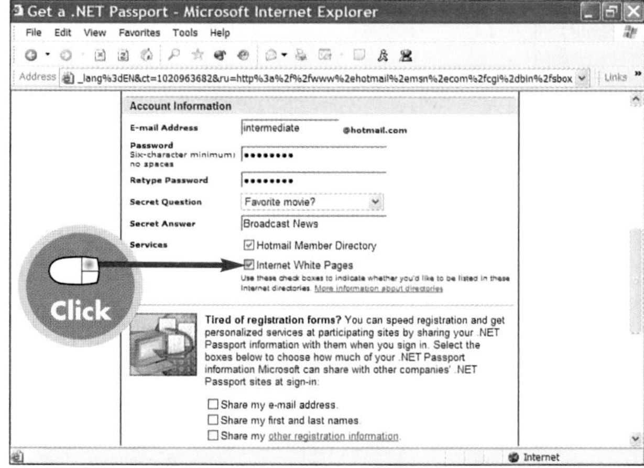

Continued 9

8 Review the Terms of Use

Microsoft displays the terms of use to which you must agree before an account will be created. If you agree, scroll to the bottom of the page and click the **I Agree** button to join Hotmail.

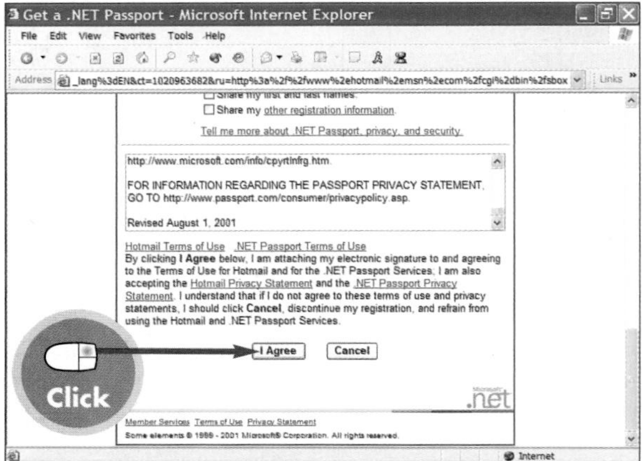

9 Choose Another Username

Because millions use Hotmail, you may find it difficult to find a unique username. If your choice is taken, you'll see a list of suggestions for alternative usernames. Click a radio button to choose that suggestion, or click the last radio button and type another username in the adjacent text box. When you're done, scroll down and click **I Agree** again.

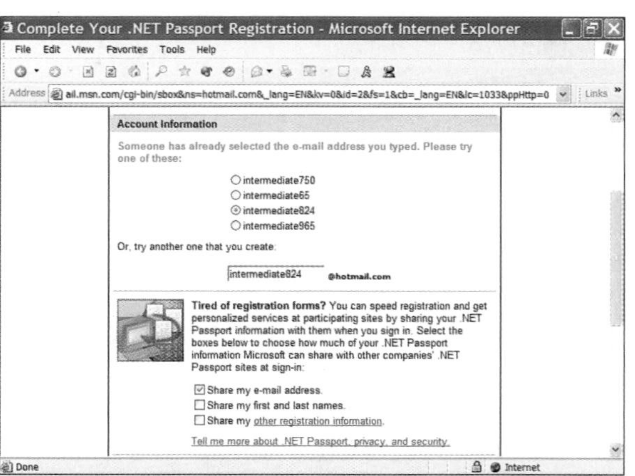

10 Continue Sign-Up

After you have found a username, Hotmail displays a page indicating that you have successfully signed up for a Microsoft .NET Passport. Your Hotmail username and password can be used at any site that supports Passport. Click the **Continue** button.

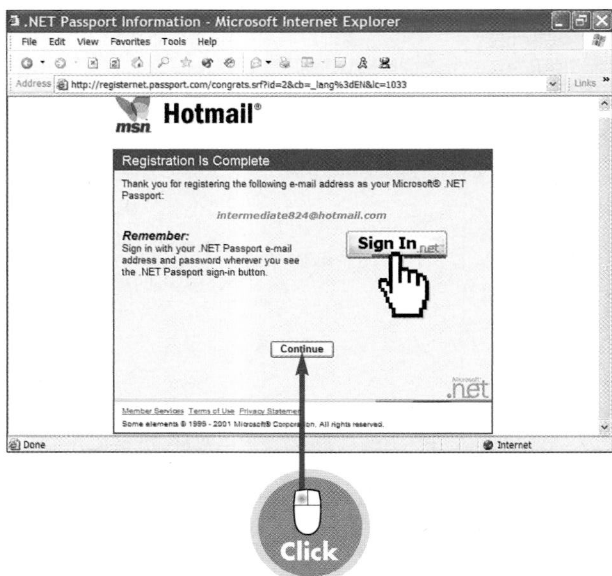

11 Choose a Subscription

Although Hotmail is free, there's also an expanded account available for $19.95 a year that offers more storage space for your mail and other benefits. If you want to join, click the **Continue to Billing Information** button. To stick with the free account, don't click anything yet.

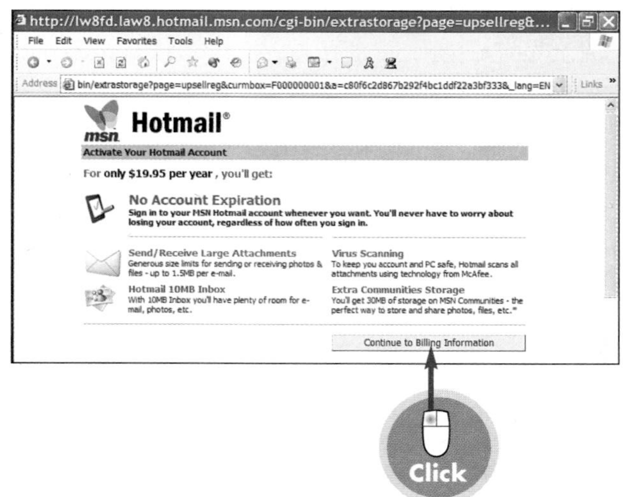

12 Use the Free Service

At the bottom of the page, Microsoft describes the pay and free Hotmail subscriptions. To choose the free option, click the **Click here** hyperlink.

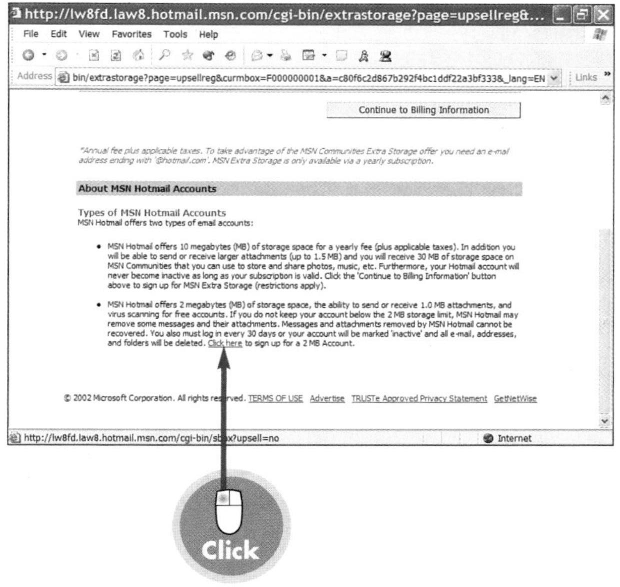

13 Pick WebCourier Services

After you pick a subscription (and pay for it, if necessary), Hotmail enables you to sign up to receive free WebCourier email newsletters. Hover your mouse over a newsletter's check box to read about the service in an adjacent area of the page. To subscribe to the service, enable the check box.

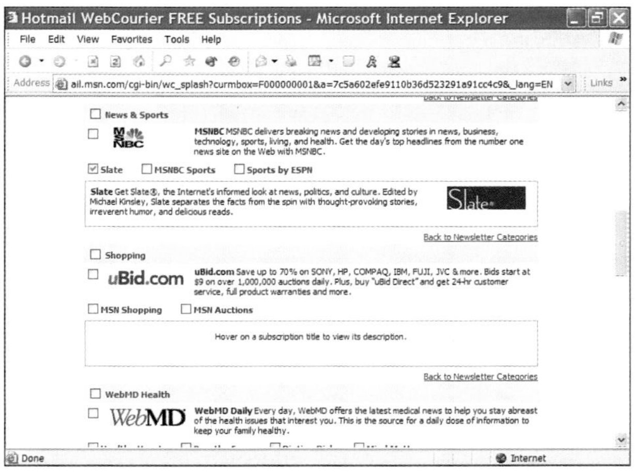

14 Complete Sign-Up

After you have decided whether to join any of the WebCourier email newsletters, scroll to the bottom of the page and click the **Continue** button.

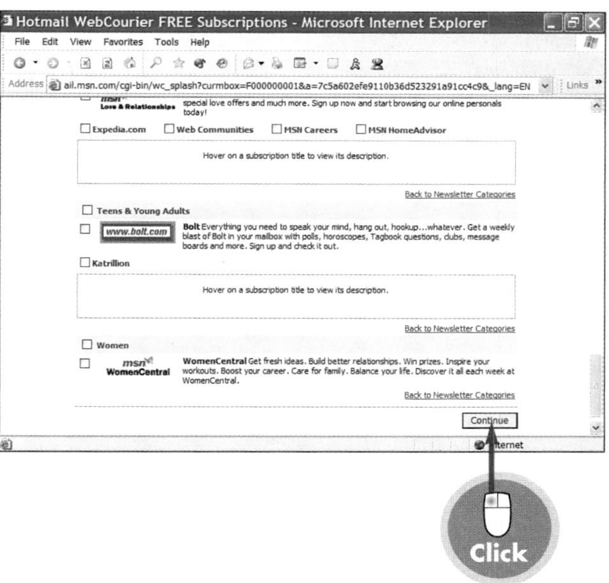

15 Choose Special Offers

To receive email offers on topics in entertainment, shopping, and other categories, enable the check boxes for the desired categories. When you're done, click **Continue to Email**. You can start using your new Hotmail account immediately in Internet Explorer or set it up in Outlook Express.

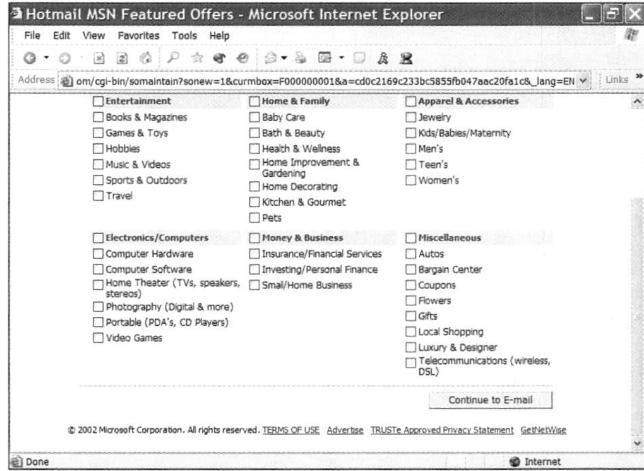

How to Set Up Hotmail in Outlook Express

You can use Hotmail to send and read your email can be in two different ways. One is to use Internet Explorer or another Web browser by visiting the URL `http://www.hotmail.com` and logging in with your username; you can employ this method regardless of where you are or whose computer you're using. Alternatively, you can use Outlook Express on your own computer to send and read your Hotmail email without ever running your browser. After you sign up for a Hotmail account (as explained in the preceding task), you can set up Outlook Express to work with this account. Hotmail won't interfere with any other email accounts that already use Outlook Express.

1 Run Outlook Express

To get started, run Outlook Express. Click the **Start** button and choose **Email**. When Outlook Express is running, open the **Tools** menu and choose **Accounts**. The **Internet Accounts** dialog box opens.

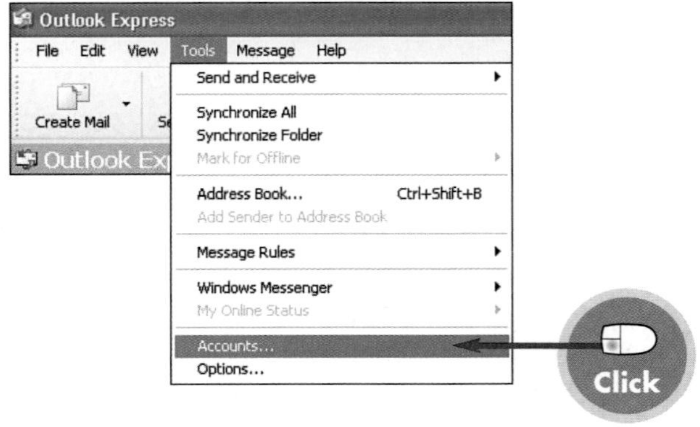

2 Add an Account

The **Internet Accounts** dialog box displays the accounts that currently are set up in Outlook Express. To add your Hotmail account, click the **Add** button and choose **Mail**. The **Internet Connection Wizard** starts.

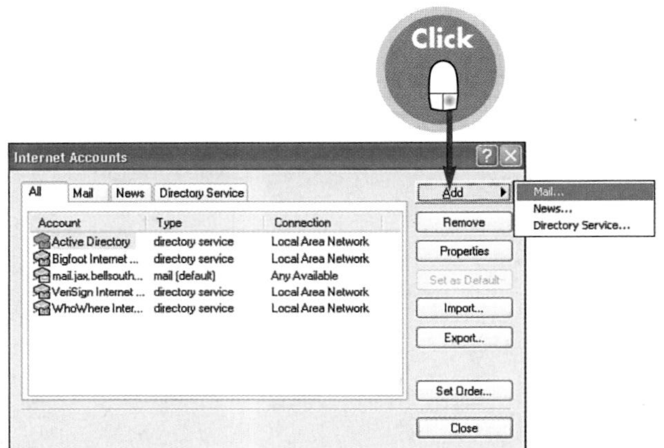

3 Identify Yourself

Type the name you want to use on your outgoing mail in the **Display name** text box; most people use their real names, but that's not required. Click **Next** to continue.

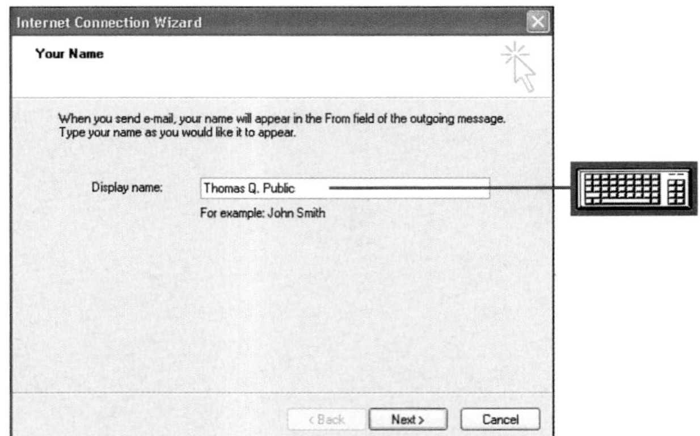

4 Provide Your Address

Type your Hotmail email address—which you set up in the previous task—in the **Email address** text box and click **Next**.

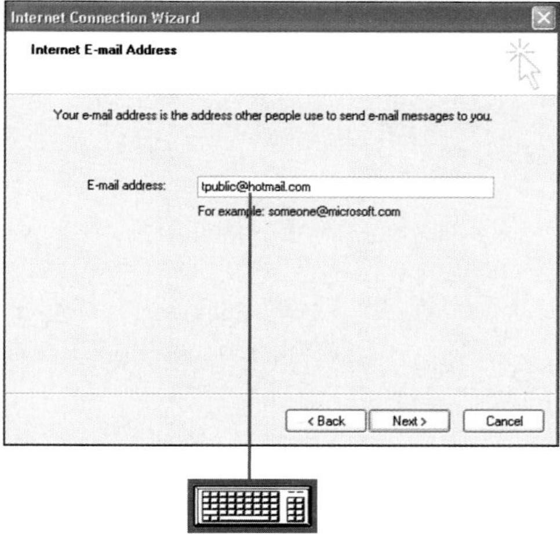

5 Confirm Your Settings

Because you entered a Hotmail address, the **Internet Connection Wizard** assumes that you are using an HTTP server with **Hotmail** as your provider. The wizard is correct—click the **Next** button without changing anything on this screen.

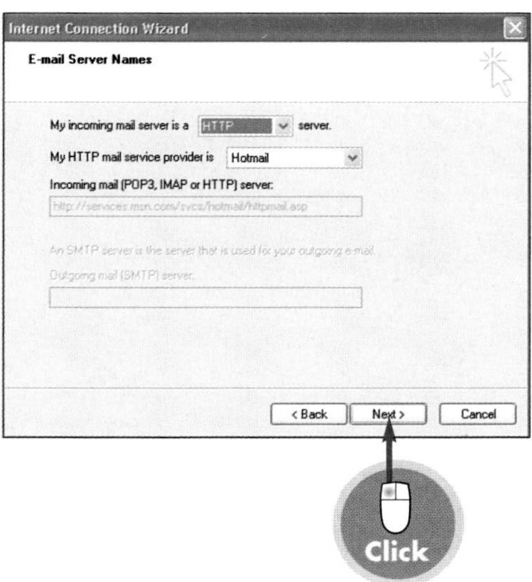

6 Provide Login Information

Outlook Express must log in to Hotmail. To make this possible, type your Hotmail email address again in the **Account name** text box and your password in the **Password** box. Then click **Next**. The wizard informs you that the account is ready to set up—click **Finish**.

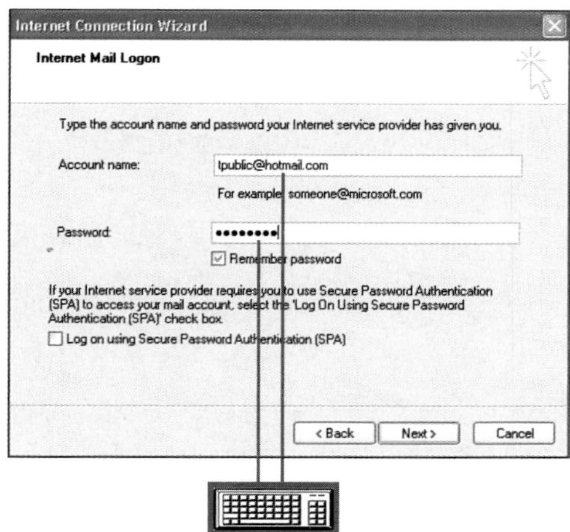

7 Close Your Settings

Your Hotmail account will be displayed in the list of accounts that are set up in Outlook Express. Click the **Close** button. A dialog box appears asking whether you want to download folders from Hotmail. Click the **Yes** button. Now you'll have a new set of folders in which you can store Hotmail mail, separate from any other mail.

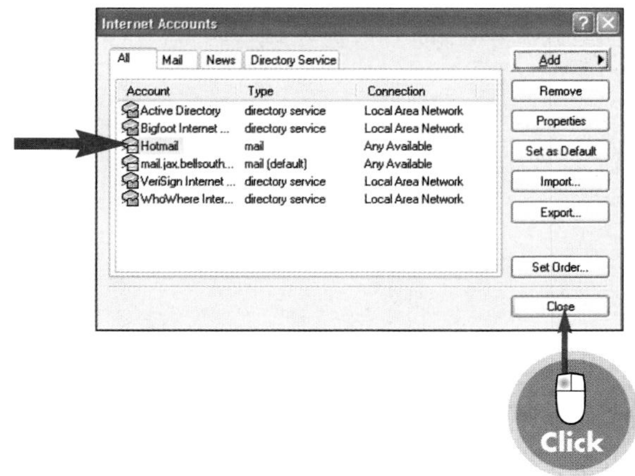

How to Use Your Free Web-Based Email Account

The preceding task described how to set up a free Hotmail account with Outlook Express. After you've done this, Hotmail service is fully integrated into all the features of Outlook Express. You can send and receive email through your Hotmail account and any other accounts you have set up. Hotmail messages are stored apart from your other Outlook Express mail in separate **Inbox**, **Sent Items**, **Deleted Items**, **MSN Announcements**, and **Bulk Mail** folders.

1 Check Your Hotmail Account

Start Outlook Express: Click **Start** and choose **Email**. To check for messages sent to your Hotmail account, click the Hotmail **Inbox** folder icon in the top-left pane of the window. (If you don't see this icon, click the **Hotmail** icon. A dialog box opens asking if you want to view available folders. Click **Yes**.)

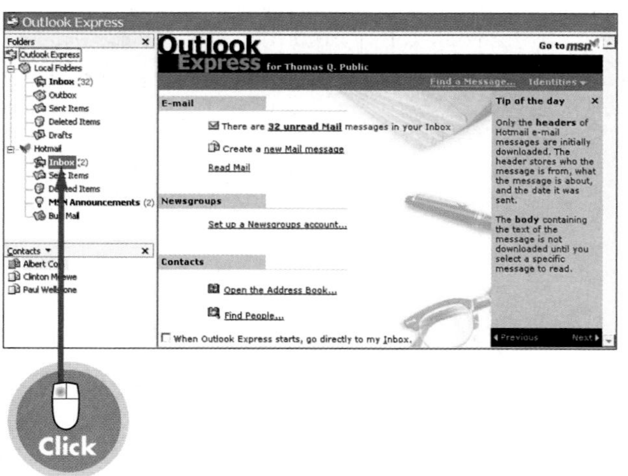

2 Start a New Message

Start a new message with Hotmail: Click the **Create Mail** button in the toolbar at the top of the screen. A **New Message** window opens.

3 Choose an Account

Click the arrow to the right of the **From** drop-down list and select the address from which the message should be sent. (If your copy of Outlook Express is configured to use only one email account, the **From** list box will not appear in the **New Message** window.) The **From** list box contains your Hotmail account and any other email accounts you may have set up.

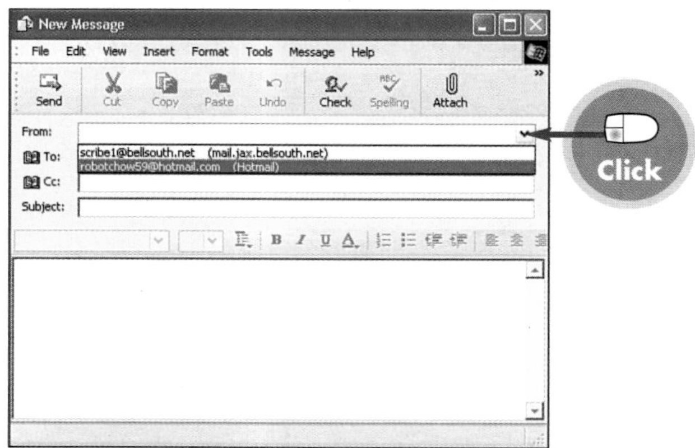

4 Send the Message

After you have specified the recipient of your message in the **To** text box and typed the body of your message, click the **Send** button to deliver the message using Hotmail. If the recipient replies to the message, the reply will be received in your Hotmail **Inbox** folder.

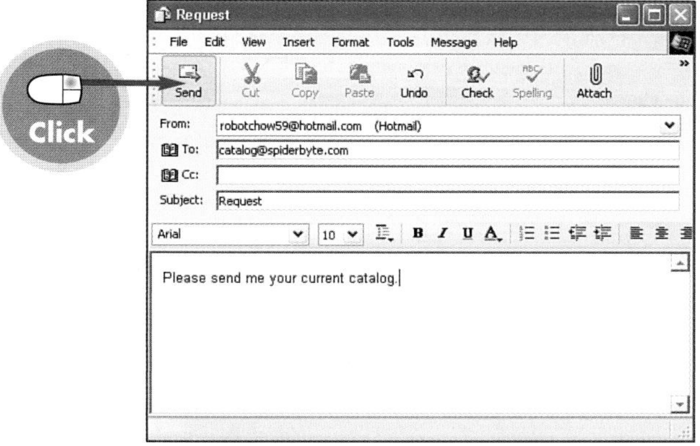

5 Change Mail Settings

If you want Hotmail to be your primary mail service, you can change your Outlook Express settings to make that happen. From the **Tools** menu, choose **Accounts**. The **Internet Accounts** dialog box opens.

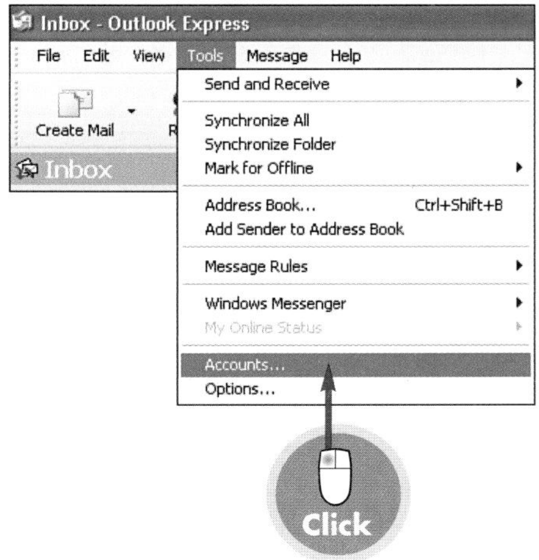

6 Choose a Default

Click the **Mail** tab to bring that screen to the front. All your mail accounts are listed. To make your Hotmail account the default, click the **Hotmail** list item and then click the **Set as Default** button.

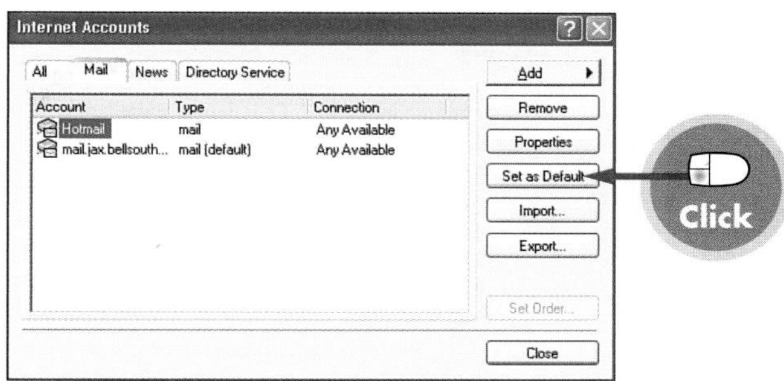

How to Hint

Using Hotmail As Your Public Email Address

One of the biggest annoyances for people who use email is the growing problem of *spam*—unsolicited commercial email that is sent to thousands of Internet users at the same time. This electronic junk mail often is sent to promote disreputable or obscene businesses. It can take a lot of your time and patience to read and delete these messages. You may want to use a Hotmail address as your public email address—the one you use on Web sites, Usenet, and other places where a spam sender might find it. Another email address, such as the one provided by your Internet service provider, can be your private email address—given only to friends, relatives, and business colleagues. Hotmail stores all incoming mail believed to be spam in a **Bulk Mail** folder so you can deal with it more easily.

How to Print an Email Message

You can print email from Outlook Express using the standard Windows printing interface. Because email you receive from Outlook Express (and many other types of mail software) can contain the same kind of content as a Web page, printing a message is similar to printing a Web page. You can print the current message, print all the hyperlinks it contains, and print a collection of linked pages. Messages can be sent to a printer, sent out using a fax modem, or saved as a disk file.

1 Choose the Print Command

To print the message you're currently reading in Outlook Express, choose **File**, **Print**. The **Print** dialog box opens.

2 Choose a Printer

You can send Web pages to any printer or fax modem that has been installed on your system. To print the page, choose a printer from the **Select Printer** window and click **Print**.

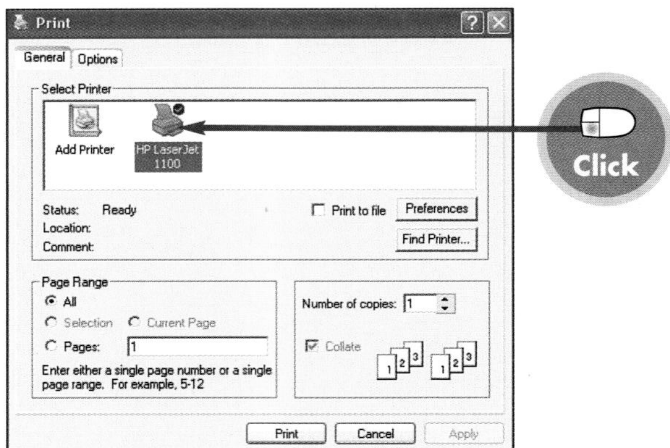

3 Customize the Print Job

You can make changes to how Outlook Express prints hyperlinks and frames (separate sections on a Web page that often have their own scrollbars and borders). To begin, click the **Options** tab to bring it to the front.

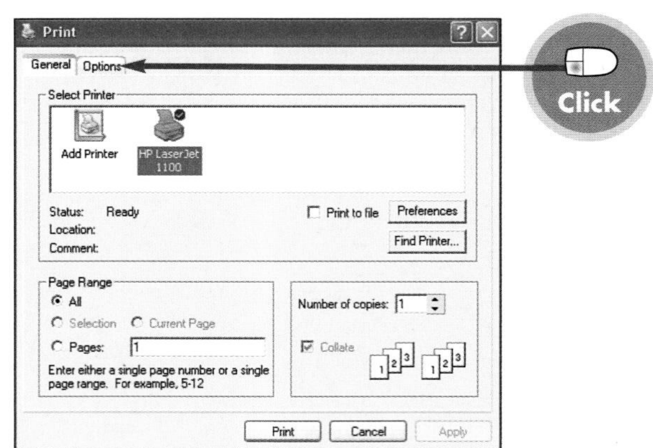

4 Print Associated Web Pages

Outlook Express can look at all hyperlinks in the current email message and print the Web pages associated with those links. Enable the **Print all linked documents** check box to print the pages that are linked to the email message.

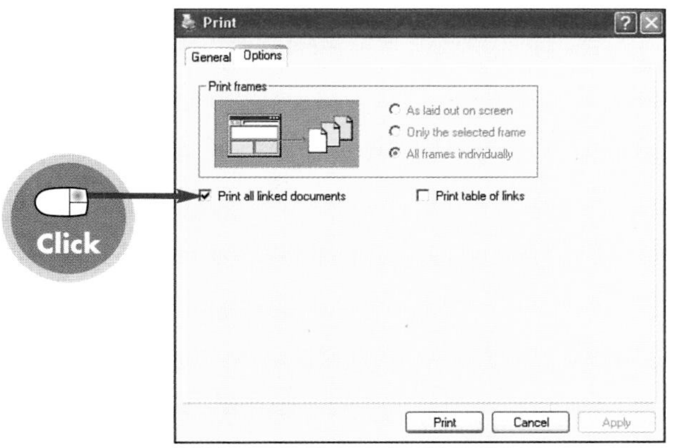

5 List All Hyperlinks

At the same time you print the email message, you can print a report listing all the hyperlinks in that message. Enable the **Print table of links** check box to print the list.

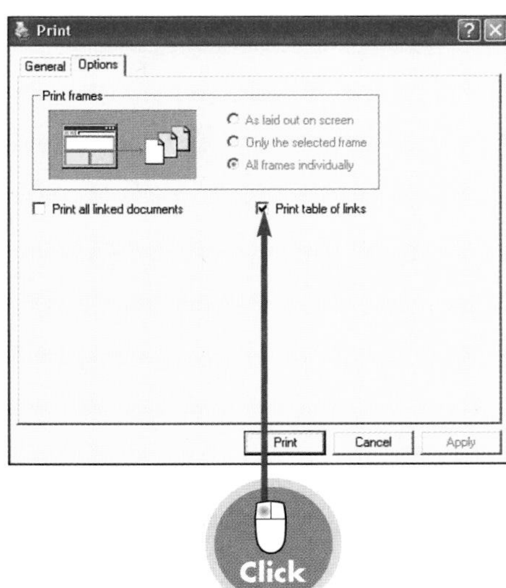

6 Print a Framed Message

Some email messages are divided into separate frames. If a message contains frames, three options will be available: Print each frame individually, print the message as it looks in Outlook Express, or print only the selected frame. To select a frame, click your mouse in that section of the message before printing the page and then select the **Only the selected frame** option.

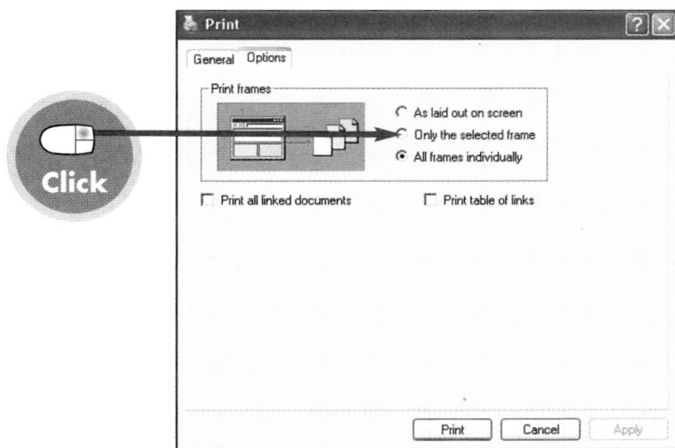

7 Print the Message

Click the **Print** button to print the email message according to the options you have selected. Your printer's dialog box opens, displaying the status of the printing operation. You should soon hear the printer working on the page.

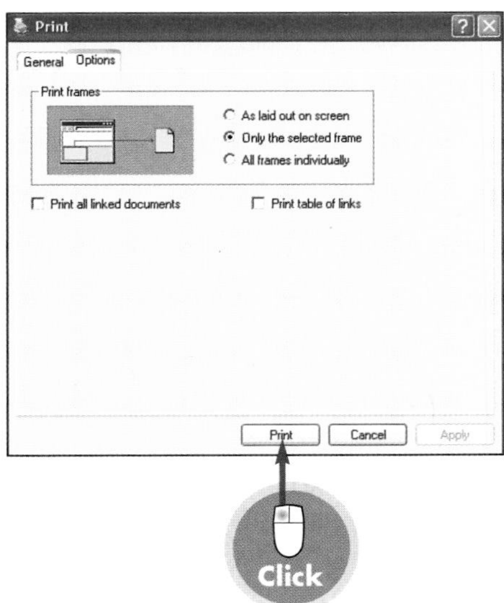

Task

6

Protecting Yourself on the Web

Part of the World Wide Web's appeal is its wide-open nature. Anyone can put a site on the Web and reach people all over the world.

This has its advantages—free speech is exercised on the Internet with great success. This also has its disadvantages—content that some people find objectionable is available in great quantity.

Another disadvantage of the Internet is that Web pages can contain interactive programs that can sometimes expose security holes that put your own computer at risk.

When you run a program in a Web browser, the program runs on *your* computer just like any other software you use. For this reason, browsers such as Internet Explorer 6 have security settings that restrict the ways a page can interact with your system.

Another way to reduce your risk is to install an antivirus program such as Norton AntiVirus 2002 and use it to scan all files you receive.

How to Choose a Security Setting

Although security risks are extremely small on the World Wide Web, you may encounter sites that try to damage files on your computer or steal confidential data. Internet Explorer 6's security settings can restrict or disable browser features that are most susceptible to abuse, such as JavaScript, Active Scripting, Java, and cookies. Restricting these features can limit your enjoyment of the Web because many popular sites rely on them, but you may feel it's a fair trade-off for a more secure computer system.

1 Configure Your Browser

Pull down the Internet Explorer **Tools** menu and select the **Internet Options** command. The **Internet Options** dialog box opens.

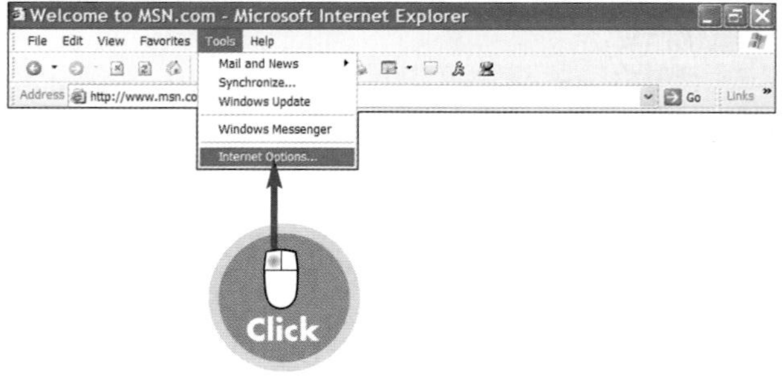

2 View Security Settings

Click the **Security** tab to view your current security settings and to make changes to those settings.

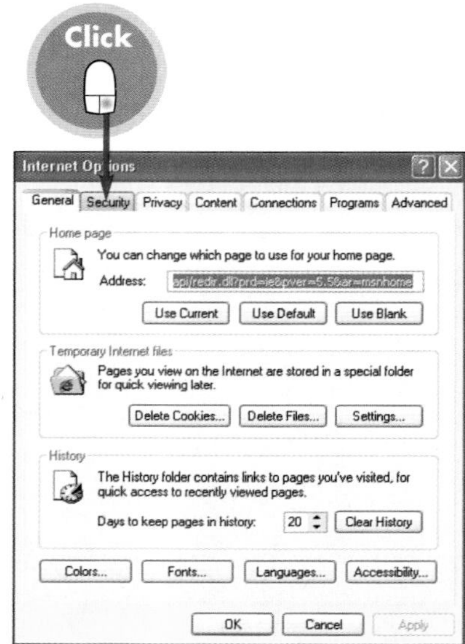

3 Set Your Internet Security

Internet Explorer enables different levels of security for sites on the Internet as well as sites on a local *intranet*—a private network of documents shared by people in a company, school, or organization. To change your Internet settings, click the **Internet** icon from the **Select a Web content zone to specify its security settings** list box.

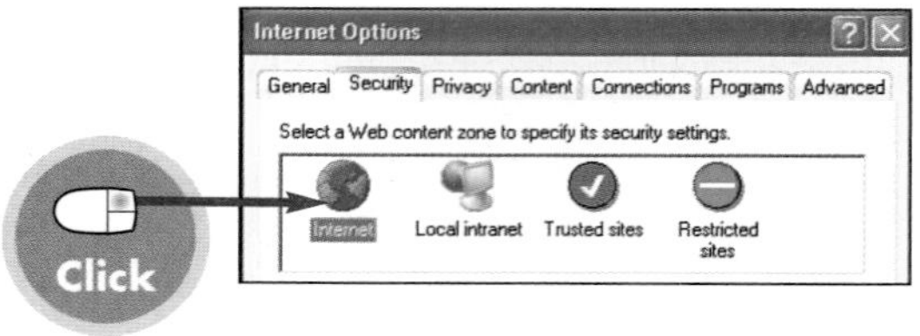

4 Pick a Security Level

There are four basic security levels: **High**, **Medium**, **Medium-Low**, and **Low**. These levels determine the kind of content Internet Explorer will load and the tasks it will restrict. To choose a security level, click the **Default Level** button and drag the slider toward the **High**, **Medium**, or **Low** setting, and release it. (The How-To Hints box at the end of this task provides some guidelines for setting a security level.)

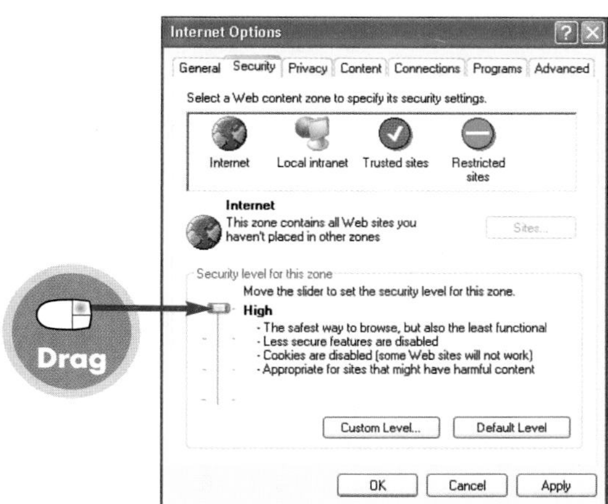

5 Oppose a Recommendation

Microsoft recommends that you use **High** or **Medium** security level while browsing the Internet. If you choose lower security level, a dialog box appears, asking you to confirm this choice. Click **Yes** if you want to disregard Microsoft's recommendation and choose a lower security level.

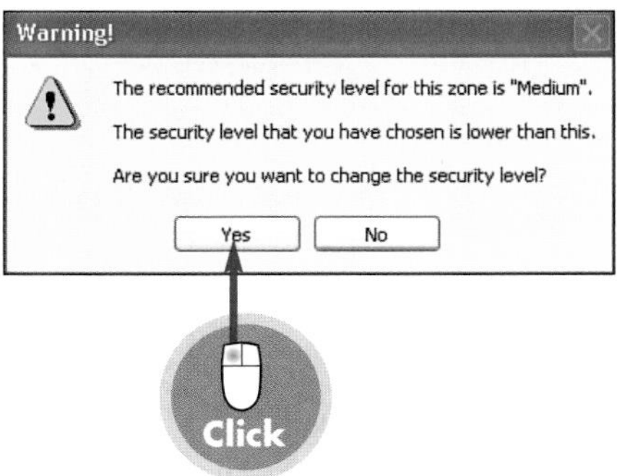

6 Restore the Default Level

If you want to restore your browser security to the level recommended by Microsoft, click the **Default Level** button.

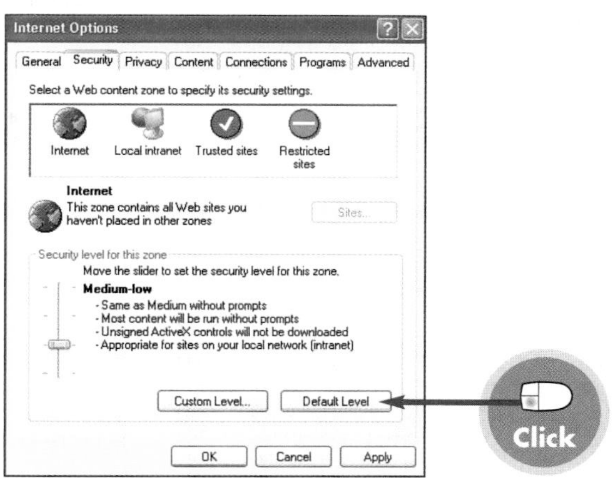

How to Hint

Deciding on a Security Level

Unless you're a Web-site developer, you probably won't have much to go on when choosing a security level. To help guide your decision, we suggest you try **High** security first. Afterward, as you're visiting Web sites, your browser and some sites will often tell you what you're missing out on because of your chosen security level. You can repeat the steps in this task to select a slightly lower security level if you want to access some of the features you've been missing.

How to Customize Your Security Setting

For most people, Internet Explorer 6's basic security levels should be sufficient. If you want more control over your browser's security, however, you can customize each of its security settings. This enables you to turn on and off specific features such as cookies, Java, JavaScript, file downloading, and some browser security warnings. Doing this can increase security risks, so you should be cautious about making drastic changes.

1 Change Your Settings

Pull down the **Tools** menu and select the **Internet Options** command to open the **Internet Options** dialog box and view your Internet Explorer settings.

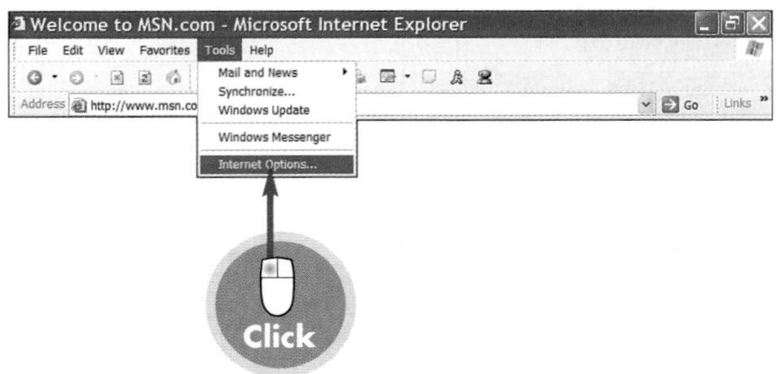

2 Choose a Custom Level

Click to see your current security settings. To change how your browser handles specific security issues, click the **Custom Level** button.

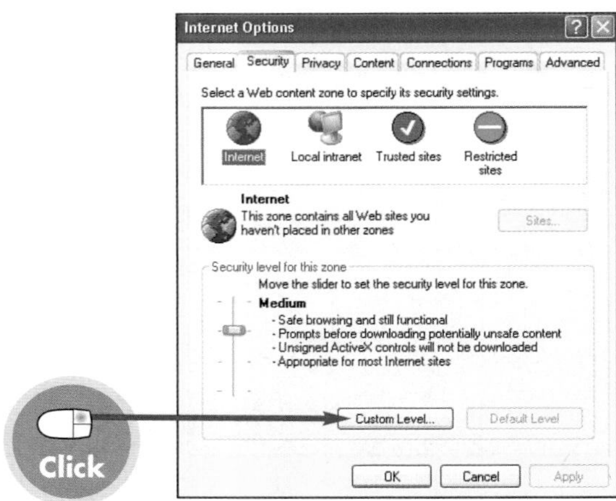

3 Set Up a Custom Level

By default, custom settings are identical to those specified by the **Medium** security level. To make them identical to a different level, click the down arrow next to the **Reset to** box and select the level you want to use as a starting point.

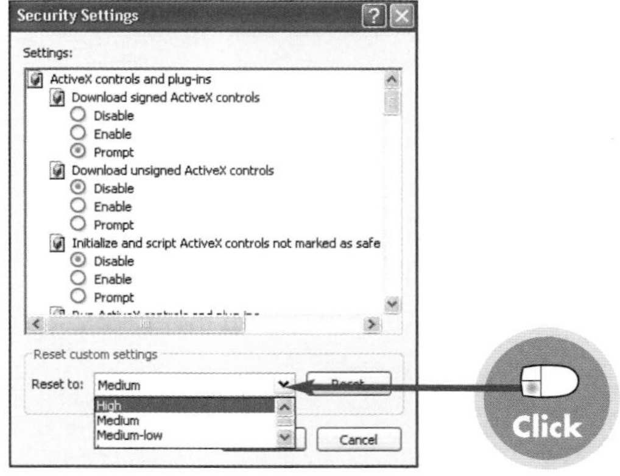

4 Reset All Settings

Click the **Reset** button to make all the custom settings the same as the level shown in the **Reset to** box.

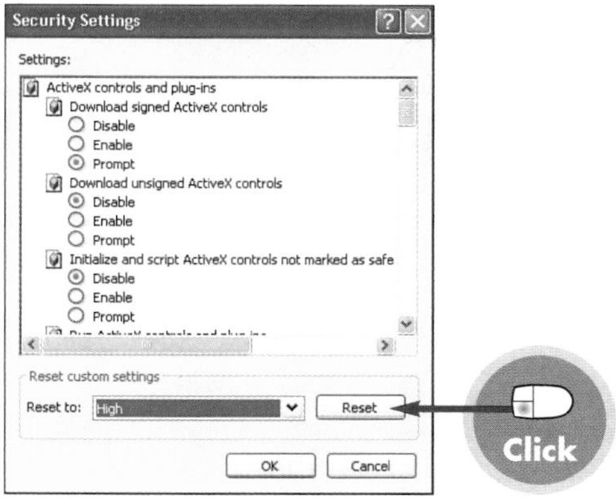

5 Customize Your Settings

Scroll through the **Settings** list box to see the various settings you can affect. To change a specific setting, click the appropriate radio button. Click **Disable** to turn off a feature, **Enable** to turn on a feature, and **Prompt** if you want the browser to ask whether a feature should be used each time it is encountered on a Web page. Click **OK** to save all your changes.

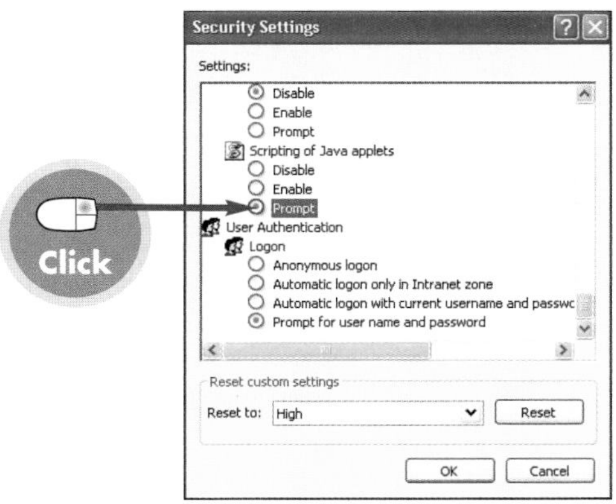

6 Undo Customization

To remove a custom security level and undo all the changes you have made since opening the **Internet Options** dialog box, return to the **Security** tab of the **Internet Options** dialog box and click the **Default Level** button.

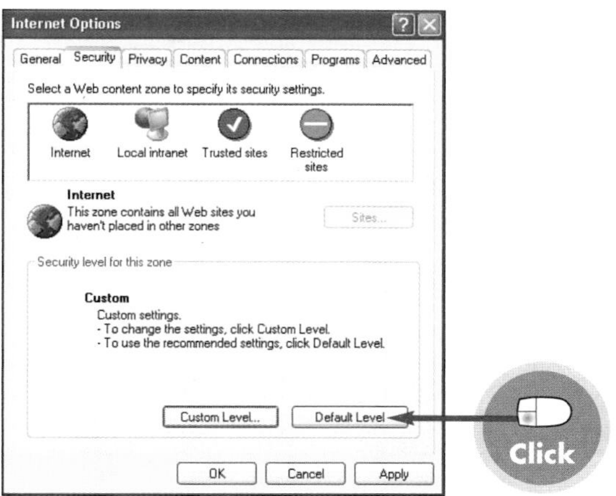

How to Hint

Turning Off Form Warnings

By default, Internet Explorer warns you before it sends data you've entered on a form that's located on an unencrypted Web server. This feature keeps you from sending private information (such as your credit-card number) without *encryption*—a way to encode data so that it remains confidential. This warning is cumbersome if you're one of those people who never reveals personal data on the Web. To turn off this warning, find the **Submit nonencrypted form data** setting in your custom settings (see step 5) and click the **Disable** radio button.

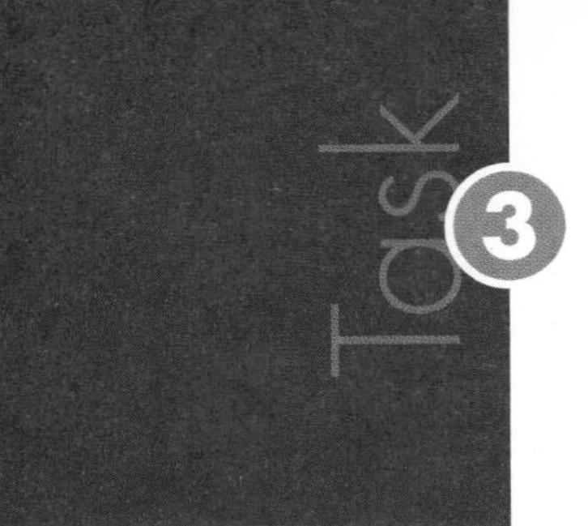

How to Block Objectionable Content from Being Viewed

To place restrictions on the material that can be viewed with Internet Explorer 6, use the browser's *Content Advisor*. The Advisor relies on RSACi ratings—an industry standard adopted voluntarily by some Web publishers to indicate their site's level of objectionable language, nudity, sex, and violence. Although the Content Advisor is far from foolproof—it relies on Web sites to honestly assess their own content—you may find it useful in conjunction with other methods of filtering the Web.

1 View Content Settings

The Content Advisor is configured with all other browser settings. Choose **Tools**, **Internet Options** from the menu bar to open the **Internet Options** dialog box. Then click the **Content** tab to view the browser's content settings. To set up the Content Advisor, first click the **Enable** button.

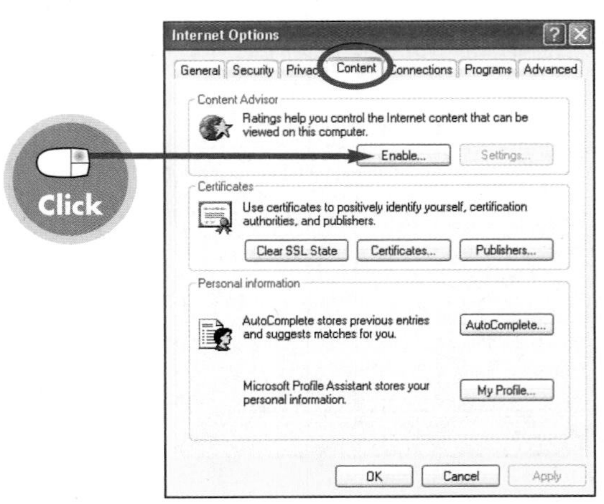

2 Set Your Content Ratings

The **Content Advisor** dialog box opens to the **Ratings** tab, ready for you to set your browser's acceptable RSACi rating. Click the RSACi category you want to set, then drag the slider to a content setting. A site must have content rated at or below all four settings to pass the Content Advisor. Pages that don't pass are not displayed.

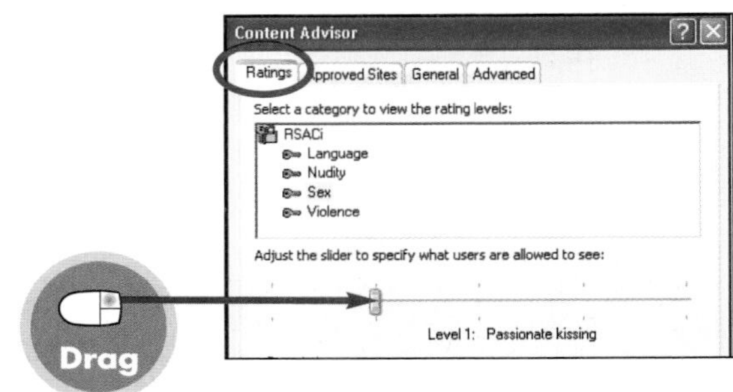

3 View Unrated Sites

By default, Web pages without RSACi ratings cannot be viewed. This keeps out unrated sites that contain objectionable material, along with thousands of sites that don't participate in RSACi. To allow unrated sites to be viewed, click the **General** tab of the **Content Advisor** dialog box and enable the **Users can see sites that have no rating** check box.

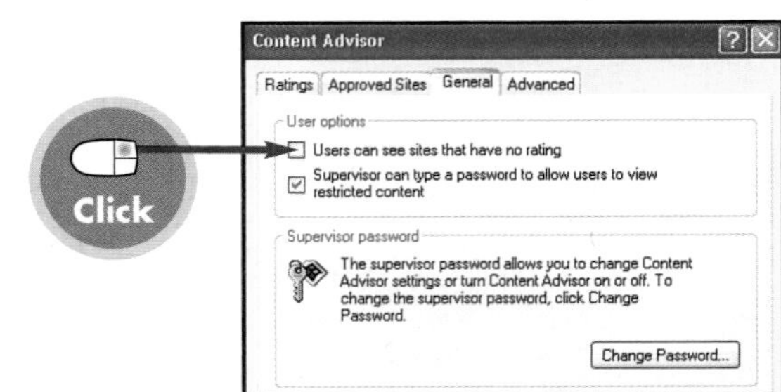

4 Approve Individual Sites

To allow individual sites to bypass the Content Advisor, click the **Approved Sites** tab, type the site's main address in the **Allow this Web site** text box, and click the **Always** button. Alternatively, you can completely restrict access to the specified site by clicking the **Never** button instead.

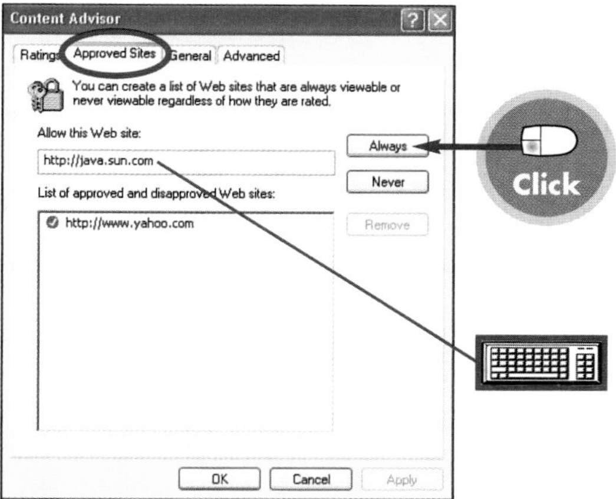

5 Save Your Changes

Click the **OK** button to save your new settings and close the **Content Advisor** dialog box. If you have imposed content restrictions, you should close Internet Explorer and launch it again. This action keeps recently visited sites from being reloaded without first being checked by the Content Advisor.

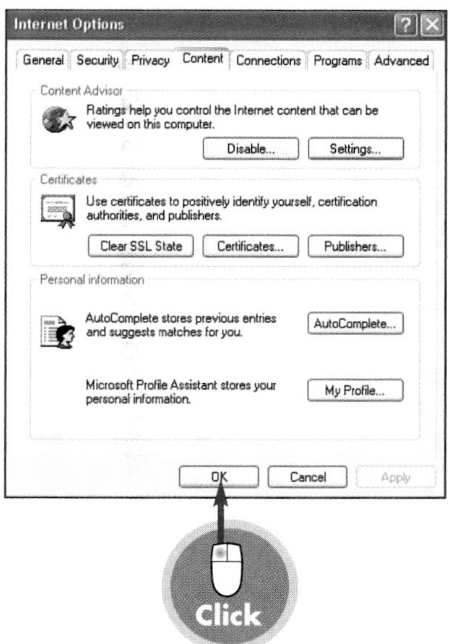

6 Choose a Password

When you save your content settings for the first time, you will be asked to select a supervisor password. This password can be used to change Content Advisor settings or turn it off completely. After you set one up, you can't modify the Content Advisor without it. Enter your password in both text boxes and click **OK** to return to the **Internet Options** dialog box.

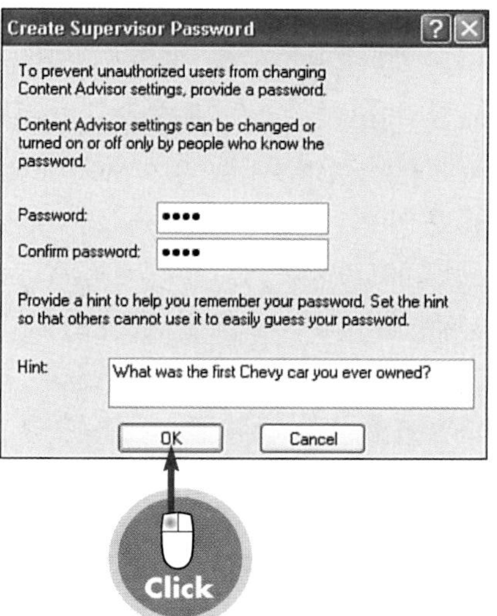

7 Turn Off the Content Advisor

To turn off the Content Advisor completely, choose **Tools**, **Internet Options** to open the **Internet Options** dialog box. Click the **Content** tab, and then click the **Disable** button. You must type the supervisor password in order to disable the Content Advisor feature.

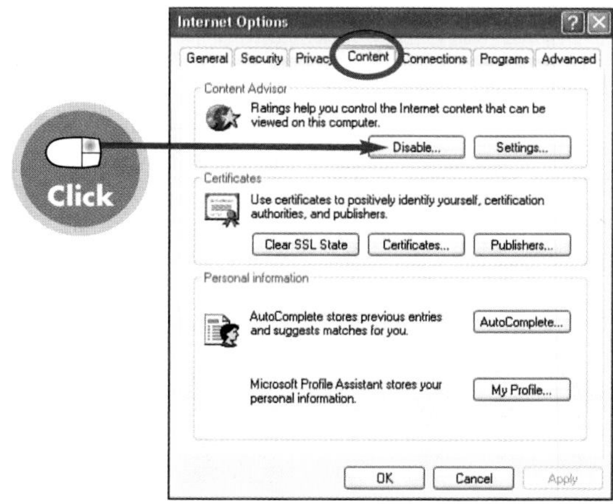

How to Use Security Certificates

As you are visiting Web sites, you may come across pages that contain interactive programs. These small programs are downloaded to your computer and run as if you installed them from a CD-ROM, but they must be approved before your Web browser runs them. Internet Explorer 6 presents a *security certificate*—a window vouching for the authenticity of the program's author. Examine this certificate and decide whether to let the program run.

1 Inspect a Certificate

When you load a page that contains an interactive program, Internet Explorer presents a dialog box asking whether the control should be installed. The author of the program is presented as a hyperlink. Click this hyperlink to find out more about the author.

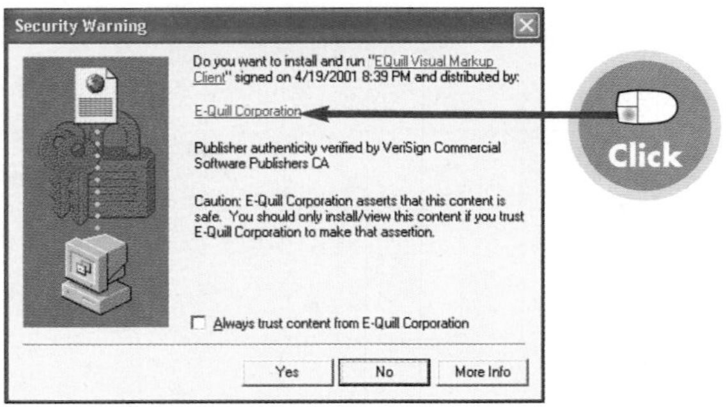

2 Determine Authenticity

The link opens a security certificate associated with the program's author. Companies such as VeriSign and Thawte create these certificates after verifying the program's authorship. Click the tabs to find out more about the certificate and the author. Click **OK** to close the window.

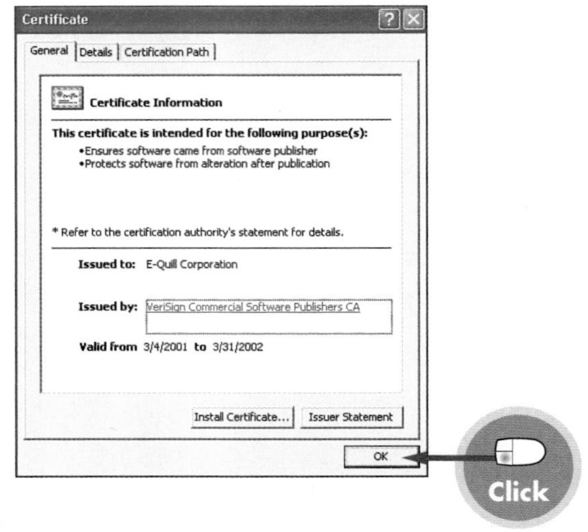

3 Always Trust an Author

If you are comfortable with the program's author, you can automatically approve the download of any programs that author creates in the future. To do so, enable the **Always trust content** check box. (You should note, however, that it's safer to approve programs individually than to issue blanket approval with this check box.)

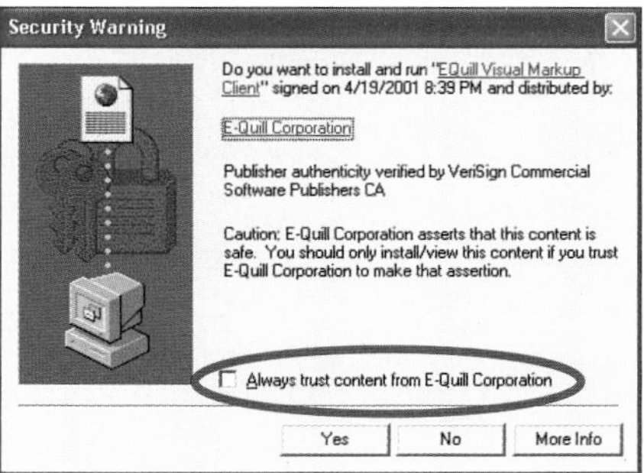

4 Reject an Author

To prevent a program from being installed, click the **No** button in the **Security Warning** dialog box. You can still use anything on the current Web page that doesn't rely on the program.

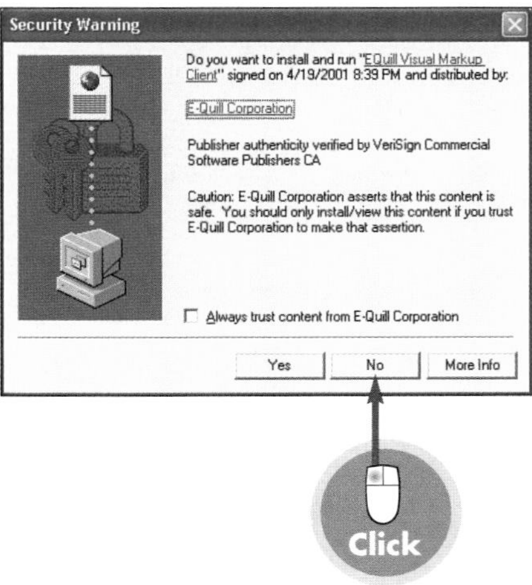

5 Approve an Author

To approve a program and run it in your browser, click the **Yes** button. The program will be saved on your system in the `Windows/Downloaded Program Files` folder so that it doesn't have to be installed again every time you visit the page.

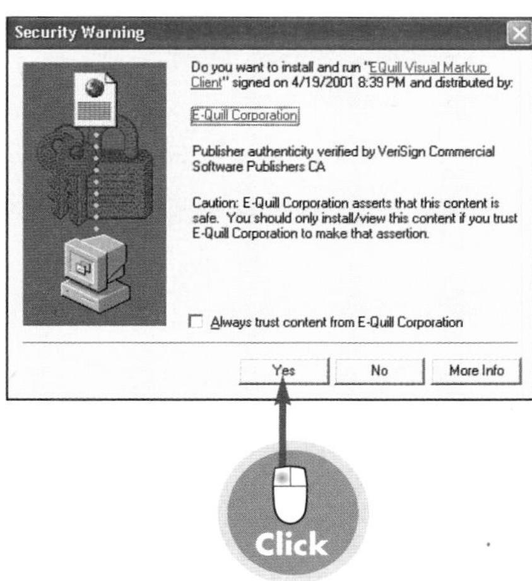

How to Hint

Restricting Programs on Your Browser

If you are never asked whether a program should be installed before it starts running on a Web page, your browser may be configured with a low security level. To check your security settings, select **Tools**, **Internet Options** to open the **Internet Options** dialog box and click the **Security** tab. Refer to Tasks 1 and 2 in this part of the book for instructions on setting and customizing a security level in Internet Explorer.

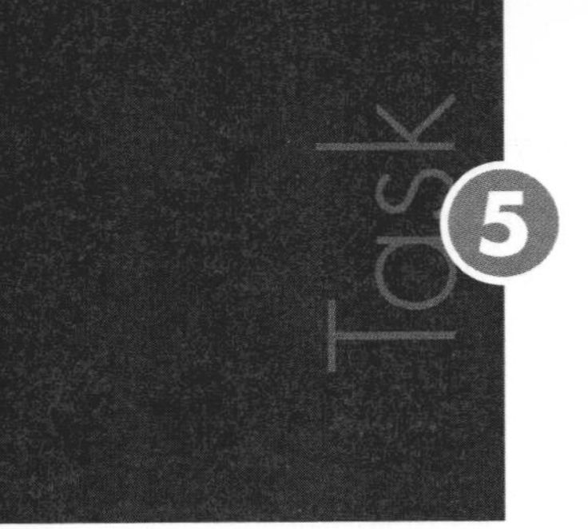

How to Disable Cookies in a Web Browser

Web sites can keep track of visitors by using *cookies*—small files that contain information collected by a site. Internet Explorer 6 saves cookie files for Web sites on your computer; when you revisit a site for which you have a cookie, Internet Explorer 6 sends the cookie file back to the site. The cookie can be used to store personal information such as your name, billing information, and similar data. By design, Internet Explorer sends a cookie file that exists on your computer only to the site that created it. Some Web sites require cookie files, but you can turn them off entirely by adjusting the browser's privacy settings.

1 Change Your Settings

Select **Tools**, **Internet Options**. The **Internet Options** dialog box opens to the **General** tab, displaying how your browser is configured.

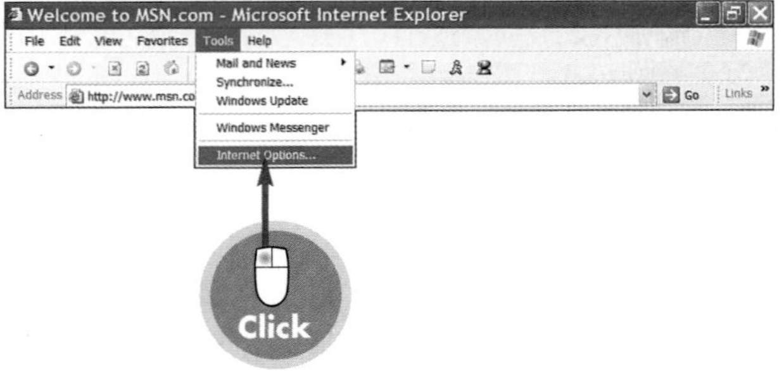

2 View Privacy Settings

Click the **Privacy** tab to bring its settings to the front of the dialog box.

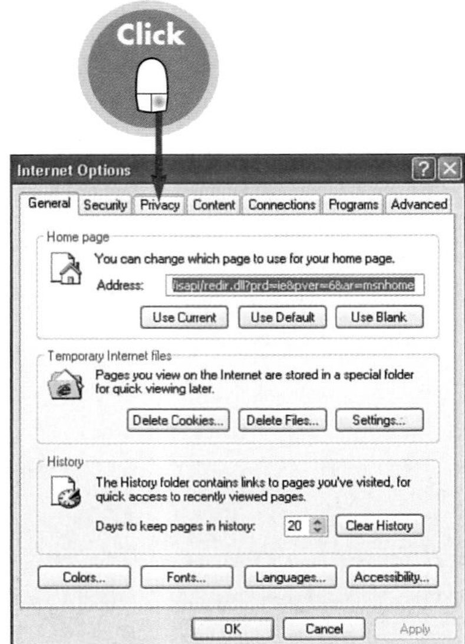

3 Block All Cookies

To block all cookies from being stored on your computer, drag the slider up to the **Block All Cookies** setting. You should note, however, that this is the strictest setting and may prevent you from using some popular sites.

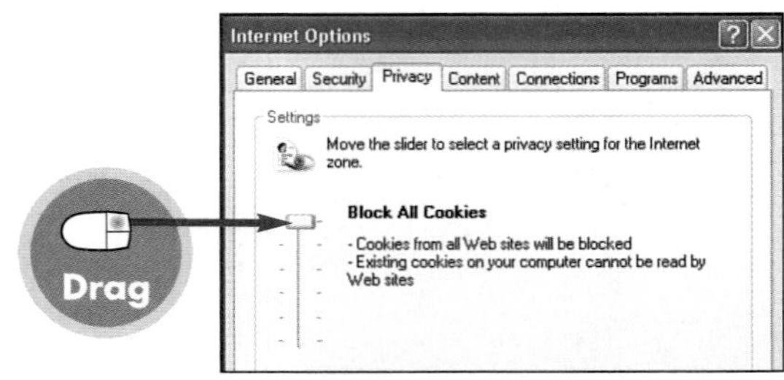

4 Block Most Cookies

To block most cookies (except for those already on your computer), drag the slider to the **High** setting. Cookies that store information related to your identity will not be stored without your consent.

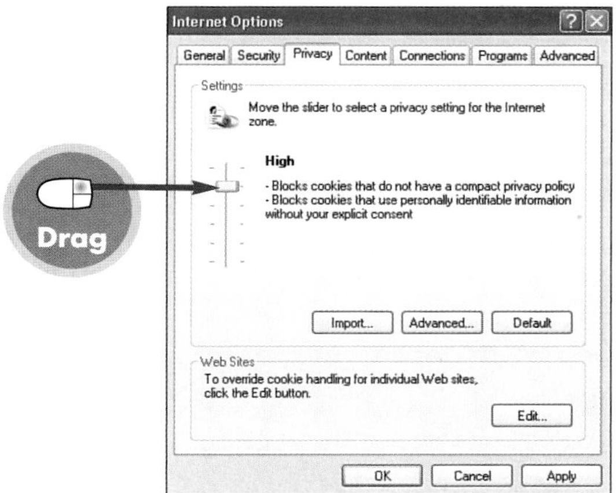

5 Block Advertiser Cookies

To block most cookies from advertisers and some others, drag the slider to the **Medium** setting. Ad cookies and cookies that identify you will not be stored unless you consent.

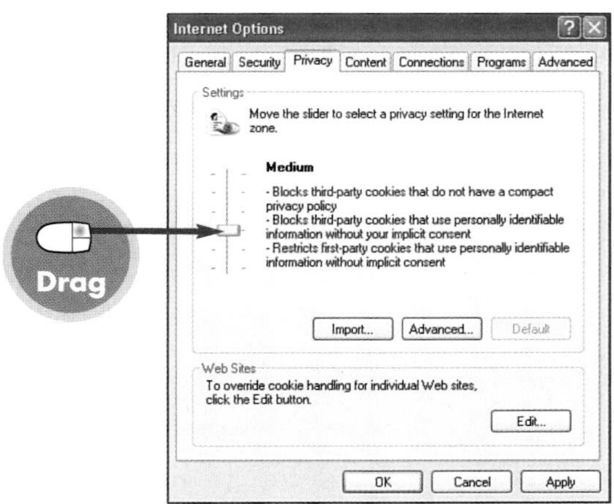

6 Save Your New Settings

To make your privacy changes take effect, click the **OK** button. Your cookie privacy settings will be in force until you change them or return to the **Privacy** tab and click the **Default Level** button.

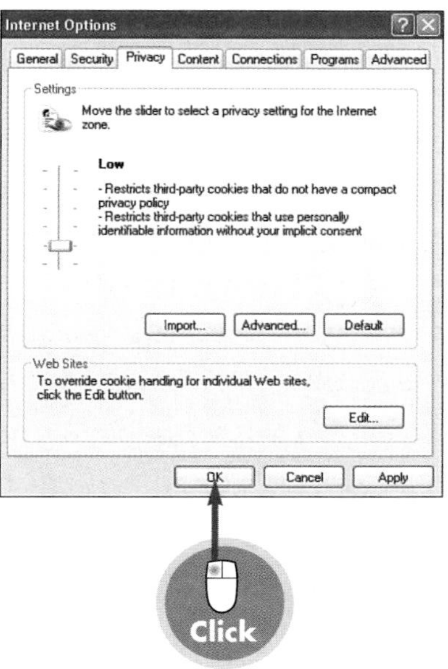

How to Hint

Approving Cookies on a Case-by-Case Basis

As you will discover after changing your privacy settings to block cookies, many of the sites you use will no longer be fully functional—especially if they offer features that are personalized specifically for you. To allow a specific site to store cookies on your computer, return to the **Privacy** tab and click the **Edit** button. The **Per Site Privacy Actions** dialog box opens. Type the main URL of the site in the **Address of Web Site** text box and click the **Allow** button. When you have finished adding sites, click the **OK** button to close the dialog box.

How to Make Your Internet Connection More Secure

When you are connected to the Internet, the Internet is also connected to you. Malicious people can use that Internet connection to look for ways to access your computer's files, programs, and devices such as printers. Although problems of this kind are relatively rare, several software developers now offer *firewalls*—programs that restrict the kind of information that can be exchanged over an Internet connection. Windows XP comes with its own protection against unwelcome intruders: the Internet Connection Firewall.

1 View Your Connections

In order to work, an Internet Connection Firewall must be associated with a network connection on your computer. (Note that the Internet Connection Firewall is available only with Windows XP.) To view your network connections, click the **Start** button, choose **Connect To**, and choose **Network Connections**.

2 Choose a Connection

The **Network Connections** folder lists the connections you have set up to the Internet and other networks. To begin adding a firewall to an Internet connection, right-click the desired connection icon and choose **Properties** from the shortcut menu that opens.

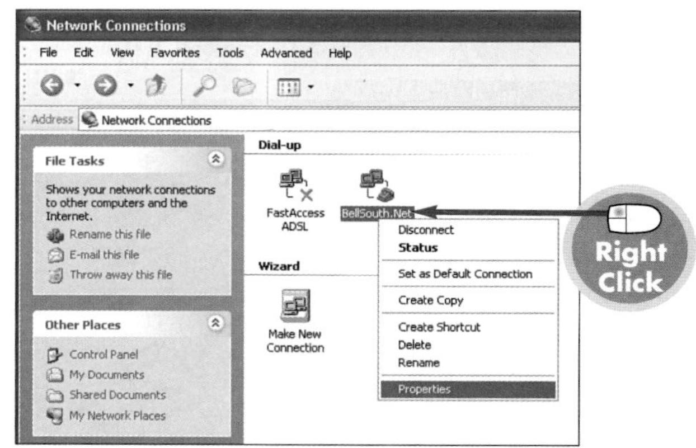

3 View Advanced Settings

The **Properties** dialog box includes five tabs that can be used to modify its settings. Click the **Advanced** tab to bring it to the front.

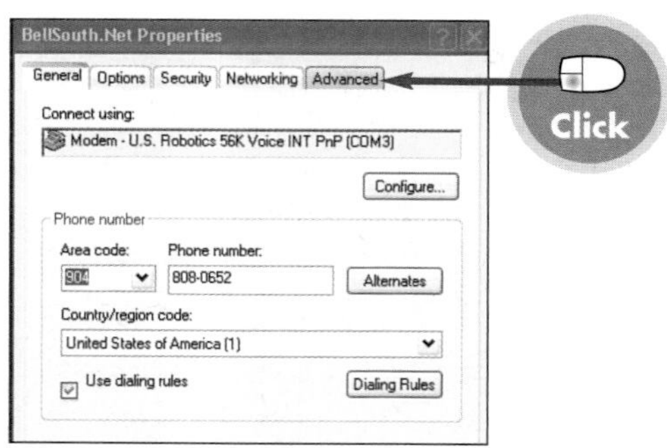

4 Turn On the Firewall

To turn on a firewall, enable the **Protect my computer and network by limiting or preventing access to this computer from the Internet** check box. To learn more about the Internet Connection Firewall, click the link of the same name.

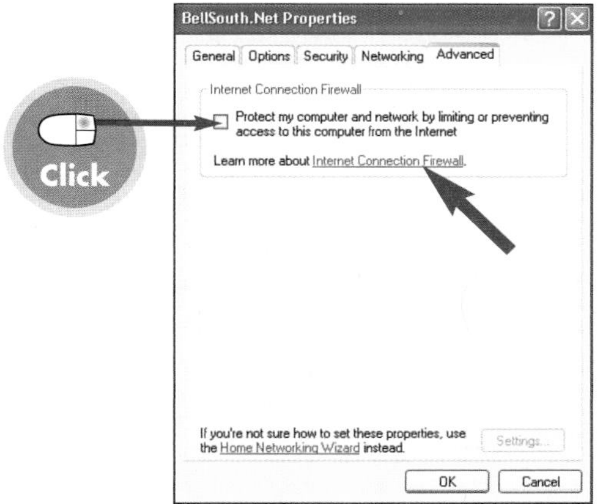

5 Save Your Settings

Click the **OK** button to save the changes you have made to your Internet connection. If you are connected to the Internet when the firewall is set up, the current connection is not protected by the firewall. Disconnect and reconnect to the Internet so that the new connection will be protected by the firewall.

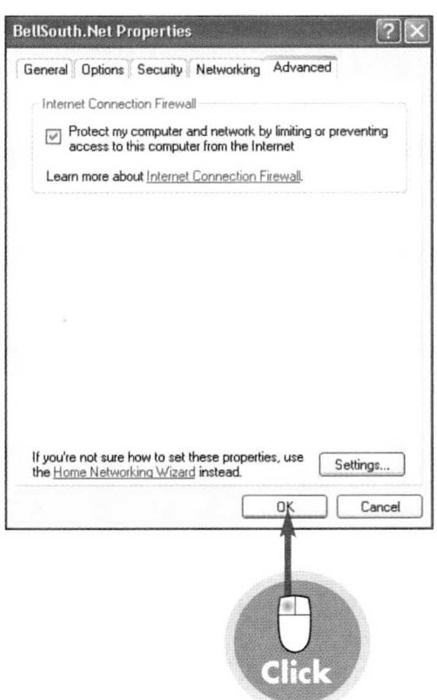

6 Connect Through the Firewall

After you have turned on the firewall, your Internet connection icon will change to show that a firewall is in place. Nothing else changes; double-click the connection icon to connect to the Internet as you normally would.

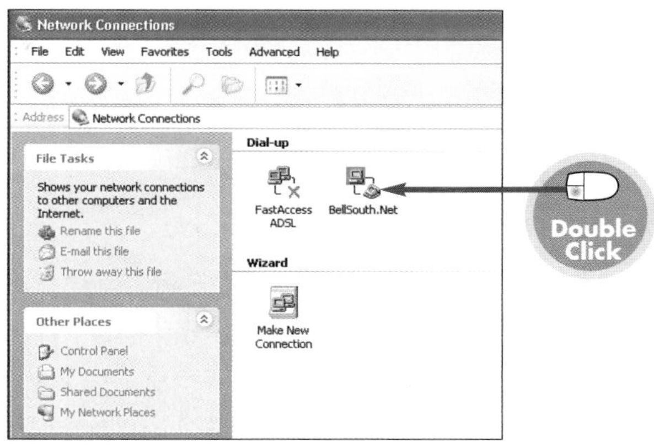

How to Hint

Choosing a Different Internet Firewall

The Internet Connection Firewall is available only on Windows XP and does not protect against some security risks. If you don't use Windows XP or want a more full-featured firewall, you might be interested in the ZoneAlarm firewall. ZoneAlarm is available in free and pay versions from Zone Labs for Windows 95, 98, Me, XP, NT, and 2000. To find out more, type the URL `http://www.zonealarm.com` in your Web browser and press **Enter**; you can then download the free version of the software if desired.

How to Install Antivirus Software

It's only a matter of time before your computer is exposed to its first *virus*—a harmful program that runs without permission, tries to spread itself to other computers, and may damage or delete your files. Viruses infect millions of computers each day on the Internet. To avoid them, you should buy an antivirus program that can check files for viruses before you open them, even as they arrive in email. One of the best is Norton AntiVirus 2002, which sells for $39 at many software retailers. Most computer and office superstores sell the software, including Office Max, Staples, and CompUSA.

1 Load the Wizard

When you place the Norton AntiVirus 2002 CD in your CD drive, it loads automatically. To begin installing the program, click the **Install Norton AntiVirus** link. An installation wizard starts.

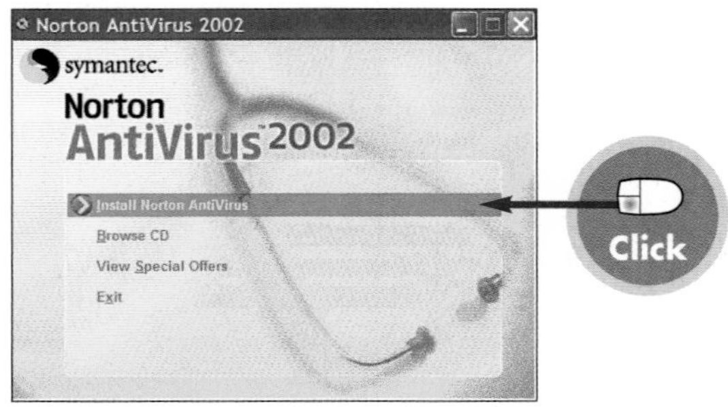

2 Run the Wizard

If possible, you should close all other programs before installing Norton AntiVirus 2002. After you have done so, click **Next** to run the installation wizard.

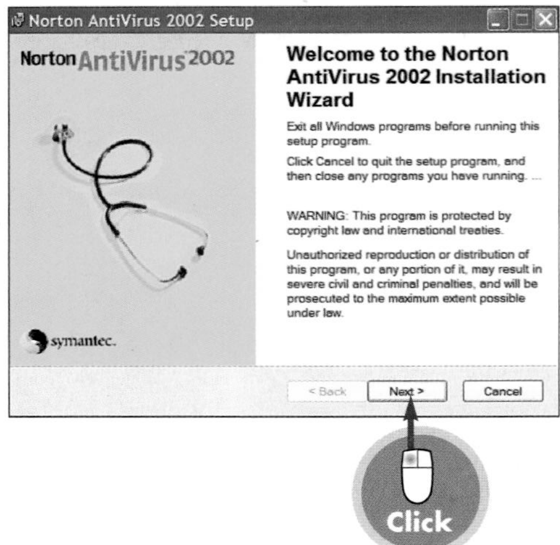

3 Review the License

The wizard presents the software's license agreement. If you agree to its terms, select the **I accept the license agreement** radio button and click **Next**.

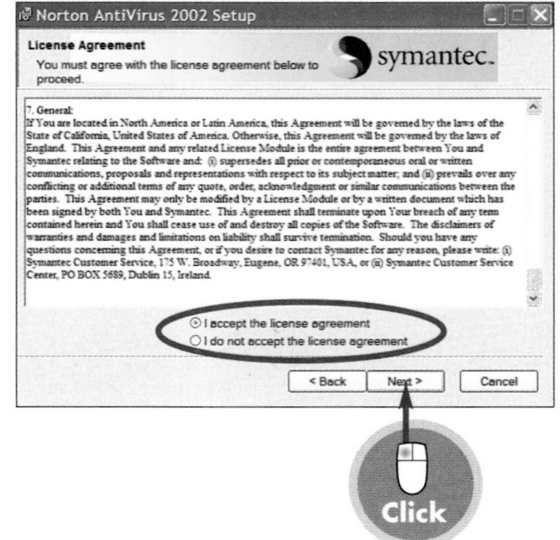

4 Choose a Folder

The wizard recommends a folder for the software: **\Program Files\Norton AntiVirus**. Click **Next** to accept this. (To pick a different folder, click the **Browse** button, use the **File** dialog box to choose a folder, and click **OK**, then click **Next**.)

5 Confirm Your Choice

The wizard displays the folders where Norton AntiVirus 2002 and related files will be installed. Click **Next**. Some last-minute information is displayed. After reading it, click **Next**.

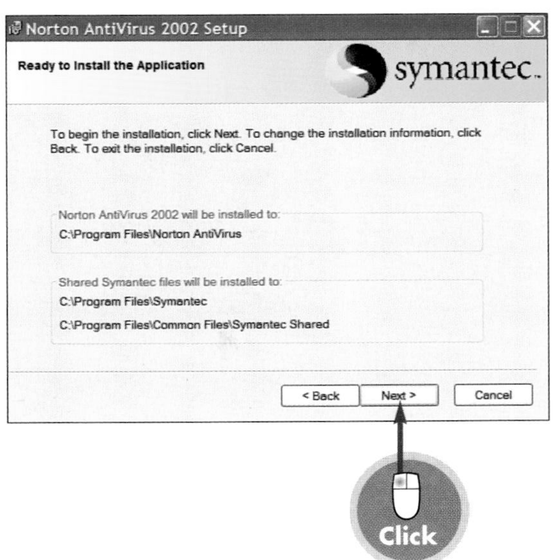

6 Begin Registration

The software will be installed. Click **Finish**. An information wizard opens; use it to register your name, email address, and mailing address with Norton, and then click **Next**.

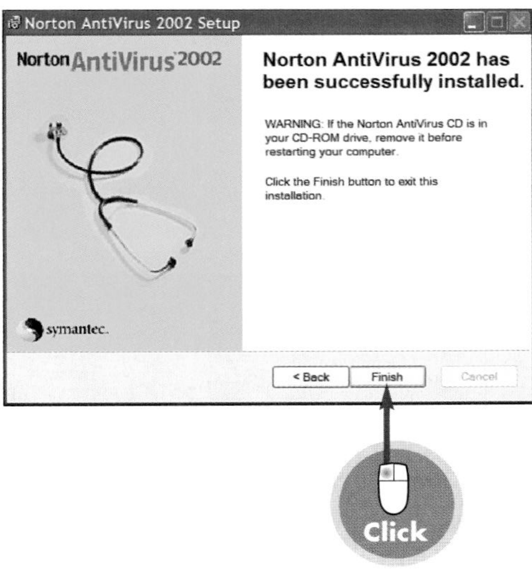

How to Hint

Avoiding Virus Infection on Your Computer

If you install antivirus software such as Norton AntiVirus 2002 or McAfee VirusScan 6.0 and keep its virus database current, you should be able to avoid any problems with viruses on your computer. That said, you always should be careful about the programs you install and the files you open while using the Internet. Don't open files sent to you via email by people you don't know—even if the files appear to be something innocuous such as a digital photograph. Also, if an email from someone you know contains a file and seems a little suspicious, don't open it until checking with the person. If that person's computer is infected with an email virus, it may have sent the mail to you. Virus programmers count on tricks like this to spread viruses around the world.

7 Use LiveUpdate

Norton AntiVirus 2002 includes a free one-year subscription to LiveUpdate, a service that keeps your computer up-to-date on new virus threats and keeps the program current. After reviewing the dates of your subscription, click **Next**.

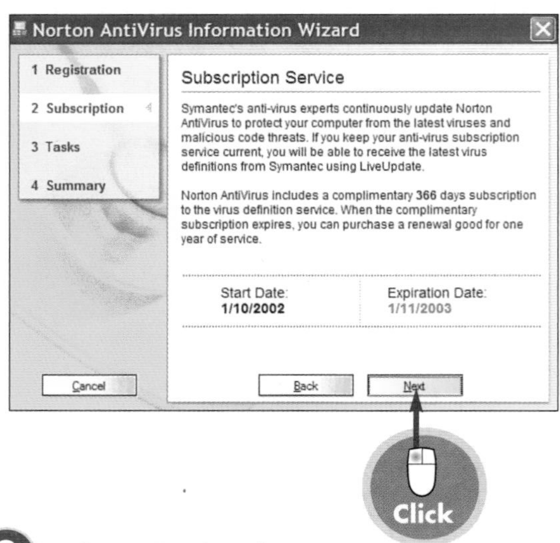

8 Set Up Tasks

Enable the check boxes for tasks you want Norton AntiVirus 2002 to undertake. (Choosing all three is a good idea.) When you're finished, click **Next**.

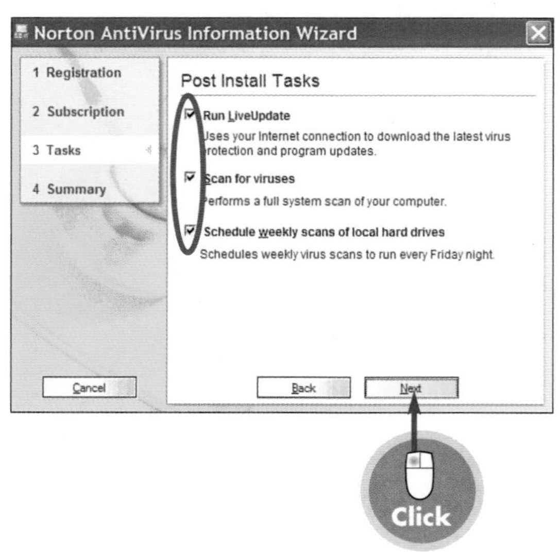

9 Review the Tasks

Review the tasks you have enabled and click **Finish**. Norton AntiVirus 2002 does a lot of the work automatically, including a Friday-evening scan of your entire computer.

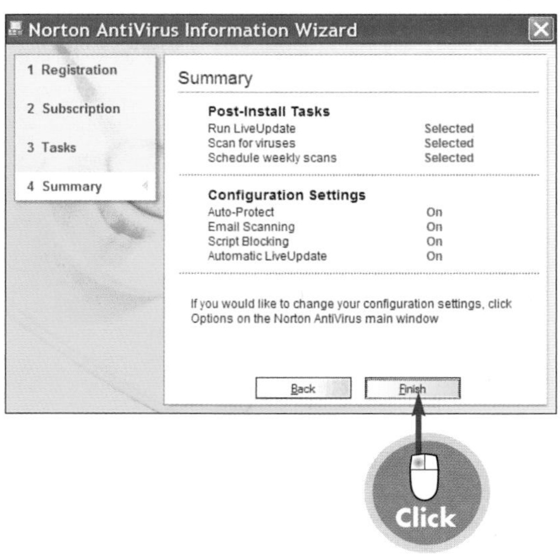

10 Look for Updates

If you chose to run LiveUpdate, it begins immediately. Connect to the Internet (if you aren't already online) and click **Next**.

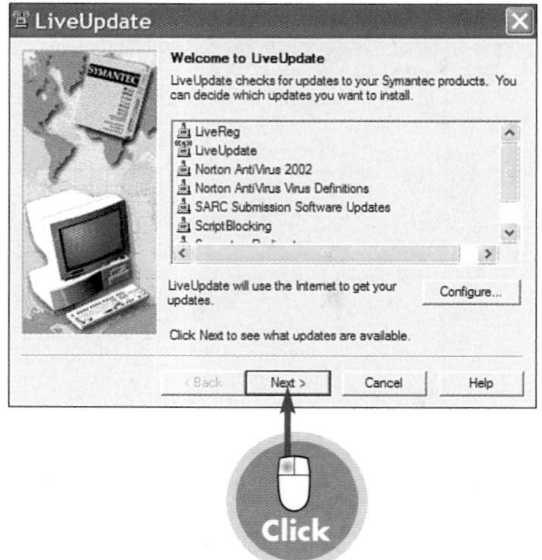

11 Select Updates

LiveUpdate connects to Symantec's Internet site and lists the things that need to be updated on your computer, with check marks next to each one. To install them, click **Next**.

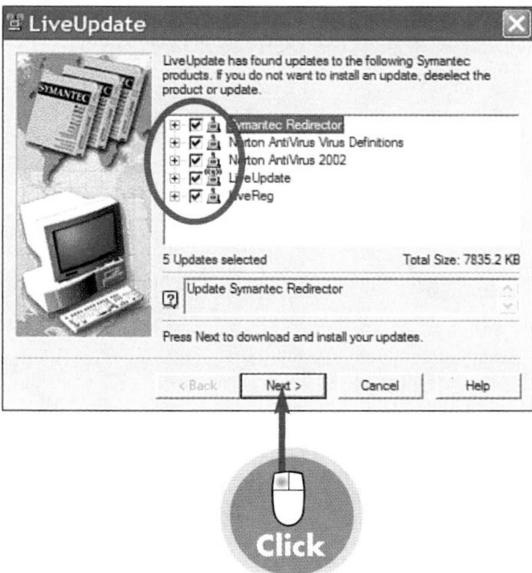

12 Close LiveUpdate

LiveUpdate downloads and installs each selected update and presents a status report. (You may also see a dialog box telling you to run LiveUpdate several times, as discussed in the next step.) Click **Finish** to close the program.

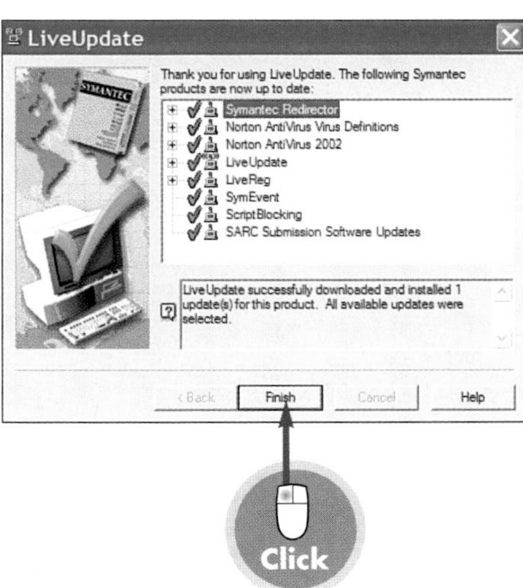

13 Run LiveUpdate Again

You are encouraged to run LiveUpdate several times when you first install Norton AntiVirus, just to make sure you get everything up to date (including LiveUpdate itself). To run the program, click **Start**, choose **All Programs**, choose **Norton AntiVirus**, and click **LiveUpdate—Norton AntiVirus**.

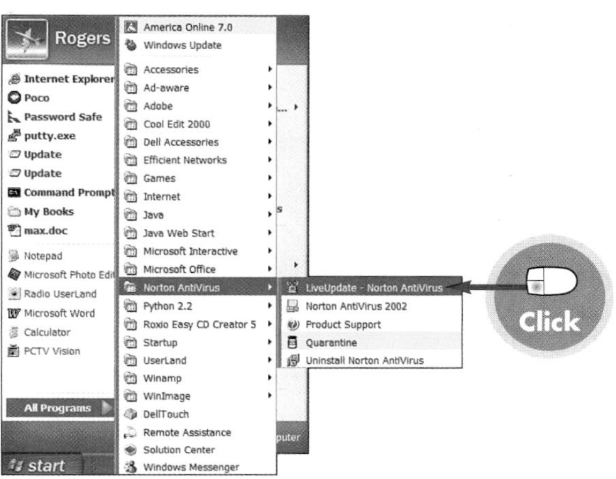

14 Look for Updates

The process of running LiveUpdate is the same as before; connect to the Internet and click **Next** to begin. Keep running LiveUpdate until you are told that no more updates are available. After that, LiveUpdate will run automatically while you are subscribed.

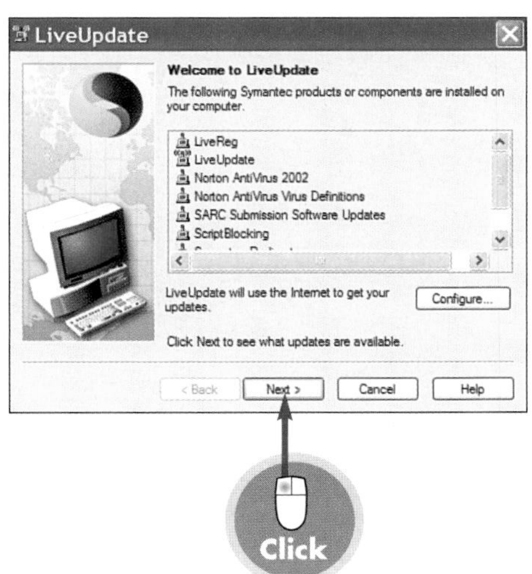

How to Check Your Computer for Viruses

After you install antivirus software such as Norton AntiVirus 2002 (described in Task 7), you should immediately use the software to look for viruses on your computer. This is called a *scan*. Norton AntiVirus 2002 conducts its own scan automatically every Friday evening if your computer is on during that time. The software also scans all incoming email, reporting immediately if any file that arrives is infected with a virus.

1 Run the Program

Click the **Start** button, choose **All Programs**, choose **Norton AntiVirus**, then click **Norton AntiVirus 2002**.

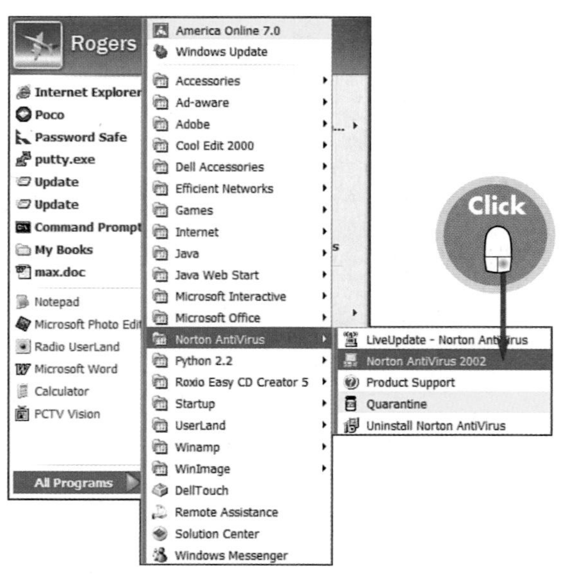

2 Begin a Scan

Norton AntiVirus 2002 presents a status report, which may contain items you need to handle. To scan your computer, click the **Scan for Viruses** link.

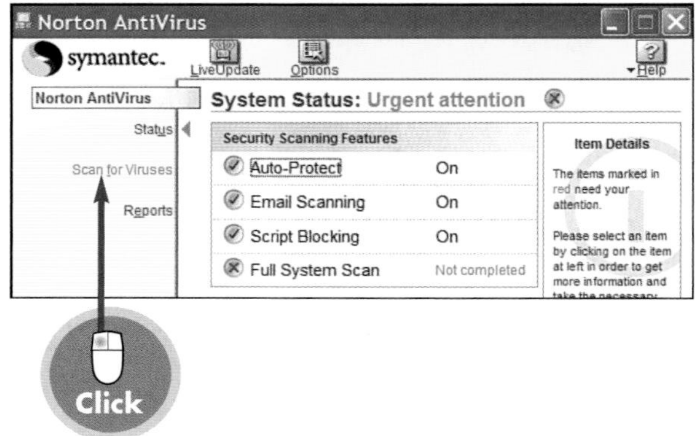

3 Choose What to Scan

You can scan your entire computer, or scan specific parts of it such as a drive, folder, or file. For a full scan of your entire computer, click the **Scan my computer** link.

4 View the Summary

A complete scan can take an hour or more. If any viruses are found, a dialog box opens, advising you to either delete the file or put it in quarantine—a special folder with files that can't be opened. Click **Finished** to close the program.

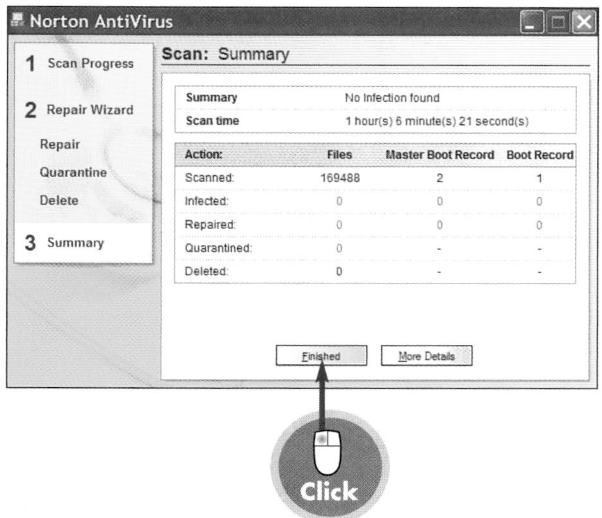

5 Deal with a Virus

If a virus is emailed to you in a file, Norton AntiVirus 2002 opens automatically and asks you to deal with it immediately. Click **Quarantine** to put the file in the quarantine folder (or **Delete**, if that option is offered).

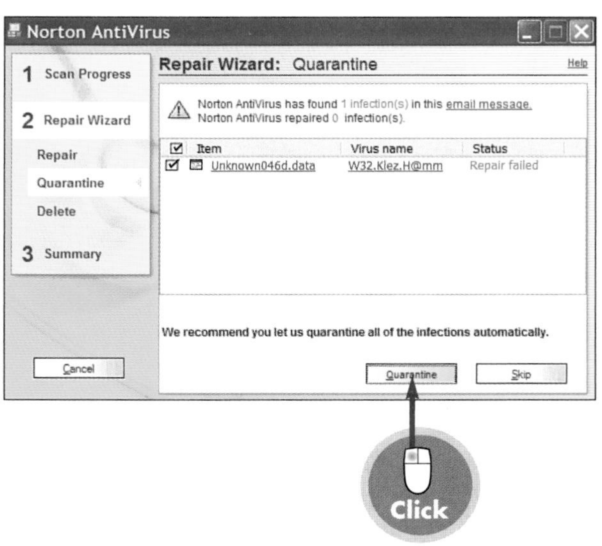

6 Close the Program

After Norton AntiVirus 2002 deals with the virus according to your instructions, click **Finished** to close the program.

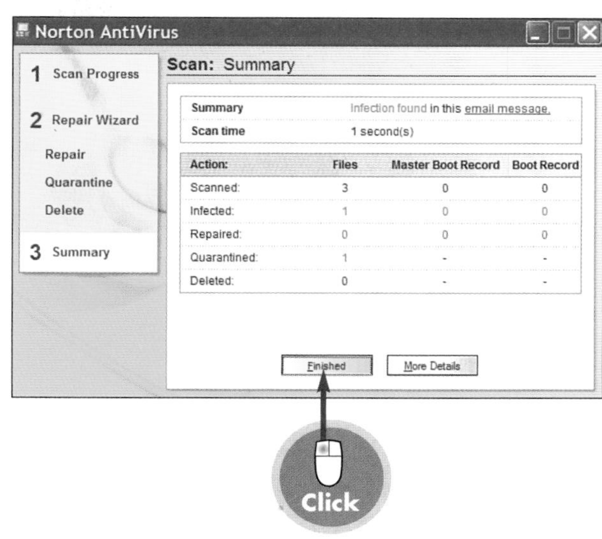

How to Hint

Scan a File for a Virus

Because a full scan of your computer can take an hour or longer, you will probably be reluctant to do one when you are concerned about an individual file and want to check it out before opening it. To scan a single file quickly, open the folder that contains the file, right-click its icon, and select **Scan with Norton AntiVirus** from the pop-up menu that appears. A quick scan will be performed of only that file.

Task

7

Participating in Usenet Discussion Groups

One of the most popular communities on the Internet is Usenet, a collection of public discussion groups on a diverse range of topics. Usenet groups, which also are called *newsgroups*, are distributed by thousands of Internet sites around the world.

Newsgroups function in a manner similar to electronic mailing lists. Subscribers join a group in which they are interested, read the messages written by other subscribers, and contribute their own messages. When you post a message in a Usenet newsgroup, it is copied by all servers connected to Usenet that carry the newsgroup.

The decentralized design of Usenet gives it a unique personality. Messages can't be removed from all those servers after they are sent. Although a small number of Usenet newsgroups have a moderator who must approve messages before they are distributed, most newsgroups are unrestricted.

This freedom leads to many discussions that might never take place anywhere else but on Usenet. Of course, it also does little to discourage things that shouldn't be taking place at all.

How to Set Up Outlook Express for Usenet Newsgroups

Outlook Express supports Usenet newsgroups in addition to email. To participate in Usenet, you must have access to a *news server*—an Internet site that can send and receive newsgroup messages. Many Internet service providers offer Usenet as part of a subscription. If yours does, the provider must give you the name of its news server. You also can subscribe to Usenet with services such as Supernews and NewsGuy. Before you can set up Outlook Express to work with Usenet, you must have the name of your news server. If your server requires a username and password, you also must have this information to get started.

1 Run Outlook Express

Launch Outlook Express: Click the **Start** button and choose **Email**.

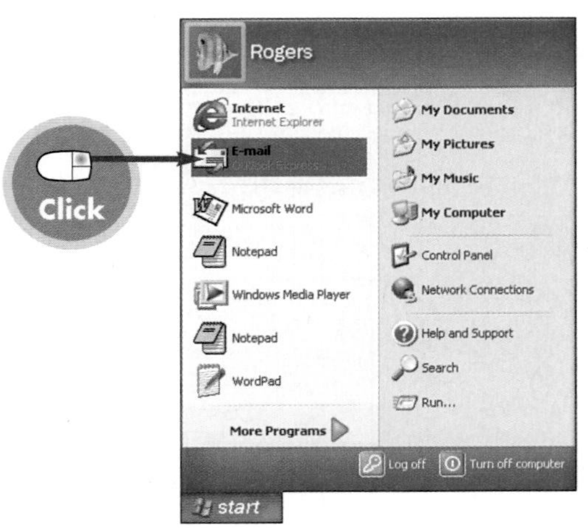

2 Set Up Newsgroups

If Outlook Express has not already been set up to work with Usenet, a **Set up a Newsgroups account** hyperlink will be displayed. Click this hyperlink to start the **Internet Connection Wizard**.

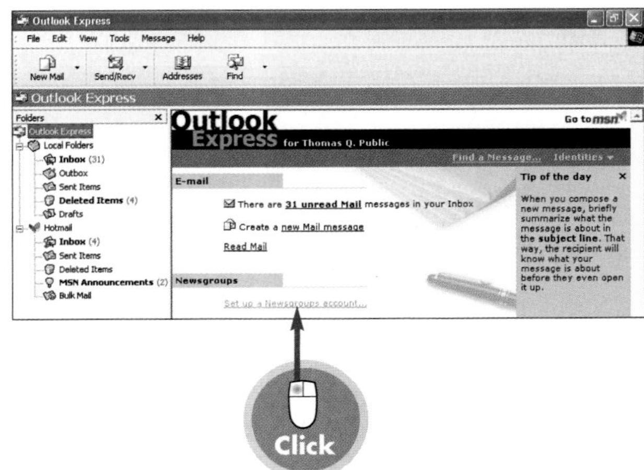

3 Identify Yourself

A name will be displayed on all the messages you post in Usenet newsgroups. In the **Display name** text box, type the name, or *handle*, that will identify you. Unlike email, where real names are the norm, on Usenet it is commonplace for people to use a nickname or similar pseudonym when posting messages. Click **Next** to continue.

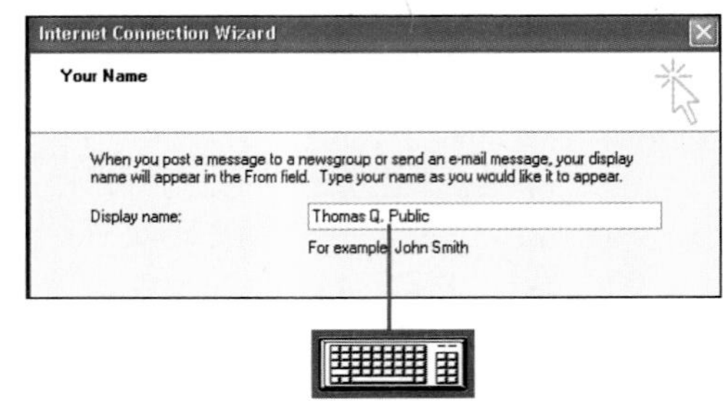

4 Identify Your Address

An email address also will be displayed on your Usenet messages. In the **Email address** text box, type your email address and click **Next** to continue.

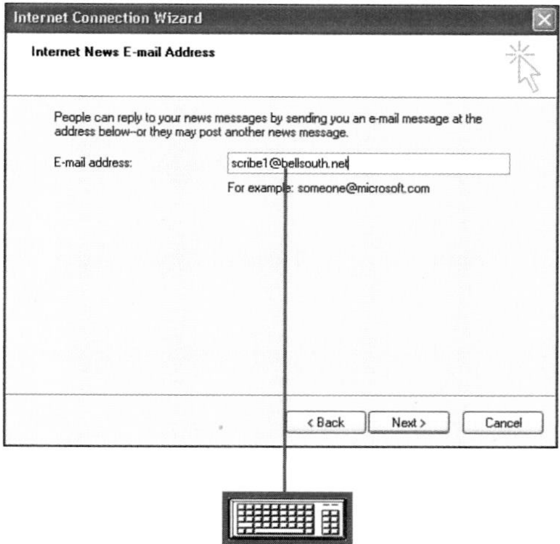

5 Identify Your Server

Type your server's name in the **News (NNTP) Server** text box. Most news servers do not require a username and password. If your server does not require you to log on, click **Next** to finish setting up your Usenet service. If your news server does require you to log on (your ISP will have told you so), check the **My news server requires me to log on** box. When you click **Next** to continue, you'll be asked for your username and password for the news server.

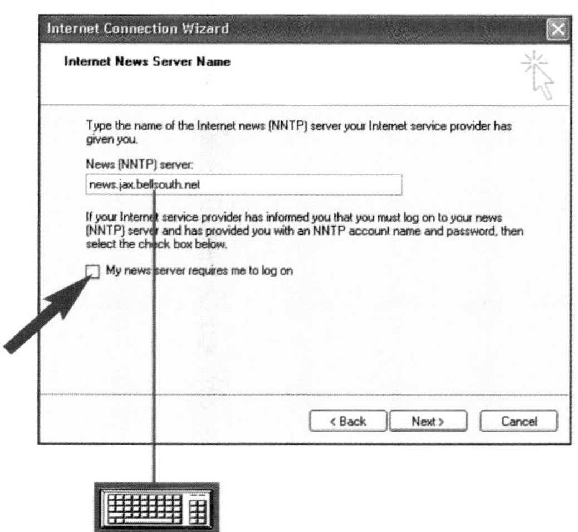

6 Set Up the Usenet Service

After you have created a Usenet account, you are asked whether you want to download newsgroups from your server. This step is needed so that you can find discussion groups on topics of interest. Click the **Yes** button to download them. Many servers offer more than 20,000 different newsgroups, so it may take five minutes or more to download the list of groups.

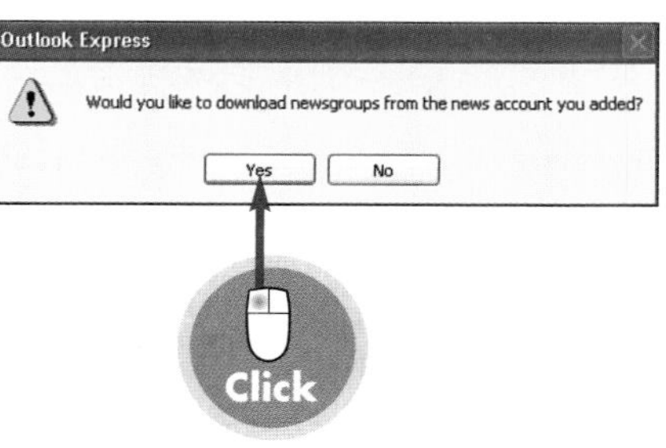

How to Hint

Subscribing to a Usenet Service

If your Internet service provider does not offer Usenet, you can subscribe to a Usenet news service. Charging from $5 to $15 per month, services usually offer more newsgroups than the free Usenet servers provided by ISPs. Visit the following Web sites to find out more:

- **Supernews**: `http://www.supernews.com`
- **NewsGuy**: `http://www.newsguy.com`

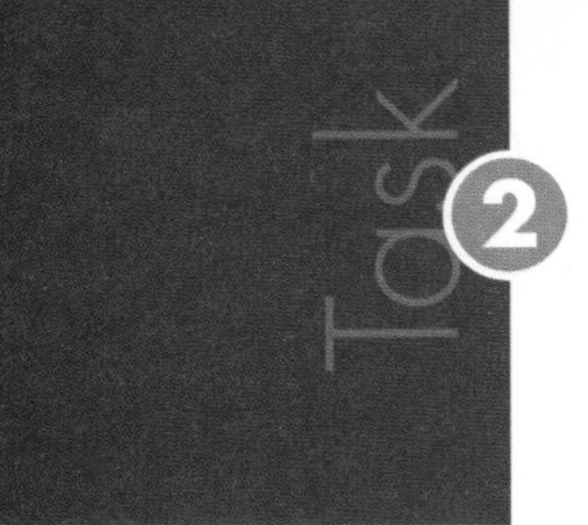

How to Read a Newsgroup

After you have set up Usenet service in Outlook Express, you're ready to read *news*—public messages contributed to the various newsgroups. There are more than 54,000 newsgroups on many Usenet servers, and some of the more popular groups receive more than 100 messages a day. If you find a newsgroup you'd like to read on a regular basis, you can subscribe to it and keep up with the group more easily.

1 Read Usenet Messages

To begin reading newsgroups in Outlook Express, click the **Start** button and choose **Email** to launch Outlook Express. Then, click the **Read News** hyperlink.

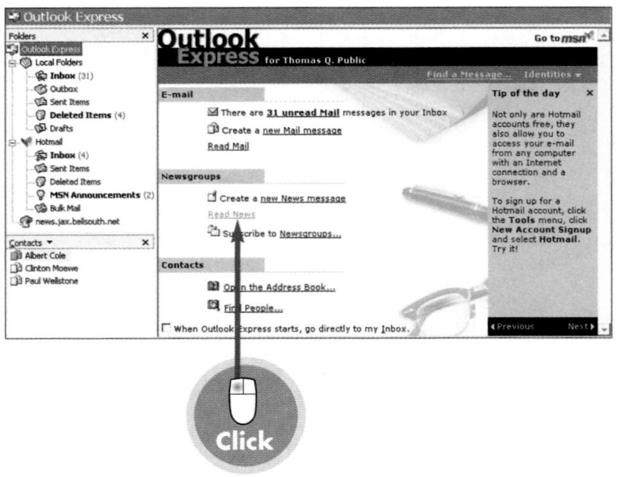

2 View Newsgroups

If you have not yet subscribed to any newsgroups, you'll be asked whether you want to see a list of available groups. Click the **Yes** button to display the **Newsgroup Subscriptions** dialog box. (If you have subscribed to any groups, you can view available groups by clicking the **Newsgroups** button in the news window when it opens.)

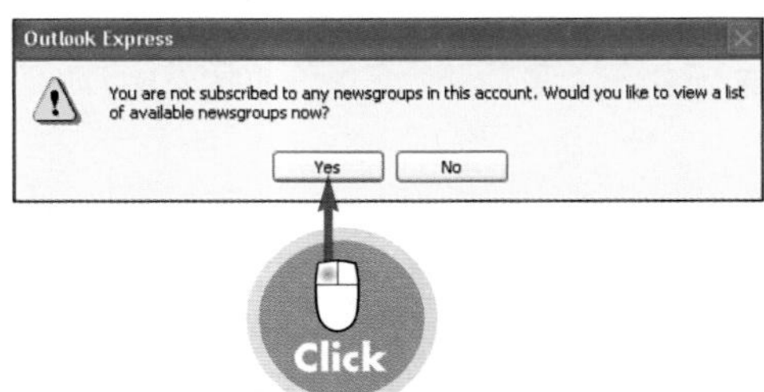

3 Search Newsgroups

Usenet newsgroups are given names that describe their purpose. To search for groups on a topic, type the topic in the **Display newsgroups which contain** text box. As you type, matching groups will be listed in the bottom pane of the window.

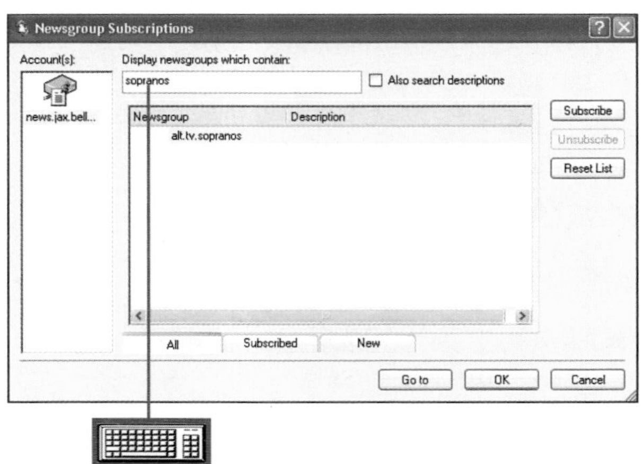

4 Choose a Group

If you want to read the messages in one of the newsgroups that is listed as a result of your search term, click the newsgroup name and then click the **Go to** button.

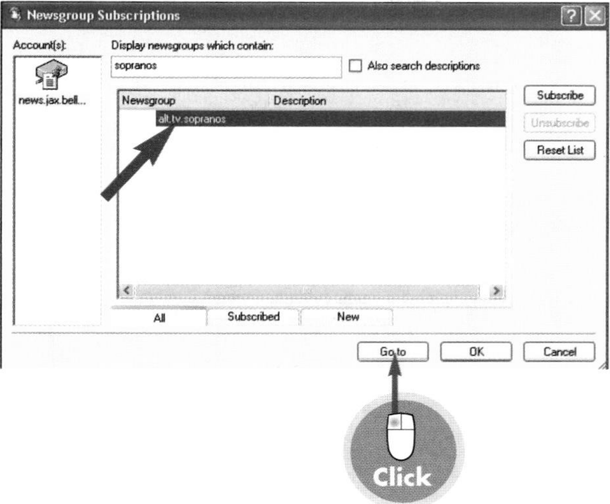

5 Read Messages

Outlook Express displays Usenet messages similarly to the way it displays email messages. Click the subject of a message to view that message in the Outlook Express window; alternatively, double-click the subject to view the message in a new window.

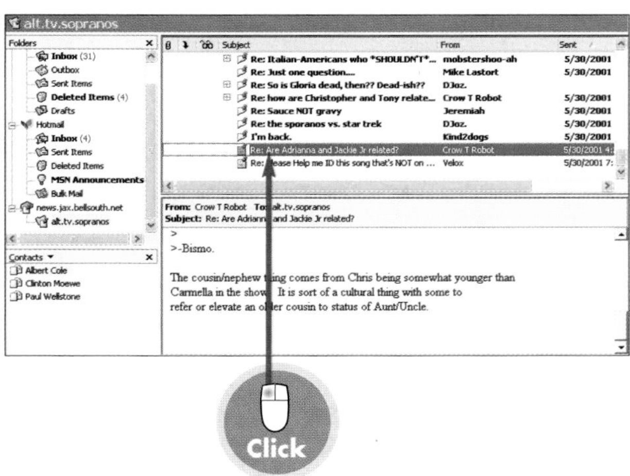

6 Subscribe to a Group

The easiest way to read Usenet newsgroups is to subscribe to the groups you frequent. To subscribe to a group while reading it, right-click the group name in the **Folders** pane and select **Subscribe** from the context menu that appears. The next task explains how to read news for newsgroups you've subscribed to.

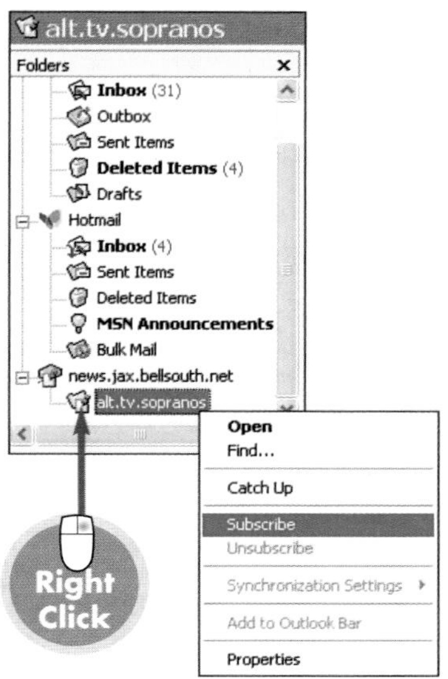

How to Hint: Finding Groups by Their Descriptions

Many newsgroups also have brief descriptions that provide more information about the group. To search through these descriptions as you're looking for newsgroups, enable the **Also search descriptions** check box in Step 4. The first time you enable this option, descriptions must be downloaded, which may take five minutes or more depending on the speed of your Internet connection.

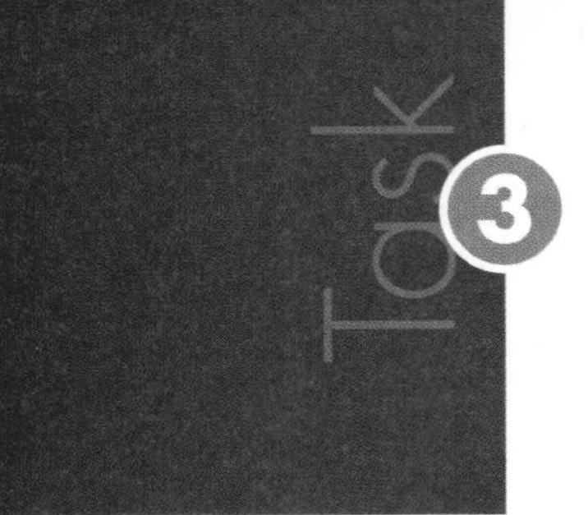

How to Read Newsgroups You Have Subscribed To

The most convenient way to read Usenet newsgroups is to subscribe to them. The preceding task explained how to subscribe to a newsgroup with Outlook Express. Outlook Express keeps track of your subscription internally and makes it easy to follow new discussions. After you have subscribed to a group, you can automatically download new subjects and messages with the synchronization feature.

1 View Newsgroups

After you have subscribed to a newsgroup, you can read the news for that group at any time. Click the **Start** button and choose **Email** to open Outlook Express; then click the **Read News** hyperlink to begin setting up synchronization. A new window opens; Outlook Express uses the name of your news server as the window's title when you read news.

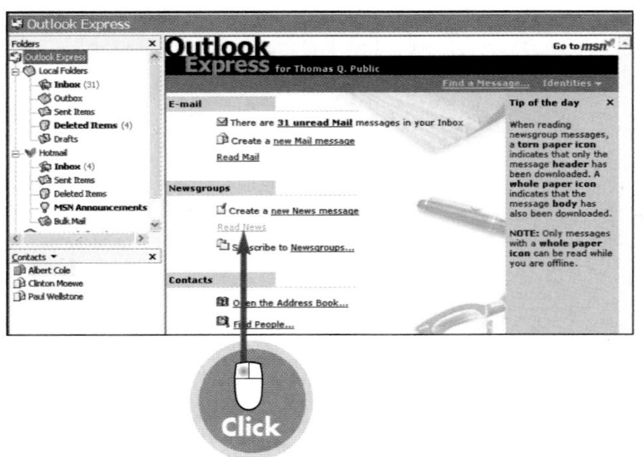

2 Set Up Newsgroups

The synchronization feature in Outlook Express determines how a subscribed newsgroup will be updated. To set up a group so that new subject headings are downloaded, click the name of the newsgroup in the right pane of the window, click the **Settings** button, and then choose **Headers Only** from the drop-down list.

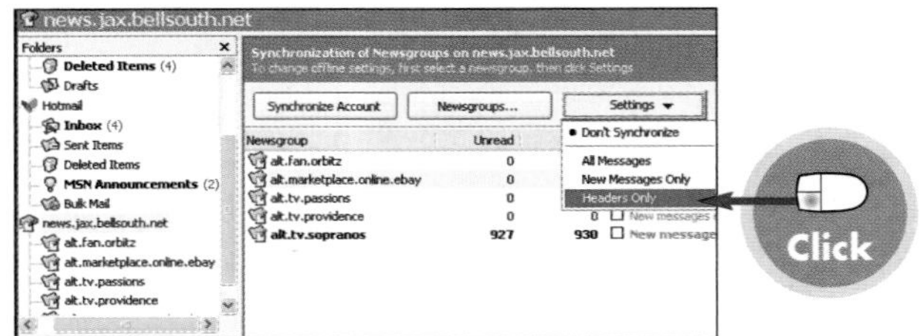

3 Download All Messages

To set up a group so that all messages are downloaded automatically to a Usenet folder in Outlook Express, click the group name, click the **Settings** button, and then choose **All Messages**. This is the most time-consuming option, especially for a popular and active newsgroup.

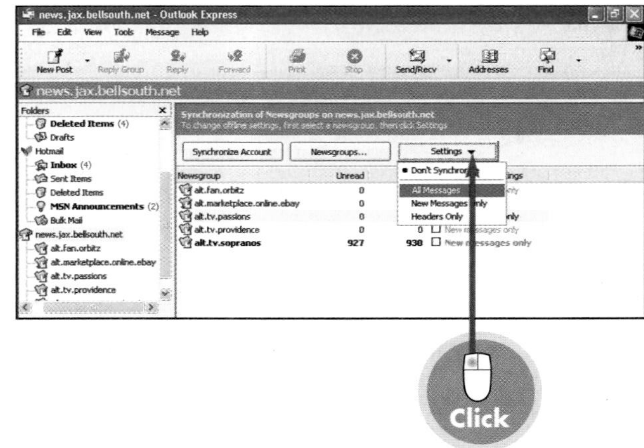

4 Download New Messages

To set up a group so that new messages are downloaded as they arrive, click the group name, click the **Settings** button, and then choose **New Messages Only**.

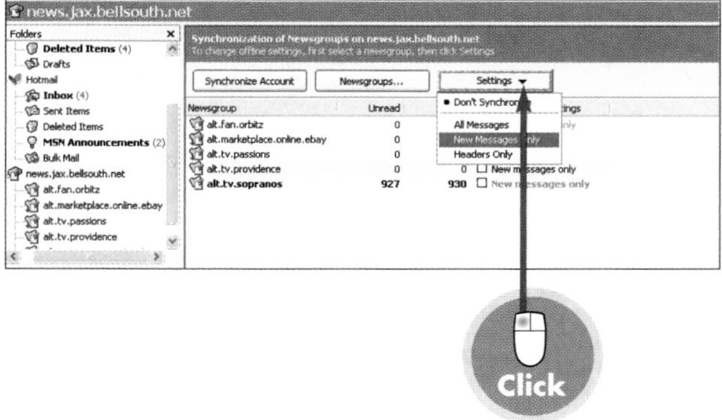

5 Synchronize Newsgroups

After you have specified how you want to synchronize your newsgroups, click the **Synchronize Account** button to retrieve messages based on the settings specified in the **Settings** column. Click this button every time you want to check your server for new Usenet messages in your subscribed groups.

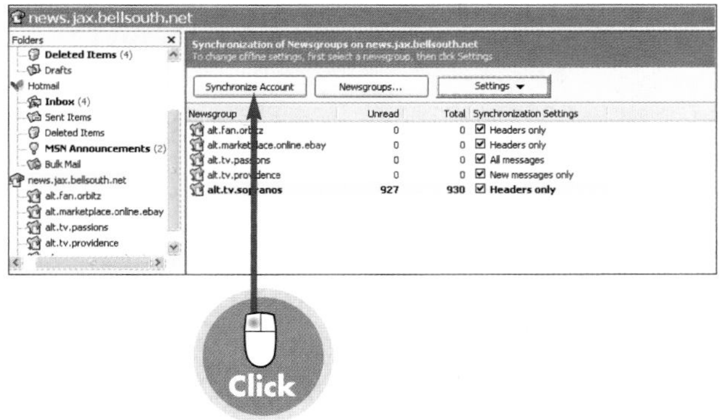

6 Retrieve Messages

As Outlook is synchronizing newsgroups and downloading messages, it displays a progress dialog box. Click the **Details** button to see more information on what Outlook Express is retrieving.

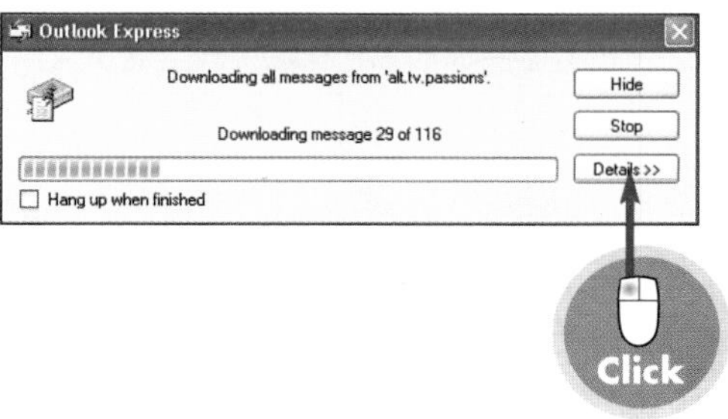

How to Hint

Stopping the Retrieval of Messages from a Group

If you want to put a Usenet subscription on hold for a while, choose the group, click the **Settings** button, and choose **Don't Synchronize**. You'll remain subscribed, but you won't retrieve any messages or subject headings until you change the **Settings** option for that group.

How to Post a Message to a Newsgroup

Anyone who reads a Usenet newsgroup can participate in its discussions by posting a message. Your message may be distributed to thousands of servers around the world, depending on the newsgroups you're posting to. One thing you'll become acquainted with as you post messages is the concept of *netiquette*—commonly accepted standards for behavior on the Internet. Although you can post a Usenet message to as many groups as you like, established netiquette says you should post to four groups or fewer.

1 Post a New Message

After you have decided which newsgroup(s) you want to post a message to, click the **new News message** hyperlink in Outlook Express. A **New Message** dialog box opens.

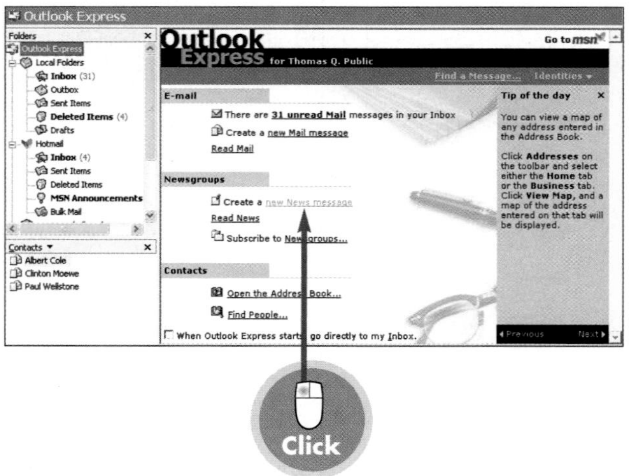

2 Choose Newsgroups

In the **Newsgroups** text box, type the name of the group to which you want to post this message. You can specify more than one newsgroup if you separate the group names with commas.

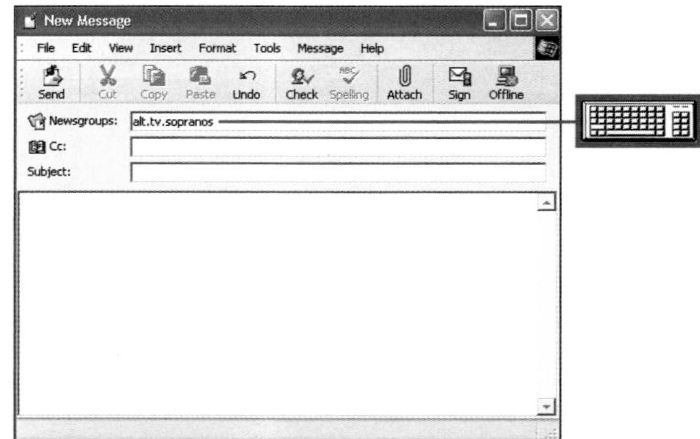

3 Send a Copy by Mail

You also can email a copy of your newsgroup posting to anyone who has an Internet email account—regardless of whether that person reads the newsgroup you're posting to. Type the recipient's email address in the **Cc** text box.

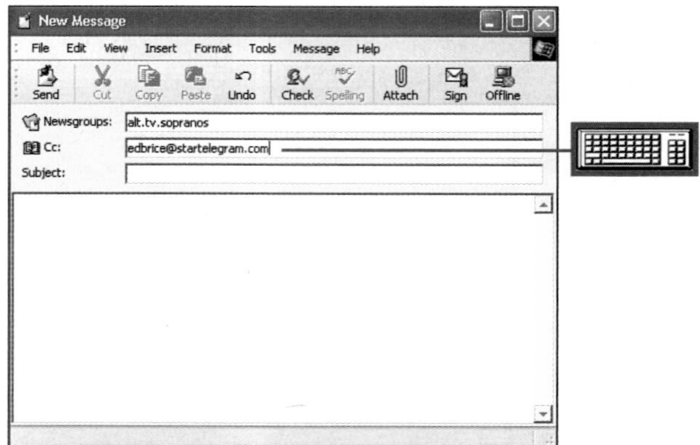

4 Describe Your Message

In the **Subject** text box, type a succinct description of your message. The subject helps Usenet news readers skim a Usenet newsgroup looking for topics that interest them.

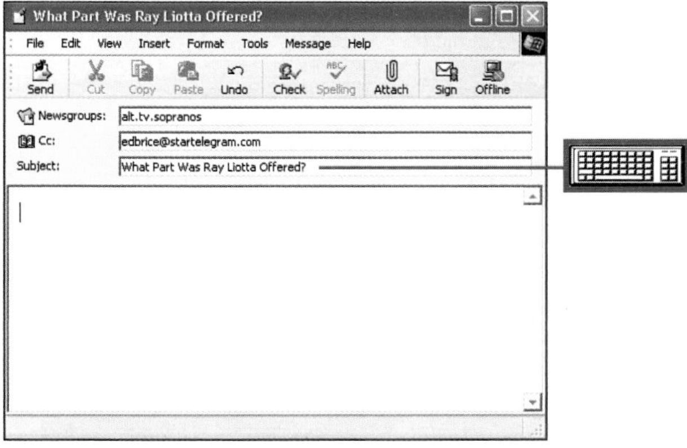

5 Send Your Message

Type the text of the message you want to post and then click the **Send** button. Your message will be submitted to the newsgroup on your news server and distributed to servers around the world.

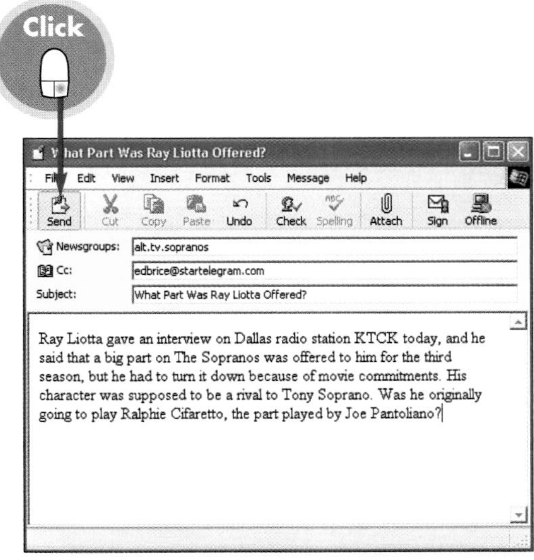

6 Reply to a Message

You also can post messages on Usenet by replying to a message you're reading. With the message selected and displayed in the message pane in the lower-right portion of the Outlook Express window, click the **Reply Group** button. A modified **New Message** window opens. (If you want to reply by email to the author of a Usenet message rather than replying to the entire newsgroup, click the **Reply** button.)

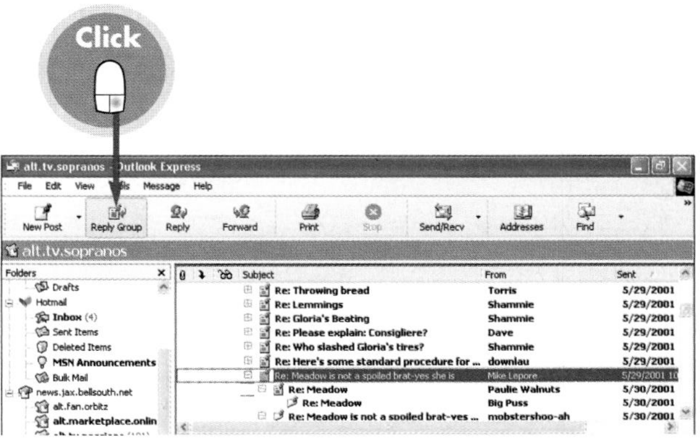

7 Send Your Reply

The text of your reply starts out with the name of the newsgroup you're responding to in the **Newsgroups** box, the **Subject** line filled in, and the text of the original message. If the original message is lengthy, netiquette dictates that you delete any text that is not relevant to your reply. Type your reply and click the **Send** button to distribute the message to the newsgroup.

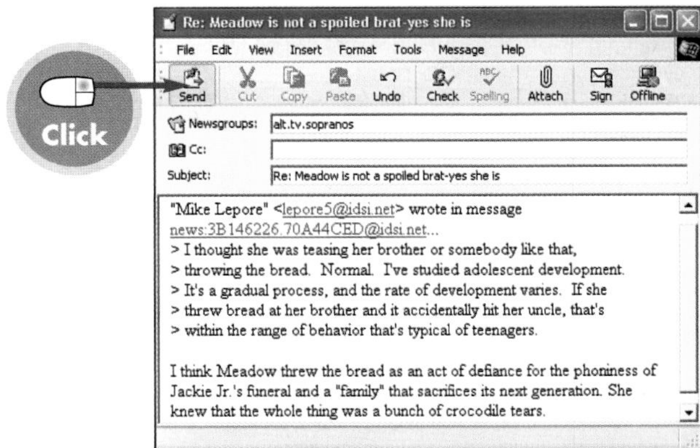

Task 5

How to Find a Newsgroup

As you're searching for newsgroups in Outlook Express, you may be dismayed to find that there are no groups devoted to a topic you're interested in. There's a chance, however, that you can find a relevant newsgroup elsewhere, since no single Usenet server carries all newsgroups. Currently, there are more than 54,000 Usenet newsgroups; more than a dozen new ones are created every day. After you've searched for a group using Outlook Express, you can use sites on the World Wide Web such as Google to find other newsgroups.

1 Search in Outlook

Start by looking for newsgroups in Outlook Express. Click the **Start** button and choose **Email** to open Outlook Express; then click the **Newsgroups** hyperlink. The **Newsgroup Subscriptions** dialog box opens.

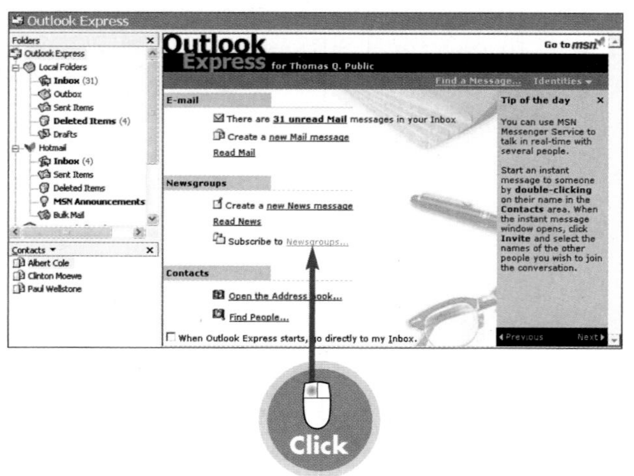

2 Search for Newsgroup Names

To search for specific text in a newsgroup name, type the text in the **Display newsgroups which contain** text box. Outlook Express displays results as you're entering text. To subscribe to a group, click its name, and then click the **Subscribe** button.

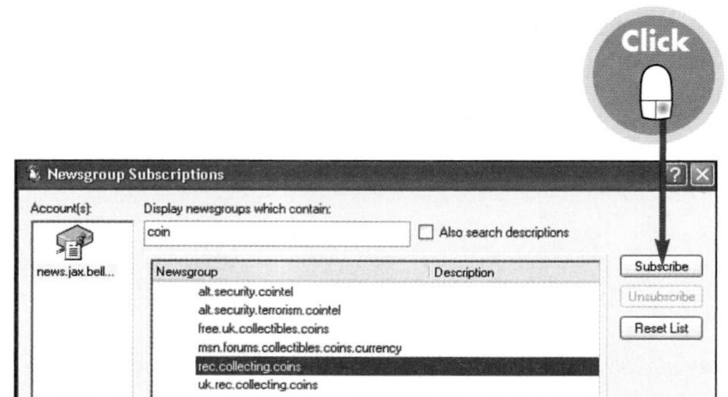

3 Search Descriptions

To search for text in both newsgroup names and descriptions, check the **Also search descriptions** box. The first time you select this option, descriptions are downloaded from your Usenet server to your local machine to speed up the search process.

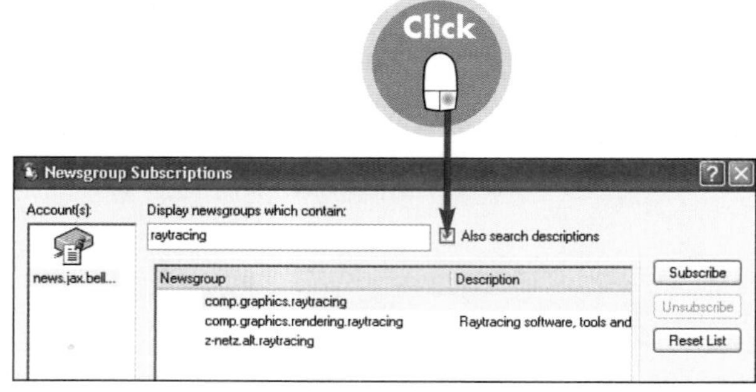

4 Find Other Groups

Several World Wide Web sites offer directories of Usenet groups. To use Google Groups Usenet directory, for example, launch your Web browser, type the URL `http://groups.google.com` in the browser's **Address bar**, and press **Enter**.

5 Search the Directory

When the Google Groups home page opens, type the text you're looking for in the search box and click the **Search** button.

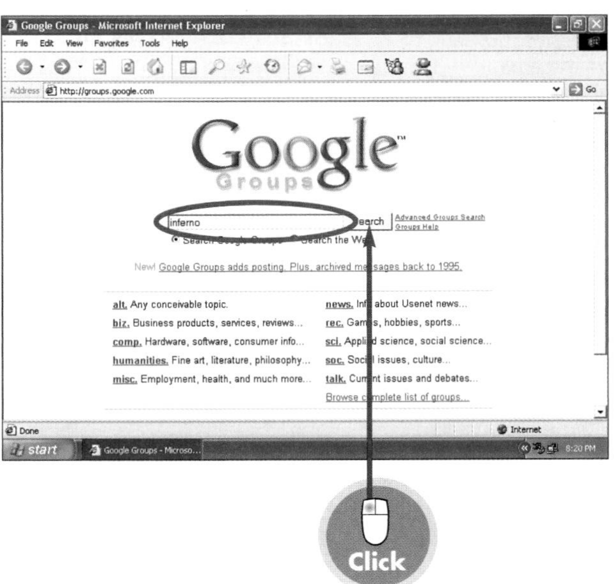

6 Read Newsgroups

If Google finds any groups that match the text you typed, they are listed above a list of Usenet messages that also contain that text. Click the newsgroup's name to use your browser to view a list of recent messages posted in the newsgroup.

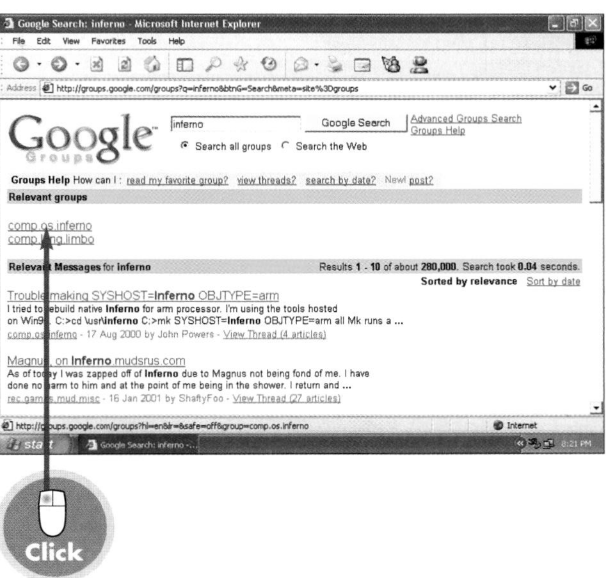

How to Hint: Comparing Your Usenet Server to Others

One of the best reasons to search a Web directory of Usenet newsgroups is because many groups will be completely unknown to you. No single Usenet server offers a full assortment of the more than 54,000 newsgroups currently available, and many servers carry only those groups that have been specifically requested by users. For more information on how to search Google Groups for newsgroups and other information, see the next task, "How to Search an Archive of Past Newsgroup Discussions."

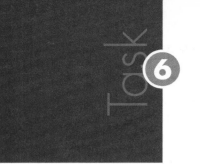

How to Search an Archive of Past Newsgroup Discussions

An important thing to note about Usenet is that it's routinely archived. Messages you post to newsgroups are saved by several Web sites which make their archives searchable by topic and by author. Google Groups, the most popular archive, has Usenet discussions that date back to 1981. The Google archive is a good place to find newsgroups you aren't familiar with. It's also a great research tool on many subjects—especially technical subjects related to the Internet and computers.

1 Visit Google Groups

To visit the Google Groups home page, start your Web browser, type the URL **`http://groups.google.com`** into the **Address bar**, and press **Enter**. The Web page opens in your browser window.

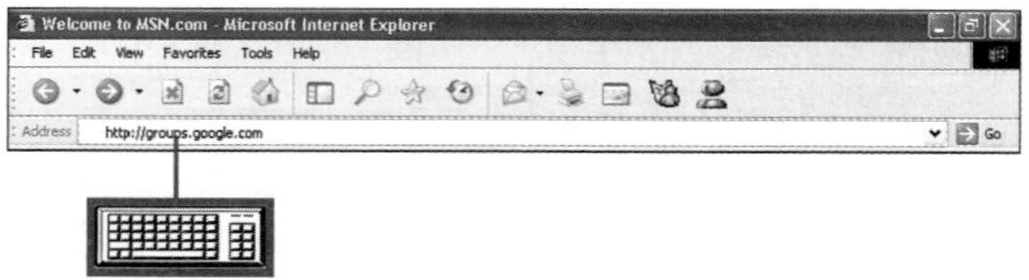

2 Search the Archive

Type the text you're looking for in the search box and click **Search** to begin a search.

3 Read Messages

In the results list, Google lists the subjects and some text of messages that match the text you are searching for. To read a message, click the appropriate hyperlink.

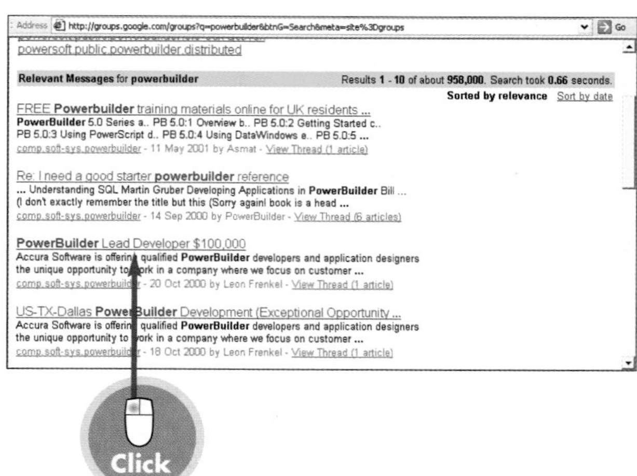

4 Conduct an Advanced Search

For a more advanced search, return to the main Google Groups page and click the **Advanced Groups Search** hyperlink next to the **Search** button.

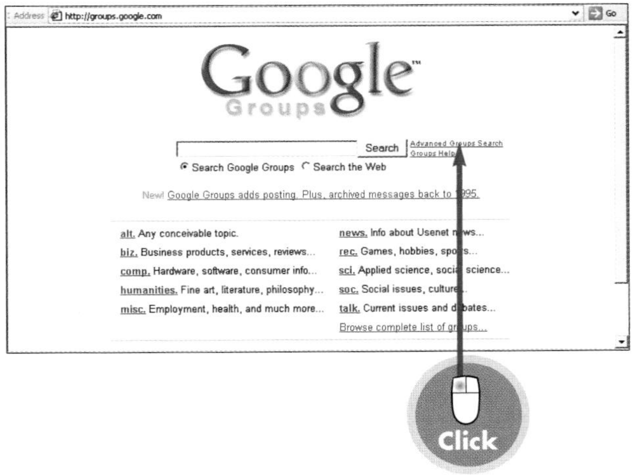

5 Conduct a Search

The Advanced Search feature supports some common searching techniques. Type your search text in one of four **Find messages** boxes and click the **Google Search** button.

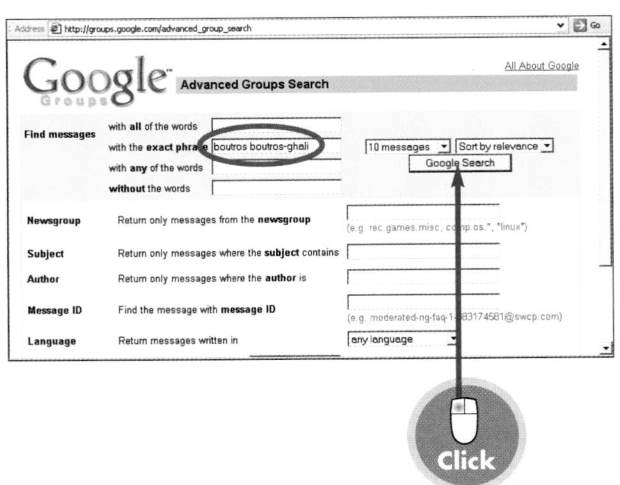

6 Search for Recent Messages

Google Groups normally sorts messages based on how well they match the text you are searching for. To arrange messages by date, beginning with the most recent and going backwards, change the **Sort by relevance** drop-down menu selection to **Sort by date**.

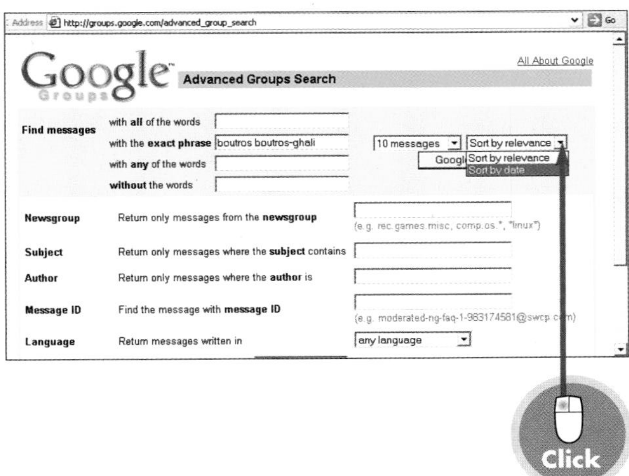

How to Hint

Reading Usenet on Google

Because Google has the most comprehensive archive of Usenet discussions, it's a convenient place to read newsgroups not available on your Usenet server. Simply load the Web site's home page and use the directory of newsgroups.

Keeping Posts Out of Google

All the Usenet messages you post are archived by Google—if its server receives them. To keep a message out of the archive, type the text `X-No-Archive: Yes` on a line of its own as the first line of your message.

How to Decrease the Junk Email You Receive

When you start contributing to Usenet, you can count on receiving more email as a result. Unfortunately, almost all of it will be *spam*—unsolicited advertising email. Marketers who rely on spam to promote their products often build their mailing lists by scanning Usenet messages. You can deter them by posting with a fake email address. Your real address can be placed in a *signature file*—text that is automatically appended to email, Usenet postings, and similar documents.

1 Set Up Options

Start by creating a signature file in Outlook Express. From any screen in Outlook Express, open the **Tools** menu and select the **Options** command. The **Options** dialog box opens.

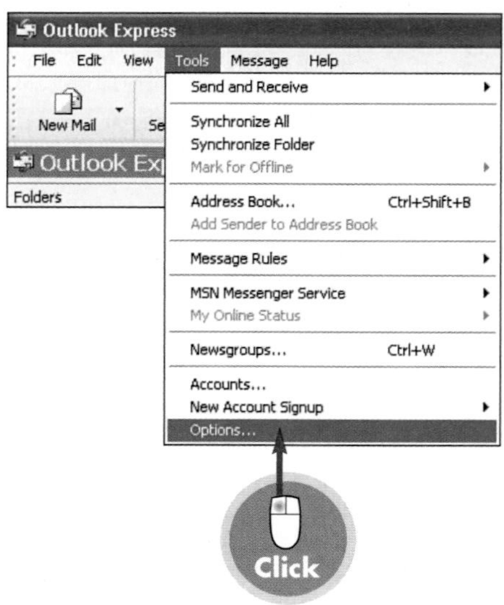

2 Create a Signature

Click the **Signatures** tab to bring that screen to the front of the dialog box. Click the **New** button to create a new signature file. The default signature filename (**Signature #1**) appears in the **Signatures** list box.

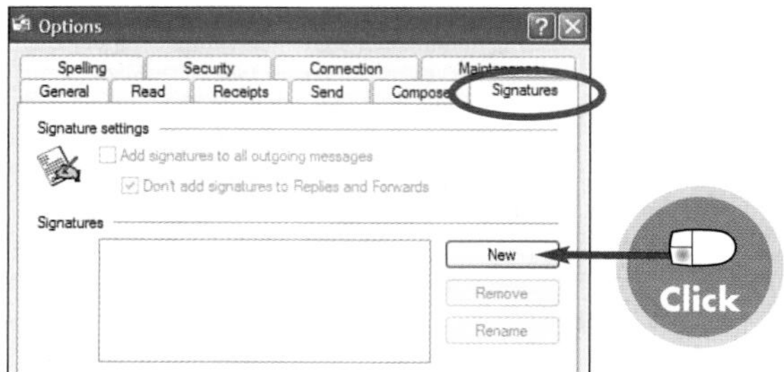

3 Edit the Text

A signature file usually contains your name, email address, personal Web site, and similar personal information. In the **Text** box at the bottom of the dialog box, type the text for your signature file—including your real email address—and click the **Advanced** button. The **Advanced Signature Settings** dialog box opens.

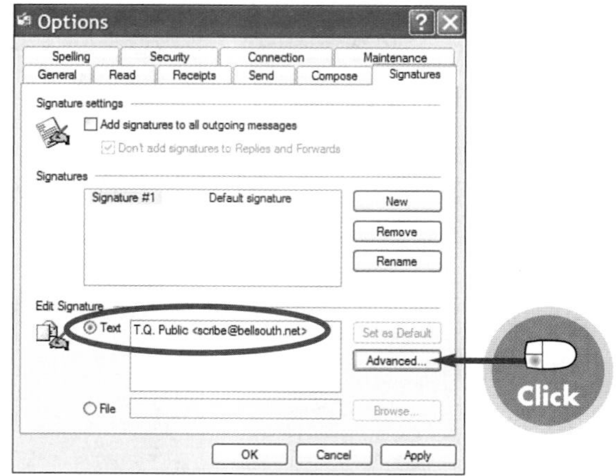

4 Use a Signature

In the list box, enable the check box in front of the Usenet account for which you want to use your new signature file. If you want to use the signature file with other Outlook Express accounts, enable those check boxes also. Then click the **OK** button. Next, close the **Options** dialog box by clicking the **OK** button.

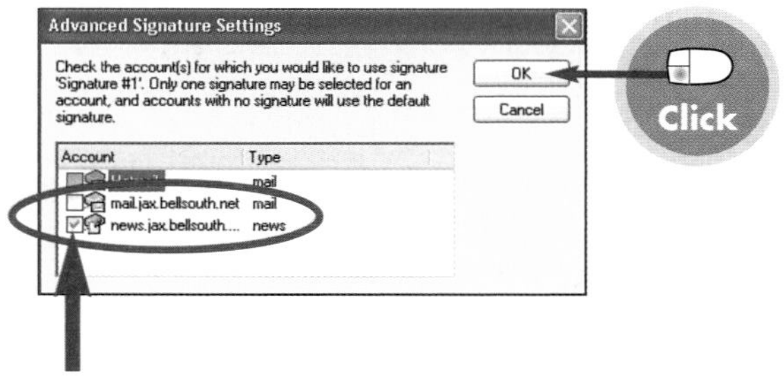

5 Change Your Address

After creating a signature file, you should remove your real email address from your Usenet account. To do so, open the **Tools** menu and choose the **Accounts** command to open the **Internet Accounts** dialog box.

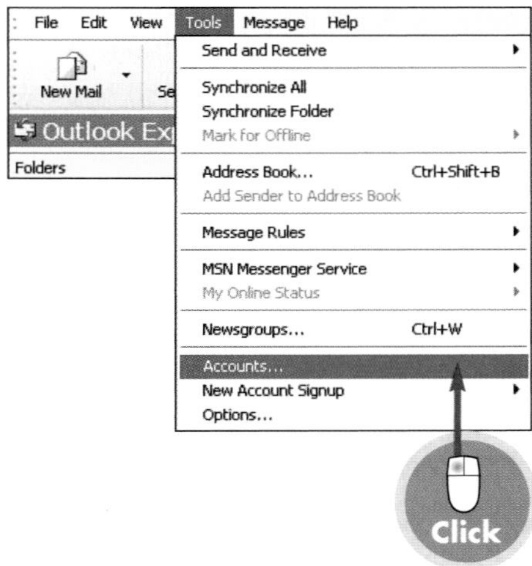

6 Adjust Your Account

Click the **News** tab to view your Usenet newsgroup accounts. Select the account you want to change and then click the **Properties** button. The **Properties** dialog box opens.

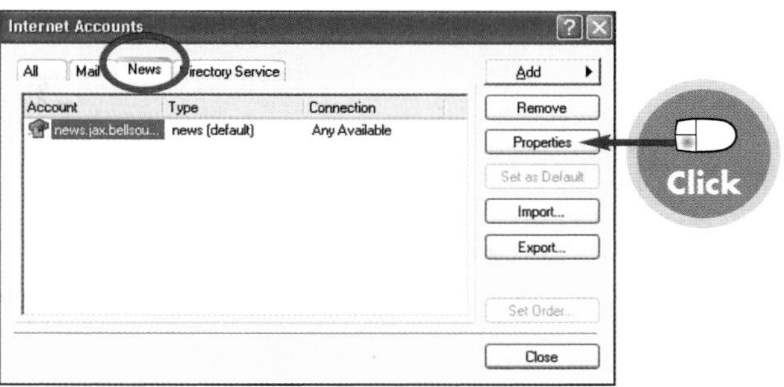

7 Falsify Your Address

In the **Email address** text box on the **General** tab, type an obviously false email address (the address `see_my_sig@fake_address.com` is suitable for this purpose). Click **OK**. Usenet participants who want to send you mail will know to look for a signature if they want to contact you personally. Spammers will add the fake address to their mailing lists, and you'll never get unsolicited mail from vendors who picked up your email address from the newsgroup.

Task

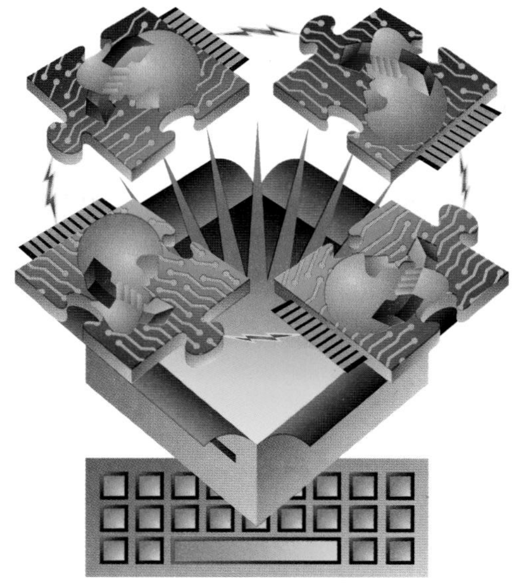

8

Sending and Receiving Instant Messages

There are more than a dozen different ways to chat, including America Online's member-only chat rooms and World Wide Web chat pages. Some of these chat options are described in Part 9, "Participating in Chat and Online Communities." You also can use the free instant-messaging services offered by AOL, Microsoft, and others.

Instant messaging is a style of chat in which you can keep track of people you know who are using the same software. A server tells you when selected people are online and provides the same information about you to others. You can send private messages that are received instantly on another user's computer.

Windows XP includes Windows Messenger, instant-messaging software you can use to communicate with other people who employ the same software. Other Windows users can download the program free from Microsoft at the Web address **`http://messenger.msn.com`**.

Task 1

How to Add Someone to Your Contact List

Before you run Windows Messenger, you must set up a Microsoft Passport. If you don't have one yet, follow the instructions in Part 3, Task 4, "How to Set Up a Microsoft Passport Account." When Windows Messenger is running, it adds its icon to the *system tray*—the area of the Windows taskbar closest to the current time. You can display Messenger's main window by double-clicking the Messenger icon in the system tray. One of the ways to use the program is to keep in touch with people you know who are also Messenger users. You can track whether they are online by adding them to your contact list.

1 Open Windows Messenger

To run Windows Messenger for the first time, click the Messenger icon in the Internet Explorer toolbar. The main Windows Messenger window opens.

2 View Your Contacts

The main Windows Messenger window lists all the contacts you communicate with using the software (if you're just getting started, this window will contain no contacts). To begin setting up your contact list, click the **Add a Contact** link. The **Add a Contact Wizard** opens.

3 Add a New Contact

If you know the email address of someone you want to contact using instant messages, choose the **By email address or sign-in name** option and click the **Next** button. (The **Search for a contact** option is covered in the next task.)

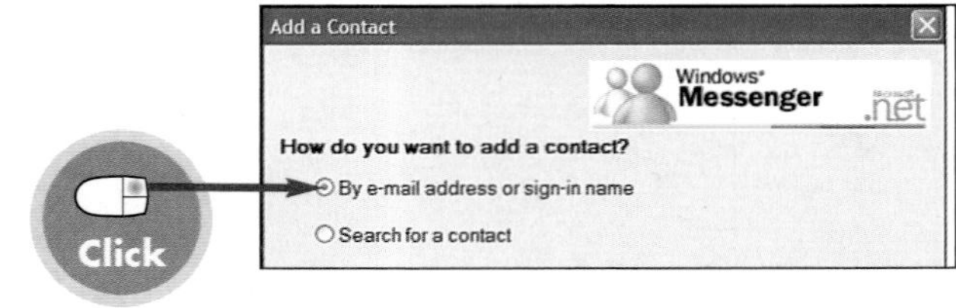

Enter the Address

You can add people to your contact list whether or not they currently use Windows Messenger. To add a contact to your list, type the person's email address in the text box and click the **Next** button.

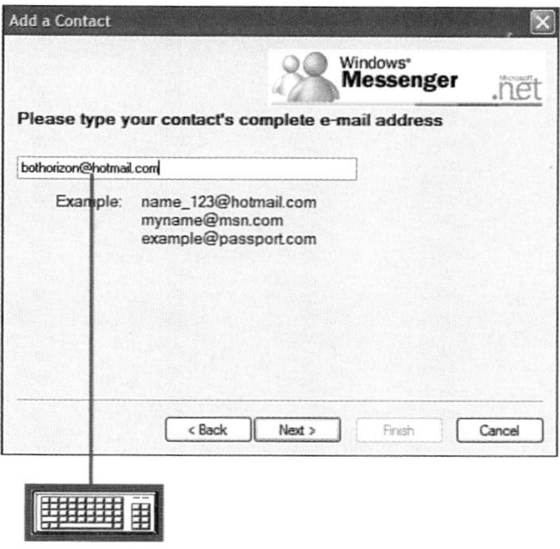

Notifying a Contact

Windows Messenger doesn't immediately recognize whether your contact uses Messenger or not. You have a chance to send an email message to the person about Messenger, even if it isn't necessary. Click the **Next** button to continue.

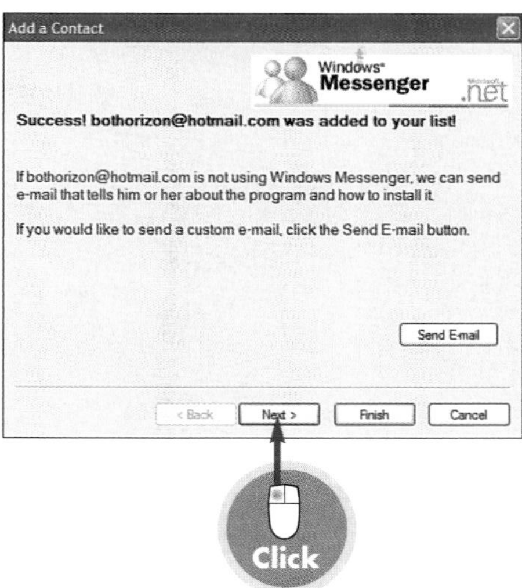

6 Add Another Contact

If you have another contact to add to your list, click the **Next** button. Otherwise, click the **Finish** button to return to the main **Windows Messenger** window.

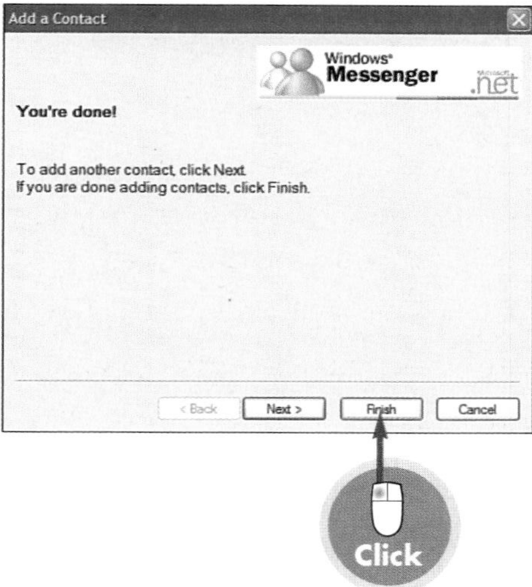

How to Hint

Trying Other Instant-Messaging Software

Millions of people use other instant-messaging software from AOL, Yahoo!, and other companies. Note that you can't communicate with those people directly from Windows Messenger; to send instant messages, you must be using the same software as the person with whom you want to chat. To try these other instant-messaging programs, type one of these addresses in your browser's **Address bar** and press **Enter**:

- **Yahoo! Messenger**: `http://messenger.yahoo.com`
- **AOL Instant Messenger**: `http://www.aim.com`
- **ICQ**: `http://www.icq.com/download`
- **Jabber.com**: `http://www.jabber.com/downloads`

Task 2

How to Invite Someone to Use Messenger

Although Windows Messenger has more than 25 million users, you're likely to find that many people you'd like to chat with aren't yet using the software. More than 50 million people use instant-messaging programs from AOL and Yahoo!, and many others don't use any messaging software at all. If you add someone to your contact list who does not use Messenger, the program makes it easy to send an email message telling that person how to get the appropriate software.

1 Open Windows Messenger

To open the Windows Messenger program, double-click the Windows Messenger icon in the system tray. The main **Windows Messenger** window opens.

2 Add the Person

To look for someone you'd like to contact using Messenger, click the **Add a Contact** link. The **Add a Contact Wizard** appears.

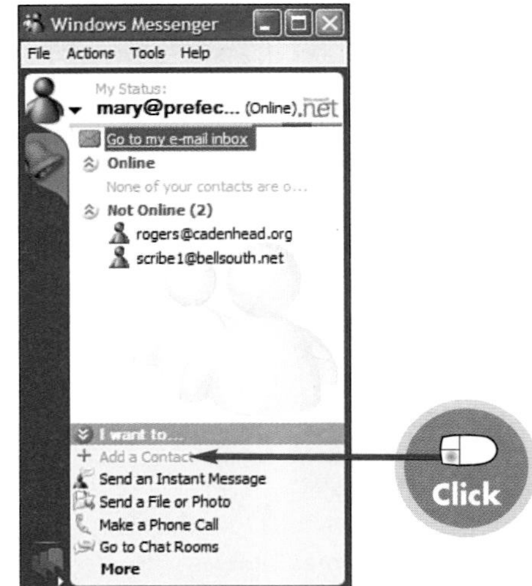

3 Search for a Contact

If you don't know the person's email address but do know that he or she uses Hotmail, you can search Hotmail's member directory. Choose the **Search for a contact** radio button and click the **Next** button.

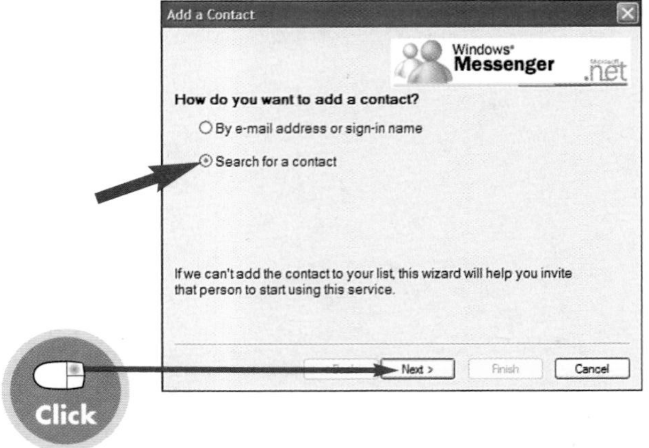

4 Look in Hotmail

Type the person's name in the **First Name** and **Last Name** text boxes. To narrow a search, fill out the **Country/Region**, **City**, and **State** boxes. Make sure that **Hotmail Member Directory** is selected in the **Search for this person at** drop-down list and click **Next**.

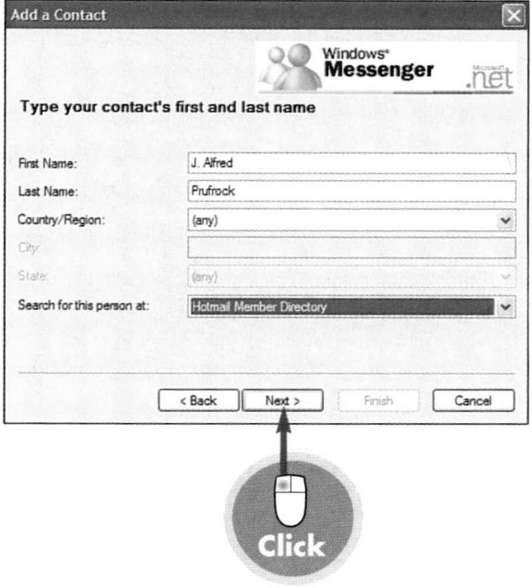

5 Find the Right Person

The **Search Results** dialog box lists everyone who matches the fields in your search. If you think you have found the right person, choose his or her name from the results list and click the **Next** button.

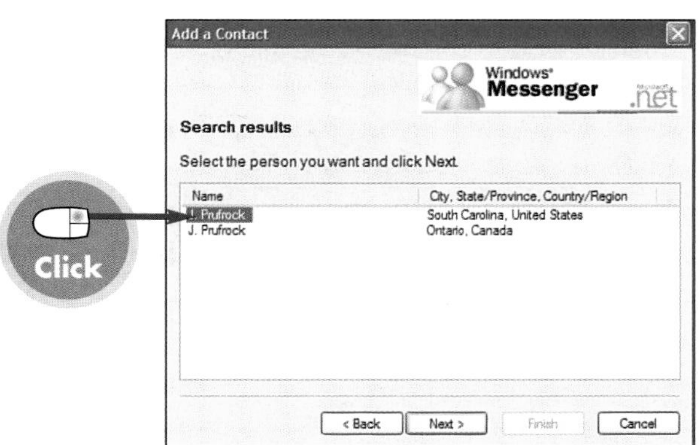

6 Notify the Person

Hotmail won't release a person's email address if you find it in the directory, but it can send an email to that person on your behalf describing Windows Messenger. If you'd like to do this, click the **Next** button.

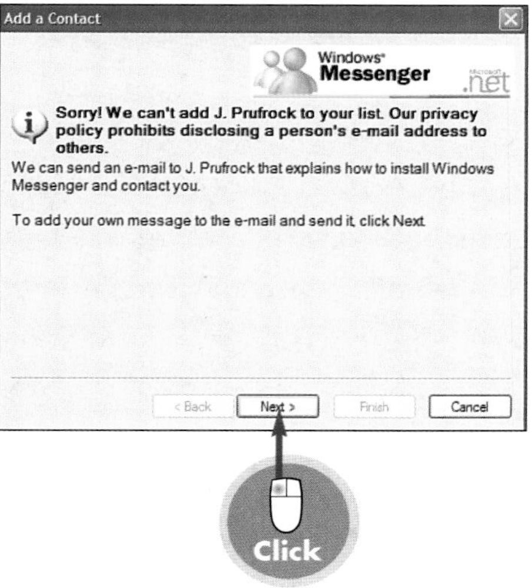

7 Send an Invitation

You can read the message that Microsoft will send on your behalf touting Windows Messenger and add a note of your own. Type your message in the top text box. When you're done, click **Next** to send it (or **Cancel** if you have decided not to send an email message). Click **Finish** to exit the wizard.

Task 3

How to Send Someone an Instant Message

After you have added some people to your contact list, you can use Windows Messenger to send private messages to them. Messages are delivered instantly if the person is connected to Messenger. Two things happen when new messages arrive: A distinctive sound is played and the message appears briefly above the system tray. If you try to send a message to someone who isn't connected, Messenger asks whether you want to send an email message instead of an instant message.

1 Run Windows Messenger

To run Windows Messenger, double-click the Windows Messenger icon in the system tray. (You also can run the program by clicking the Windows Messenger icon on the Internet Explorer toolbar.) The **Windows Messenger** main window opens.

Double Click

2 Choose a Contact

You can send an instant message to anyone in your contact list who is listed under the **Online** heading. To send a message, double-click the contact's name. If you double-click a contact in the **Not Online** list, a dialog box opens asking if you want to send an email message instead.

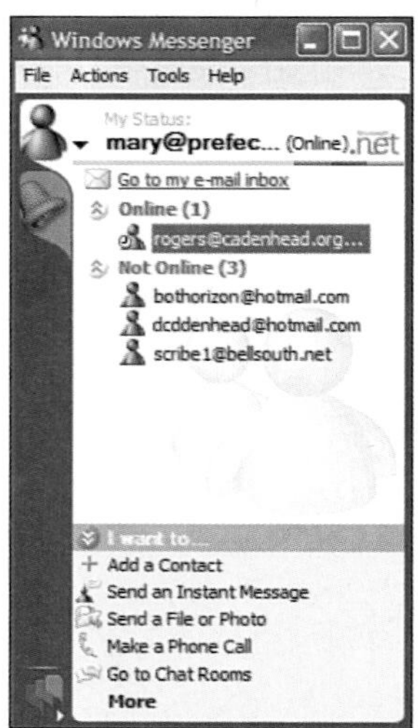

3 Write a Message

You use the **Instant Message** window to compose an instant message. The recipient of the message is the person listed in the window's title bar. Type your message in the text box at the bottom of the window.

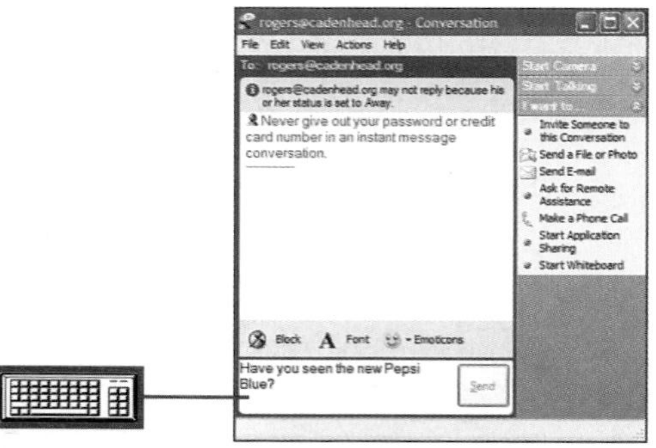

Send the Message

To send your message, click the **Send** button. If this button becomes grayed out before you can click it, that means the recipient has disconnected from Windows Messenger, making it impossible for you to send a message.

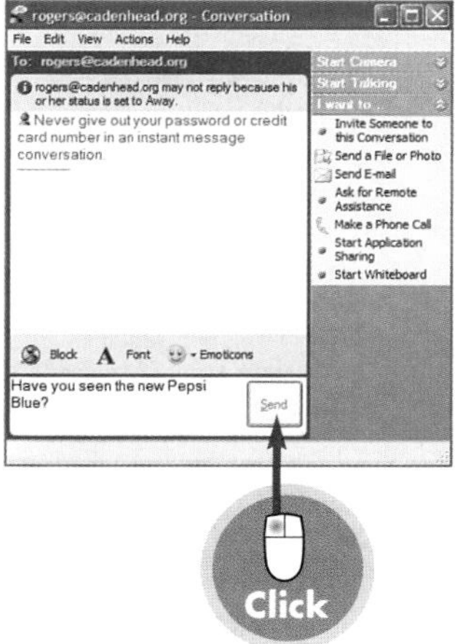

5 End the Chat

The top window displays your messages along with any replies that you receive. When you're finished chatting, close the window by clicking the **x** button in the window's title bar.

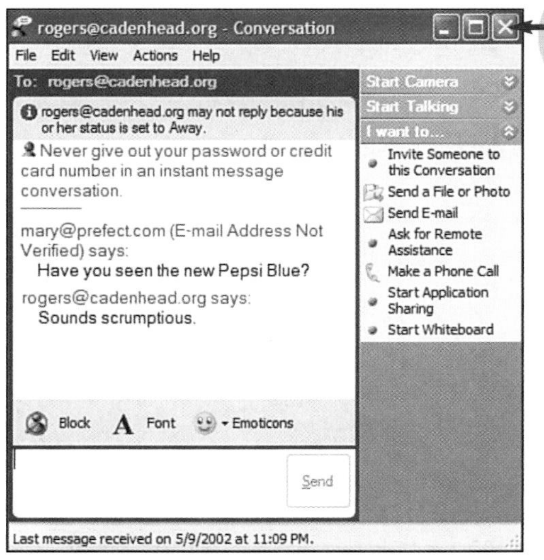

How to Hint

Sending Messages to Other People

You can send instant messages to people who are not on your contact list. Click the **Send an Instant Message** link on the main Windows Messenger window and choose the **Other** tab. A dialog box opens that can be used to enter the recipient's email address. The instant message can be delivered only if the recipient is online with Windows Messenger.

Sending Photos and Other Files

You also can send a file to someone on your contact list if they currently are online. Click the **Send a File or Photo** link. The **Send a File** dialog opens with a list of your contacts. Click the name of a contact and click **OK**. A dialog box opens that enables you to find a file on your computer. Click the name of the file to send it.

Asking for Remote Assistance

The Windows Messenger version on Windows XP has a feature called *Remote Assistance* that enables a person you're chatting with to control your computer over the Internet. One way to use this: Get a technically minded friend to help you fix something.

To use this feature, both of you must have Windows Messenger on Windows XP. Begin a chat with the person, and then click the Ask for Remote Assistance link in the Conversation window to request assistance.

Task 4

How to Prevent Someone from Sending You Messages

As is true with email and other forms of communication on the Internet, instant messaging is open to abuse. There's nothing to prevent people from sending you unsolicited commercial advertisements (for scam products or worse), abusive comments, and other unwelcome messages. Windows Messenger can be set up to block specific users from ever contacting you again. You also can block all messages temporarily when you are too busy to chat or away from the computer.

1 View a Message

Windows Messenger can receive instant messages even when you're not actively using the program. When a message arrives, the first few lines are displayed briefly in a small window near the system tray. Click the message text to read it.

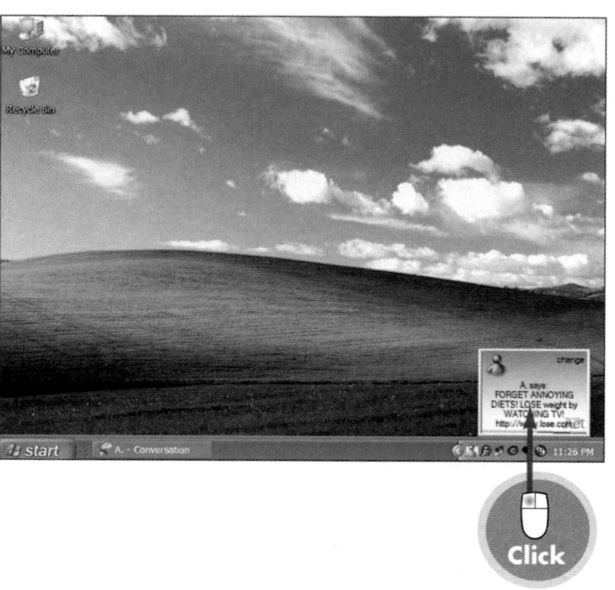

2 Open a Message

After an instant message arrives, if you don't open it right away, its window is minimized on the Windows taskbar. Click the message's taskbar button to read the message.

3 Block Someone

If you read an instant message and decide that you don't want to receive more messages from the sender, click the **Block** button. A dialog box may open asking you to confirm your decision to block messages from this sender.

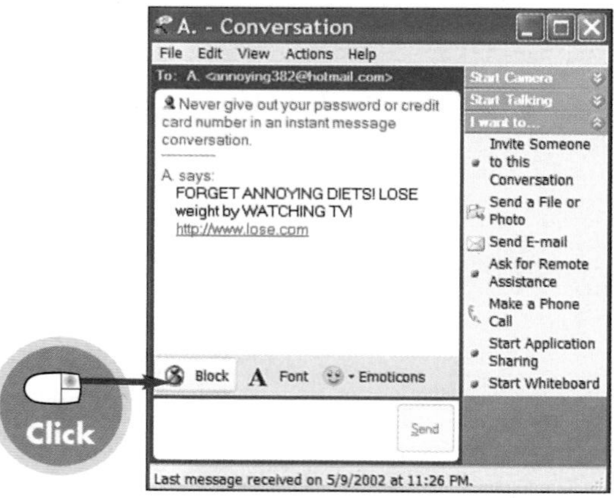

4 Confirm the Block

If you see a confirmation dialog box, click **OK** to block the sender. You will appear to be offline to that person at all times, and no more messages from him or her will be delivered to you. Windows Messenger does not inform the person that you are blocking messages.

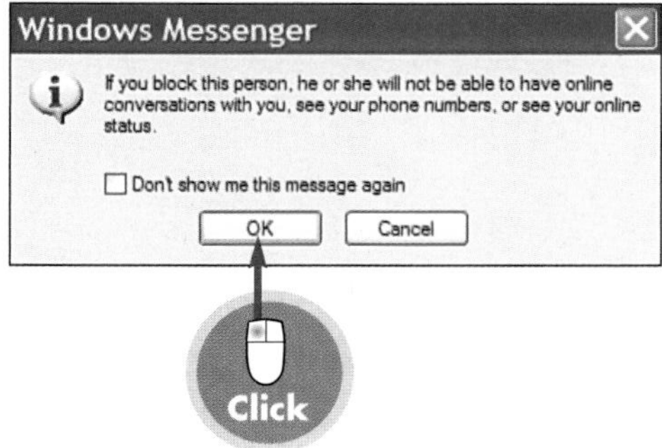

5 Discourage Messages

To let people know when you can't chat, open the main **Windows Messenger** window and click your email address. From the menu of options that appears, choose **Busy, Be Right Back**, **Away**, **On the Phone,** or **Out to Lunch**. This text and a special icon will appear next to your name on the contact list of people you chat with. Any messages that are sent to you while you are busy still come to you in the normal way; the sender just gets a message indicating that you can't respond immediately for the reason you specified.

6 Prevent All Messages

You still can receive messages if you have selected **Busy** or one of the other choices in step 5. To stop receiving instant messages, click your email address in the main **Windows Messenger** window and choose **Appear Offline**. Now people on your contact list will think you are no longer connected to Messenger.

How to Hint

Letting People Know You Can Chat

After you choose **Busy**, **Be Right Back**, or one of the other message-discouraging options in Windows Messenger, you should let people know when you're back and available to talk again. To do so, click your email address in the main Windows Messenger window and choose **Online**.

Task

9

Participating in Chat and Online Communities

There are thousands of World Wide Web sites where you can hold conversations with other people. Some of these sites are chat rooms, where people send and receive messages that are delivered immediately to each other. Everyone talks at once, several conversations can occur at the same time, and it can be hard to keep track of what's going on. After you become familiar with using chats, however, it will be easier for you to follow the many threads of conversation in a room.

Other sites are message boards, where people can post messages that are presented on a page for others to read and respond to by writing their own replies.

There are a variety of ways and places to chat on the Internet: Web sites, America Online, Internet Relay Chat (IRC), and instant-messaging services such as Windows Messenger and ICQ.

MSN, the Web portal offered by Microsoft, offers chat rooms and message boards for everyone with a Microsoft Passport.

How to Create an Account to Chat on MSN

On MSN Chat, a feature of Microsoft's MSN Web site, there are hundreds of chat rooms in which people gather to talk in groups of 2–35 people. You can hold conversations with people who share a common interest, age, city, or lifestyle. Topics include current events, politics, sports, dating, music, and software. These chats are informal and lively. Before you can set up an account on MSN Chat, however, you must have a Microsoft Passport. If you don't have one yet, read Part 3, Task 4, "How to Set Up a Microsoft Passport Account."

1 Visit MSN Chat

To visit the Chat section of the MSN site, type the URL **http://chat.msn.com** into your browser's **Address bar** and press **Enter**. A page opens listing a directory of chat rooms and some upcoming chats with celebrities that will take place soon.

2 Present Your Passport

Before you chat, you should sign in to your Microsoft Passport account. If you haven't done so yet, click the **Sign In** button at the top of the page.

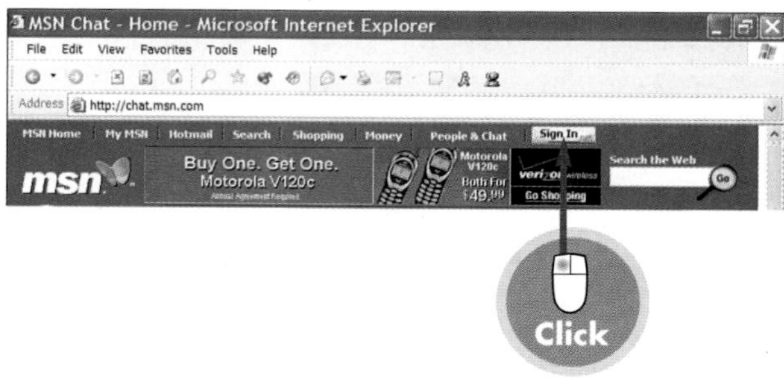

3 Provide Your Age

If this is one of the first times you have used your Microsoft Passport, you may be asked for your birth date. Use the drop-down boxes to choose your birth month and day then type your year in the adjacent text box. When you're finished, click **Continue**.

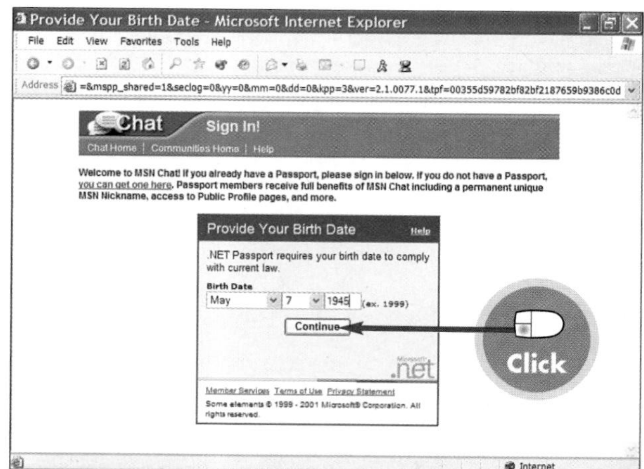

4 Choose a Nickname

MSN Chat identifies you using a nickname of your choosing rather than your email address or real name. Microsoft suggests several nicknames; click a name to use it or click the **More Suggested Names** link to see more suggestions. To choose your own nickname, type it in the text box and click **Register Nickname**.

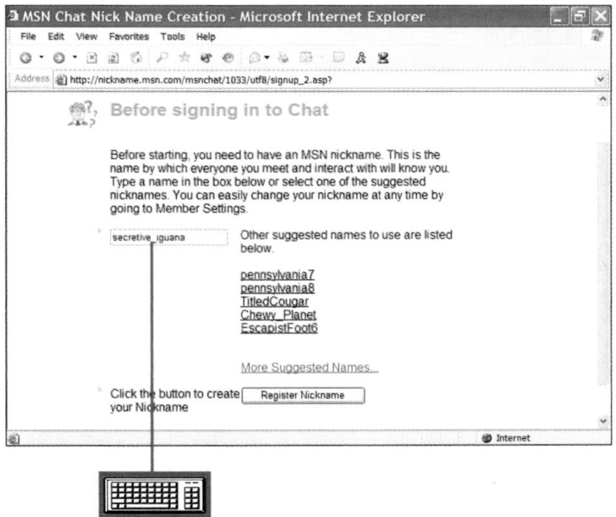

5 Create a Profile

Every participant in MSN Chat has a public profile that can be viewed by others. To make sure that you're revealing only the things you want to reveal, click the **Create a public profile** button.

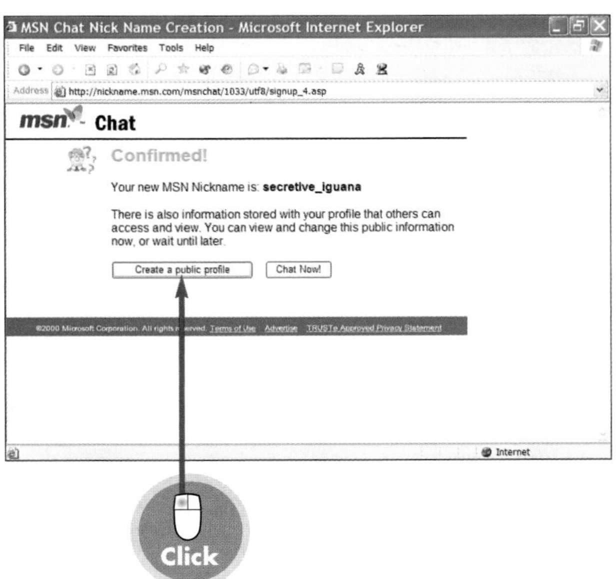

6 Identify Yourself

Fill out all the items in the **About Me** section (these items are required to set up an MSN Chat account). To protect your privacy, however, don't type your full name in the **Display name** text box. Scroll down to see the rest of the form.

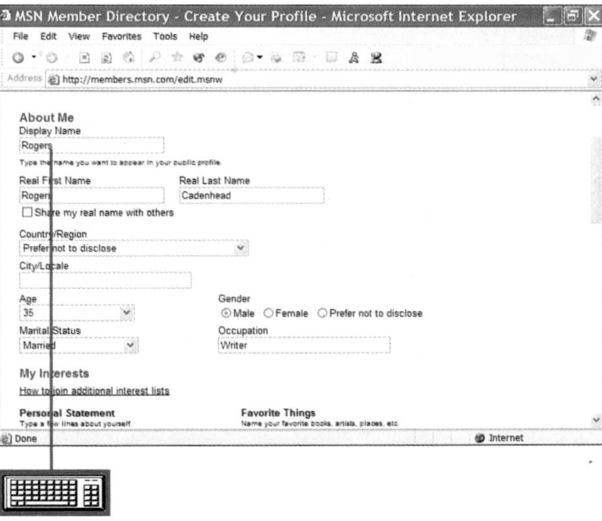

7 Complete Your Profile

Finish the form by filling out the **Permissions** section. Click the **Code of Conduct** link to review the site's rules; enable the **I accept** box if you agree. Finally, click the **Save** button to set up your MSN Chat account.

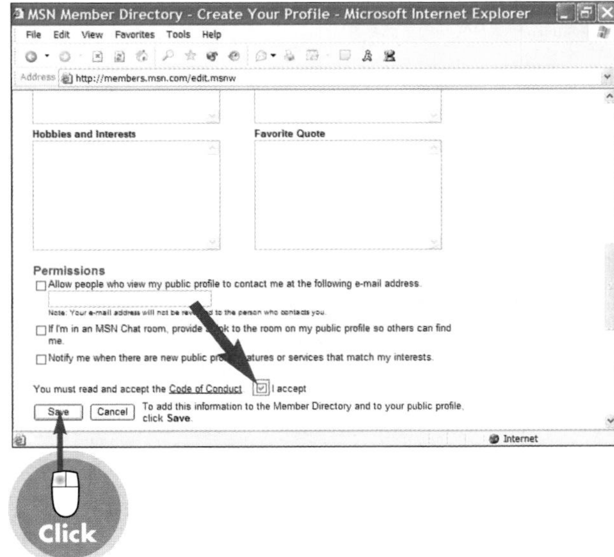

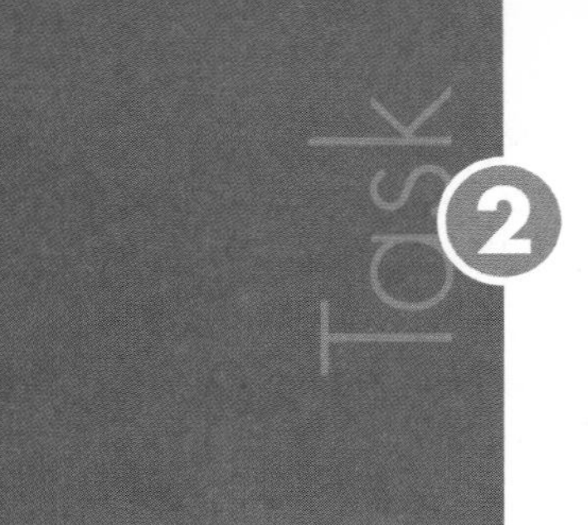

How to Chat for the First Time on MSN

As you will discover quickly when you participate in a chat room, chats are a part of the Internet that's susceptible to abuse. Although most chat users are friendly, you should be extremely cautious about what you reveal in any chat room. The term *phishing* refers to efforts to steal a password or credit-card information in a chat or instant message, and scams like that are relatively common. To be safe when chatting on the Internet, you should never reveal personal information such as your phone number, address, credit-card number, or passwords.

1 Visit MSN Chat

To visit the Chat section of the MSN site, type the URL `http://chat.msn.com` into your browser's **Address bar** and press **Enter**.

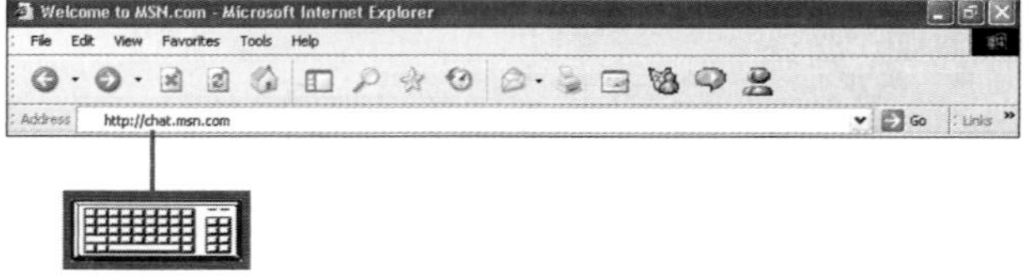

2 Sign In To Passport

You can't join a chat without signing in to MSN, which requires your Microsoft Passport. If you aren't signed in, click the **Sign In** button at the top of the page.

3 Identify Yourself

You may be asked to sign in to your Passport account. Choose your email address from the drop-down box and type your password in the **Password** text box. When you're finished, click **OK**.

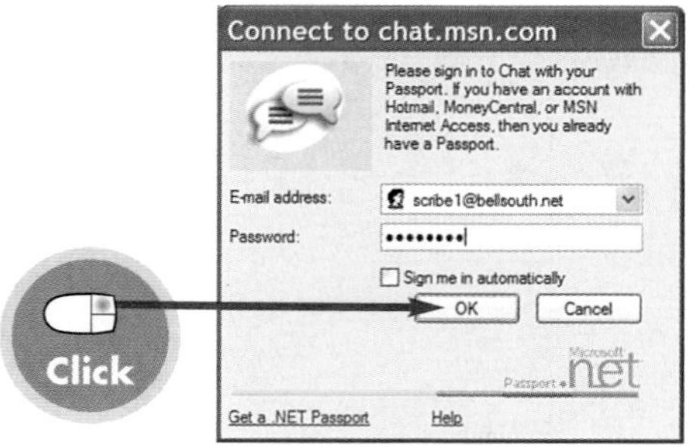

4 Choose a Chat Category

MSN Chat organizes chat rooms by topic. To see the chat rooms in a specific category, click the hyperlink for a category (such as **News**). A page opens listing chat rooms that are currently open in that category.

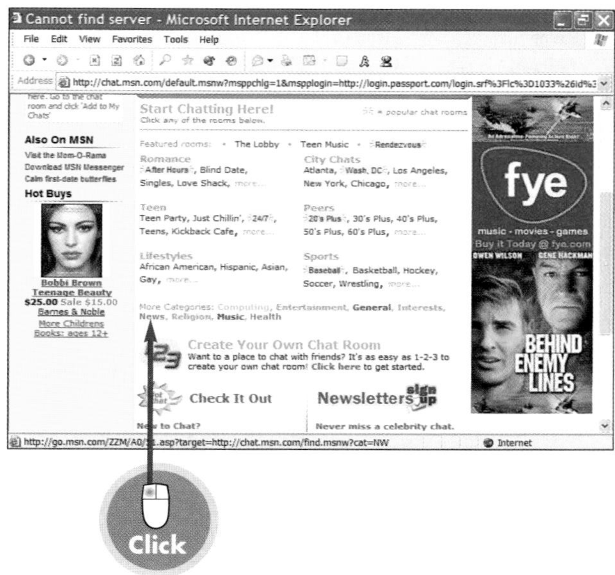

5 Choose a Chat Room

Rooms can be created by MSN or chat users. To visit one of the listed chat rooms, click its name. **Headlines** is one of the permanent rooms in the **News** category, as indicated by a MSN butterfly icon. Click the **Headlines** link to join an ongoing discussion of current news.

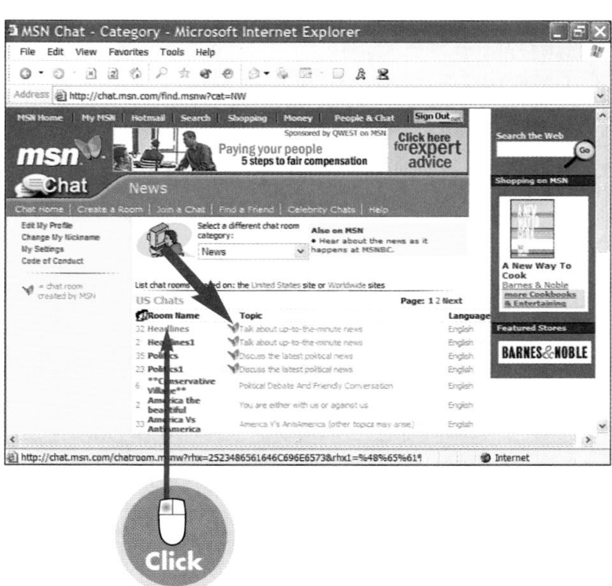

6 Download Software

If you have never participated in an MSN Chat, your browser may require special software that works with Internet Explorer. In that case, the **We are now downloading MSN Chat software** text appears. (If you're not using Internet Explorer, you'll be directed to a "this feature requires Internet Explorer" page.) A **Security Warning** dialog box appears after the download is finished.

7 Install Software

MSN Chat Control is software that works in conjunction with Internet Explorer to present chat rooms. To install the software, click the **Yes** button. To participate in your first chat, proceed to Task 3.

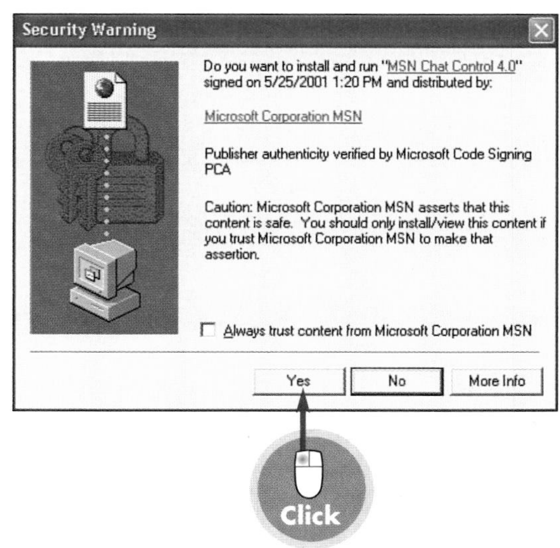

How to Participate in a Chat on MSN

If you have never participated in an MSN Chat, follow the instructions in the preceding task, "How to Chat for the First Time on MSN," before you start to chat. After MSN Chat Control is set up to work with Internet Explorer, it appears whenever you enter a chat room on MSN. To find a chat room, type the URL `http://chat.msn.com` in your browser's **Address bar** and press **Enter**, click the link of a chat category such as **News**, and then click the name of a room.

1 Write a Message

In an MSN chat room, all messages sent by people using the room appear in a large chat window along with the nickname of the sender. To write your own message, type it in the box at the bottom of the chat window.

2 Send a Message

To send your message to everyone in the chat room, click the **Send** button. Your message appears along with your nickname (also called your display name) at the bottom of the chat window.

3 Ignore a User

To ignore all messages sent by a particular user, click that user's nickname in the list of people in the room on the right side of the page, and then click the **Ignore** button.

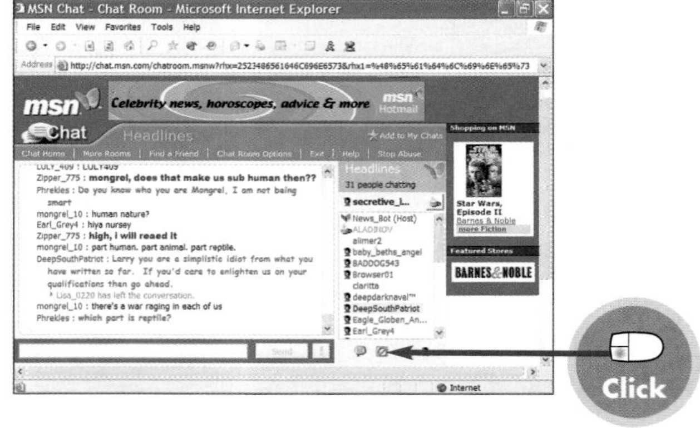

4 Begin a Private Chat

You can speak to a chat room participant privately while in MSN Chat. To begin a private conversation, double-click the person's nickname in the list of people in the room. A **whisper** window opens in which you can conduct a conversation away from the rest of the room.

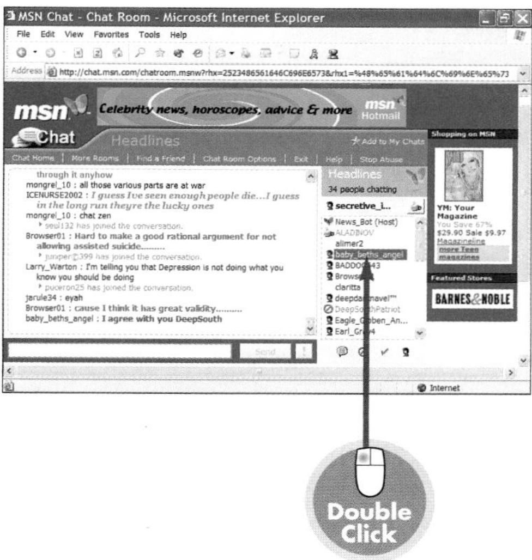

5 Send a Private Message

In the **whisper** window, type the private message in the text box at the bottom of the window. When you're ready, click **Whisper** to send the message. The message does not appear in the chat room window; instead, it is sent only to the specified recipient.

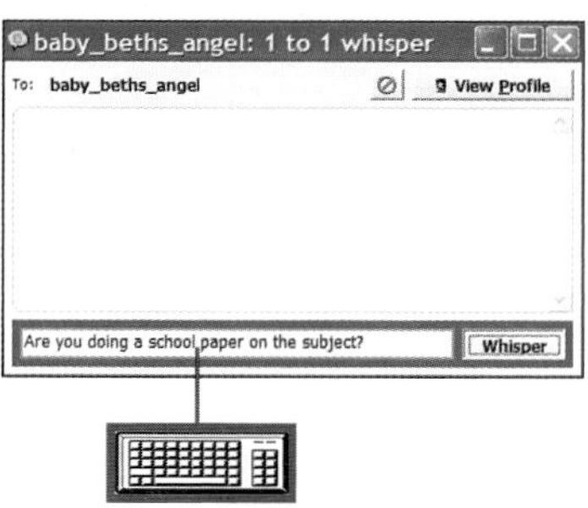

6 Read a Response

Your private messages and the replies you receive will appear in the **whisper** window's top text box. To continue the private conversation, type text in the bottom box and click **Whisper**. When you're done chatting privately, click the **x** button on the **whisper** window's title bar to close the window and return to the main chat room.

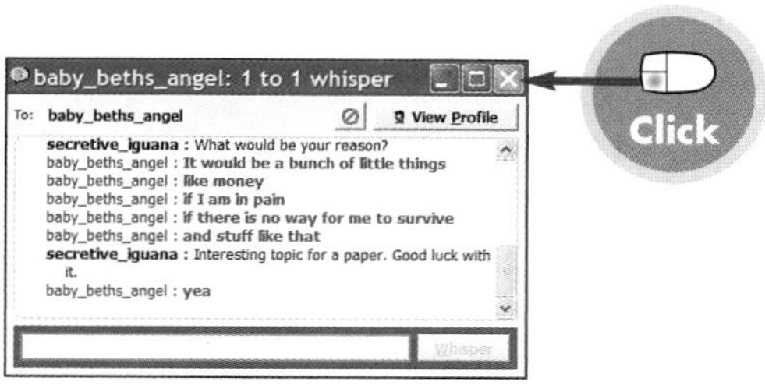

How to Hint

Chatting with People on Yahoo!

Yahoo! offers chat rooms that are similar to those featured on the MSN portal. You can participate in live chats with celebrities, join rooms created by Yahoo! and other users, and talk privately with other participants. To use a Yahoo! account to participate in these chats, type the URL **http://chat.yahoo.com** into your browser's **Address bar** and press **Enter**.

Task

4 How to Join a Community on MSN

If the pace of a chat room is not to your liking or you'd like to participate in more formal discussions, you may be interested in message boards and other discussion Web sites. Message boards are Web pages where you can read messages posted by others and write your own responses. MSN offers this feature in its **Communities** section, where hundreds of people create and maintain boards on various topics. Joining an MSN community requires a Microsoft Passport account. To set one up, read Part 3, Task 4, "How to Set Up a Microsoft Passport Account."

1 View Your Communities

To see the communities associated with your Microsoft Passport account, type the URL `http://communities.msn.com` in the browser's **Address bar** and press **Enter**.

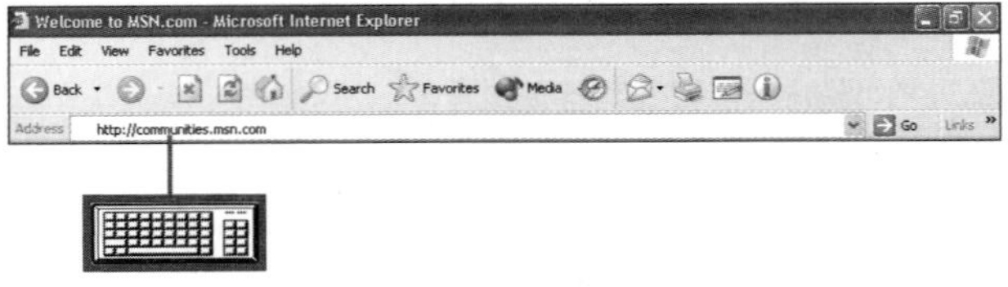

2 Provide Your Passport

The **MSN Communities** home page highlights some of the coolest communities you can join. If you haven't yet signed in to your Microsoft Passport account, click the **Sign In** button at the top of the page.

3 Find a Community

MSN has a directory of communities, but the fastest way to find one of interest is to search for it. Type text to look for in the **Find a Community** text box and click the **Go** button. A page opens listing communities whose names match the text you typed.

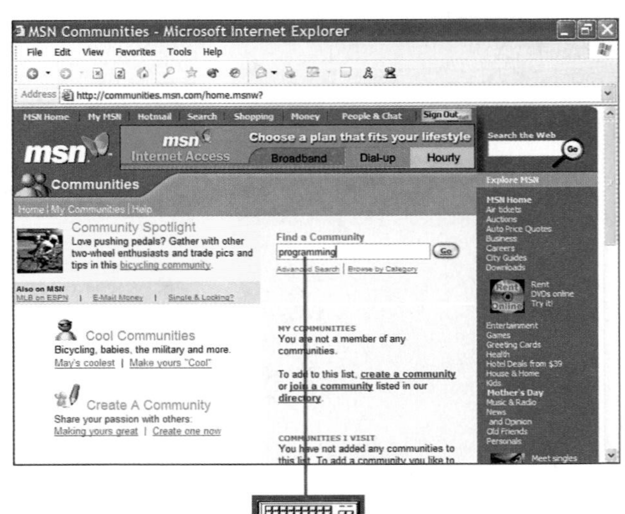

4 Visit a Community

MSN offers public communities and private ones. Each community that turns up in a search is open for the public to visit. To take a look at one of these communities, click its hyperlink.

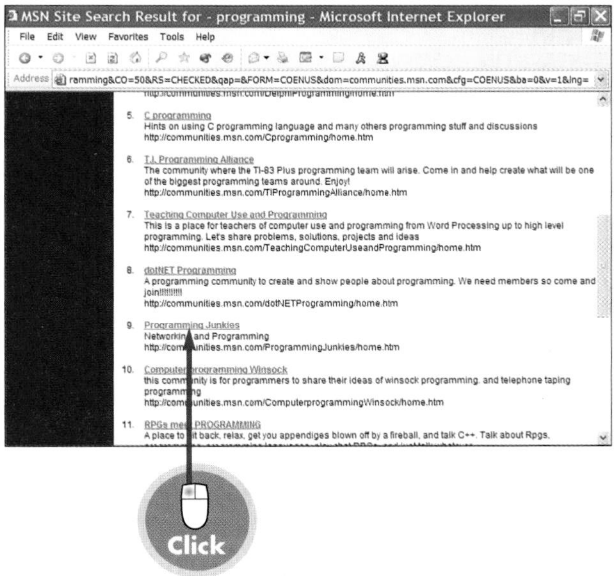

5 Join a Community

To join a community, click the **Join Now** hyperlink in the column along the left side of the page.

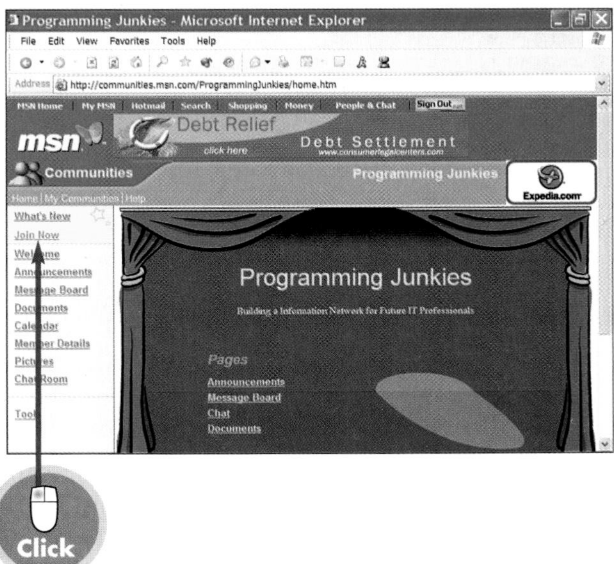

6 Identify Yourself

Type a nickname you would like to use in the community in the first text box and your email address in the second text box. Choose an option for how you would like to receive messages.

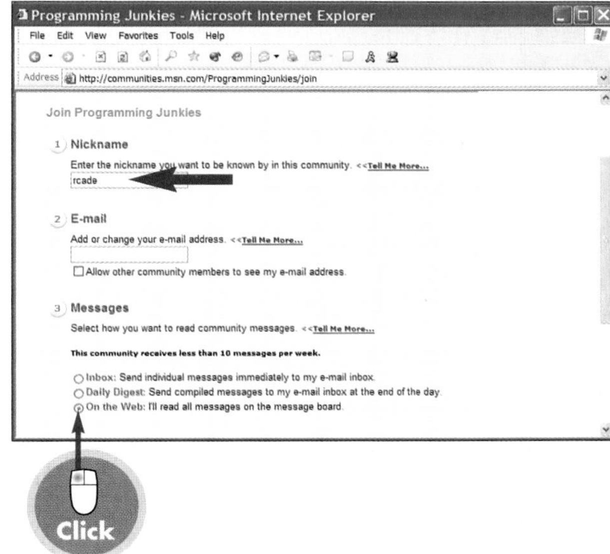

7 Send Your Application

Before joining a community, you must review the MSN conditions of membership by clicking the **Code of Conduct** hyperlink. If you accept the terms, enable the **I accept** check box. When you're finished, click the **Join Now** button. You'll be added to the community if it allows public membership.

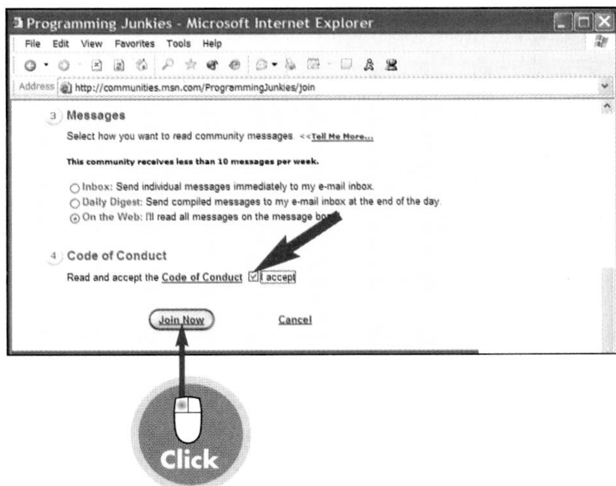

Task 5

How to Read and Send Messages in an MSN Community

Because MSN Community message boards can be read and replied to at your leisure, the discussions are often more formal than those you find in a chat room. In some ways, a message board is like a discussion taking place in e-mail, except that everything is published for others to read. On its community message boards, MSN publishes the messages you post with your chosen nickname rather than with your email address or any other identifying information.

1 View Your Communities

To see the communities you have joined (or created) on MSN, type the address `http://communities.msn.com/MyWebSites` in your browser's **Address bar** and press **Enter**. A page opens with links to each community.

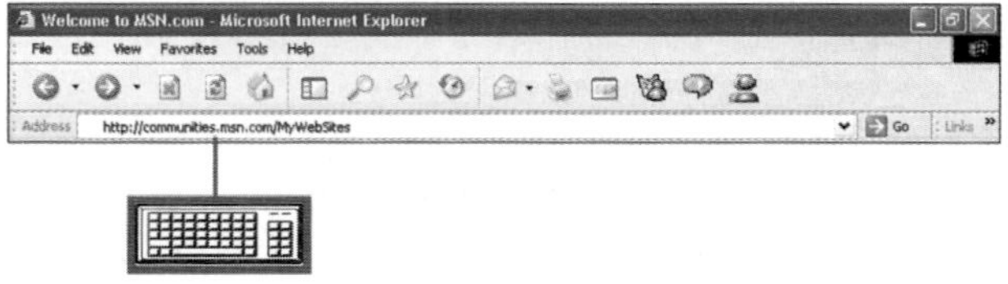

2 Visit a Community

To visit one of the communities you have joined, click its hyperlink. If you'd like to look for other communities instead, click the **Home** hyperlink at the top of the page.

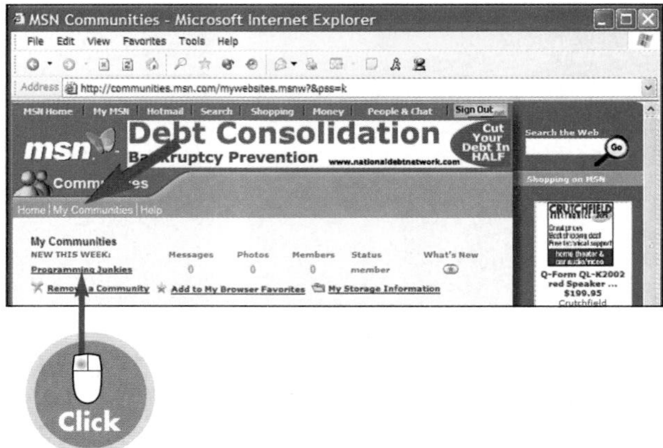

3 View a Message Board

Click the **Message Board** hyperlink to see a community's message board. If a community has more than one message board, a page opens where you can choose a specific board by clicking its link.

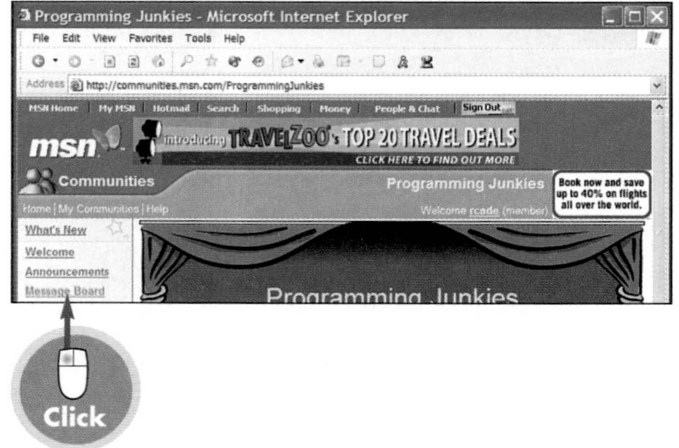

4 Read Messages

Discussions are organized by subject. To read a discussion, click a link in the **Subject** list. You also can start a new discussion of your own: Click the **New Discussion** hyperlink.

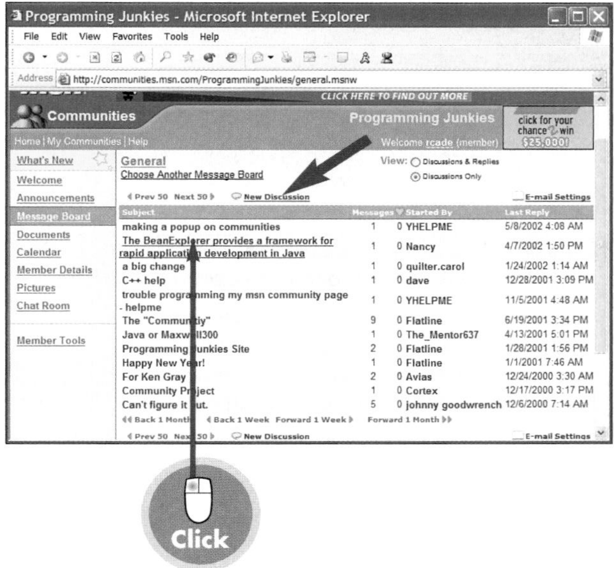

5 Reply to a Message

Every message you read has a **Reply** hyperlink you can use to post a public message in response to the original message. Click this link to reply to the message you are reading. A window opens where you can type your message and send it.

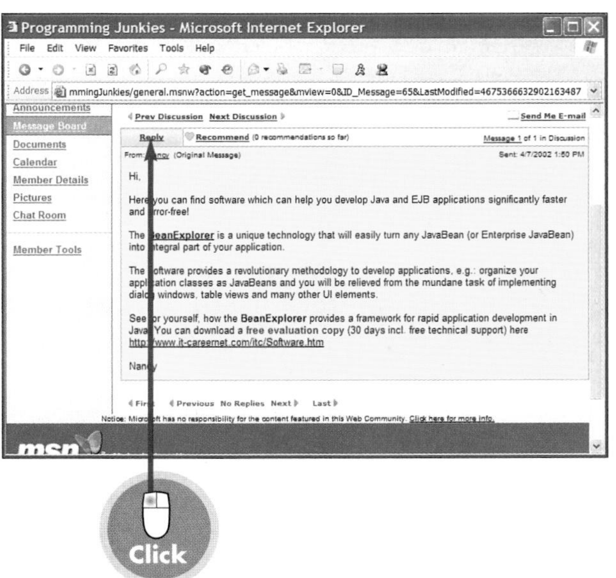

6 Compose a Reply

Type your message in the text box. When you're finished, click the **Send** button. Within a minute or two, your message should show up on the community's message board.

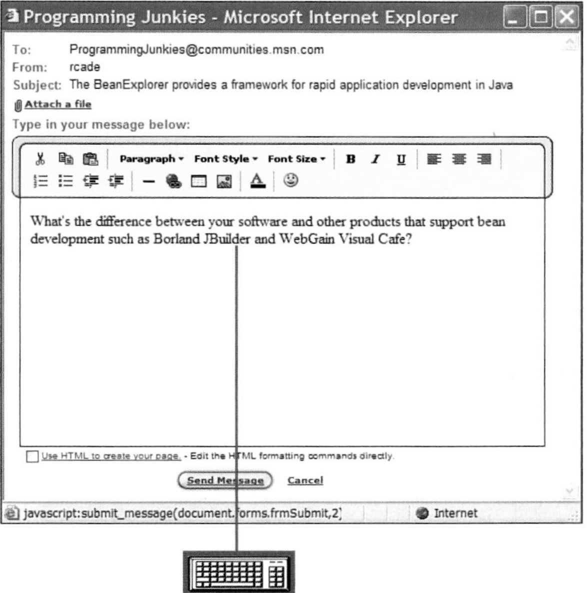

How to Hint

Creating Your Own Message Board

If you don't find an MSN community on a topic that interests you, you can build your own. Anyone with a Microsoft Passport account can create a community with a message board and other features and decide whether to make it available to the public or restrict its membership. To find out more, read Part 14, "Creating Your Own Web Site."

Visiting a Weblog Community

Some communities on the Web are organized to exchange links to interesting sites and news stories. These sites are called *weblogs* because they present a daily log of site links. One of the most popular is the 14,000-member MetaFilter, a weblog established by Matt Haughey that's frequented by Web developers, programmers, political aficionados, and others. To visit, type the URL **`http://www.metafilter.com`** in your browser's **Address bar** and press **Enter**.

Task

10

Using America Online's Internet Capabilities

Like other online services launched before the popularization of the Internet, America Online takes a more hands-on approach than most Internet service providers today. Instead of selling a connection to the Internet and letting you set up your own email, instant messaging, and chat software, America Online integrates these services into its own software.

America Online offers access to the World Wide Web through a version of Internet Explorer that is integrated into the service. You also can run other Web browsers while connected to America Online.

There are two ways to connect to the service: by using your modem to dial up a local America Online access number or by using another Internet service provider's connection. The latter approach requires a secondary account with the other Internet provider, but your America Online subscription is discounted. You might want to use both AOL and another ISP if you find that AOL has services you can't get anywhere else but you want to use another ISP for other reasons—such as faster access, for example.

How to Install America Online

Before you can use America Online, you must install its software on your computer. The easiest way to install the current version of AOL is by using one of the CDs that the company frequently includes in magazines and other giveaways. If you can't find one (they're often available at Target and Blockbuster Video stores), you can request a free CD by mail—call (888) 265-8002. If you already have Internet access, you can also download the software from AOL's site by visiting the address `http://free.aol.com`; doing so ensures that you get the most recent version—but be aware that it might take a while to download.

1 Choose America Online

To begin installing America Online, open the folder that contains the AOL setup software. (If you're installing from a CD, put the CD in its drive, click the **My Computer** icon on your desktop, and then click the CD icon.) Double-click the **SETUP.EXE** icon.

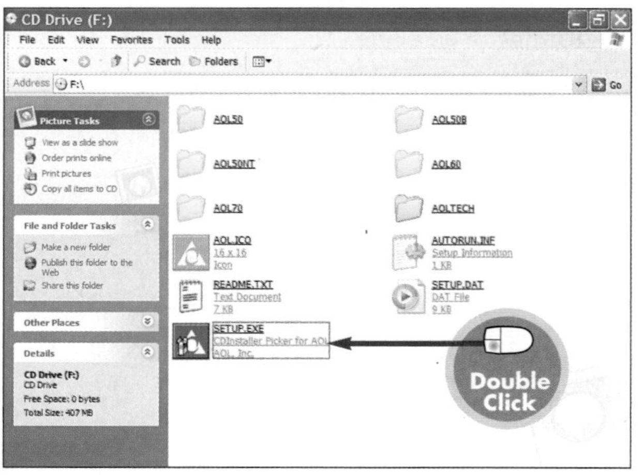

2 Start a New Account

After a moment, the America Online installation program starts and opens a **Welcome to America Online!** dialog box. If you are not a current member, click the **New Members** button to set up an account.

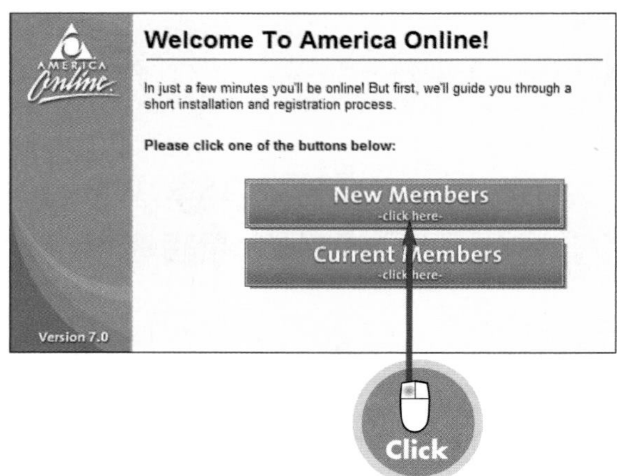

3 Choose a Folder

The next screen indicates where AOL will be installed. The default folder is **C:\Program Files\America Online 7.0**. It's best to go with the default unless you have a good reason not to. (If you want to install AOL somewhere else, click the **click here** hyperlink and choose a different folder.) Click **Next**.

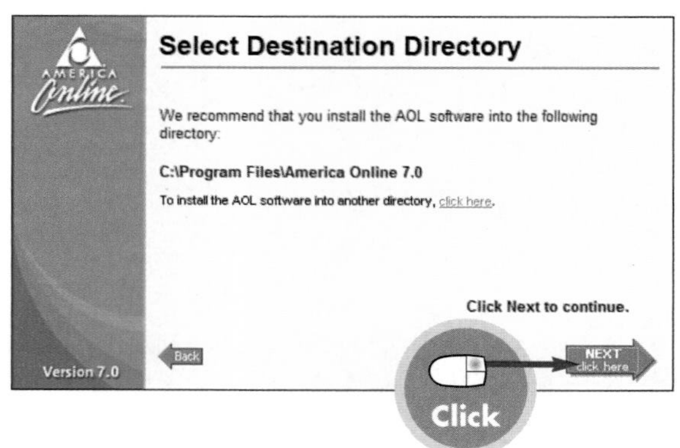

4 Install AOL

After AOL is installed, it must be set up to work on your computer. Click the **Next** arrow to begin.

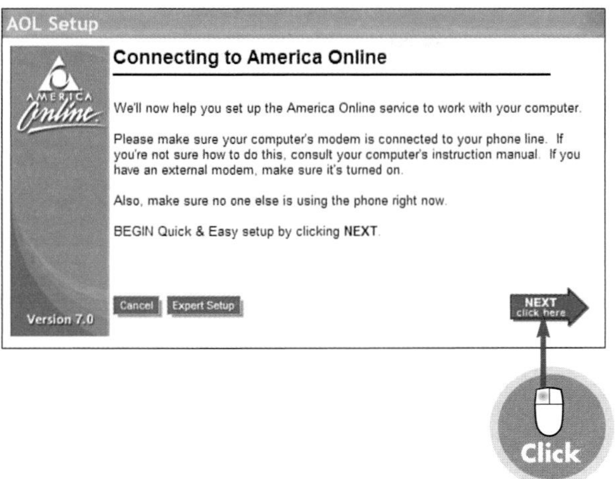

5 Select Your Connection

The **Select Your Connection** dialog box lists the different ways your computer can connect to AOL. If you plan to use AOL as your Internet service provider, select **Modem** from the list. If you already have a provider, choose **TCP/IP**. Click the **Next** arrow to continue.

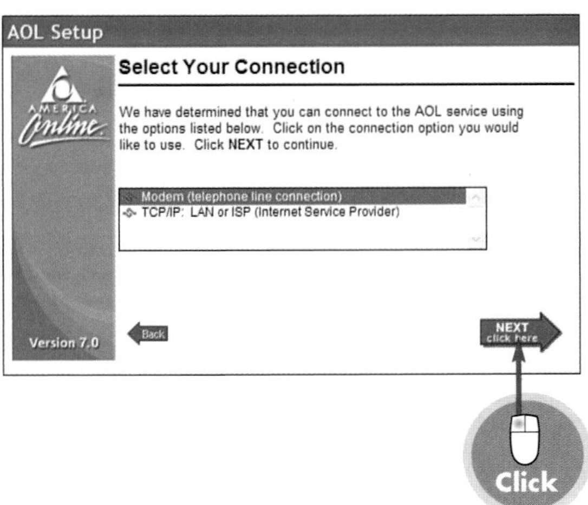

6 Identify Your Location

If you are using AOL as your Internet service provider, you must find the closest access number to your home. Type your telephone area code in the **Area Code** box, choose your location from the **Country/Region** drop-down menu, and then click **Next**. AOL will use your modem to retrieve the current list of access numbers.

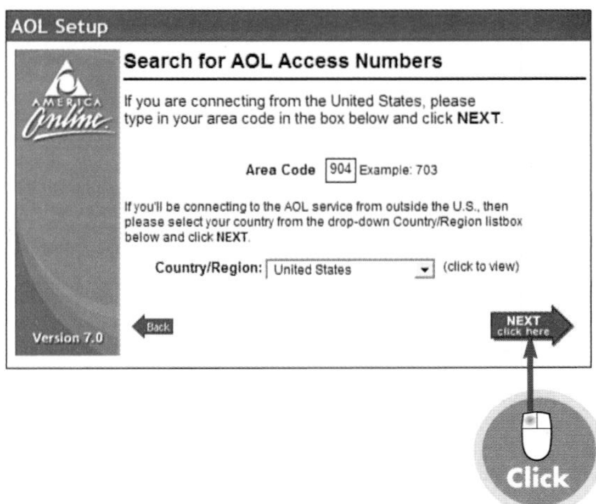

7 Set Up Your Phone

For AOL to use your modem correctly, you must indicate any special dialing requirements that are needed (such as dialing 9 to reach an outside line in an office). Enable the check boxes that apply to your location and click Next.

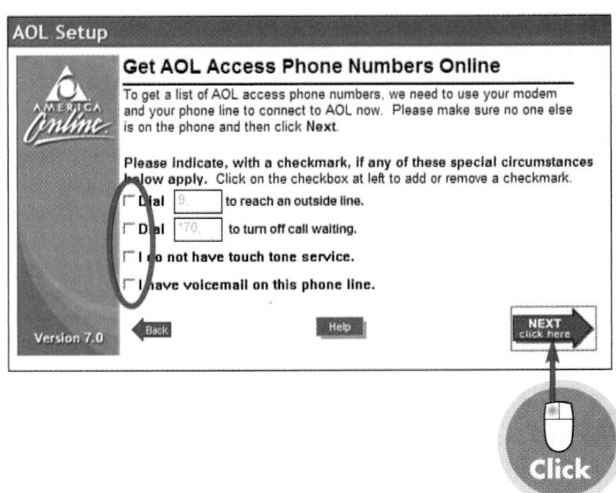

8 Choose an Access Number

The access numbers closest to your home are listed. Enable the box next to a number to choose it (you can pick up to three). Make sure that you pick numbers that are local calls. Otherwise, you must pay long-distance charges for the time you spend on AOL, which can be enormously expensive. Click **Next** to continue.

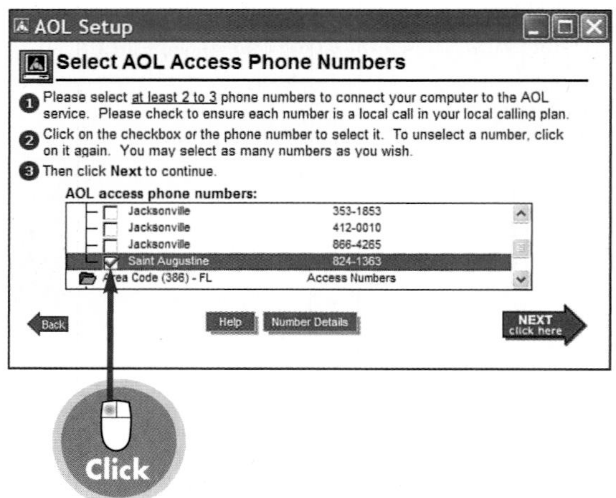

9 Choose Calling Options

If your phone requires any special dialing sequences to reach an outside line or to turn off call waiting, click a **Dial** check box and type the required dialing sequence in the box next to it. It's often helpful to include a comma in the sequence, which causes the computer to pause for a few seconds before continuing to dial the access number. Click **Next** to continue.

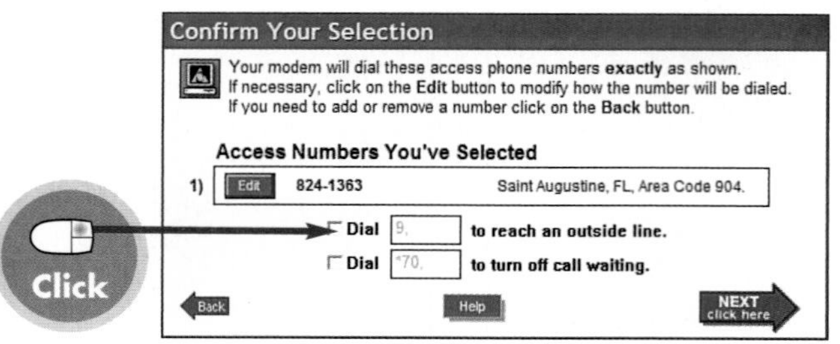

10 Set Up an Account

You will be asked for your name, address, and the credit card or checking account to bill when your free period expires. You also must choose a *screen name*—a handle that will identify you on the service—and a password that you will use. To begin, choose **New User** in the **Select ScreenName** list box and click **SIGN ON**.

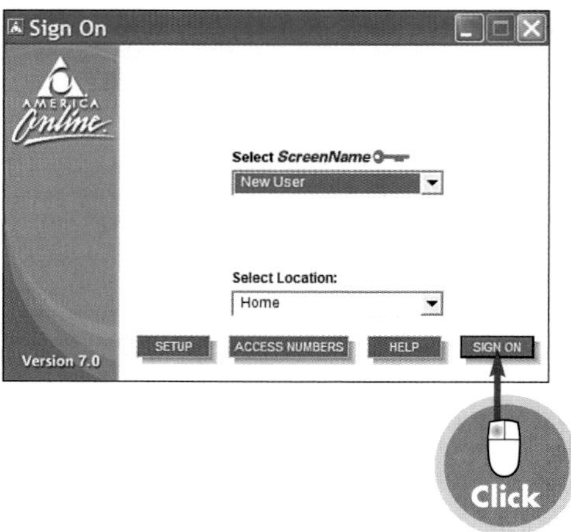

11 Enter Your CD Code

If you installed AOL from a CD, it came with a registration number and password. Provide both in the **Registration Number** and **Password** text boxes and click the **Next** arrow.

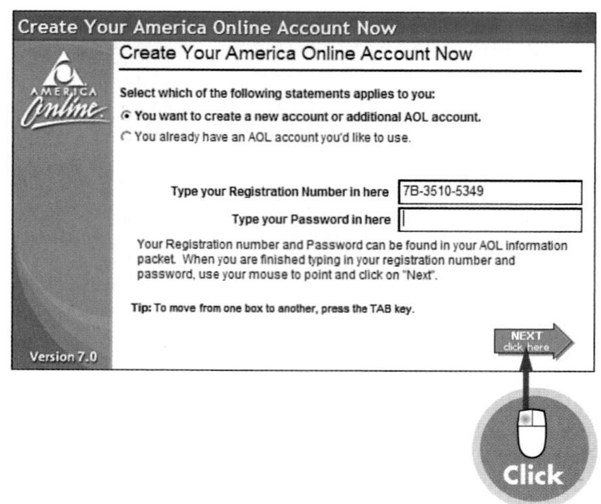

12 Provide Your Address

AOL requires your name, mailing address, and day and evening phone numbers. (Don't worry—none of this information will be published on the service.) After filling out the form, click **Next**.

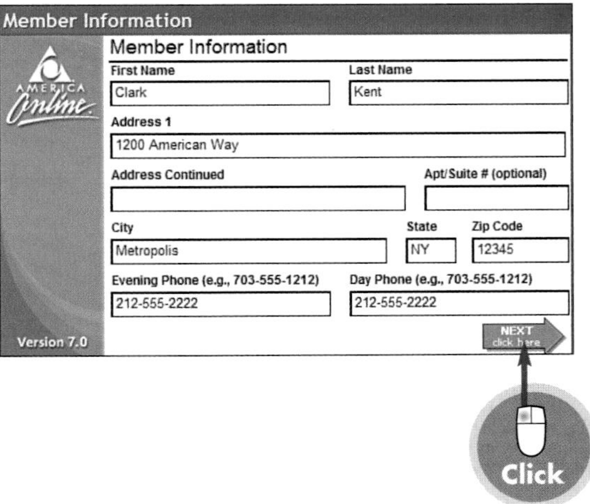

13 Pay for Service

Although AOL is free for the first 30 or 45 days, you must provide a credit- or debit-card number (or click **Other Billing Options** to arrange other payment). Your card will be charged automatically each month when your free subscription expires. Fill out the billing form and click **Next**.

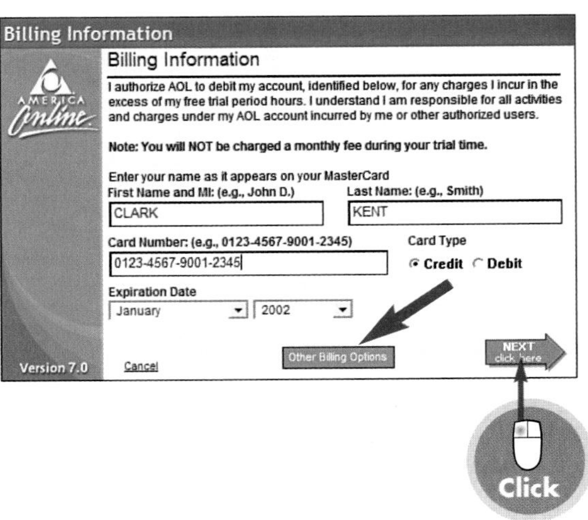

14 Review the Rules

AOL's conditions of membership must be accepted before you can join. To review them, select the **Read Now** radio button and click **Next**. After you look them over, assuming you agree to AOL's terms, click **I Agree** and click **Next**.

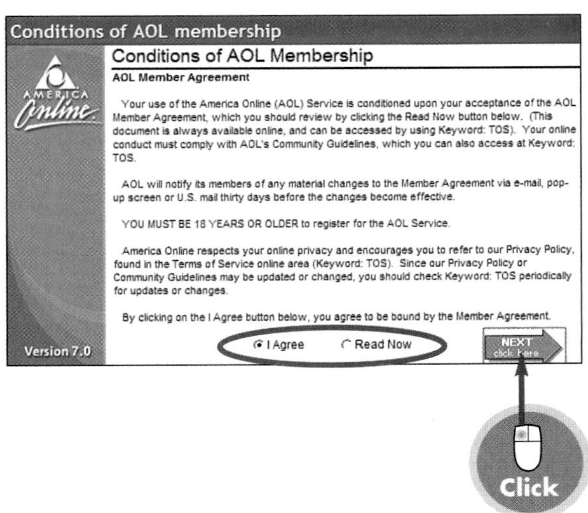

15 Choose a Screen Name

Your screen name identifies you in email, instant messaging, and chat. Type your desired name in the **Screen Name** box and the password you want in the **Password** and **Re-enter Password** boxes. When you find an unused screen name, your account will be set up and you can begin using AOL.

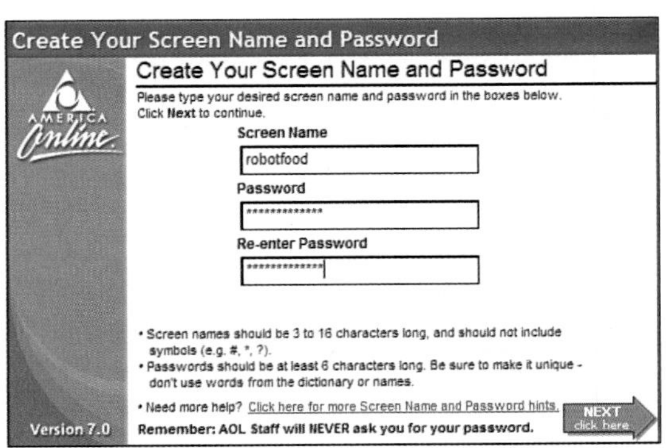

Task 2

How to Send AOL Mail

Although most Internet service providers require users to get their own email software (such as Microsoft Outlook Express or Qualcomm Eudora), America Online supports email as part of the service. You can send and receive email and attached files with anyone on the Internet while you are connected to America Online. If new mail arrives while you are using the service, a sound file alerts you to the event.

1 Sign On to AOL

To run America Online, choose **Start**, **All Programs**, **America Online 7.0**. The **Sign On** dialog box opens. Choose your screen name in the **Select ScreenName** list box and type your password in the **Enter Password** box, then click **SIGN ON**.

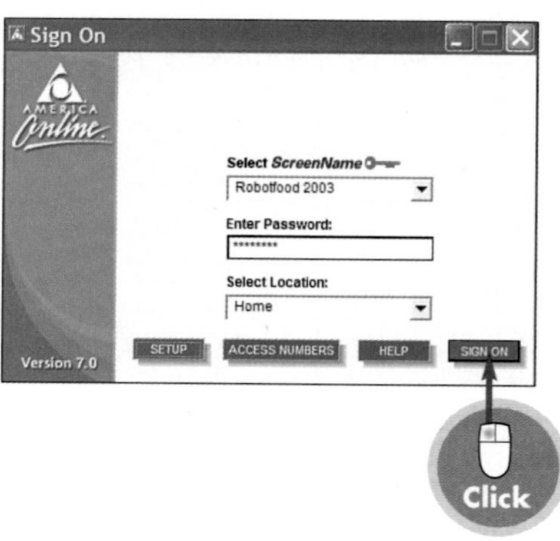

2 Click the Write Button

To send an email on AOL, click the **Write** button on the toolbar. The **Write Mail** window opens. Incidentally, you can also compose email messages while you're offline and send them later—a great strategy if you want to minimize your time online.

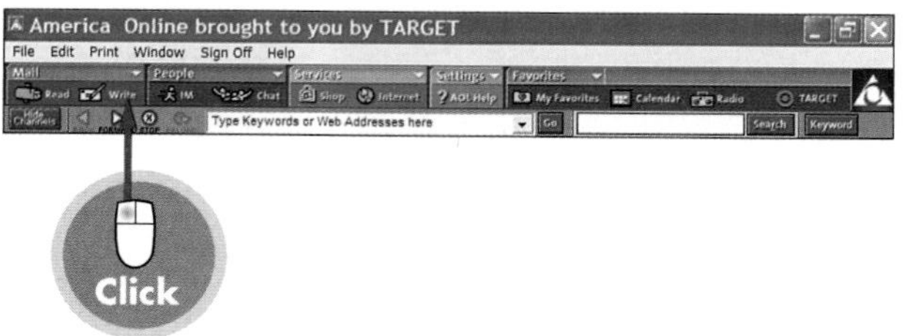

3 Enter a Screen Name or Email Address

In the **Send To** box, type the recipient's screen name or Internet mail address. (If you want to type several addresses, separate them with commas.) It doesn't matter if you type the address in uppercase letters, lowercase letters, or a mixture of the two.

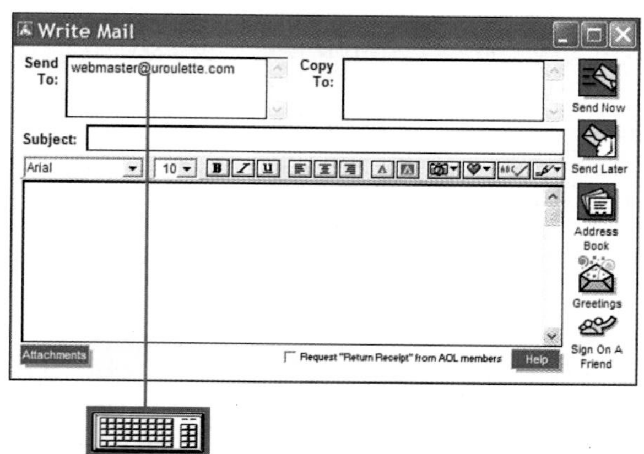

4 Send Carbon Copies

If you want to send a *carbon copy* of your message to another person, type his or her address in the **Copy To** box. (To specify several recipients, separate their email addresses with commas.)

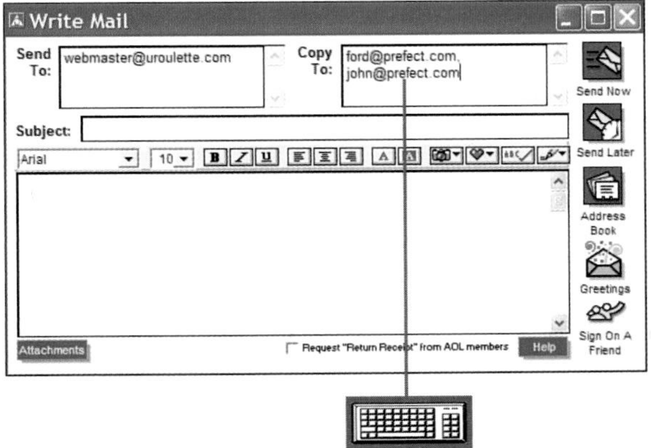

Type a Subject and Message

Type a subject for your message in the **Subject** box. Your recipients see this text before opening your message. In the large box at the bottom of the window, type your message. Use the arrow, **Backspace**, and **Delete** keys to review and edit the message. When you finish addressing and composing your message, click **Send Now** to send it right away.

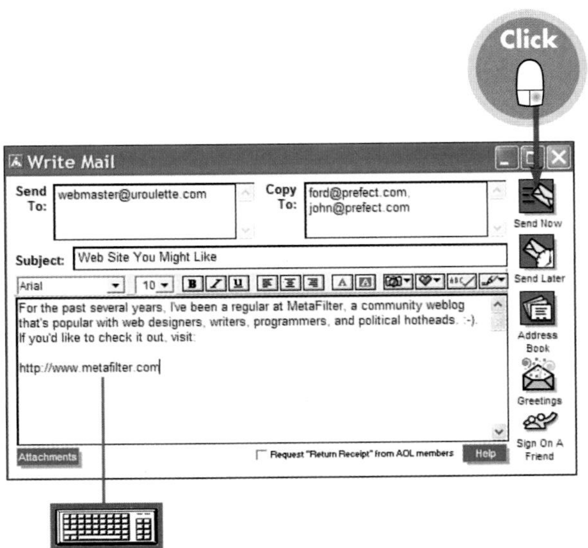

6 Unsending Messages

If you send a message and then have a change of heart, you *might* be able to unsend it, depending on whether the recipient is an AOL member and whether he or she has read the message yet. Click the **Read** toolbar button and choose the **Sent Mail** tab. (If you're already in your mailbox, just click the **Sent Mail** tab.) In the list of recently sent messages, highlight the message or messages you want to unsend and click the **Unsend** button.

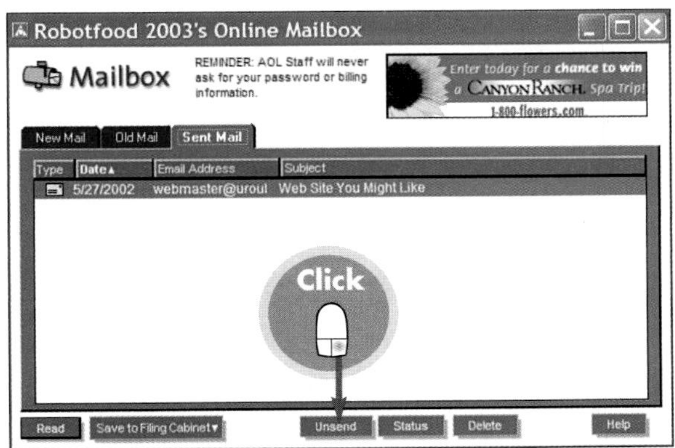

How to Hint

Finding Screen Names

If you're unsure of a recipient's screen name, try finding it in AOL's Member Directory. Click the arrow on the **People** section of the AOL toolbar, then choose **People Directory**. You can search the directory by name or by the person's interests (if he or she has filled out a public membership profile).

Internet Email Addresses

If you're an AOL member, your Internet email address is your screen name, minus any spaces, followed by `@aol.com` (for example, if your screen name is `robotfood2003`, your Internet email address is `robotfood2003@aol.com`). To use your AOL account to send email to someone who is not on AOL, you'll need to use his or her full Internet email address. Internet email addresses are usually in the format `username@sitename`. It can sometimes be difficult to guess a person's username—it's usually easier to ask for a person's Internet email address or to have that person send you an email message so that you can read the address in the message's **From** line.

How to Read Usenet Newsgroups on AOL

Another built-in feature of America Online is support for Usenet newsgroups—the thousands of public discussion groups hosted on computers around the world. When you begin using Usenet, America Online subscribes you automatically to several newsgroups. You can remove these groups and add others based on topics that interest you. One of the default newsgroups on America Online is `news.announce.newusers`, a good place for beginners to find out more about Usenet and the Internet.

1 Choose Newsgroups

To begin, log in to America Online. When you are connected, click the **more** arrow next to **Services** in the toolbar at the top of the screen, choose **Internet**, and then select **Newsgroups**. The **Newsgroups** window opens.

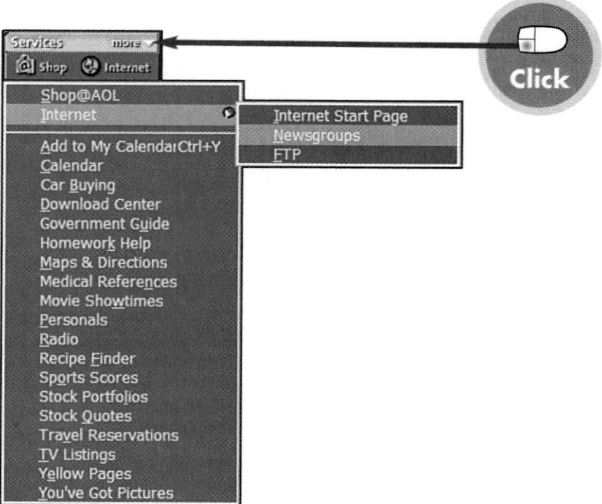

2 Read Newsgroups

Click the **Read My Newsgroups** button to read newsgroups you have subscribed to. The **Read My Newsgroups** window opens.

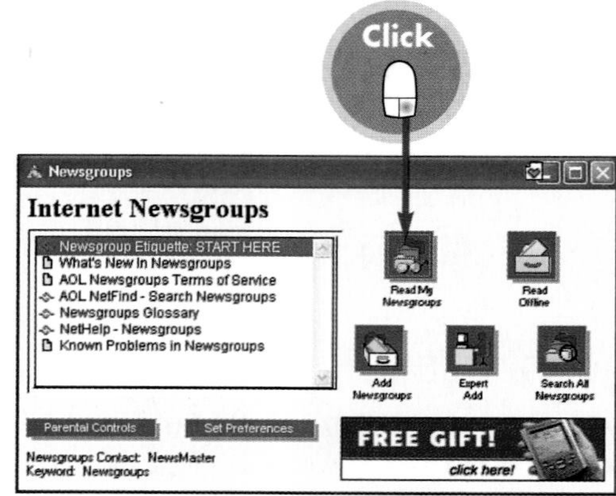

3 List Messages

You can list all the messages for a newsgroup or just the messages you have not yet read. Select the name of the newsgroup you want to peruse from the **My Newsgroups** list and click **List All** to see all the message subjects. Alternatively, click **List Unread** to see only the subject lines of messages you haven't read yet.

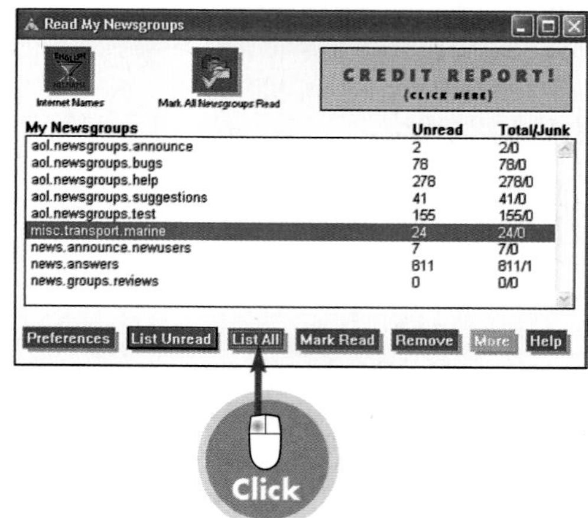

4 Read a Message

From the list of subjects for the selected newsgroup, select the subject of the message you want to read and click the **Read** button. The message appears in a new window.

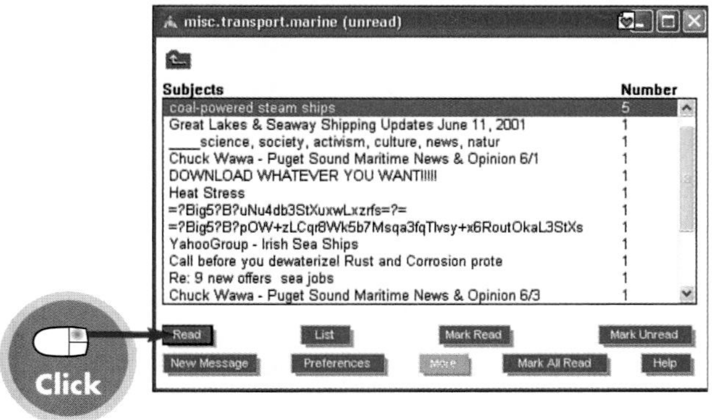

5 Add a Newsgroup

If you want to subscribe to a newsgroup and you know its name, click the **Expert Add** button in the **Newsgroups** window. The **Expert Add** dialog box opens.

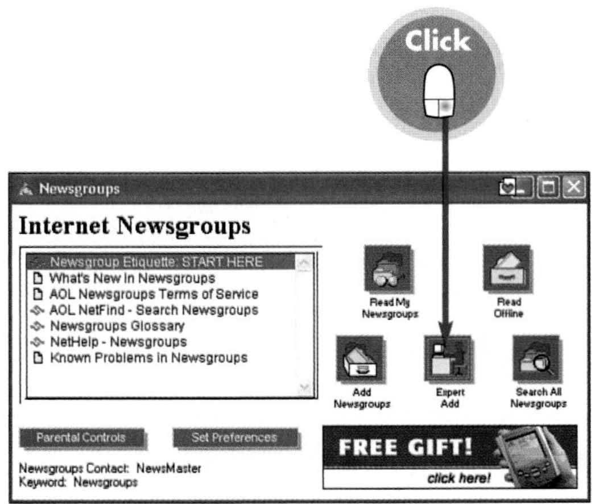

6 Subscribe to the Group

Type the newsgroup's name in the **Internet Name** text box and click the **Subscribe** button. If America Online offers the newsgroup, it will show up the next time you click **Read My Newsgroups** to read Usenet messages.

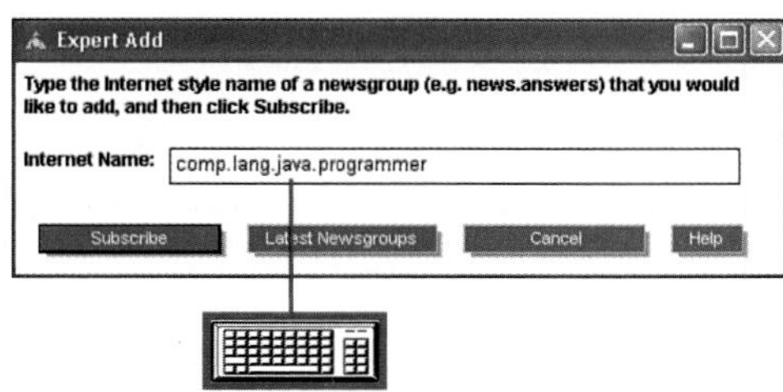

7 Filter the Group

Newsgroups can be filtered in several ways. If you're reading a group, you may want to enable the **Hide binary files** box so you don't receive any pictures or program files in the group (downloading a file from a Usenet group is generally a bad idea). Click **Save** when you're done.

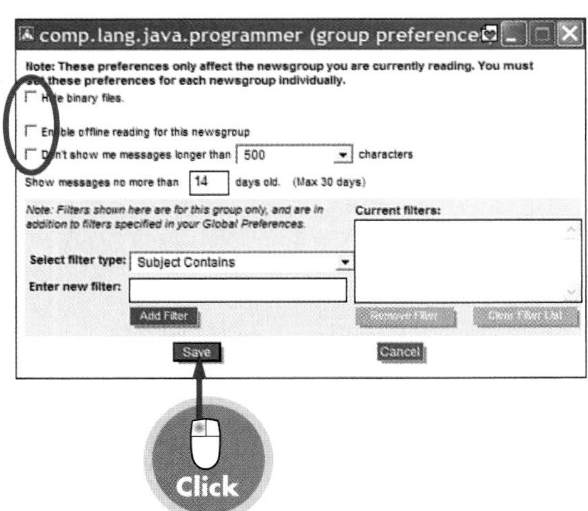

How to Use AOL's Chat Features

The **People** area of America Online offers more than just the opportunity to chat in small groups in chat rooms. AOL chat helps you meet people, find out information about them (by reading their member profiles), and even send them Instant Messages—all without leaving your chat room. Because sometimes people rub you the wrong way, you even have the option to ignore people you just don't want in your conversation. AOL's wealth of features allows you to personalize your AOL chat sessions.

1 Enter a Chat Room

Make sure that you're signed on to AOL. Click the **more** arrow next to **People** in the AOL toolbar and choose **Find a Chat**. The **Find a Chat** window opens.

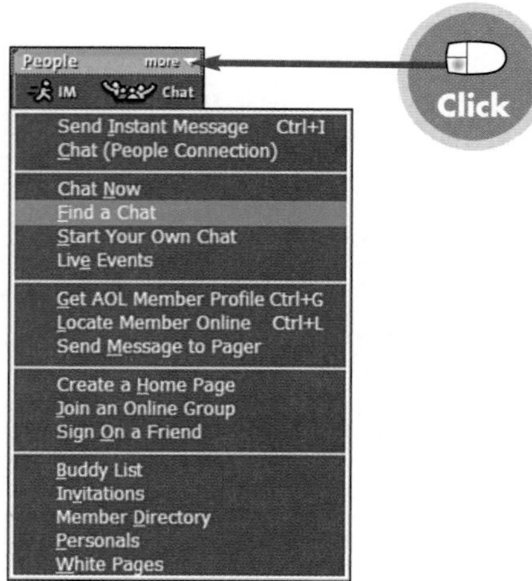

2 View Chat Rooms

Chat rooms are organized into categories. To see the chat rooms associated with a category, select a category from the list on the left side of the window and click the **View Chats** button. A list of chat rooms in that category appears in the pane on the right side of the window.

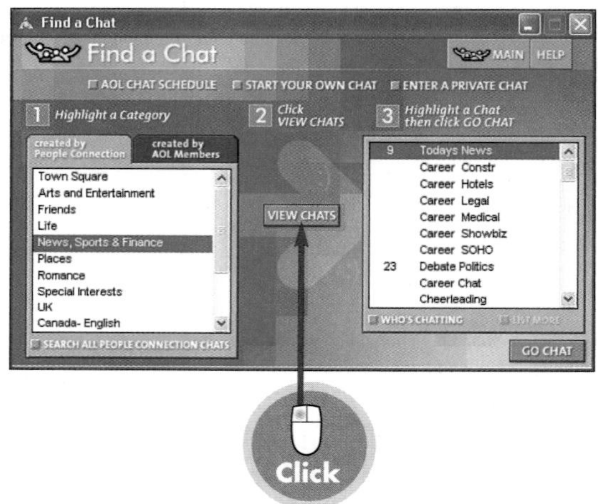

3 Join a Chat Room

To join a chat room, select the name of the room from the list in the right pane and click the **Go Chat** button. A new window opens, showing the ongoing discussion in the selected chat room.

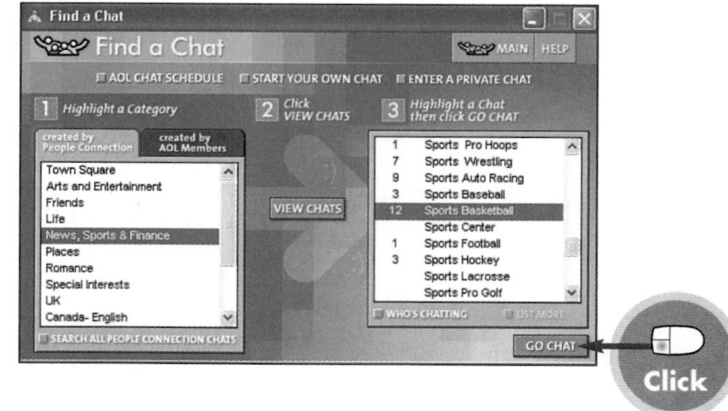

4 Say Something

The main chat window displays comments made by other people in the room. In the window, each user's screen name appears followed by a colon and the comment made by that user. To say something, type your comment in the box at the bottom of the window and click the **Send** button.

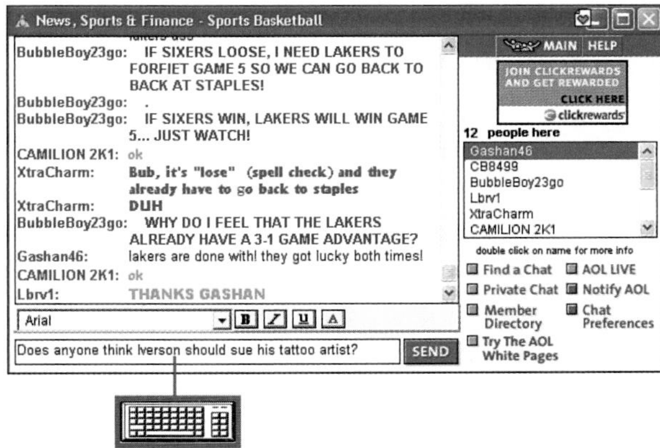

5 Ignore Someone

If you'd like to stop seeing comments made by a specific user in a chat room, double-click that user's screen name in the **people here** list on the right side of the window and select the **Ignore Member** option. Comments made by that person are no longer displayed on your screen.

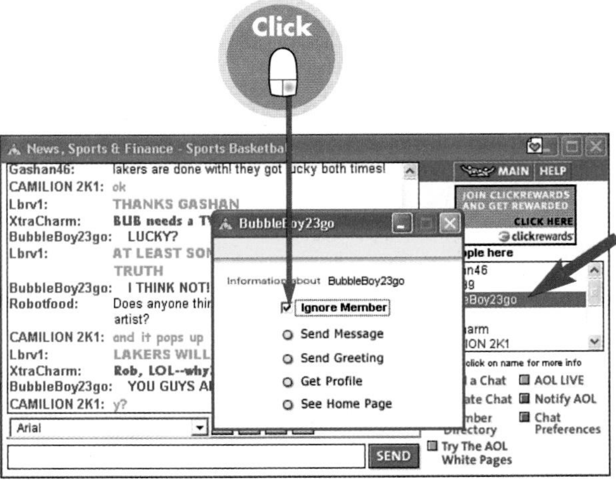

6 Send an Instant Message

To send an Instant Message to someone in a chat room, double-click the person's screen name in the **people here** list and click **Send Message**. In the **Send Instant Message** dialog box that appears, type your comment and click the **Send** button. This message appears only on the selected individual's screen; no other members will see that message.

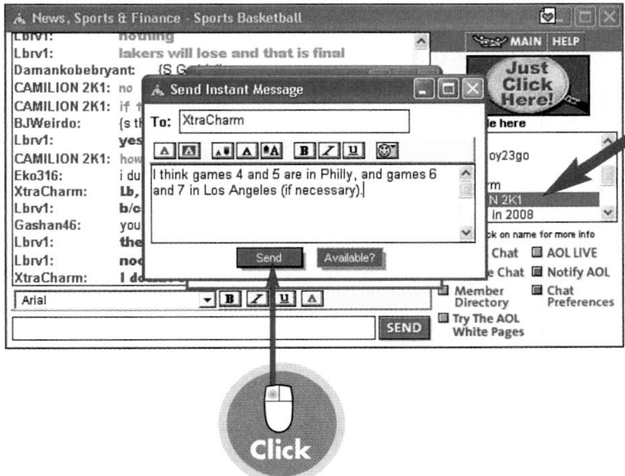

How to Hint

Starting a Chat Room on a New Topic

You can start your own chat room devoted to any topic. Click the **more** arrow next to **People** on the toolbar and choose **Start Your Own Chat**. As other America Online users show up in the room, their screen names will be listed in the **people here** text box. Your new room remains active as long as there is at least one person in the room.

Handling Inappropriate Messages

If you find that a member's messages are inappropriate, click the **Notify AOL** button in the lower-right corner of the chat-room window. This feature acts much like the **Notify AOL** button available in Instant Message windows (described in the next task).

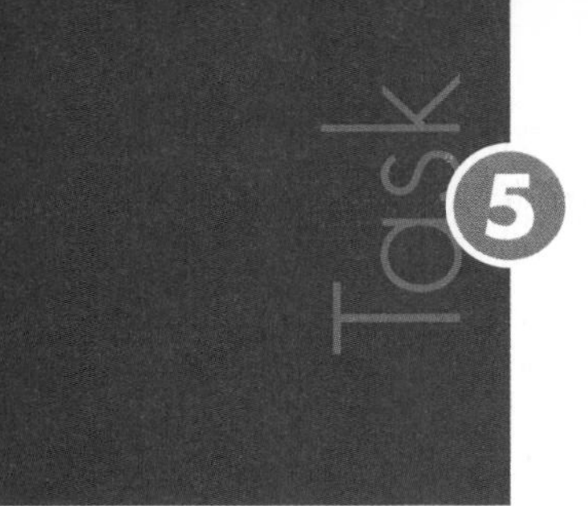

How to Send Instant Messages on AOL

Instant Messages are a great way to get someone's attention—to invite a person to join you in a chat room, ask a quick question, or just start a conversation. Each Instant Message is a private, person-to-person communication. Unlike email, Instant Messages are live interactions between two AOL members; you can send these messages only to someone who is online. The only real delay is how long it takes to type your response and send it.

1 Open an Instant Message Window

To open an Instant Message window, click the **IM** button on the AOL toolbar. The **Send Instant Message** window opens.

2 Type the Screen Name

In the **To** box, type the screen name of the person to whom you're sending a message. (Note that you can send Instant Messages only to other AOL members.) To see whether your acquaintance is online before you send the message, click the **Available?** button.

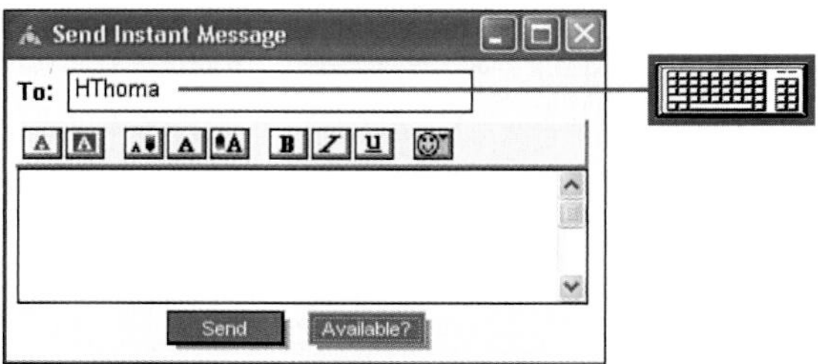

3 Check Whether Person Is Online

A dialog box opens, informing you whether the person is online (you can't send Instant Messages to people who aren't online). Click **OK** to close this box.

4 Type and Send the Message

In the **Send Instant Message** dialog box, type your message in the text box and click **Send**.

5 Respond to an Instant Message

Your acquaintance will receive the message in an **Instant Message** window that lists you as the sending party. There's a good chance he or she will write you back, in which case you'll see the message in the upper pane of an **Instant Message** window like the one shown here. (You may also hear a tone to alert you to the incoming message.) To respond to an Instant Message, just type your response in the lower pane and click the **Send** button. If you do not want to respond to the message, click **Cancel**.

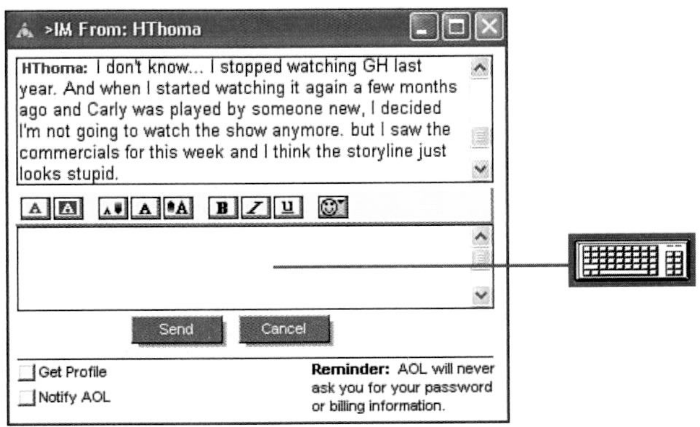

6 Continue the Exchange

Continue exchanging messages with your acquaintance by entering your responses in the lower pane and clicking **Send**.

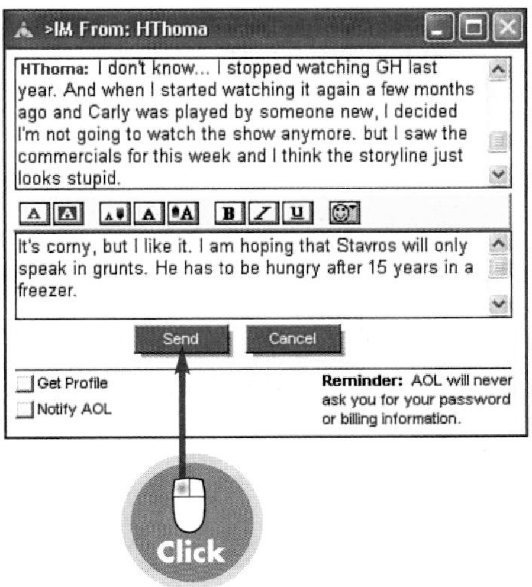

How to Hint

Reviewing Instant Messages

If you want to review your Instant Message exchange, use the scrollbar in the upper pane of the **IM From** window. The window contains every message you have sent or received in the conversation since the window opened.

How to Add Someone to Your AOL Buddy List

The easiest way to chat with people you know on America Online is to put them on your **Buddy List**, a feature that enables you to keep track of friends, co-workers, and other acquaintances who also use AOL (or a separate software called AOL Instant Messenger). After you add an AOL user to a Buddy List, AOL will notify you when that person has connected to AOL so that you can send him or her an Instant Message.

1 View Your Buddy List

When you join AOL, an empty Buddy List is created for you. To see your list so that you can add people to it, click the **more** arrow next to **People** on the AOL toolbar and choose **Buddy List**. The **Buddy List** window opens.

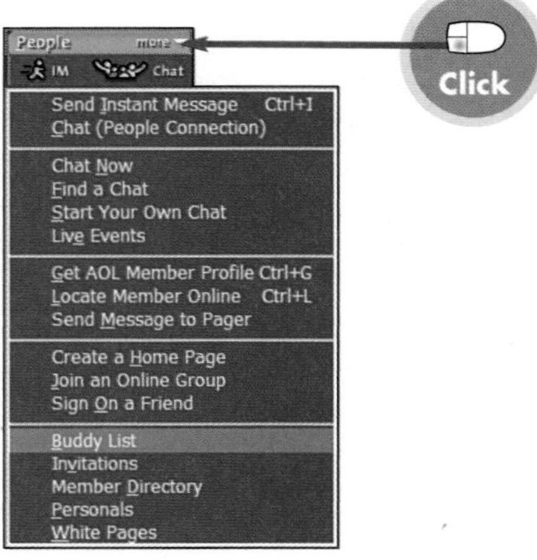

2 Set Up a List

When your Buddy List is created, it has three groups: **Buddies**, **Family**, and **Co-Workers**. To add a buddy to any of these groups, click the **Setup** button. The **Buddy List Setup** dialog box opens.

3 Work On a List

If you know the screen name of the person you'd like to add to your Buddy List, choose one of the three groups and click the **Add Buddy** button.

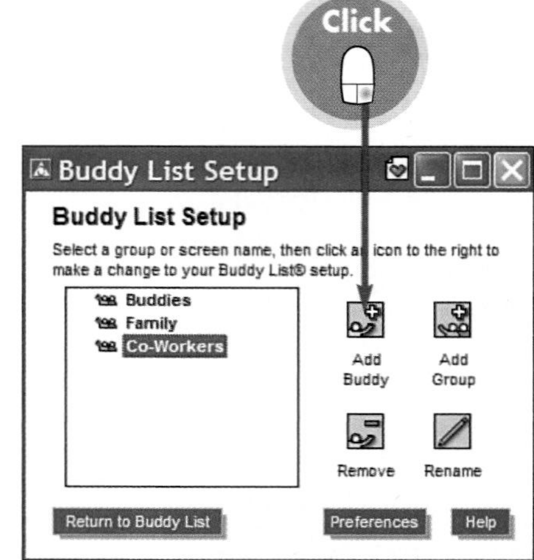

4 Add a Buddy

In the **Enter New Buddy's Screen Name** text box, type the screen name of the person you want to add to your Buddy List and click **Save.**

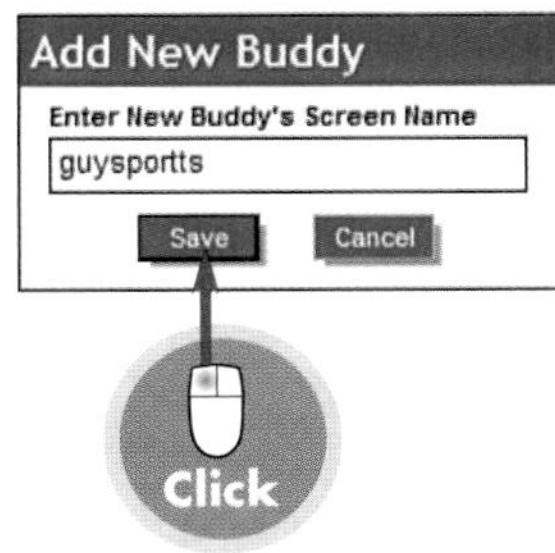

5 Close the Setup Window

After you have finished adding buddies, click **Return to Buddy List** to close the dialog box.

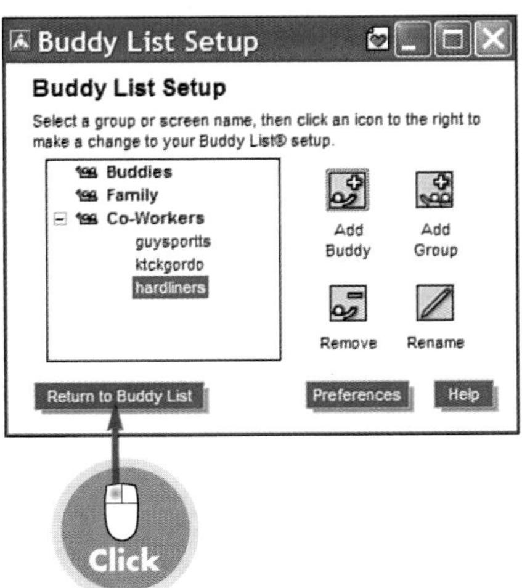

6 Send a Message to a Buddy

Because you are connected to AOL, the **Buddy List** window displays the screen names of the buddies who are online. To send an instant message to one of these people, click the appropriate buddy category (**Buddies**, **Family**, or **Co-Workers**) to see a list of buddies in that group. Click the screen name of the person you want to chat with and then click the **Send IM** button.

How to Hint

Letting Others Know You're Too Busy to Chat

If you are too busy doing something on America Online to chat with your buddies, you can let them know by using the **Away Message** feature. To do so, first open the **Buddy List** window (click the **more** arrow next to **People** on the AOL toolbar and choose **Buddy List**). Then click the **Away Message** button. A dialog box opens from which you can choose a message that explains why you are unavailable for instant messages.

How to Block Objectionable Content from Your AOL Account

Like many aspects of the Internet, America Online offers features you may not think are suitable for younger audiences. If you're sharing an America Online account with a child, you can set up a more restricted version of the online service by utilizing AOL's parental controls. To use these controls, you must create a new screen name for the child to which the controls will be applied. You can have up to seven screen names with your America Online 7.0 account.

1 Establish Controls

To begin setting up a restricted America Online screen name, click the arrow next to **Settings** on the AOL toolbar and choose **Parental Controls**. The **AOL Parental Controls** dialog box opens.

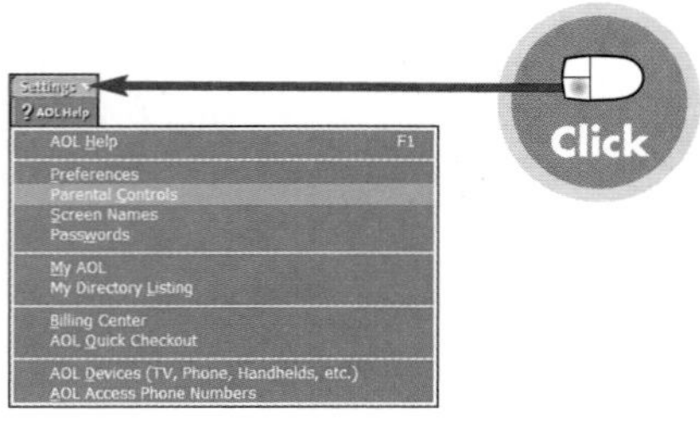

2 See Screen Names

Click the **Create Screen Names** link near the bottom of the screen to open a window where you can see your current screen names, find out more about names, or create a new one. In this new window, click the **CREATE a Screen Name** link. You will be presented with several windows explaining how parental controls operate. Read the information that appears in these windows until you come to the **Step 1 of 4** window.

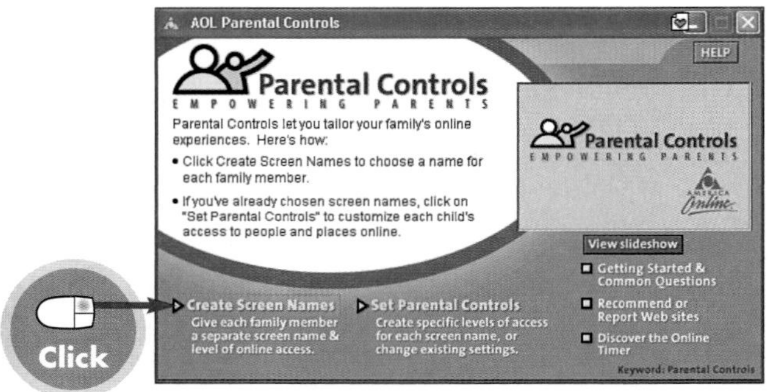

3 Choose a Name

Screen names can be as many as 16 characters long. Type the name you want to use and click **Continue**. In this example, the new screen name `Jax Jaguars 2002` will have parental controls applied to it.

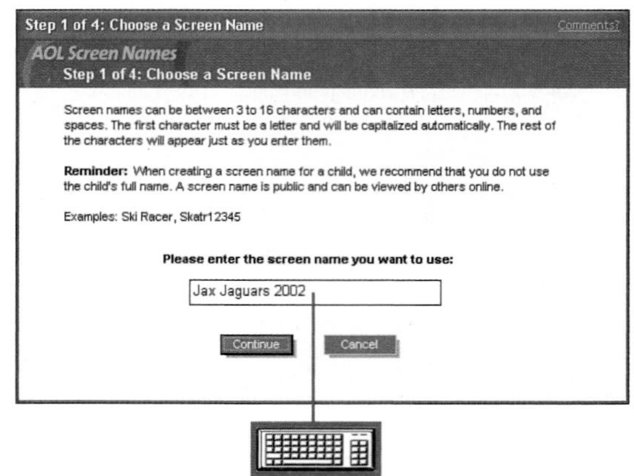

4 Choose a Password

In the first text box, type the password you want to use with this screen name. (The password you type for this username should be different from the one on your main America Online account.) In the second text box, verify the password by typing it again. Click **Continue**.

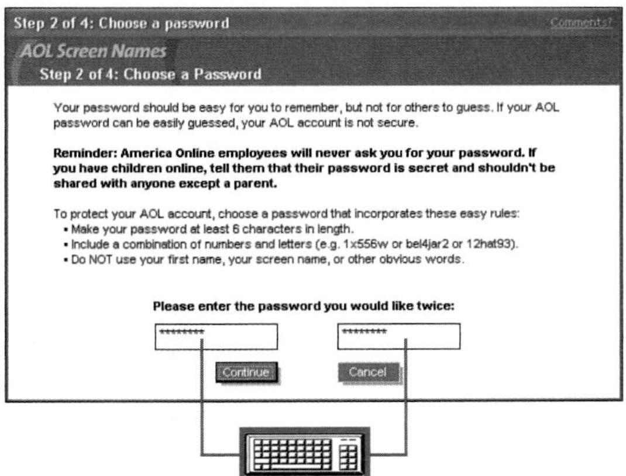

5 Choose a Category

AOL offers four parental-control categories, each with a different combination of restrictions. Click the radio button next to the category you want to restrict this screen name to and click **Continue**.

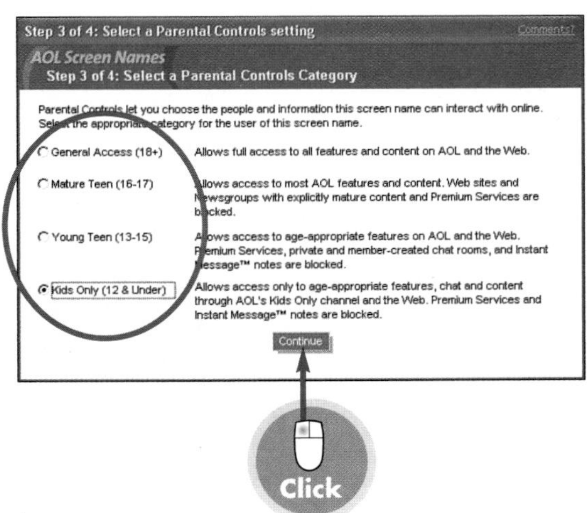

6 Set Up Controls

To set up parental controls exactly as they were described in the category you picked, click the **Accept Settings** button. To make specific changes to the controls, click the **Customize Settings** button.

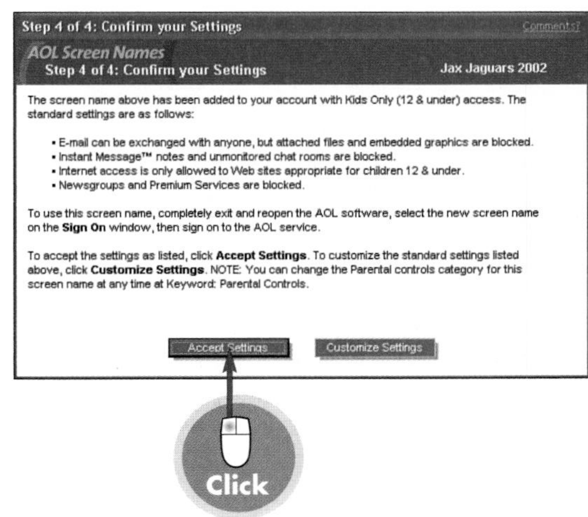

7 Test the Controls

The best way to see whether your parental controls are suitable is to try them out. From the menu bar at the top of the screen, choose **Sign Off**, **Switch Screen Name**. Log in to America Online using the restricted screen name and password, and then use chat, the World Wide Web, Usenet newsgroups, and instant messaging.

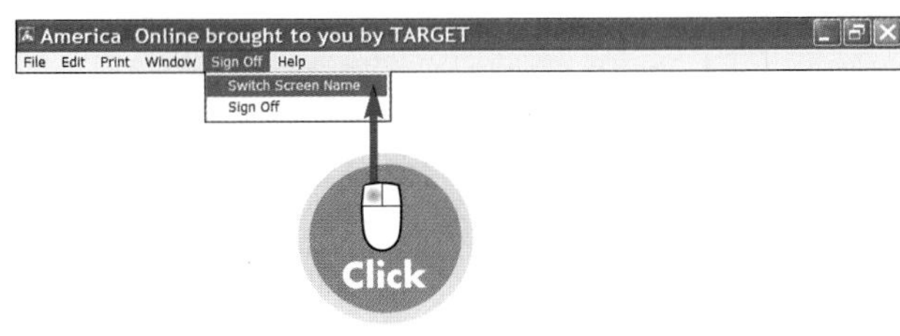

Task

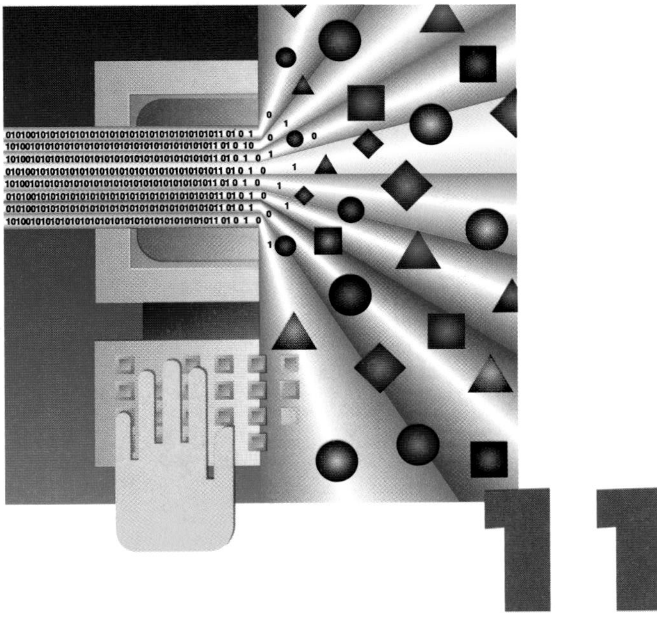

11

Listening to Audio and Viewing Video over the Internet

One of the best reasons to have high-quality speakers on your computer is the Internet. MP3 (short for *MPEG-1 Audio Layer 3*) is a popular format for presenting recorded sound on a computer.

Sound is also presented on the Internet as *streaming audio*, which begins playing immediately rather than at the end of a complete download.

Video is available on the Internet in several popular formats: Microsoft Audio-Visual Interleave (AVI), Apple QuickTime, and Moving Pictures Expert Group (MPEG)—a video technology pioneered by the same group as MP3. Two free software programs you can use to play audio and video files are Windows Media Player 7, which is included with Windows XP, and Winamp, a popular free MP3 player by AOL's Nullsoft division.

How to Find Windows Media Audio and Video Files

Windows Media Player 7, the version included with Windows XP, can play audio and video files in several formats, including Windows Media (WMA) and MP3 files. It supports streaming audio and video in the WMA format. The Media Guide feature of the software makes it easy to find ways to use the software; a mini-browser included in the player presents new audio and video of interest. You can also use the Windows Media Guide on the Web: Type `http://windowsmedia.msn.com` in your browser's **Address bar** and press **Enter**.

1 Start the Player

To start Windows Media Player 7, click **Start** and choose **Windows Media Player** (or choose **Start**, choose **All Programs**, and choose **Windows Media Player**).

2 Find New Music

Windows Media Player displays a Media Guide in a Web browser inside the player. Click a category's hyperlink.

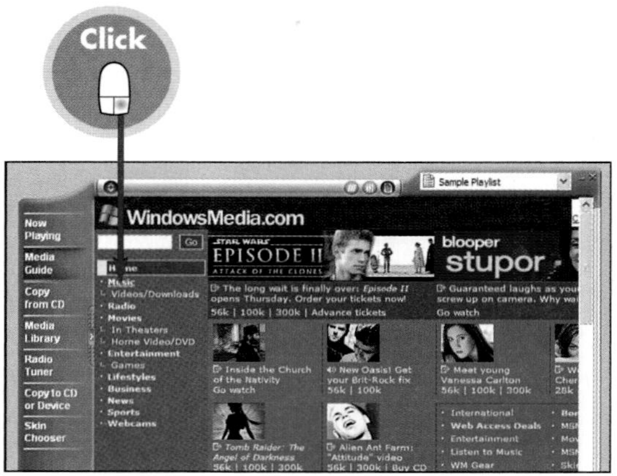

3 Choose Something

To load a file, click the hyperlink associated with your modem speed (people using a dial-up modem should choose **28k** or **56k**; others can choose **100k** or higher).

4 Visualize the Song

Songs can play in the background while you're using the player's browser to view Web pages. Click the **Now Playing** button to see Windows Media Player 7's *visualizations*, animations that change in response to the MP3 file being played.

5 Choose a View

The name of the visualization is displayed at the bottom of the animation. Click one of the arrows next to the name to see a different visualization.

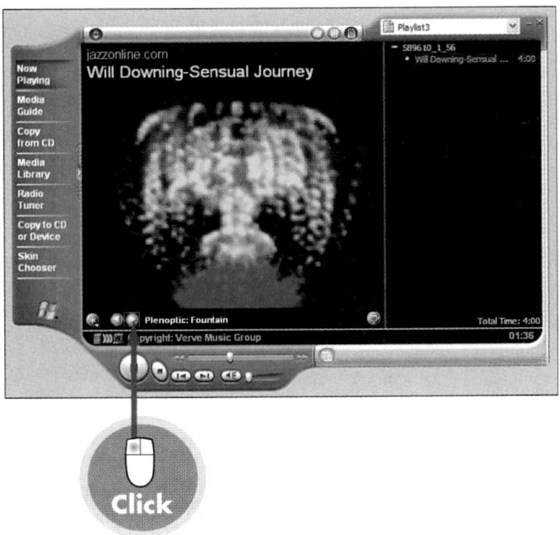

6 Find More Music

To find more audio and video files in Windows Media format, return to the Media Guide by clicking the **Media Guide** button.

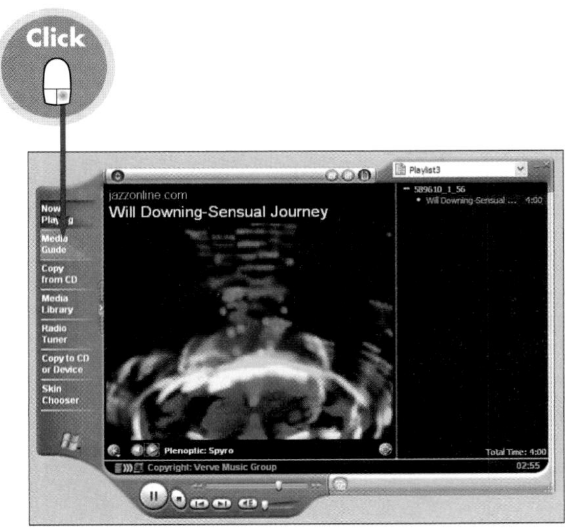

How to Hint

Changing the Appearance of the Player

Windows Media Player 7 supports a feature called a *skin* that lets you change the appearance of the player. To choose a new skin for the player, click the **Skin Chooser** button along the left edge of the player (you might have to use the down-arrow button to see this button). Click a skin's name to see a preview of it and then click the **Apply Skin** button to choose it. Click **More Skins** to open a Microsoft Web site offering more than 100 additional user-defined skins.

How to Listen to Web Radio Stations

Thanks to the Internet, you are no longer relegated to listening to local radio stations. These days, thousands of radio stations around the world reach a global audience by streaming audio over the Internet. In addition, there are hundreds of new stations that exist only on the Net. Windows Media Player 7 includes a Radio Tuner that can help you find many of these stations, whether you're looking for a specific station; trying to find news, sports, or another format; or just randomly searching the dial.

1 Open the Radio Tuner

Open the Windows Media Player by choosing **Start**, **All Programs**, **Windows Media Player**. To tune in a radio station, click the **Radio Tuner** button.

2 Try a Station

The Radio Tuner lists several popular radio stations in the **Featured Stations** list. To tune in to one of these stations, click the name of the station to expand its listing, and then click its **Play** hyperlink. The station begins playing in Windows Media Player.

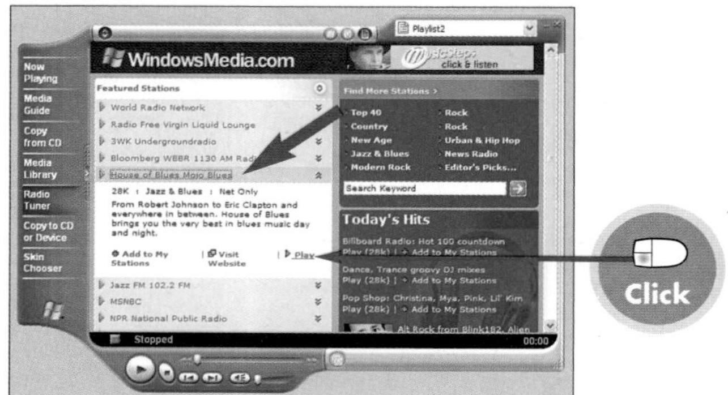

3 Add a Preset

Like a real radio, Media Player can be set up with *presets*, shortcut links to your favorite stations. Click a station's **Add to My Stations** hyperlink to make it one of your presets.

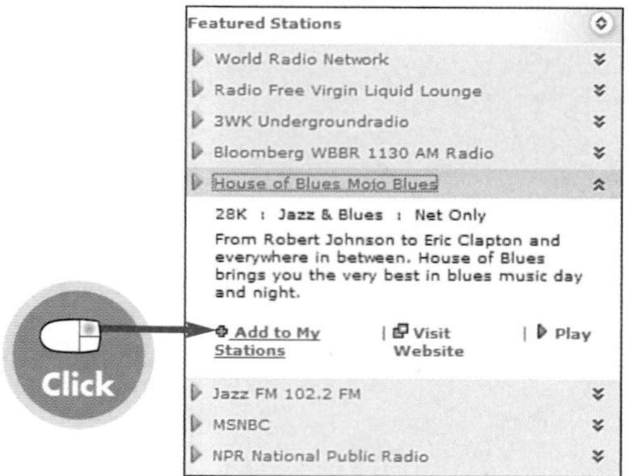

4 Find a Station

The Radio Tuner's **Find More Stations** section contains links to stations organized by format such as **Country**, **Rock**, and **Top 40**. To search for other formats (or specific stations), type a format or station in the text box and click the arrow button next to the box.

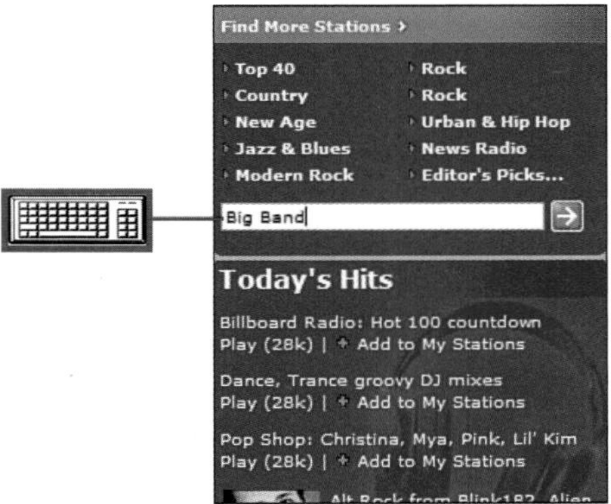

5 Listen to a Station

Radio Tuner lists all stations that match the text you are searching for. To listen to a station, click its name to expand its listing, and then click its **Play** link if one is available. Otherwise, click **Visit Website** to play it.

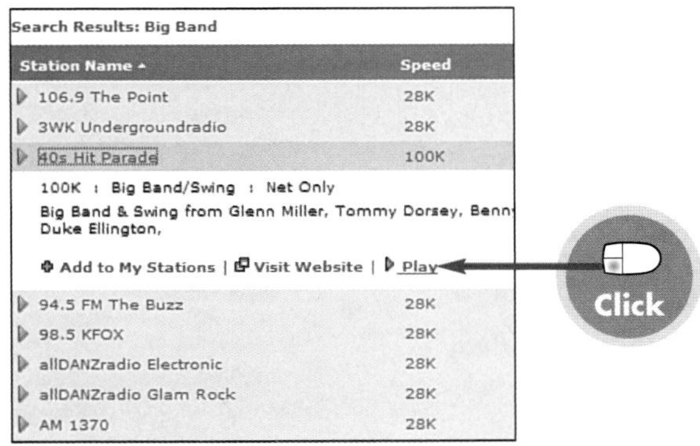

6 View Your Presets

All station listings in the Radio Tuner include **Add to My Stations** links so you can quickly compile a list of your favorites. To see your list, click the **Return to My Stations** hyperlink.

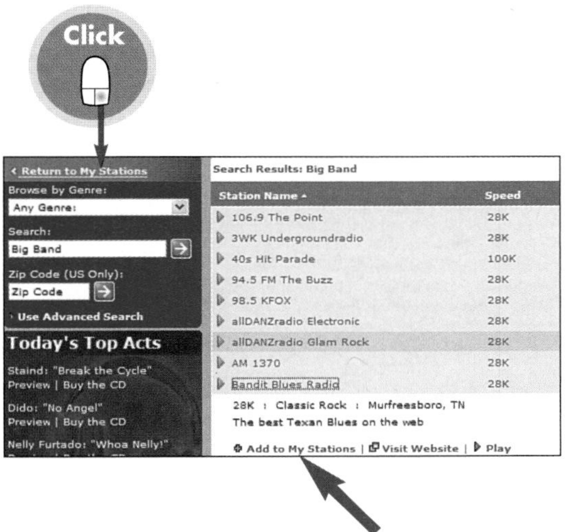

7 Listen to a Preset

To listen to your favorite station, click its name to expand the station listing and then click its **Play** or **Visit Website** link.

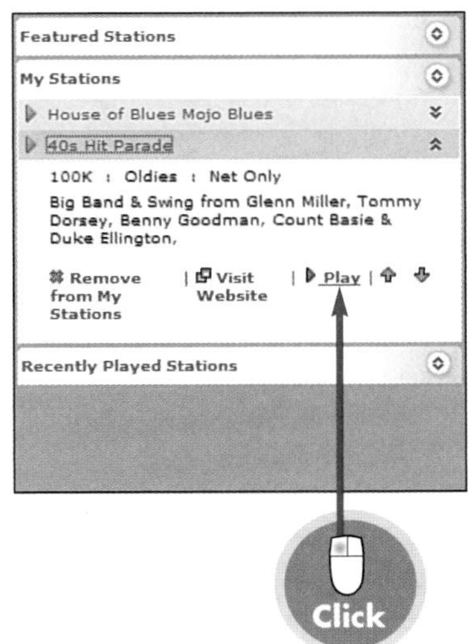

How to Install an MP3 Player

The most popular way to present recorded music on the Internet is in MP3 format, an audio standard that can store roughly one minute of music per megabyte of disk space. To play MP3 files, you must have one of the software programs that support this format. Winamp, a free program from AOL's Nullsoft division, is one of the most popular MP3 players. Winamp comes in Full, Standard, and Lite versions. The full version includes support for Windows Media Audio, the format designed for Windows Media Player; the Standard version includes visualizations.

1 Find the Download Page

Launch your browser, type `http://www.winamp.com/download` in the **Address bar**, and press **Enter**. A Web page opens offering several versions of the Winamp MP3 player.

2 Choose a Version

The Winamp download page lists the features of each version of the software. Select the radio button at the bottom of the page for the version you want to use and click **Begin Download**.

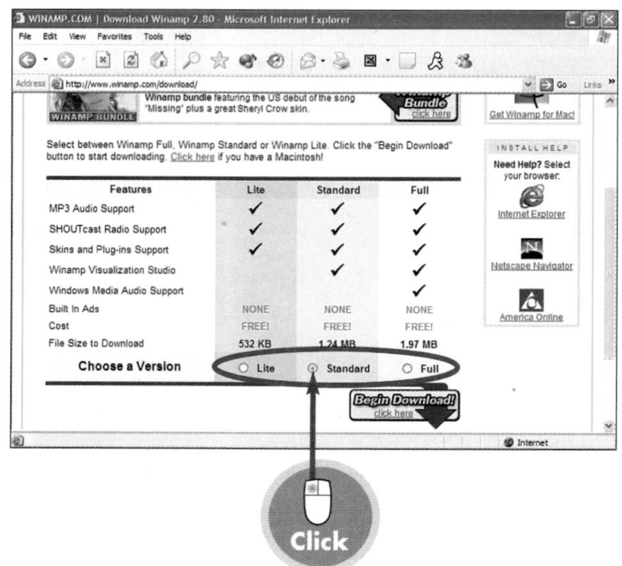

3 Install from the Web

A **File Download** dialog box opens before the download begins. To install Winamp directly from the Web, click the **Open** button. When the download is complete, review the software's license agreement and click **Next** if you agree to its terms.

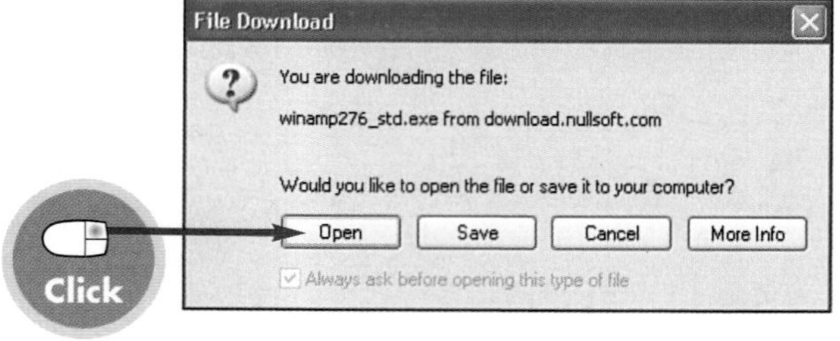

4 Choose Winamp Settings

Choose the components you want to install by enabling check boxes or by selecting a prearranged setup from the **Select the type of install** drop-down box. Most users should leave these settings as is. Click **Next** to continue.

5 Choose a Folder

Accept the recommended folder in which Winamp will be installed or click the **Browse** button to select a different location. Click **Next** after choosing a folder.

6 Review the Settings

Choose where Winamp icons should be placed on your computer and other installation settings. Enable the **Associate with audio CDs** check box if you want Winamp to play musical CDs you put in your CD drive. (Otherwise, Windows Media Player will play them.) Then click **Next**.

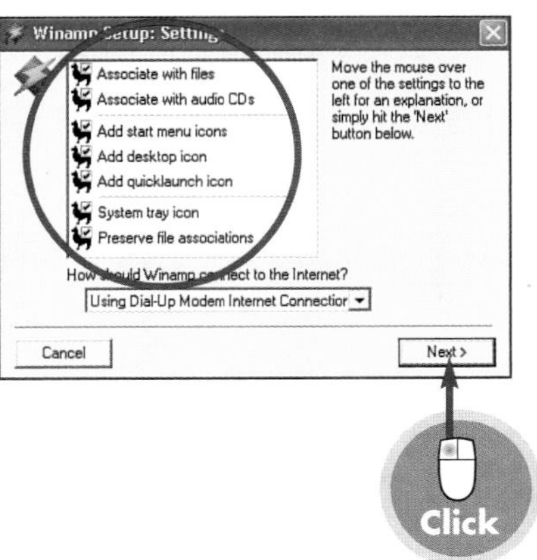

7 Identify Yourself

Type your email address and ZIP Code in the text boxes and use the check boxes to sign up for any of several optional services. Make sure that you deselect the check boxes for services you don't want. Click **Next;** a dialog box appears to indicate that Winamp has been installed.

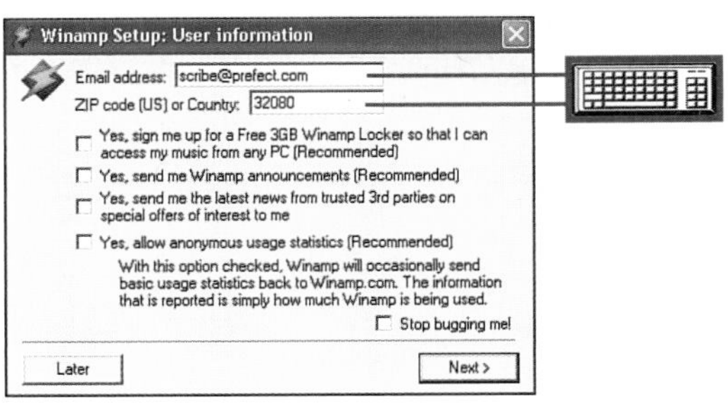

Task 4

How to Listen to an MP3 File

There are dozens of different sound-file formats, including WAV for recorded sound, RealAudio for streaming audio, and MIDI for sounds played by computer-generated instruments. MP3 has become enormously popular in a short time because it can approximate CD-quality audio in a relatively small file size and because numerous MP3 players and CD recorders are available. Several companies make portable MP3 players that can handle the same files you play with a program such as Winamp.

1 Load an MP3 File

To play an MP3 file with Winamp, open the folder that contains the file and double-click its icon. The Winamp window opens and the file begins playing immediately.

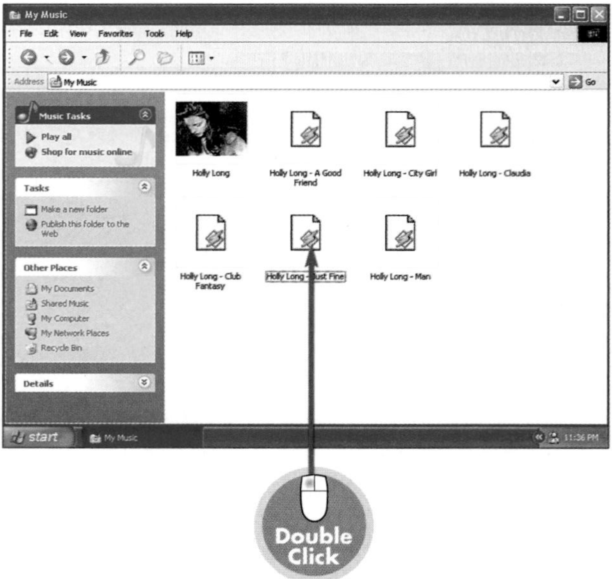

2 Add to the Playlist

Winamp includes an equalizer, a playlist manager, and a mini-browser. To add an MP3 file to the current playlist so that you can "queue up" several songs to play in succession, click the **Add** button and then click **Add File**.

3 Choose a File

Using the **Add file(s) to playlist** dialog box, open the folder that contains the file you want to add to your playlist, click the file, and then click the **Open** button. The file will appear on the Winamp playlist and will be played in sequence with the other listed files.

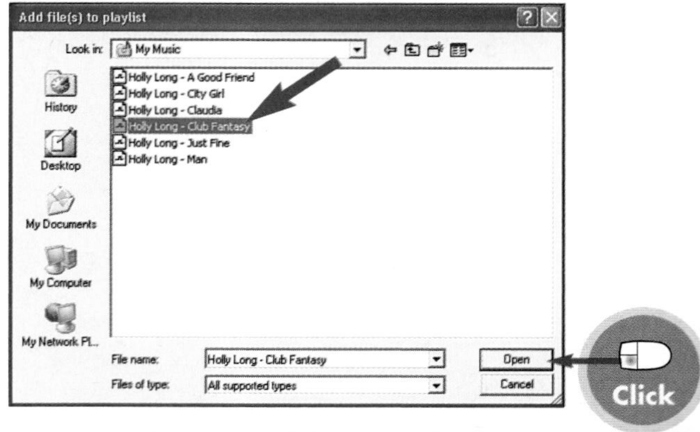

4 Save a Playlist

You can save playlists to a file so that you can replay them later. Click the **List Opts** button in the **Playlist** window and then click **Save List**.

5 Name the Playlist

In the **Save playlist** dialog box that opens, type a name for the playlist in the **File name** text box, then click the **Save** button.

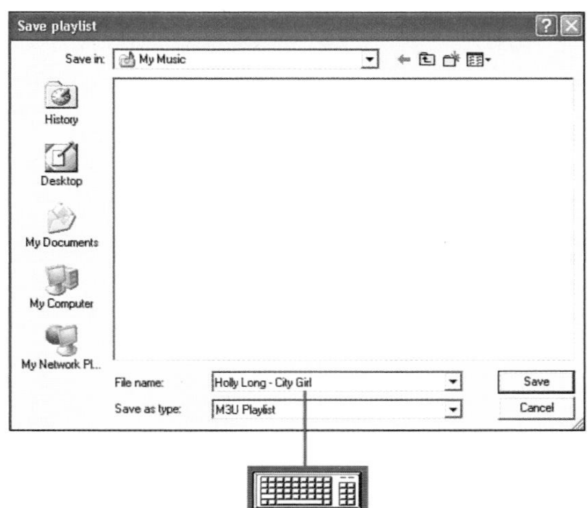

6 Play a List

To play the songs in a stored playlist, open the folder that contains the playlist and double-click its icon. Winamp opens with the playlist loaded and begins playing the first song in the playlist.

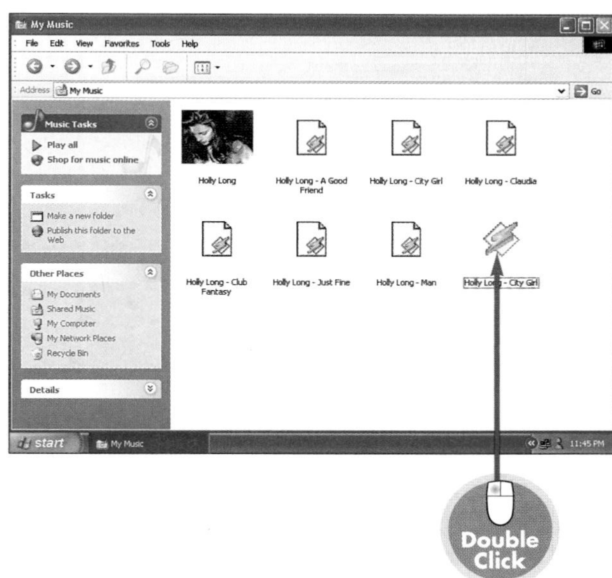

How to Hint

Evaluating Other MP3 Players

The World Wide Web site MP3.com has links to several MP3 players you can download. Type the URL **http://help.mp3.com** into your browser's **Address bar** and press **Enter** to visit this site. Click the **Download a player** hyperlink.

Sharing MP3 Files with Others

The most popular use for MP3 audio on the Internet is *file sharing*, downloading MP3 files from other people and making your own MP3 files available to others. In fact, more than 15 million people use file-sharing programs such as KaZaA and WinMX or services such as AudioGalaxy and Gnutella. Their popularity is controversial because these services do nothing to stop people from exchanging copyrighted music by popular musicians. The ZeroPaid Web site covers file-sharing news and offers links to popular software. To visit, type the URL **http://www.zeropaid.com** in your browser's **Address bar** and press **Enter**.

Task 5: How to Find MP3 Files to Download

The MP3 format does not have copy protection, so you can download a song in MP3 format and copy it to a Zip disk or to a writable CD. For this reason, many artists don't make many songs available in MP3 format on their own Web sites or on sites for online-music retailers. However, thousands of independent bands distribute their music in the MP3 format. One of the largest directories of songs in MP3 format is MP3.com.

1 Visit the Site

Launch your Web browser and type `http://www.mp3.com` in the **Address bar**. Press **Enter**. The MP3.com home page opens.

2 Browse a Genre

MP3.com is organized into different genres. Click a category hyperlink to see the most-downloaded MP3 files in that category.

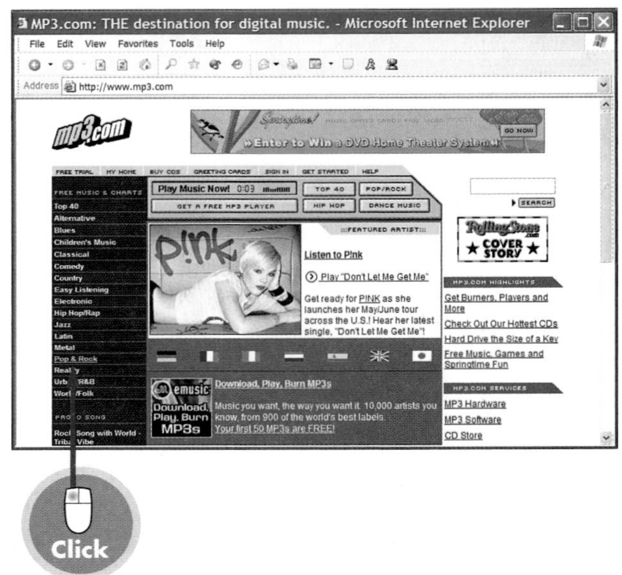

3 Search for Artists

The site is further divided into subgenres. Click a hyperlink to see artists in that category. To search for a particular artist, type the name in the box at the top of the page and click the **Search** button.

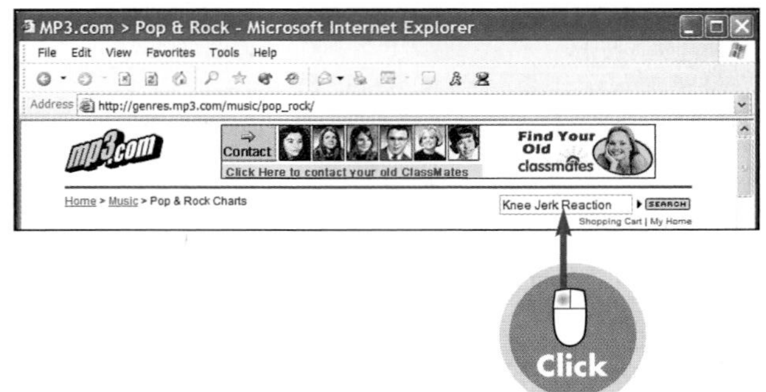

4 Visit the Artist's Page

A search-results page opens listing all artists that match the text you're looking for. Click a hyperlink to visit an artist's page on MP3.com.

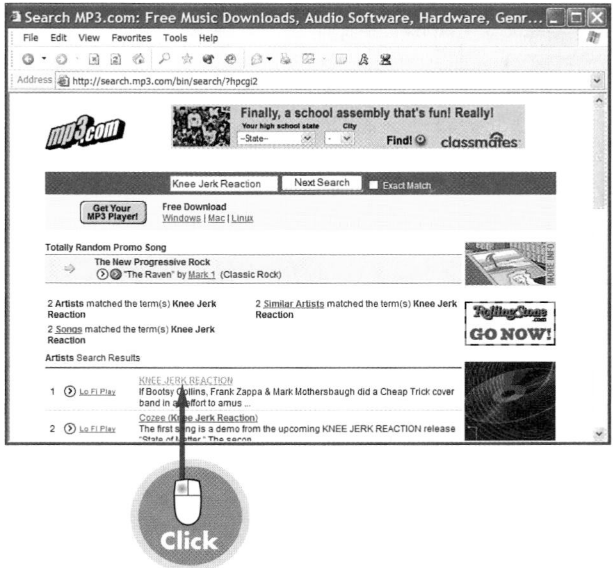

5 Open a Song File

When you find a song you'd like to listen to, click the **Download** hyperlink. Before you can download an MP3 file, however, you must answer a few questions about yourself.

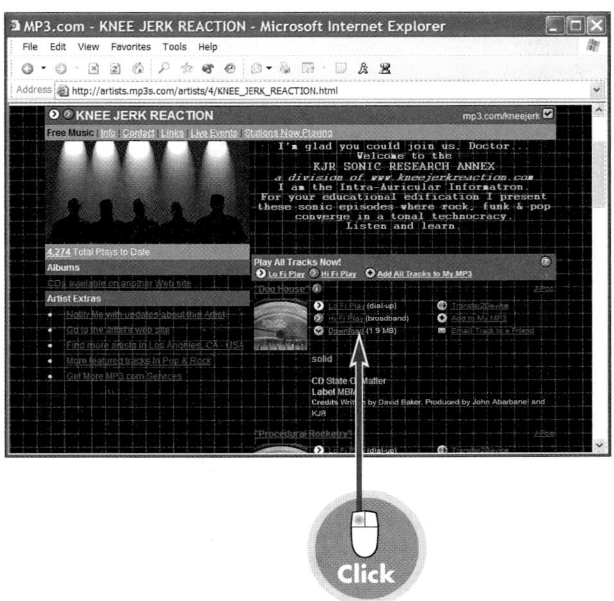

6 Identify Yourself

Type your email address in the **Email Address** box, answer the remaining questions, and click the **Get Free Music!** Button. A dialog box opens asking whether you want Internet Explorer to play the song. Click **Yes** to hear the song in the browser; click **No** to hear it in Winamp.

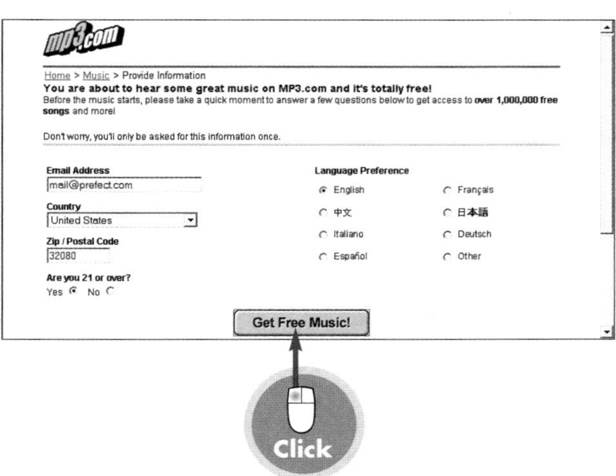

How to Hint

Saving MP3 Files Permanently from MP3.com

After you have downloaded an MP3 file from MP3.com, you may be able to save it to a folder on your computer instead of playing it (this feature is available only for certain songs). Right-click a song's **Download** link and choose **Save Target As** from the shortcut menu that appears. A dialog box opens, which can be used to choose a folder and filename for the song.

How to View Windows Media Video Files

As faster Internet connections such as cable modems and DSL become more popular, Web sites are catering to this audience by offering video files. Internet Explorer 6 can play video in three formats: Windows Media, Real, and QuickTime. Some files are broadcast as part of a Web page, while other files open in a separate window and begin playing. You can also find video files in the Windows Media Guide, covered in Task 1 of this part, "How to Find Windows Media Audio and Video Files."

1 Find a Video

The Web site WindowsMedia.com offers music videos, news reports, and other video you can watch on your computer. To see what's available, type `http://windowsmedia.msn.com` in your browser's **Address bar** and press **Enter**.

2 Choose a Video

Keep your Internet connection speed in mind when selecting videos to view. Dial-up modem users should select only the **28k** or **56k** link; users of other connection types can choose the links that represent faster connection speeds. To view a video, click one of its speed links.

3 Adjust the Volume

Internet Explorer 6 can play many Windows Media videos in a separate pane as you view Web pages. To adjust the video's volume, drag the volume slider to a new position.

4 Open a Player Window

Depending on your monitor's resolution, some videos may be too small to see in an Internet Explorer pane. To open the video in a larger window, click the **New Window** button.

5 Close the Window

The video player has buttons that work just like a VCR's buttons: pause, stop, rewind, and fast-forward. Some of these buttons will be inactive for streaming video, but you can always stop and pause video playback. Click the **x** button on the **Media** window's title bar to close the player.

How to Hint

How to View Apple QuickTime Video

Another popular format for video on the Internet is QuickTime, a multimedia technology pioneered by Apple that's supported on Windows and Macintosh computers. Before you can view a QuickTime file—often called a QuickTime movie—you must install the QuickTime 5 player. To get this free software, type the URL `http://www.apple.com/quicktime/download` into your browser's **Address bar** and press **Enter**.

Finding Video Files to View

Several popular World Wide Web sites offer video files. These sites are often tailored to people with high-speed Internet connections, because video files may take a half-hour or more to download on a 28.8Kbps or 56.6Kbps dial-up connection. To view video files in AVI, QuickTime, or MPEG format, visit these Web sites:

- **Ads.com** (`http://www.ads.com`): Features current television commercials:
- **Atom Films** (`http://atomfilms.shockwave.com`): A frequently updated selection of short films in categories such as animation, comedy, drama, and world (foreign).
- **Launch** (`http://music.launch.com`): Like the Windows Media Guide, has hundreds of music videos.

Task

12

Shopping on the Internet

For a medium not used for commerce until the early 1990s, the Internet has grown up quickly as a place to buy and sell. Thousands of companies now exist strictly to sell products or services online, including Amazon.com and NetFlix. Other companies have greatly altered their marketing strategy to offer online commerce, including Dell Computer, Barnes & Noble, and Fidelity Investments.

The Internet is also enabling new kinds of commerce to take place. For example, the eBay auction site, which enables anyone to sell in public auctions, has been so successful at uniting buyers and sellers that some people make their living on the site (as many as 75,000 at one time, according to one *Time* magazine report).

As a consumer, your main hesitation before purchasing something on the Internet may be the security of the transaction. Online retailers offer several things to help reassure customers, including *secure Web servers* that keep your billing information confidential as it is transferred from your computer to the retailer's Web server. Some Internet retailers also offer you the option to phone in your credit card number rather than send it over the Web.

How to Buy a Product over the Web

Shopping on the World Wide Web is comparable to making a purchase anywhere else: You browse through the products and services offered at a site such as CDNow or 1-800-Flowers, adding items to an electronic shopping cart if you decide to purchase them. When you're ready to complete your order, you check out, removing any items from your cart that you decided not to buy after all. Amazon.com, a trendsetter in online commerce, offers a shopping experience that's typical of these Web sites.

1 Visit a Store

To visit Amazon.com, launch your Web browser, type the URL `http://www.amazon.com` in the **Address bar**, and press **Enter**. The home page for Amazon.com opens.

2 Add an Item to Your Cart

There are thousands of pages on Amazon.com describing products for sale. Browse around for a while, following links and clicking your browser's **Forward** and **Back** buttons as necessary. When you find something you want to purchase, click the **Add to Shopping Cart** button.

3 View Your Cart

When you add something to your cart, Amazon.com recommends several other items that might be of interest. To view what's in your cart, click the **Edit shopping cart** button.

4 Review Your Cart

Amazon.com displays the contents of your shopping cart when you add an item. To purchase multiple copies of the same item, type a different number in the **Qty** text box.

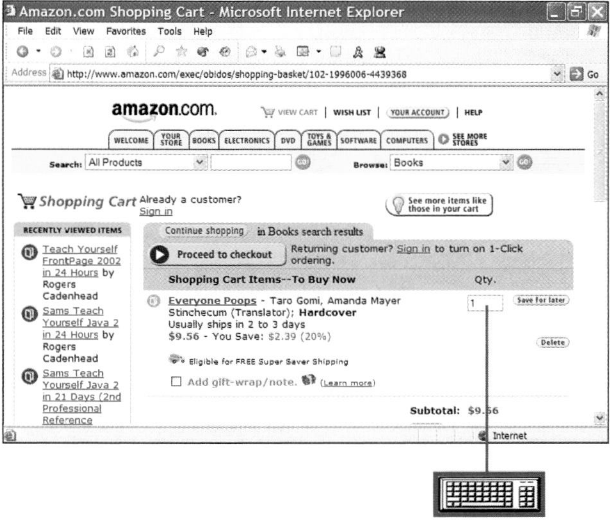

5 Remove an Item

To remove an item from your shopping cart, click the **Delete** button associated with that item.

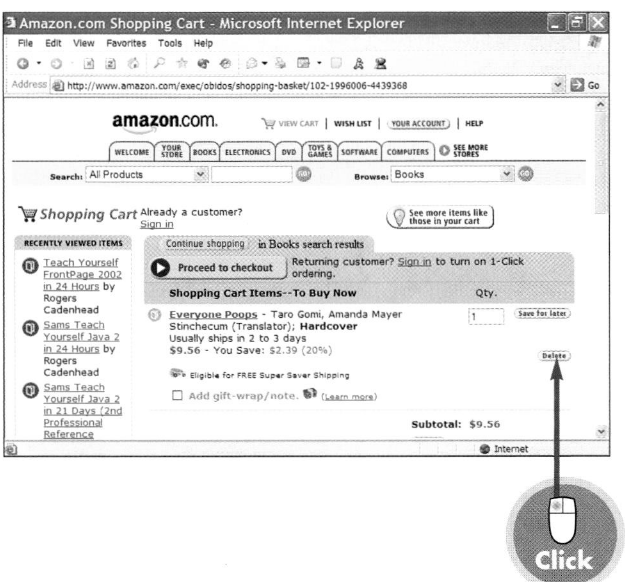

6 Proceed to Checkout

When you're ready to purchase the items in your cart, you can begin the process of buying them by clicking the **Proceed to checkout** button. (Otherwise, click **Continue shopping**.)

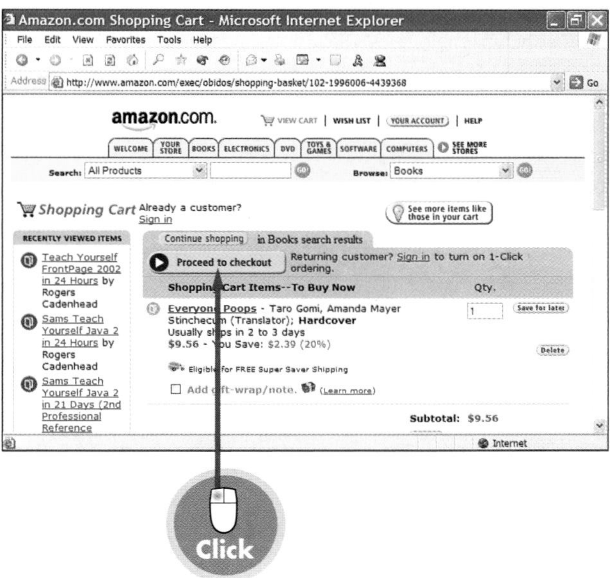

7 Identify Yourself

Type your email address in the appropriate text box. If you have never shopped at Amazon.com before, choose the **I am a new customer** radio button and click **Sign in using our secure server**.

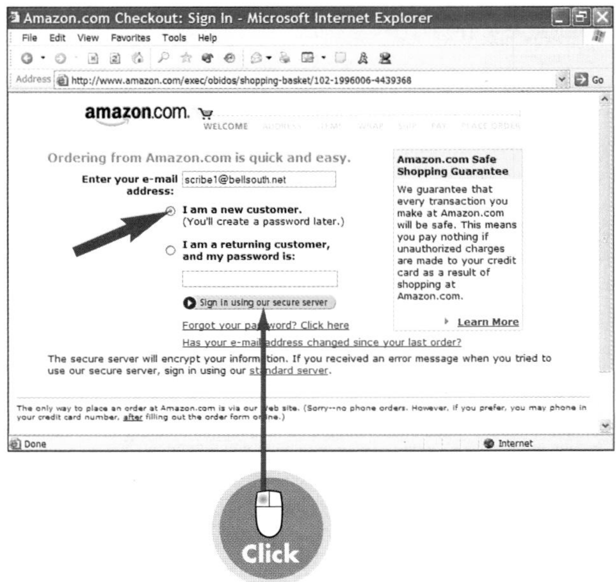

8 View Alert

Internet Explorer may display a Security Alert dialog box at this point to let you know the connection is secure. Click the **OK** button to continue.

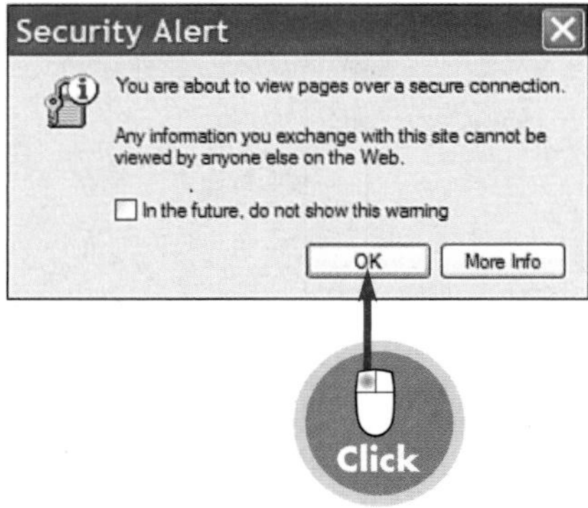

9 Check the Server

When Internet Explorer 6 loads a page from a secure server, a padlock icon is displayed in the status bar. Make sure that this icon is present before you provide confidential information such as your credit-card number on the site.

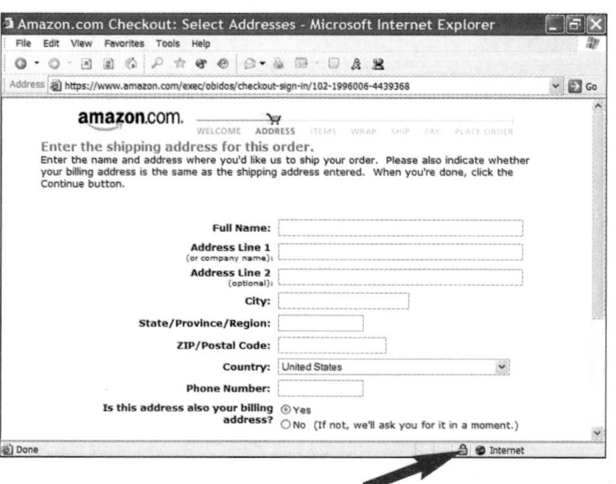

10 Provide Shipping Information

Use the text boxes to provide the shipping information requested by the store, including your name, address, country, and phone number. Click the **Continue** button to advance to the next checkout page.

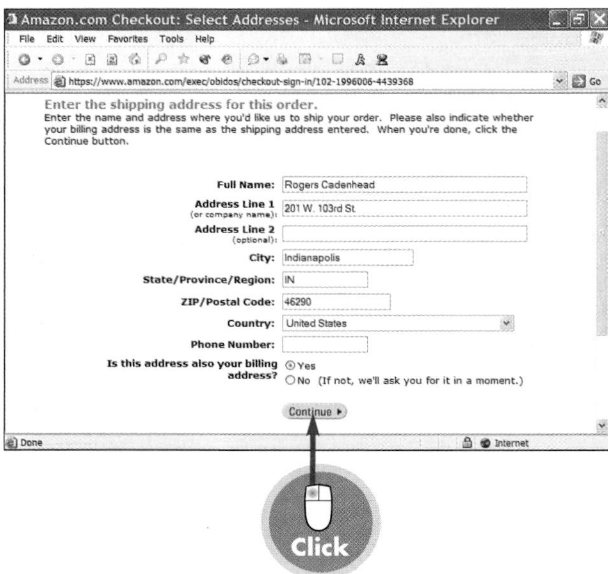

11 Select a Shipping Method

Click the radio button associated with the shipping method you want to use and then click the **Continue** button.

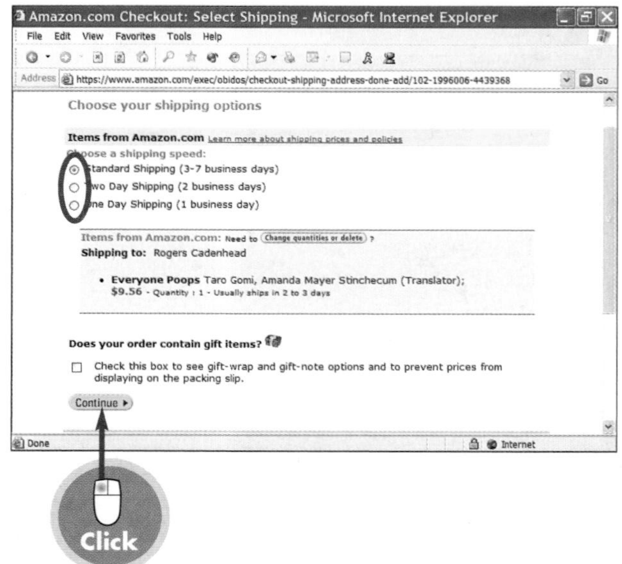

12 Select a Payment Method

You can pay Amazon.com with a credit card, check, or money order. If paying by credit card, choose a card type and then enter your card number, expiration date, and name in the appropriate text fields. Scroll down to continue.

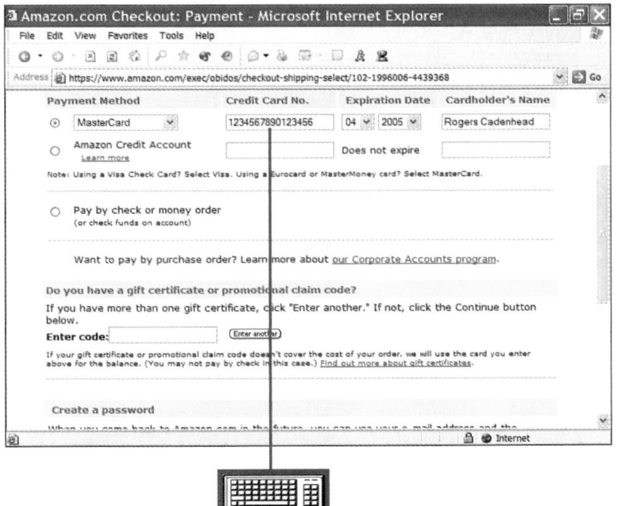

13 Choose a Password

On your first purchase, you must choose a password so you can shop more easily at Amazon.com in the future. Type a password in the **Enter a password** and **Type it again** text fields, then click **Continue**.

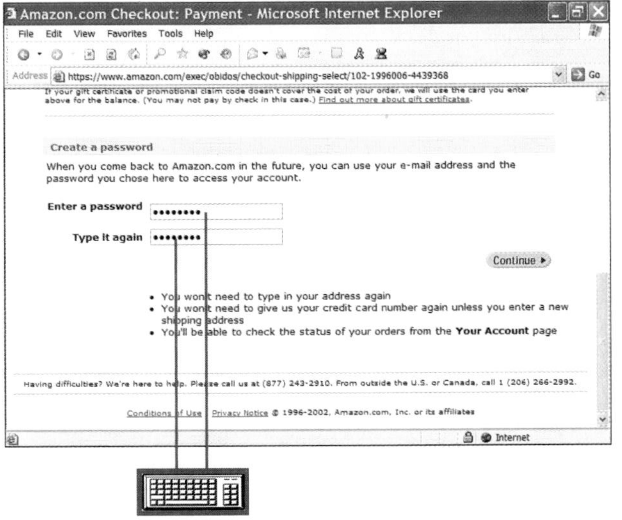

14 Confirm Your Order

Amazon.com displays the cost of your order and where it will be shipped. If everything is correct, and you want to make the purchase, click the **Place Your Order** button.

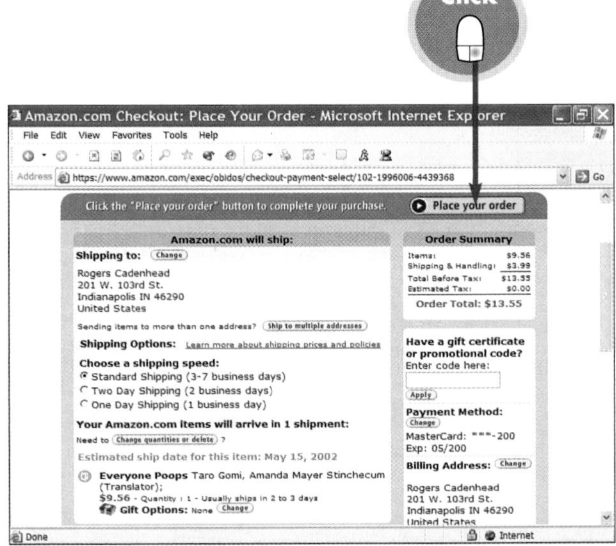

How to Hint

Tracking Orders on Amazon.com

After you order from Amazon.com, you can track when your purchases have been packed and shipped. Click the **Your Account** button at the top-right on any Amazon.com page.

Finding Stores on the Web

Each of the major portal sites offers directories of online stores; some portal sites such as Yahoo! sell products themselves. A quick way to find popular Internet retailers is to visit the Hotsheet Web site. Type the URL **`http://www.hotsheet.com`** into your browser's **Address bar** and press **Enter**, then scroll down to the **Shopping** heading.

How to Sign Up for eBay's Online Auctions

When the eBay World Wide Web site was launched, a new form of Internet shopping took hold—the world's largest garage sale. eBay acts as a middleman in online auctions, charging a small fee or a percentage from people who sell products through the site. Anyone can buy or sell items on the site, using a unique bidding system that keeps the buyer's maximum bid secret until after a sale. Users vouch for each other and report fraudulent transactions by contributing feedback ratings that are published about each seller.

1 Visit eBay

Launch your Web browser, type the URL `http://www.ebay.com` in the **Address bar**, and press **Enter**. The eBay home page opens.

2 Create an Account

Before you can buy or sell anything on eBay, you must register so that eBay can confirm that you're using a valid e-mail address. Click the **register now** button.

3 Use Your Passport

eBay accounts can be set up quickly using a Microsoft Passport. To use yours, click the **Passport Sign In** button.

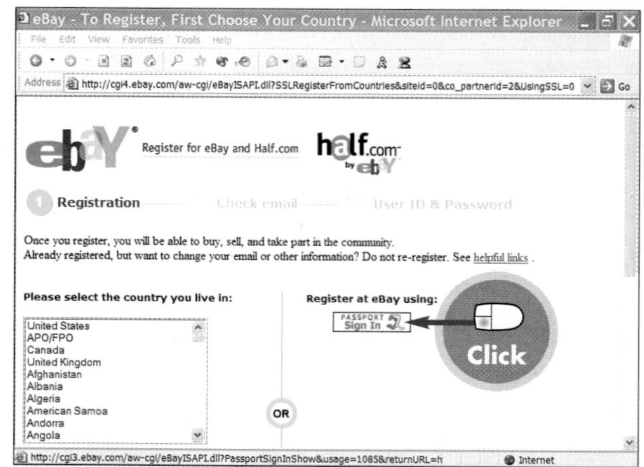

4 Provide Your Passport

Click the **Sign In** button. A dialog box may open asking for your Passport email address and password.

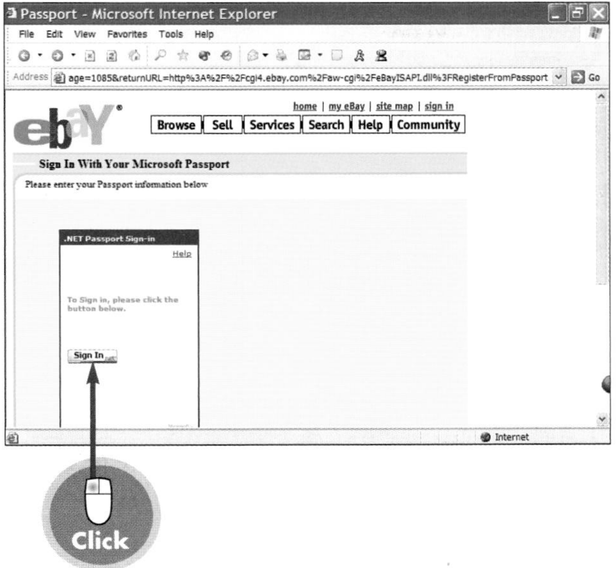

5 Choose Your Location

eBay asks for personal information in addition to what's provided by your Microsoft Passport. To begin, choose your country in the list box and click **Continue**.

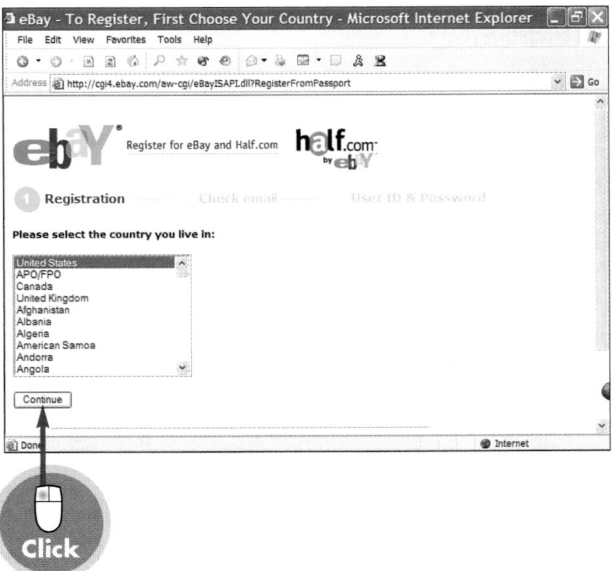

6 Identify Yourself

Fill out the registration form with your name, e-mail address, mailing address, and phone number. You also are asked several optional questions. When you're done, scroll down and click the **Continue** button. On the next page, review your information and click **Continue**.

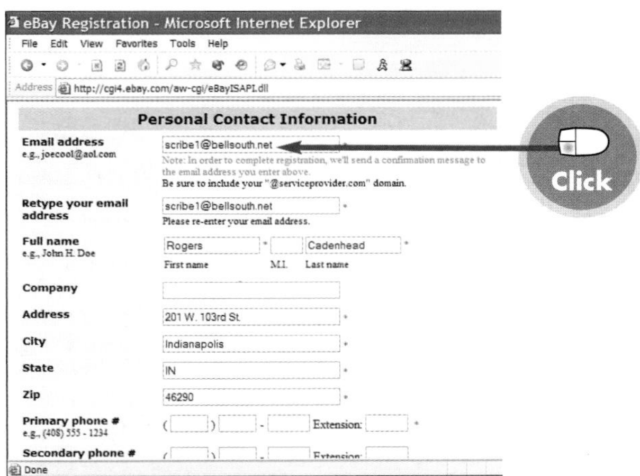

7 Complete Registration

Next, eBay displays its user agreement. If you agree to its terms, click each **I agree** checkbox and then click the **I Accept This Agreement** button. A confirmation code will be emailed to you. To join eBay, proceed to the next task, "How to Set Up a New eBay Account."

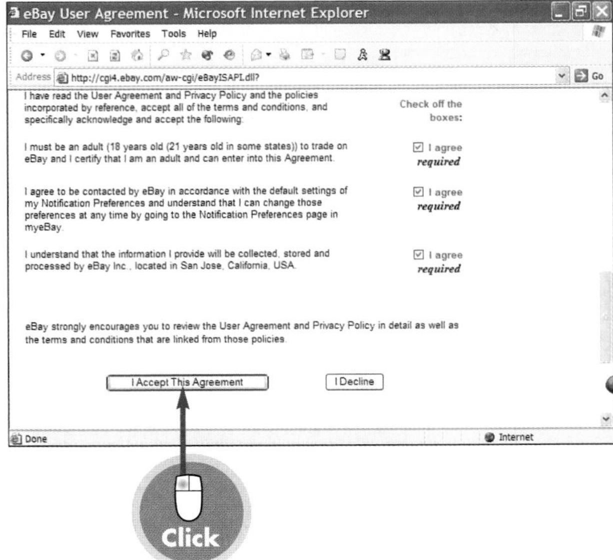

How to Set Up a New eBay Account

Before you can join eBay, you must register for an account, which is covered in the preceding task, "How to Sign Up for eBay's Online Auctions." To confirm that your email address is valid, eBay sends an email to the address you specified during registration. This confirmation letter should arrive in your inbox within 24 hours (although it can show up as quickly as five minutes after you sign up). You must click a hyperlink in this e-mail message in order to set up your eBay account.

1 Check Your Mail

Start your email program. If you're using Outlook Express: Click the **Start** button and choose **Email**. Outlook Express opens.

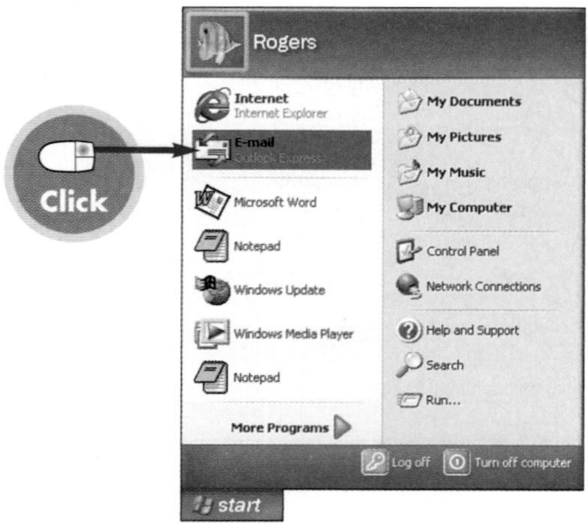

2 Read New Mail

In Outlook Express, click the **unread Mail** hyperlink to see new messages you have received. An **Inbox** window opens listing the mail in that folder.

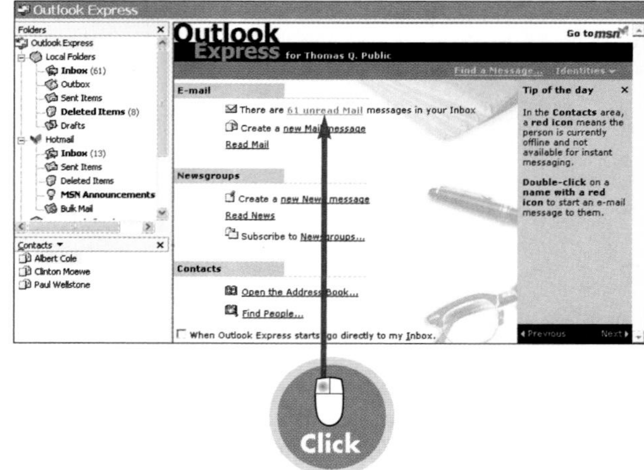

3 Read eBay's Letter

If e-mail has arrived from eBay, open it. The letter contains a hyperlink you can click to complete your eBay registration. Click this link. A Web page will load with your email address and a confirmation code already filled out.

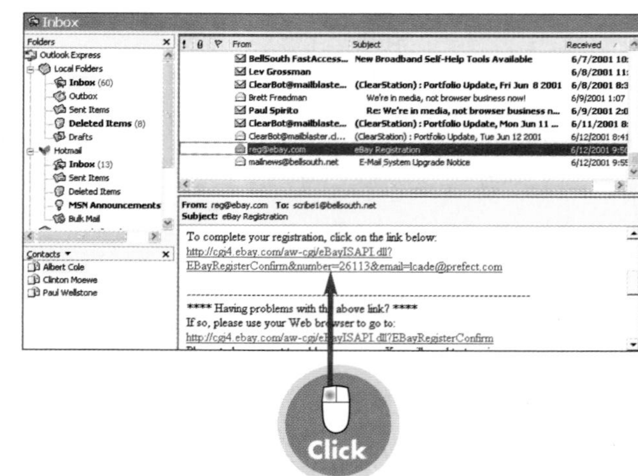

4 Choose a User ID

Type a user ID for your account in the **Your eBay User ID** text box. This ID will be used to log in to eBay and participate in auctions. It can contain letters, numbers, and some kinds of punctuation.

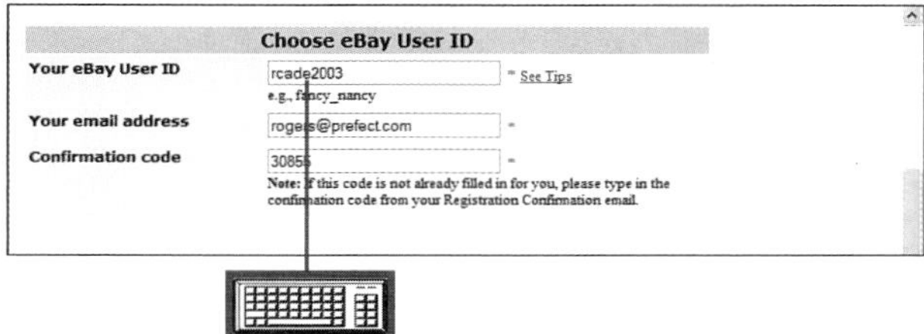

5 Choose a Password Hint

A password hint question can be used to request a new password if you've forgotten it. Type a question and answer in the boxes provided and click **Continue**.

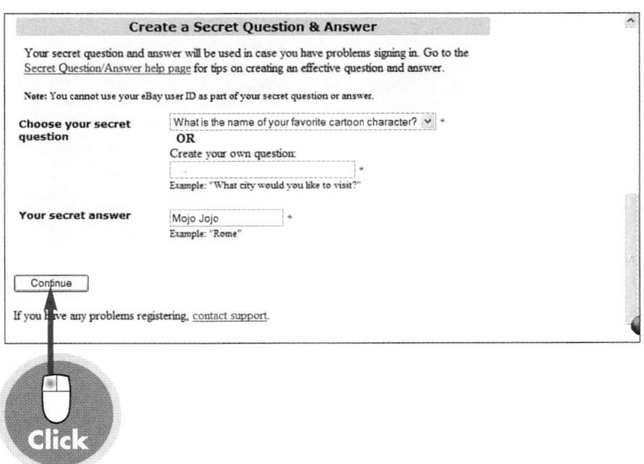

6 Choose an Alternate ID

There are 28 million eBay members, so your first choice of user ID is probably taken. If so, type a different one in the **Enter a new user ID here** box and click the **Enter** button. When you have a unique ID, eBay creates your account and you can begin using the site.

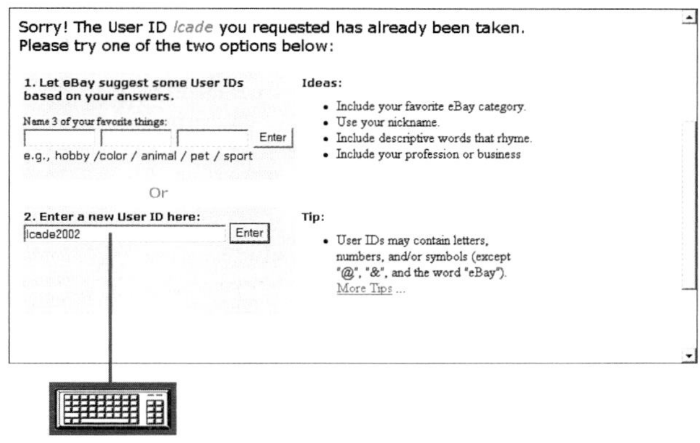

How to Hint: Choosing a New eBay Password

If you ever forget your eBay password, you can set up a new one using the secret question and answer you provided during registration. Click the **site map** hyperlink at the top of any eBay page, look in the **Services** column, and click the **I forgot my password** hyperlink. A page opens that displays your secret question and asks for the answer. If you answer correctly, you can choose a new password for your eBay account.

How to Bid in an Online Auction on eBay

After you have set up an account on eBay (which was covered in the last task), you can make bids in current auctions and sign up to sell items of your own. Bidding in auctions is free; you'll be notified by email if someone else outbids you. You also will receive an email message if you win an auction. When you win, you must contact the seller within 72 hours to arrange payment.

1 Search for Auctions

Launch your Web browser, type the URL `http://www.ebay.com` in the **Address bar**, and press **Enter**. To look for a certain item in current auctions, type the name of the item or a description of the item in the search box and click the **find it!** button.

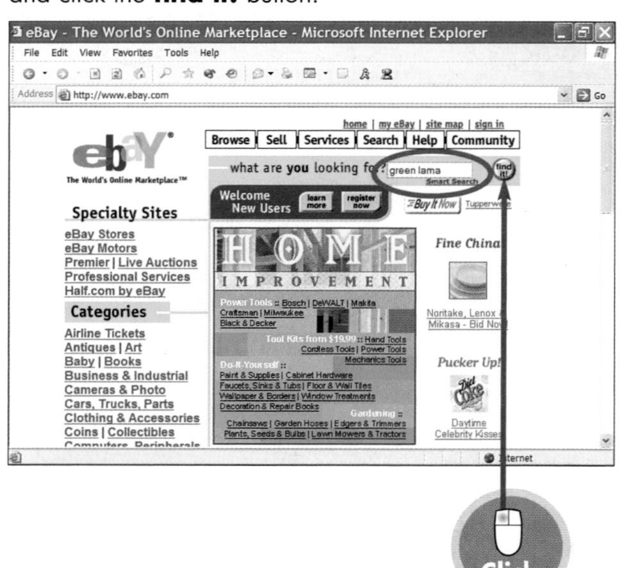

2 List Auctions

Any current auctions matching your search criteria are listed, along with the recent high bids. To find out more about an auction, click its hyperlink. You'll see a more detailed description of the item, possibly a photo of the item, and information about the history of the auction and the seller.

Picture	Current Items	Price	Bids	Ends PDT
	GREEN LAMA, Vol 1,No 5,1945, VG+ RARE	$79.00	-	May-24 04:57
	ELLERY QUEEN and GREEN LAMA RADIO SHOWS	$4.99	-	May-24 15:25
	GREEN LAMA RADIO SHOWS	$4.99	-	May-24 15:25
	vintage Tony Lama cowboy boots green leather	$20.50	4	May-24 17:05
	GREEN LAMA #6 1945	$49.95	-	May-25 14:04
	Green Lama Club Member's Kit	$36.00	2	May-27 06:15
	Green Lama #7 VG Super Bright	$40.00	-	May-27 17:24
	Green Lama #7 FN Super Bright	$60.00	-	May-27 17:31
	Green Lama #7 VG/FN Super Bright	$50.00	1	May-27 17:33

Click

3 View User Feedback

Every eBay seller has a *feedback rating*—a numeric ranking listed with his or her username. To view feedback that has been submitted about a seller, click the number next to the seller's username. You'll see a page listing comments that have been made by eBay users who have dealt with this person in the past.

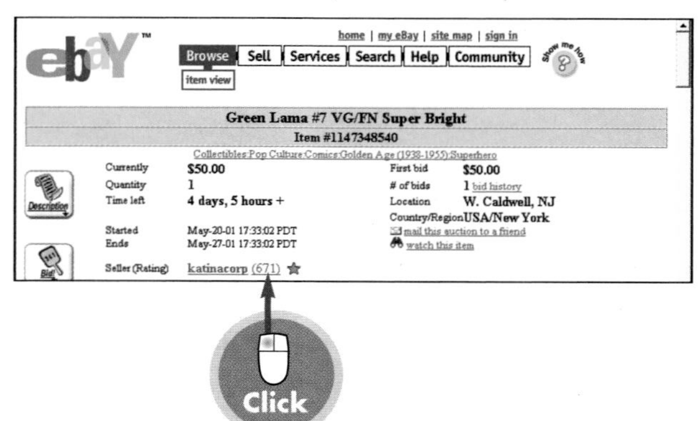

4 Place a Bid

To place a bid in an auction, scroll down the item's page until you see the **Bidding** section. Type your maximum bid in the text box and click the **Review bid** button.

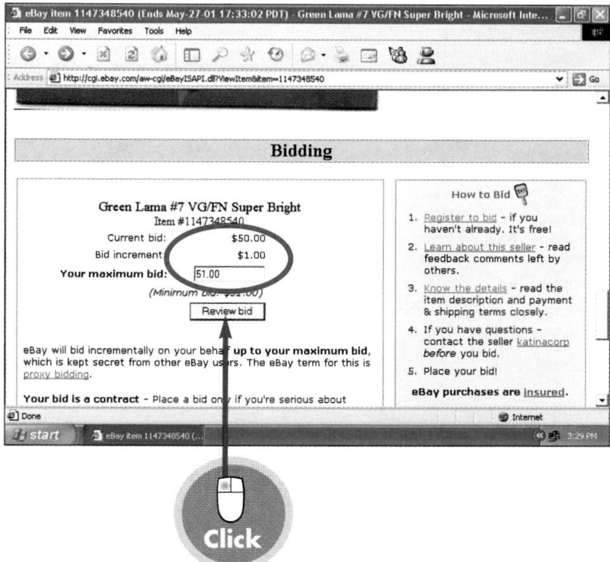

5 Confirm Your Bid

When you bid on eBay, your *maximum* bid is kept secret until after the auction. Your *actual* bid is the minimum amount needed to raise the current high bid. Click **Place bid** to confirm your bid.

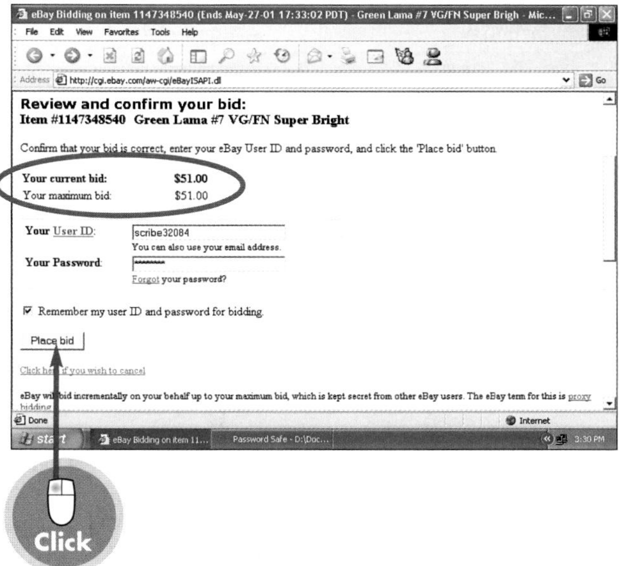

6 Bid Again

If your maximum bid is lower than someone else's, that user will outbid you automatically. You can submit a higher bid and try again: Type your new bid in the **Your maximum bid** box and click the **Review bid** button.

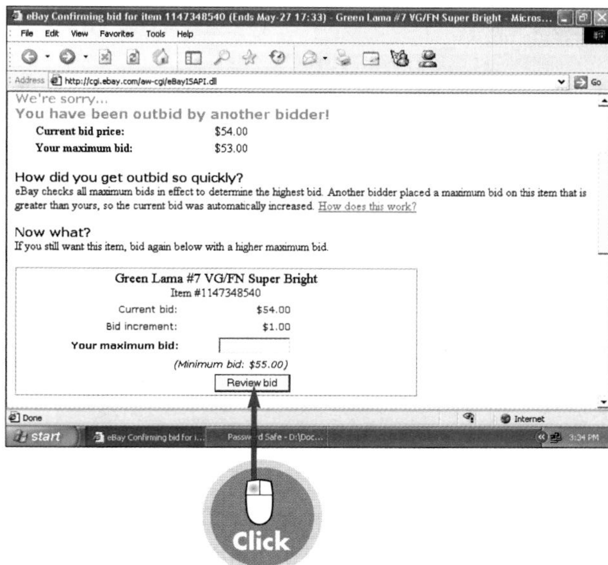

7 Bookmark an Auction

If you become the high bidder in an auction, you'll be sent an email message if another user eventually outbids you. To bookmark an auction page, make sure that the page is open in the browser, pull down the **Favorites** menu, and choose **Add to Favorites**.

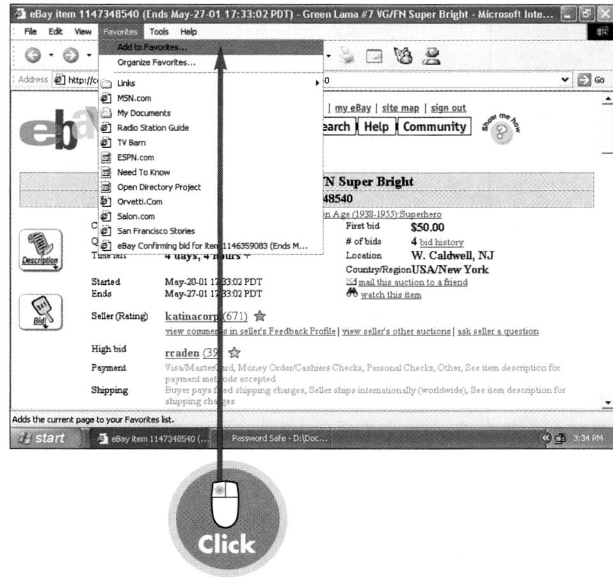

Task

13

Investigating Stocks, Taxes, and Savings on the Web

Although you can still deal personally with a broker, millions of investors are buying and selling stocks directly over the Web. They use online brokerages such as Datek and E*TRADE, placing and fulfilling an order quickly without the assistance of a professional broker. Transaction fees have dropped as low as $10.

The World Wide Web also brings information to investors that was not readily available to the public, such as technical analysis, historical data that can be immediately plugged into spreadsheets, and business news wires.

In addition to dozens of professional stock sites, you can use the Web for advice and information about other aspects of your financial well-being. These areas include taxes, savings, and mutual-fund investments.

Task

1 How to Find Current Stock Quotes

Dozens of World Wide Web sites cater to stock-market investors, including popular portals such as Yahoo!, Lycos, and the Microsoft Network. Several excellent sites offer free 15-minute–delayed stock quotes, historical stock-price information, discussion forums, and investment information. To get stock quotes without the 15-minute delay, you can join one of the online brokerages that help you trade stocks over the Web.

1 Visit a Stock Site

One free site that specializes in stock analysis is ClearStation. To visit this site, launch your Web browser, type the URL **`http://clearstation.etrade.com`** in the **Address bar**, and press **Enter**. The ClearStation home page loads.

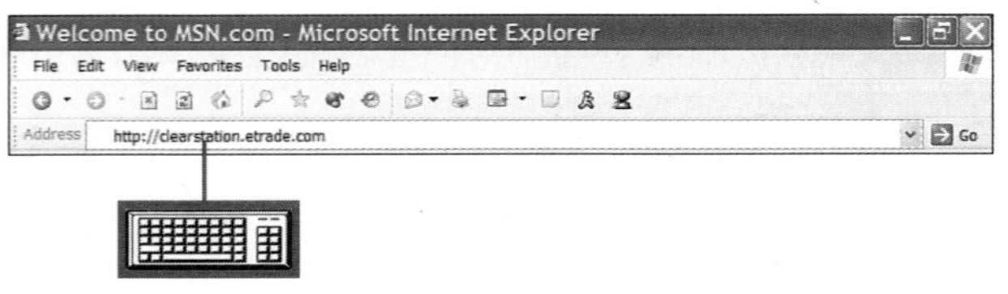

2 Look Up a Quote

You can view current stock quotes by using the stock's *ticker symbol*—a short, unique code assigned to the company by the exchange on which it trades. Type the ticker symbol in the text box and click the arrow button to the right of the box. The most recent price and a historical price graph will be displayed on a new page.

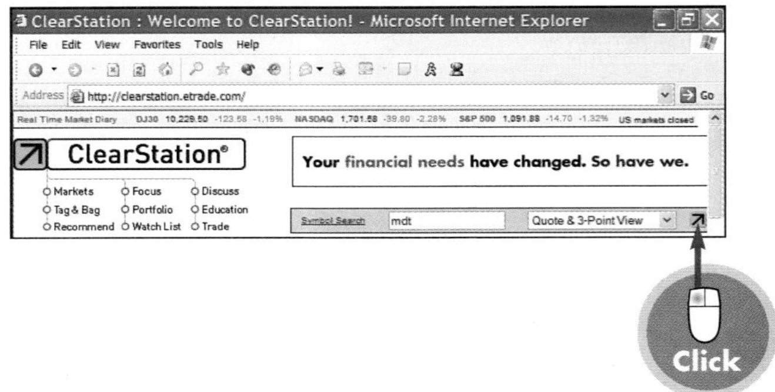

3 Read News

To see recent news stories and press releases that mention the stock you're investigating, click the **News Articles** hyperlink. Any available information is presented on a new Web page.

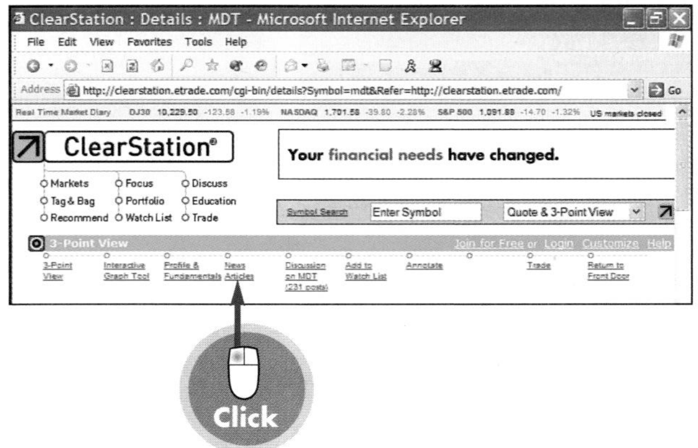

4 Find a Symbol

If you don't know a company's ticker symbol, click the **Symbol Search** hyperlink on any page in the site. A search page is displayed.

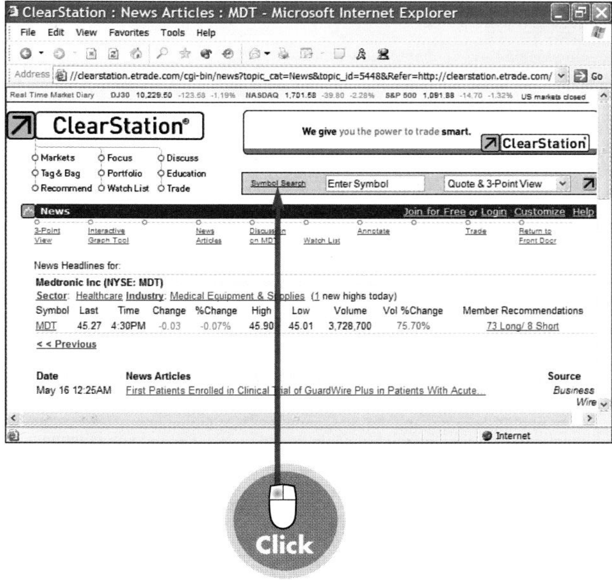

5 Search for a Company

To begin a search, type the name of the company you're looking for in the search box and then click the **Submit Query** button.

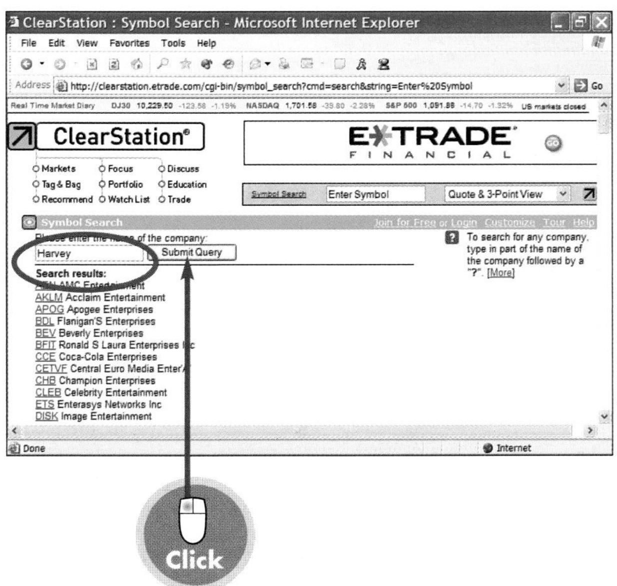

6 View Search Results

The ticker symbols for all companies that match words in the search name are listed. Click a ticker symbol to view the current stock price and other information about that stock.

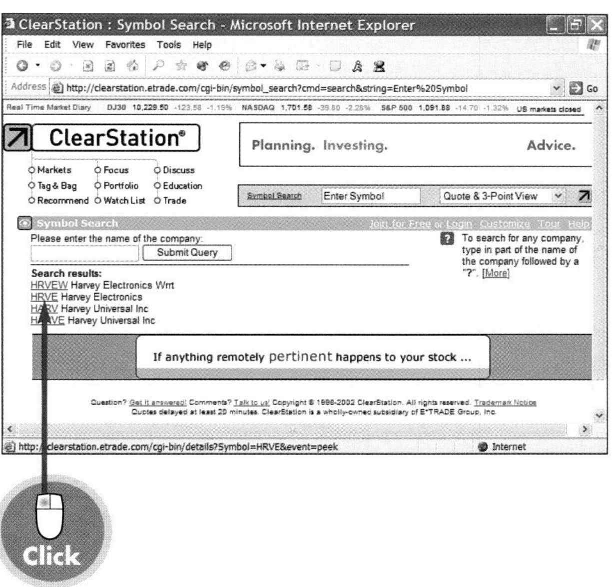

How to Hint

Finding Other Stock-Tracking Web Sites

ClearStation is a great resource for investors who make use of technical indicators such as the MACD and stochastic graphs. Depending on your investment strategy, however, you may find the services offered by other stock-information sites to be more useful. Visit the following URLs to try out other stock-market sites:

- **Yahoo! Finance**: `http://quote.yahoo.com`
- **The Motley Fool**: `http://www.fool.com`
- **Lycos Investing**: `http://investing.lycos.com`
- **MSN Money**: `http://moneycentral.msn.com`

Task 2

How to Create a Portfolio of Stocks You Track

Many World Wide Web sites that offer stock information can store a list of the stocks you're interested in—either because you own them or are thinking about buying them. If you own a stock, you can enter its purchase price and number of shares you own, and the site will display the current worth of your portfolio. To make use of these time-saving services, you must join a site to acquire your own username and password.

1 Join a Site

To join the ClearStation site, visit `http://clearstation.etrade.com`. When the home page loads, click the **Join Free** hyperlink.

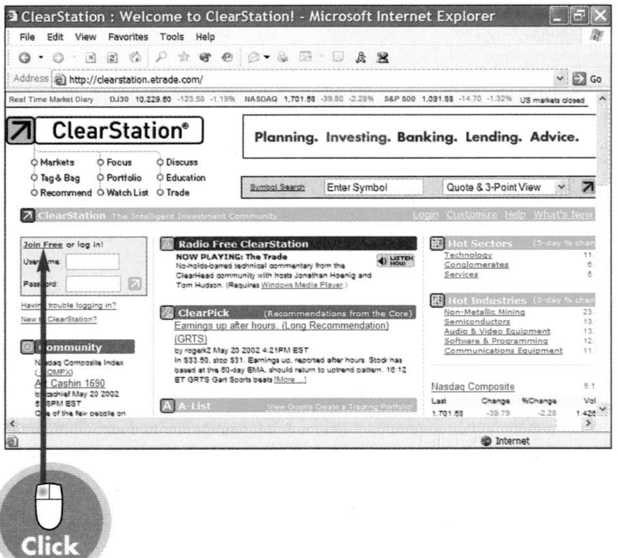

2 Identify Yourself

Fill out the text boxes on the membership form. Choose a username and password you will use on the site. When you're done, click the **Join** button. You will be presented with the site's member agreement and a short survey.

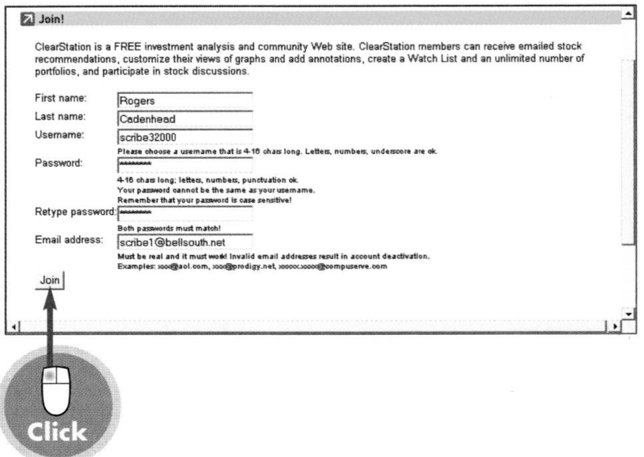

3 Set Up Your Portfolio

To start your portfolio with a list of the stocks you currently own, type each stock's ticker symbol in the **Portfolio Stocks** text box. Type a space (no commas) between symbols. Also, type a name for this portfolio in the **Portfolio Name** text box. Click the **Start Portfolio Build!** button to continue.

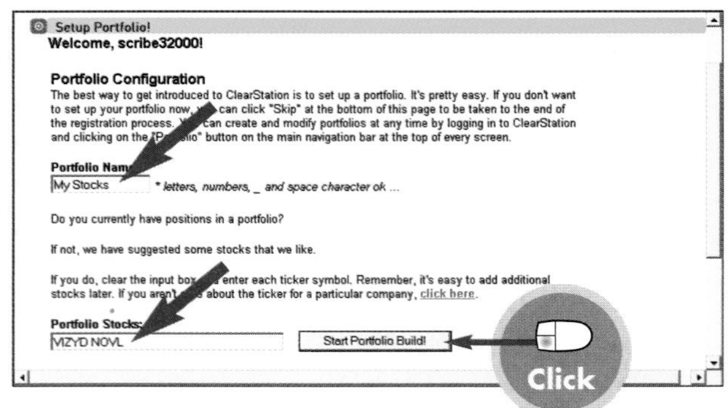

4 Describe Your Stocks

To complete your portfolio, provide price and quantity information about the stocks you have purchased. Click **Finish Portfolio Build!** when you're done. The **Watch List Configuration** page opens.

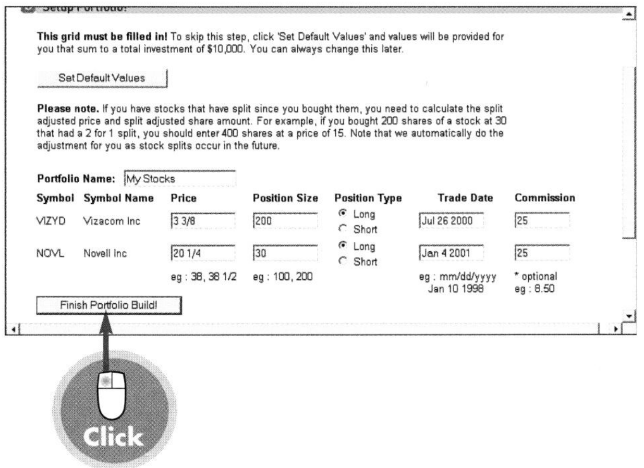

5 Set Up a Watch List

You can use ClearStation to monitor stocks you don't yet own by adding them to a watch list. To start your list, type ticker symbols in the **Watch List stocks** text box and click **Build Watch List**!

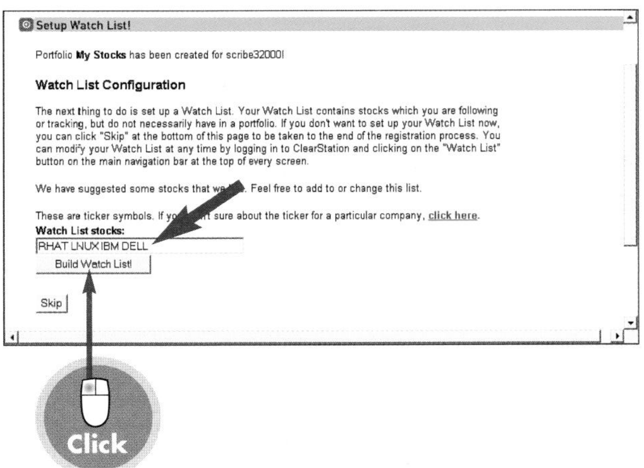

6 Create the Watch List

Click the **Finish Watch List Build!** button to add the watch list to your portfolio and to create the portfolio. A page opens with several email offers from ClearStation, including a chance to see the stock recommendations of the site's founder and several other investors.

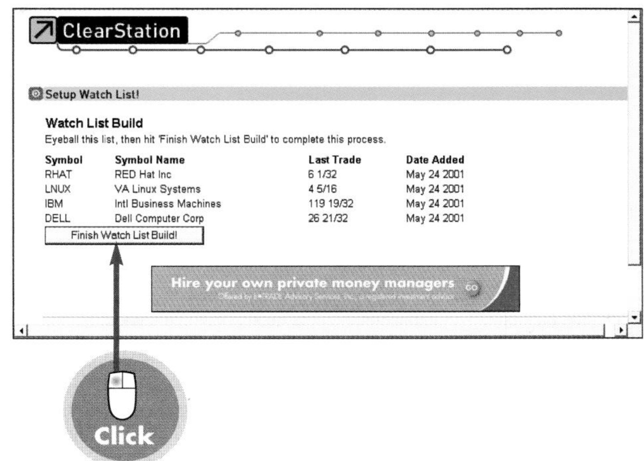

How to Hint

Entering the Purchase Price of a Stock

When you're adding a stock to a portfolio on ClearStation, you can use the fractional form of the stock price—such as 20 1/4 or 5 1/2. Many portfolio-tracking Web sites support this feature because stock prices are traditionally presented using fractions rather than decimals. Otherwise, make a note of the price as a decimal when you purchase a stock so that you can enter this price into a portfolio-management Web site.

How to Add and Remove Stocks from a Portfolio

Sites such as ClearStation and The Motley Fool offer a chance to manage a portfolio you've established with a brokerage. After buying or selling a stock through your brokerage, you make note of the purchase details on your portfolio-management Web site. On ClearStation, in addition to your actual portfolio (which is private), you can create a public portfolio of stocks that you recommend. ClearStation users can subscribe to the public portfolios of other people and will receive email whenever a change is made.

1 View Your Portfolios

Visit ClearStation at the URL **`http://clearstation.etrade.com`**. When the home page opens, log in with your username and password, then click the **Portfolio** hyperlink. A new page opens, listing your portfolios and any stocks you have recommended.

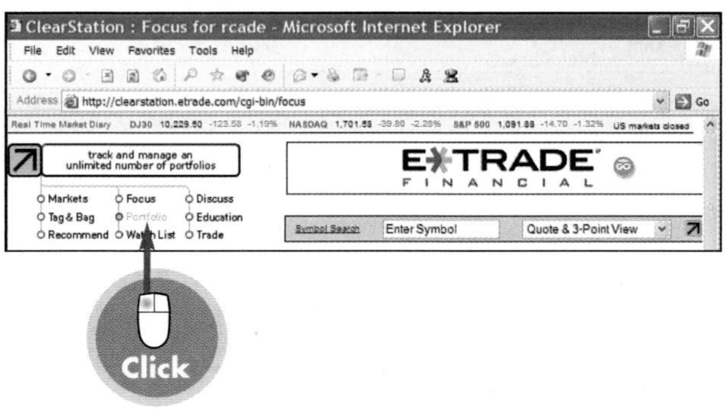

2 Choose a Portfolio

All your portfolios are displayed with their stocks' daily performances and their current values. To view a portfolio in more detail, click its name.

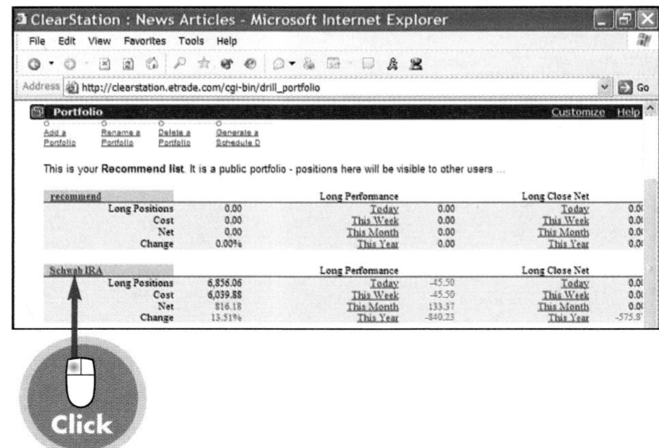

3 See a Stock

Click the ticker symbol of a stock to view more information about that stock.

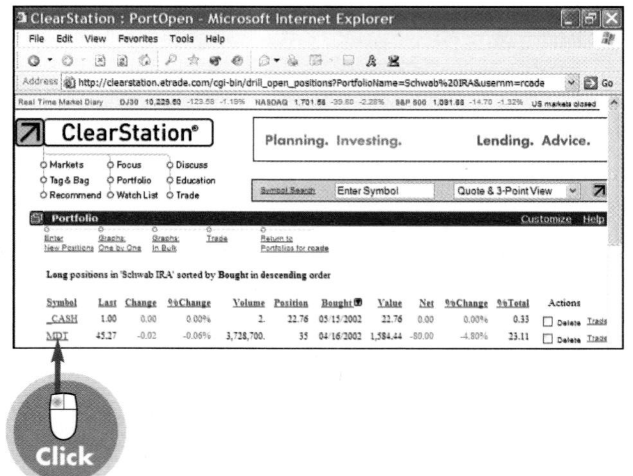

4 Delete a Stock

To remove a stock from your portfolio, return to the **Portfolio** page (shown in step 2). In the **Actions** column, enable the **Delete** check box and click the **Delete** button. A confirmation page will be displayed. Click the **Delete** button to remove the stock from your portfolio and add it to your watch list.

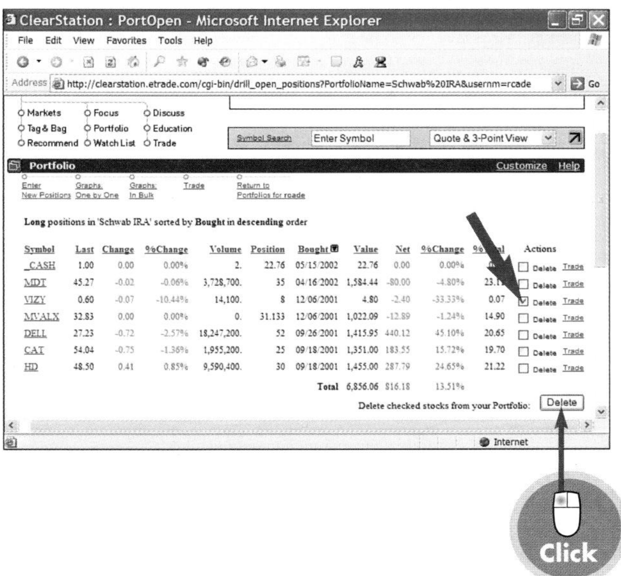

5 Add a Stock

To add a stock to your portfolio, first display your portfolio in ClearStation. Then click the **Enter New Positions** hyperlink. The page adjusts to provide an area in which you can type additions to the portfolio.

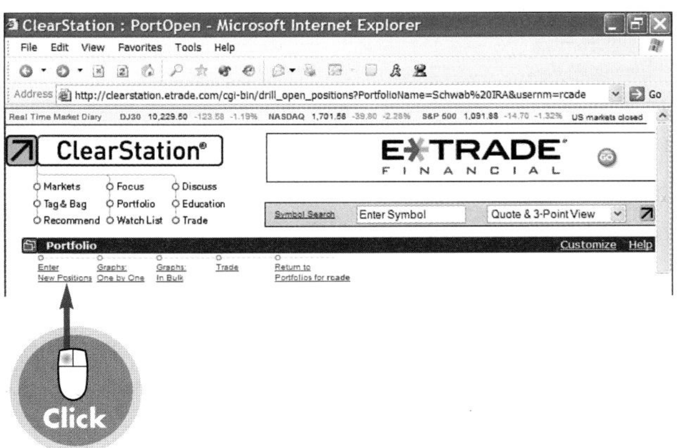

6 Enter the Symbol

Type one or more ticker symbols in the **Stocks** text box, separating the symbols with spaces, then click the **Add** button.

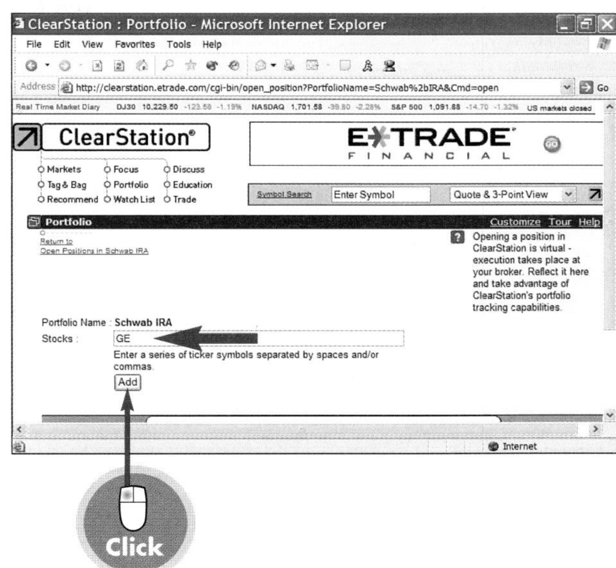

7 Describe Your Purchase

Enter the purchase price, the number of shares bought, and other details of the transaction you conducted when you bought the stock through a brokerage. Click the **Add these stocks to your Portfolio!** button.

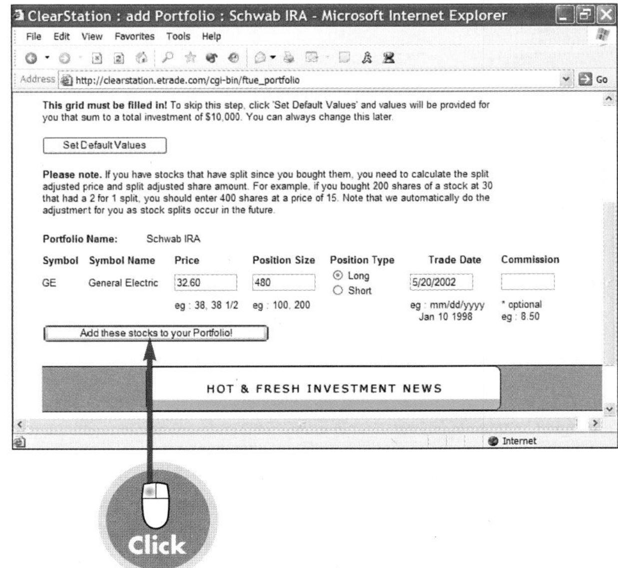

Task 4

How to Get Tax Help Online

When tax time comes around each April in the United States, one of the places you can go for help is the World Wide Web. In addition to the federal government's extensive Internal Revenue Service site, you can get information on taxes you owe—and how to reduce them—from places such as MSN Money, CNNMoney, and Yahoo! Finance.

1 Visit MSN Money

Launch your Web browser, type the URL `http://moneycentral.msn.com` in the **Address bar**, and press **Enter**. The MSN Money home page opens.

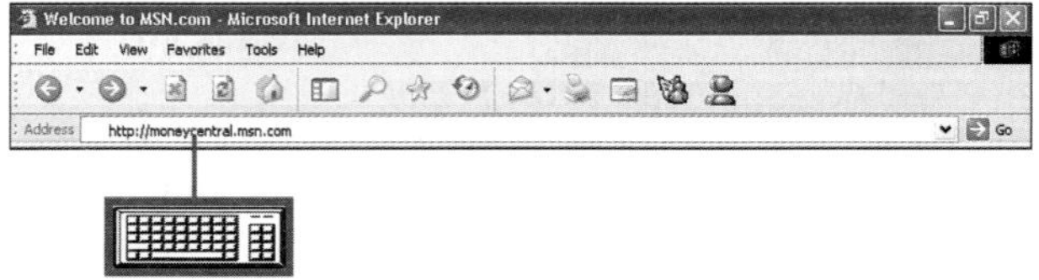

2 View Tax Information

MSN Money is divided into sections on investing, banking, financial planning, taxes, and other financial topics. Click the **Taxes** hyperlink to go to the taxes page.

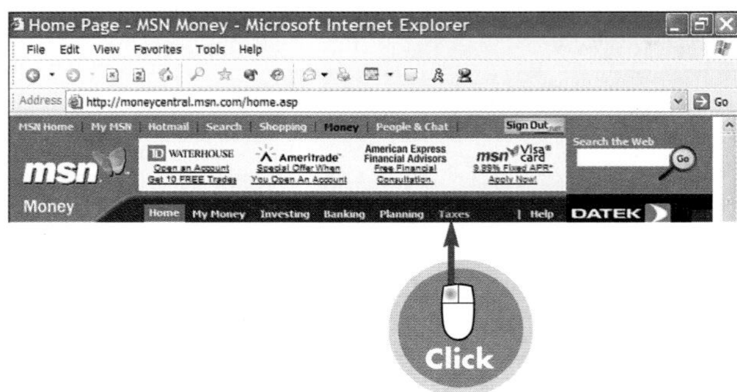

3 Estimate Your Taxes

To get an estimate of what you owe on your current taxes, click the **Tax Estimator** hyperlink. The **Tax Estimator** page opens.

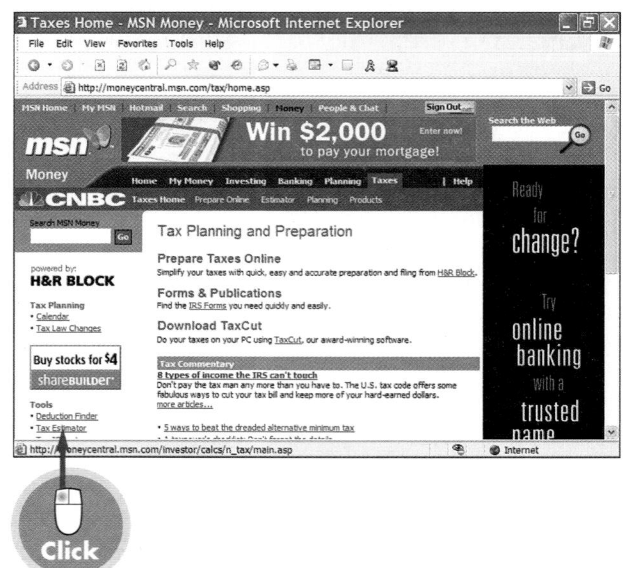

4 Get Help with an Item

The MSN Money Tax Estimator requires you to fill out several forms. Fill out the forms as they are presented. If you are unsure about an item, click that item's text box to see a description of the field in the text area to the right of the form, under the **Help** graphic.

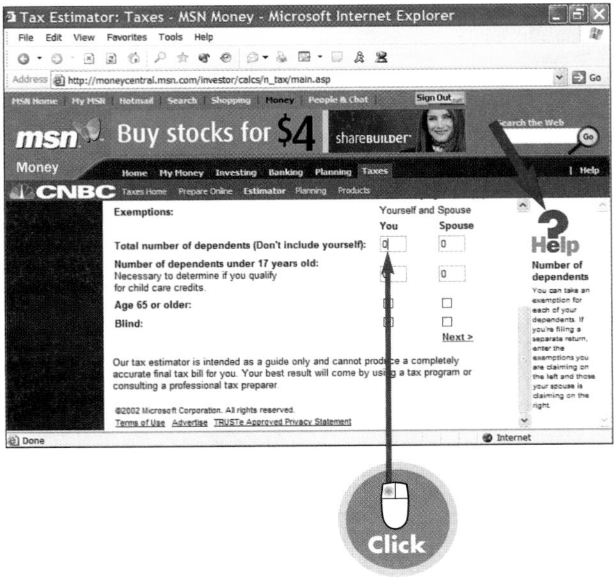

5 Download Tax Forms

The Internal Revenue Service offers tax forms you can download from the Web and print out. To find these forms, click the **Taxes** hyperlink at the top of a page to return to the main MSN Money Taxes page. Then click the **IRS Forms** hyperlink. An informational page opens.

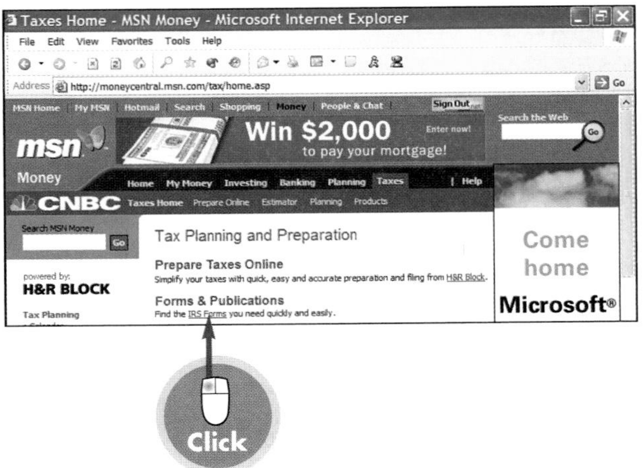

6 Visit the IRS Site

Click the **download federal forms and instructions** hyperlink to visit the forms section of the Internal Revenue Service site. You can select the forms you want to download from that site.

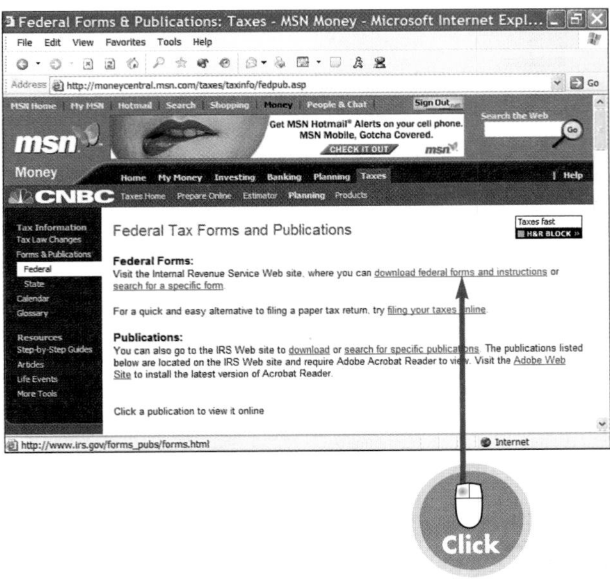

How to Hint

Finding More Information About Your Taxes

One of the most extensive World Wide Web sites devoted to taxes is the Internal Revenue Service site. To visit it directly, type `http://www.irs.gov` in your browser's **Address bar** and press **Enter**.

Staying on Top of Financial and Investment News

Several World Wide Web sites specialize in financial news and analyses written by expert commentators and journalists. To visit these sites, type the following URLs in your browser's **Address bar** and press **Enter**:

- **TheStreet.Com**: `http://www.thestreet.com`
- **Briefing.Com**: `http://www.briefing.com`
- **CBS MarketWatch**: `http://cbs.marketwatch.com`

Task 5

How to Find Savings Tips Online

The World Wide Web has thousands of sites enticing you to spend money. On many of the financial sites mentioned in the tasks in this part, however, you can find tips and tools for moving money in the opposite direction—*to* your savings. One good example of a savings tool is the retirement savings calculator offered by CNNMoney, a service of CNN and *Money Magazine*. That site also offers a searchable database of mutual funds.

1 Load the Financial Site

To use CNNMoney's retirement calculator, launch your Web browser, type the URL `http://money.cnn.com/retirement` in the **Address bar**, and press **Enter**. When the CNNMoney page opens, click the **Retirement Calculator** link.

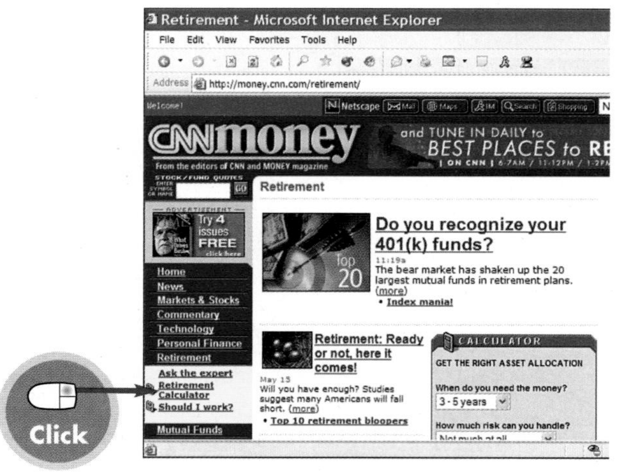

2 Use a Savings Calculator

To use the calculator, you must fill out four forms about your age, goals, and current savings. Fill out each form, and then scroll to the bottom of the page.

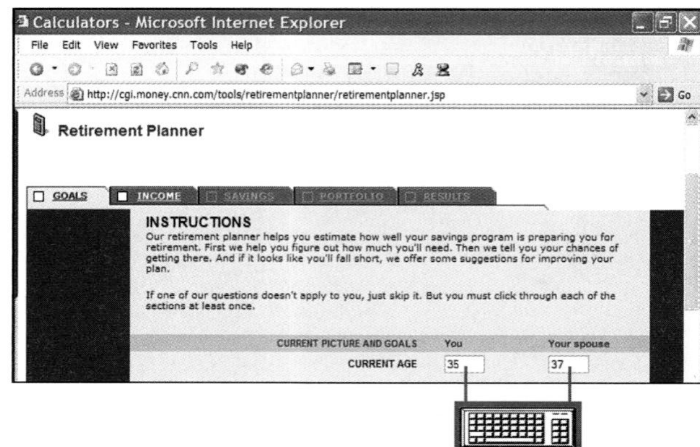

3 Complete Each Form

The calculator includes forms about your income, savings, and investment portfolio. Use your scrollbar to move down the form as you fill each part out and then click the **Next** button to continue.

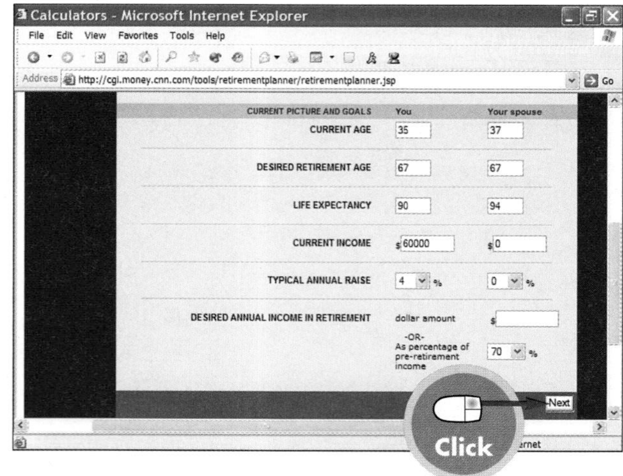

4 View the Results

After you fill out the last form, click the **Next** button to see a report estimating your retirement savings. You can go back and make changes to the answers you gave to see how those changes in your investing strategies will affect the results.

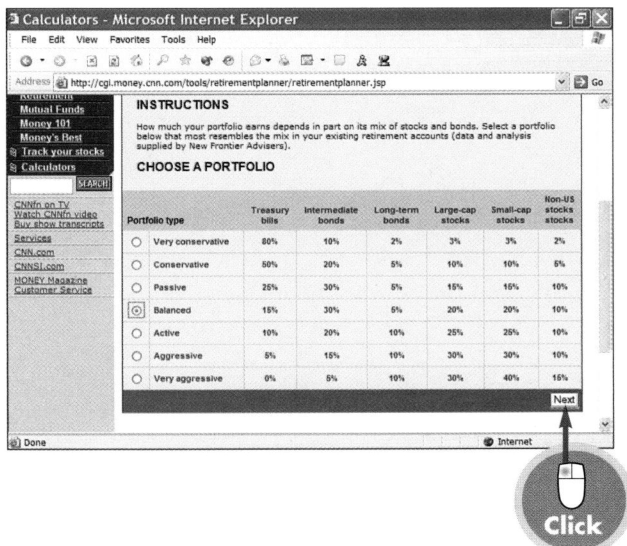

5 Research Mutual Funds

Click the **Mutual Funds** hyperlink on any CNNMoney page to search CNNMoney's database of mutual funds and to find one that meets your investment goals and matches the amount of risk you're willing to take.

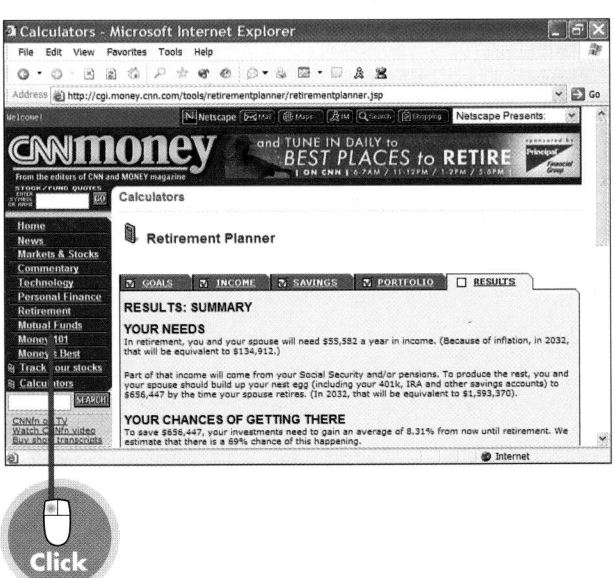

6 Search the Database

In the **Find-A-Fund** box, you can set different criteria for mutual funds you're investigating, including the type of fund, one- and three-year returns, and the expense ratio. Click the **SUBMIT** button to see a list of funds that match the criteria you've entered.

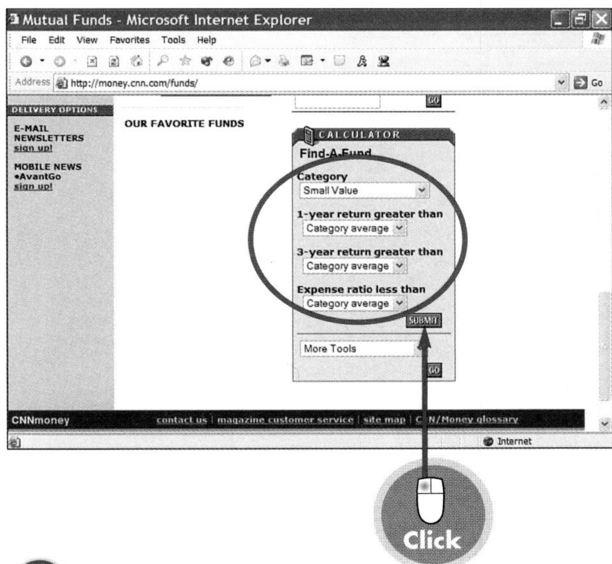

7 View a Fund

To find out more about a fund that meets your search criteria, click the ticker-symbol hyperlink next to the fund's name. A new page opens, displaying information about that particular fund.

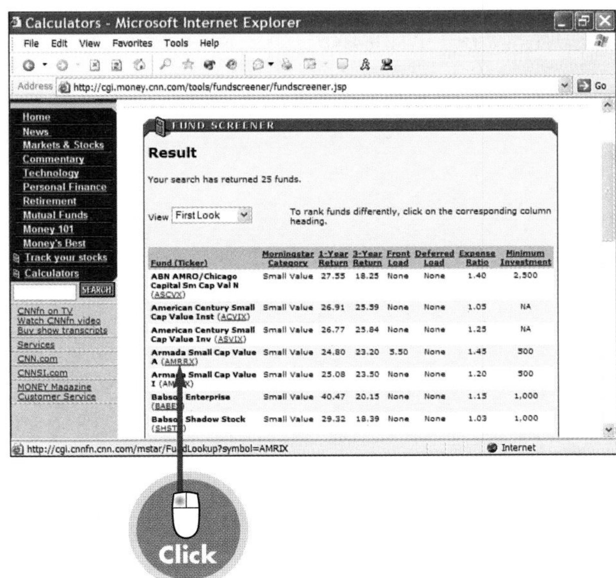

Task

14

Creating Your Own Web Site

Anyone can publish on the World Wide Web. Using the Web site features on Microsoft's MSN Web site (free to anyone with a Microsoft Passport account), you can create Web sites with features such as message boards and photo albums, add files and pages to your site, and test them in your own Web browser.

Another way to publish on the Web is to create your own *weblog*, a daily journal that contain links to pages on the Web and other personal content. In the last two years, more than 60,000 people have started publishing weblogs with tools such as Blogger, Manila, Radio Userland, and Moveable Type. One of the easiest, Manila, makes it possible to start your own weblog in less than five minutes.

Task 1

How to Create a Web Site on MSN

Some Internet service providers offer free Web hosting as part of your subscription. They provide from 1–20 megabytes of disk space for the files you want to make available on your Web site. These files must be *published*—transferred from your computer to your provider's Web server. Dozens of companies offer free Web hosting, including Microsoft, Yahoo!, and Tripod. These services require only that you have a valid email address to join.

1 Go to the MSN Home Page

Microsoft offers free Web-site hosting on MSN. You must log in with your Microsoft Passport to set up a new site. (For information about setting up a Passport account, refer to Part 3, Task 4, "How to Set Up a Microsoft Passport Account.") Type the URL `http://communities.msn.com` in your browser's **Address bar** and press **Enter**. After the MSN home page loads, click the `Sign In` button.

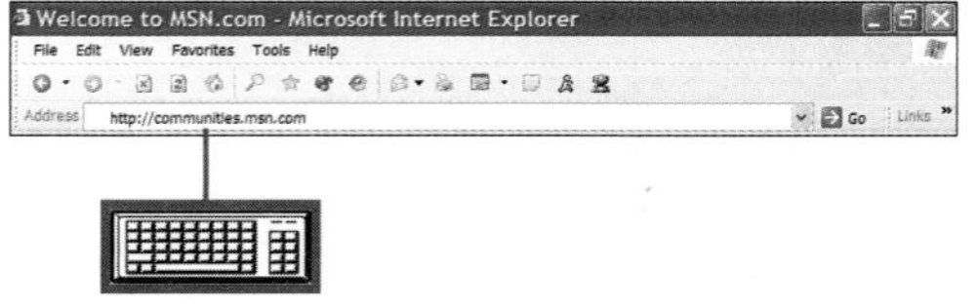

2 Create a Community

The MSN Communities page describes existing communities and lists the ones to which you belong. Click the **Create one now** hyperlink to begin your own.

3 Name Your Community

To get started, type a community name and description in the **Community Name** and **Describe your community** text boxes. Then click **Continue**.

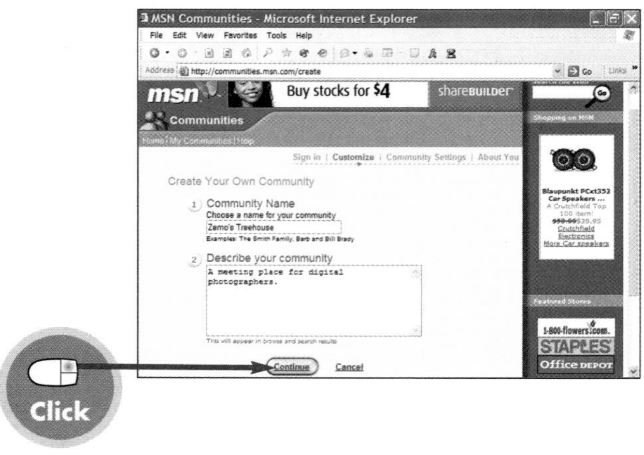

Set Policies

Use the radio buttons to choose a content rating, membership policy, and other aspects of your community. When you're done, scroll down to the rest of the page.

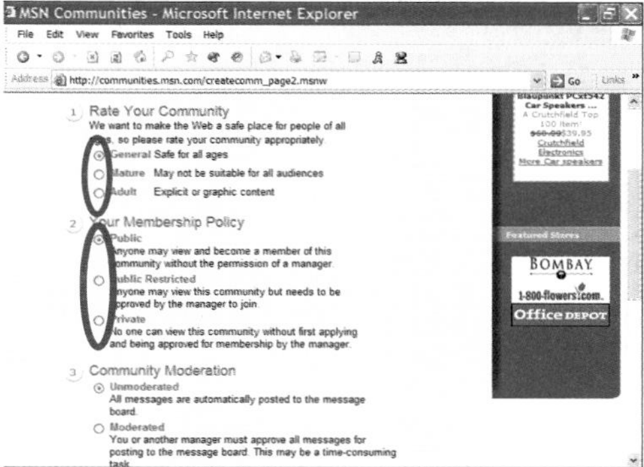

Continue Setup

Next, choose the category and subcategory where MSN should list your community in its directory (if it should be listed). When you have answered all the questions, click the **Continue** button.

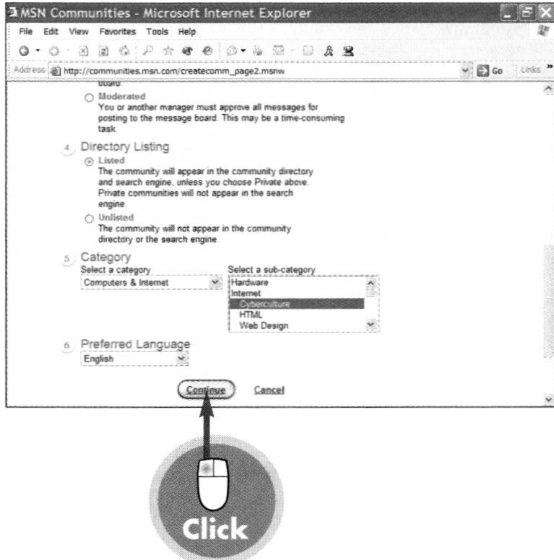

Join Your Community

The last step is to join your community: Type your email address, choose a nickname, and pick delivery options. If you accept MSN's Code of Conduct, enable the **I accept** box and click **Create my community!** Turn to the next task for information about customizing the site you've just created.

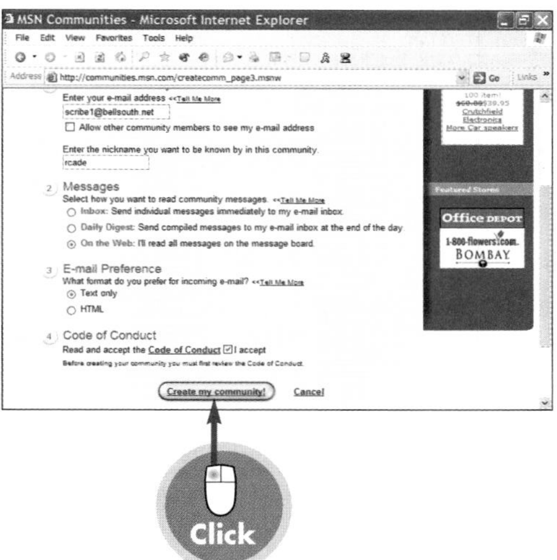

How to Hint

Choosing a Free Web Site Provider

If you're looking for a place that will host your Web site at no charge, there are numerous alternatives to MSN Communities (although it's one of the easiest to use for people creating their first site).

You may want to investigate the following Web-hosting services as an alternative to MSN:

- **Yahoo! Geocities**: `http://geocities.yahoo.com`
- **Tripod**: `http://www.tripod.lycos.com`
- **Doteasy**: `http://www.doteasy.com`
- **AOL Hometown**: `http://www.hometown.aol.com`

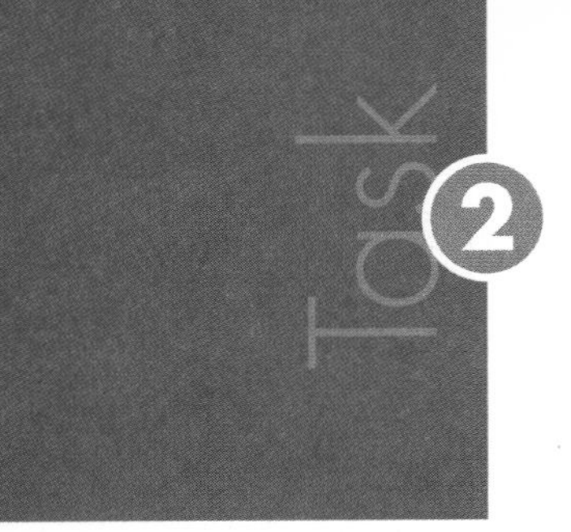

How to Work on Your MSN Web Site

After you create an MSN Web site (as described in the preceding task), it becomes available on the World Wide Web at an address that starts with **`http://communities.msn.com/`** followed by the name of your site (with no spaces between words). For example, the **Politics** community is at **`http://communities.msn.com/politics`**. MSN sites are called "communities" because of all the interactive features they offer—visitors to your site can post messages, submit photos, and make other contributions.

1 View Your Web Sites

To view your MSN sites, type the URL **`http://communities.msn.com/MyWebSites`** into your browser's **Address bar** and press **Enter**. If you are not currently logged in to your Microsoft Passport, click the **Sign In** button.

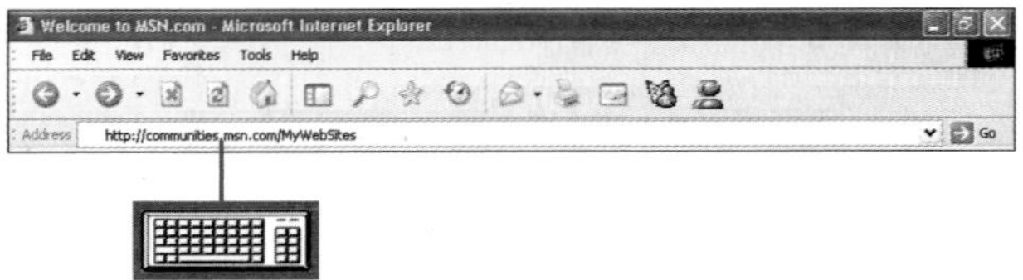

2 Edit a Community

To work on one of your MSN sites, click its hyperlink.

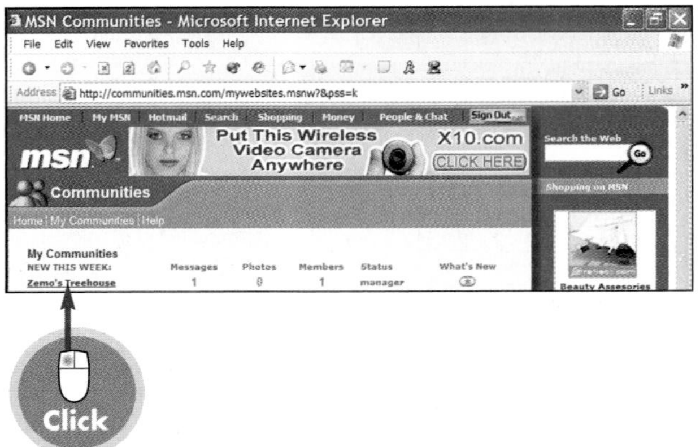

3 Describe Your Site

To help people find your MSN site, you can provide a description of the community and what it offers. Click the **Community Settings** link. The Community Settings page opens in your browser.

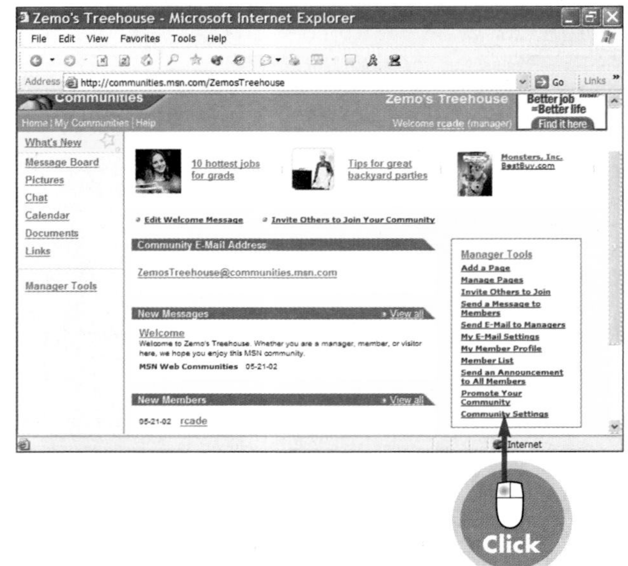

4 Write a Site Description

You can use the Community Settings page to tinker with the features of your site. For example, you can change the description of your site in the **Description** text box. When you're finished, click the **Save Changes** button.

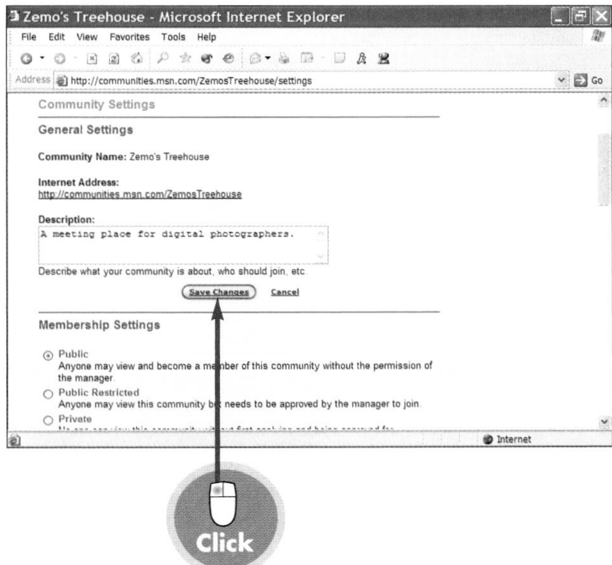

5 Greet Visitors to Your Site

Every MSN community has a welcome message that is displayed when a visitor loads that community's home page. To change the message that appears by default, click the **Edit Welcome Message** link.

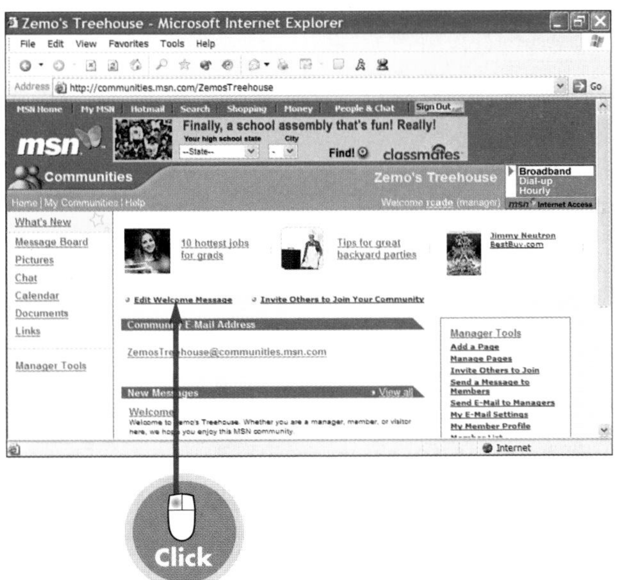

6 Edit the Welcome Message

To personalize your welcome message, type the message you want in the text box. Use the buttons above the box to add bold text, italic, hyperlinks, and other special formatting. When you're finished, click the **Save Welcome Message** button.

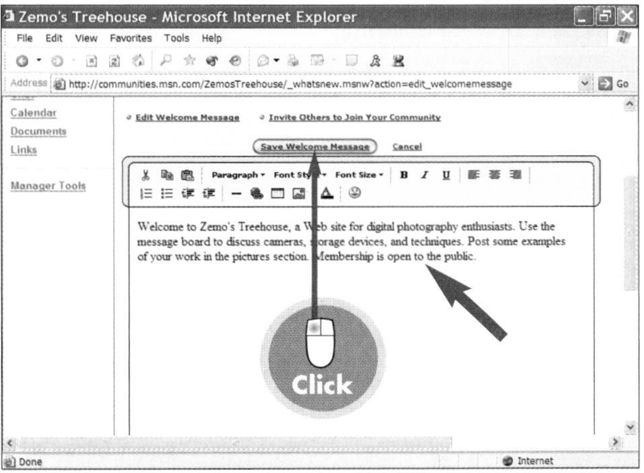

7 Work on Your Site

The Manager Tools box contains links to use when working on your site. To see a page that describes each of these tools, click one of the **Manager Tools** hyperlinks. (You'll work with these links during Task 5, "How to Add a Feature to Your Site.")

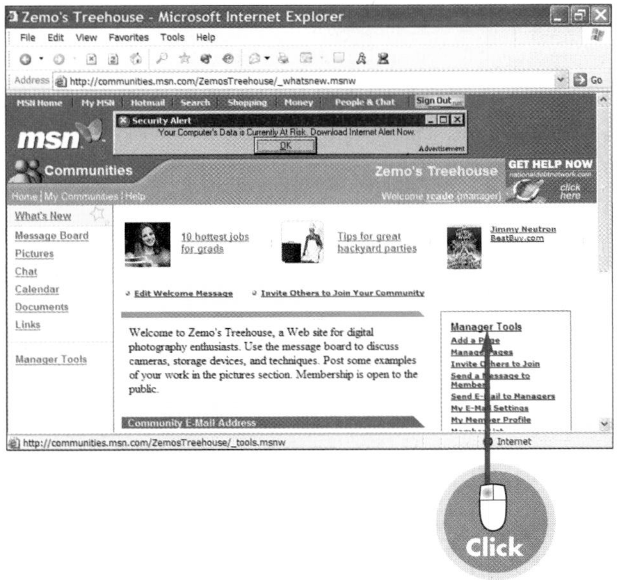

Task 3

How to Publish a Photo on Your Site

Sites you create on MSN can have one or more photo albums in which you can share your personal photos. Your MSN site must have an album before you can add any photos to it; fortunately, because your site was created from the MSN Communities home page (as described in Task 1, "How to Create a Web Site on MSN"), it does by default.

1 View Your Web Sites

Type the URL `http://communities.msn.com/MyWebSites` into your browser's **Address bar** and press **Enter**. If you haven't logged in to your Microsoft Passport, click the **Sign In** button.

2 Choose a Site

The MSN **Communities** page, customized based on your Passport, opens. To view one of your MSN sites so that you can begin working on it, click its hyperlink.

3 Open a Photo Album

Click the **Pictures** link in the column along the left edge of the page to see the photo albums that your site contains.

4 Add a Photo to an Album

Every MSN site starts off with a single photo album. To add a photo to this album, click the **Add Photos** link.

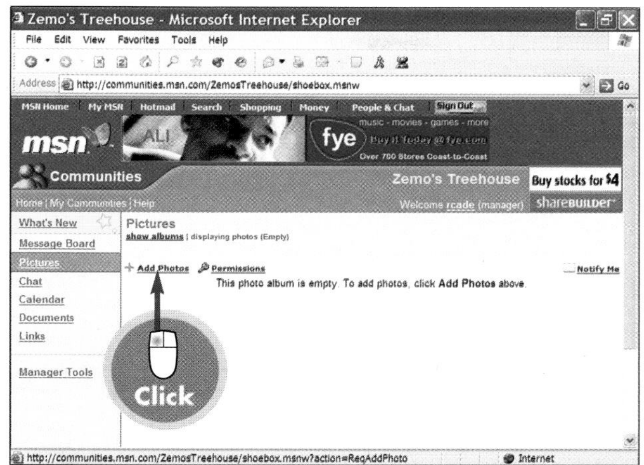

5 Install the Photo Upload Control

MSN offers a **Photo Upload** control, which you can use to add photos to your community. If you have not yet installed this control, you are given a chance to add it to Internet Explorer 6. To set up the program on your computer, click the **Install** button. A **Security Warning** dialog box appears; click **Yes** if you want to set up the program.

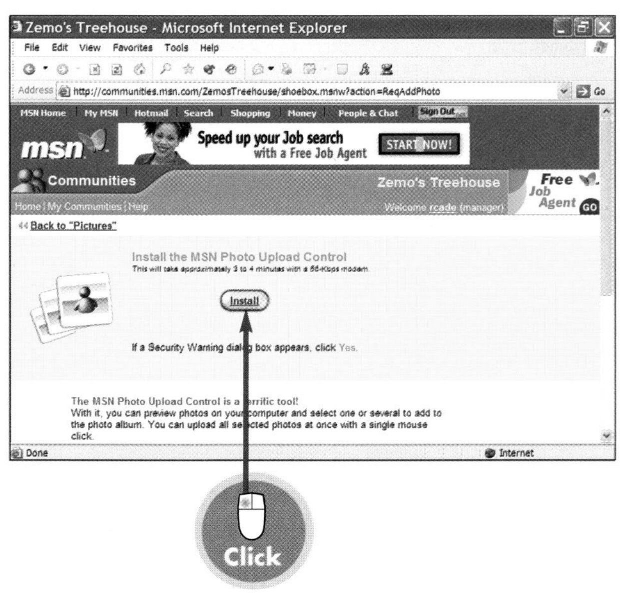

6 Choose a Photo

When the **Photo Upload** control is installed, it opens a special page when you click **Add Photos** in Step 4. From that page, you can publish any photo file that exists on your computer. In the **Select a folder with photos** list on the left side of the window, choose the folder that contains the photo or photos you want to publish. Thumbnail images of all the photos in that folder appear in the **Select photos** pane. To choose a photo you want to publish on your MSN site, click its check box; you can click multiple check boxes to publish multiple photos.

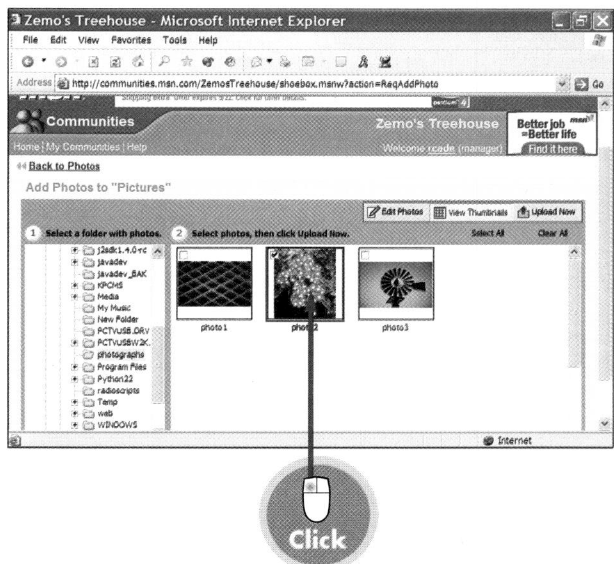

7 Upload the Photo

Copying a file from your computer to a Web site is called *uploading*. Click the **Upload Now** button to publish the photo on your MSN site. To see your photo album in your browser, click the **Pictures** link.

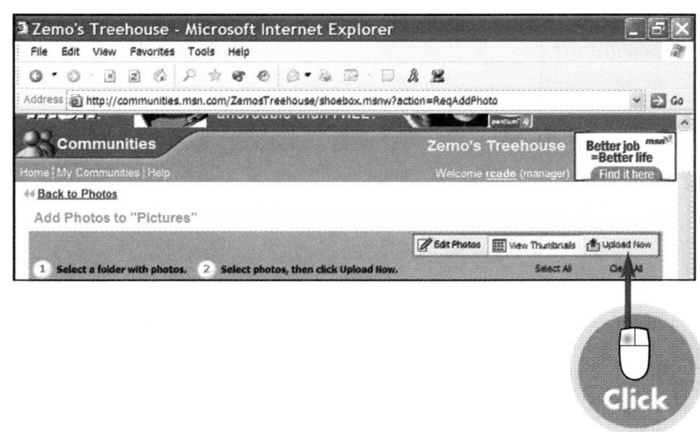

Task 4 How to Publish a File on Your Site

File cabinets on MSN work just like the photo albums described in the previous task. Your MSN site must have a file cabinet before you can add any files to it; fortunately, most sites are created with a cabinet automatically. You add files to the file cabinet using a special, required Internet Explorer add-on program called the **File Upload** control. After you add a file, it will have its own *URL* (an address that can be used to load the file with a browser such as Internet Explorer 6).

1 View Your Web Sites

To view your MSN sites, type the URL `http://communities.msn.com/MyWebSites` into your browser's **Address bar** and press **Enter**. If necessary, click **Sign In** to log in to your Microsoft Passport account.

2 Choose a Site

On your **Communities** page, click the hyperlink of the MSN community you want to work on.

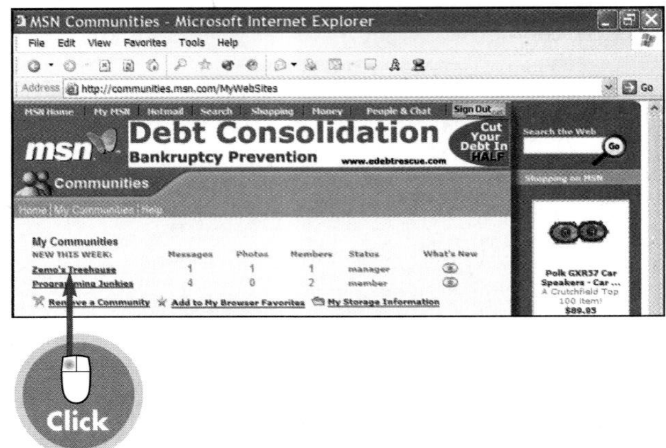

3 Open a File Cabinet

If your MSN site includes a file cabinet, the `Documents` link will be displayed in the left column on the page. Click this link to see your site's files.

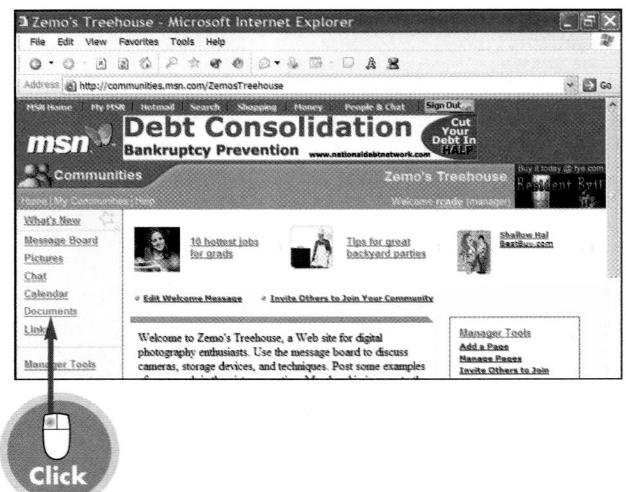

4 Set Up the File Upload Tool

To add a file, click the **Add File** link. If you have never added a file (other than a photo) to an MSN site before, you can install the **File Upload** tool for Internet Explorer 6. A **Security Warning** dialog box appears; click **Yes** if you want to set up the program.

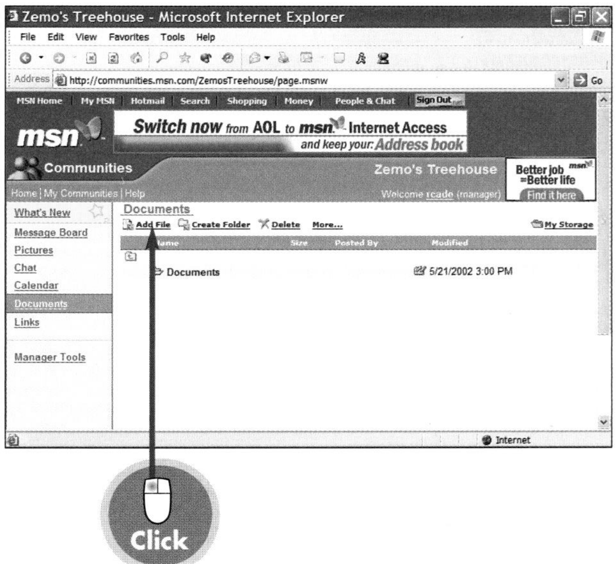

5 Choose a File

When the **File Upload** control is installed, it opens a special page when you click **Add File** in Step 4. Navigate through the file system on your computer to locate the file you want to upload to your MSN site. If you want to publish a file, click the check box for the file.

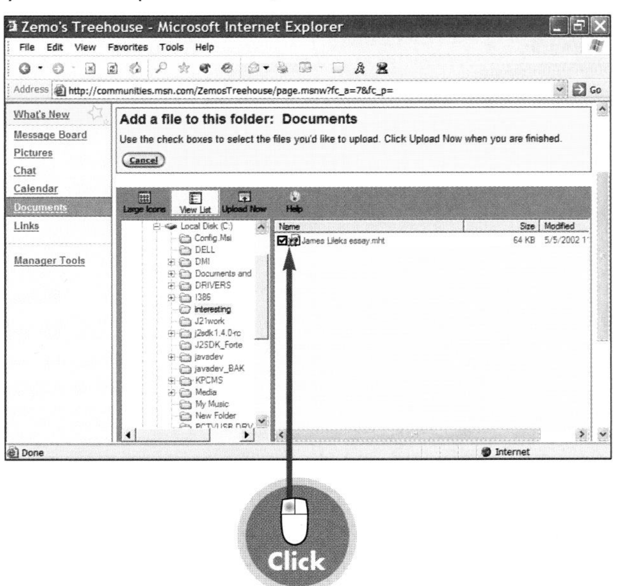

6 Upload the File

Click the **Upload Now** button to publish the file on your MSN site.

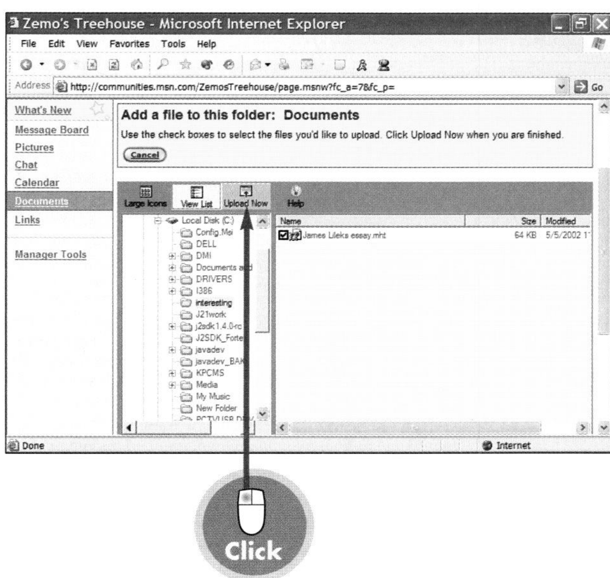

7 View the File

The **Documents** page of your MSN site lists all the files in your site's file cabinet, including the one you just published. To view the contents of a file, click its hyperlink. The URL for that link's page appears in the **Address** bar; if the file can be displayed by Internet Explorer, it will be loaded with the URL of the file in the browser's **Address** bar.

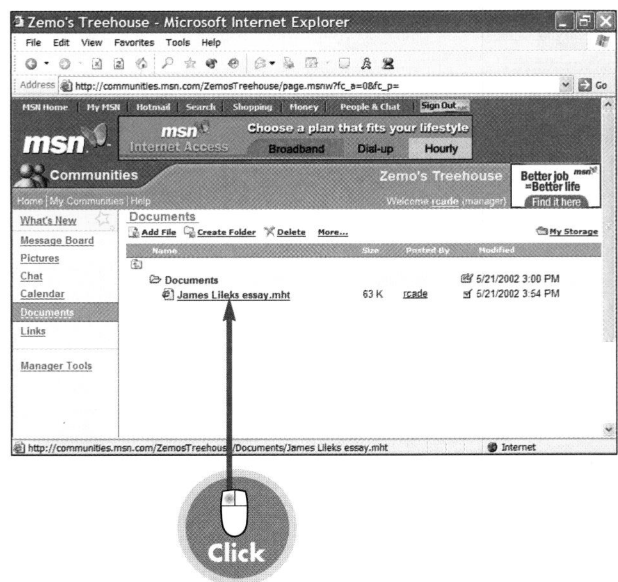

Task

5 How to Add a Feature to Your Site

Features can be added at any time to your MSN Web site. For example, if your site doesn't offer a photo album or file cabinet (these features were covered in the preceding tasks of this part), it's easy to add them now. Your site can also have message boards for discussions, calendars, lists, and other pages. All the work required to improve your site is handled in Internet Explorer 6 and shows up immediately when people visit your site.

1 Work on Your Site

Load the URL `http://communities.msn.com/MyWebSites` with Internet Explorer 6, log in with your Microsoft Passport if asked to do so, and click the link for the site you want to edit on the **Communities** page. To add a new page to the site, click the **Add a Page** link in the **Manager Tools** box.

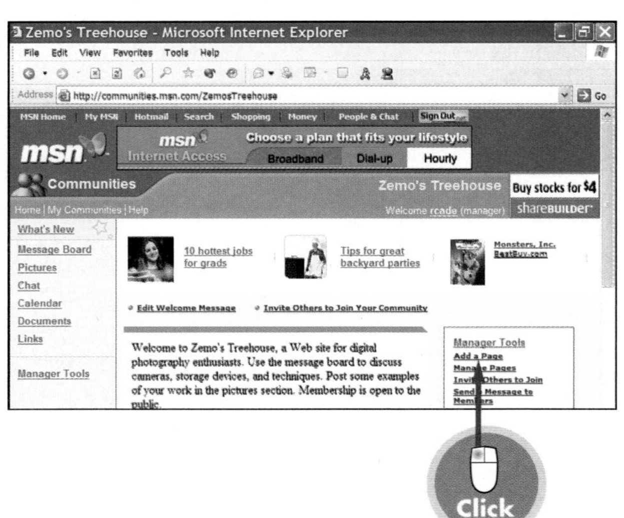

2 Choose the Page to Add

To add a list, for example, click the **A List** link. Click **A Photo Album** to add a photo album or **A Documents Folder** to add a file cabinet.

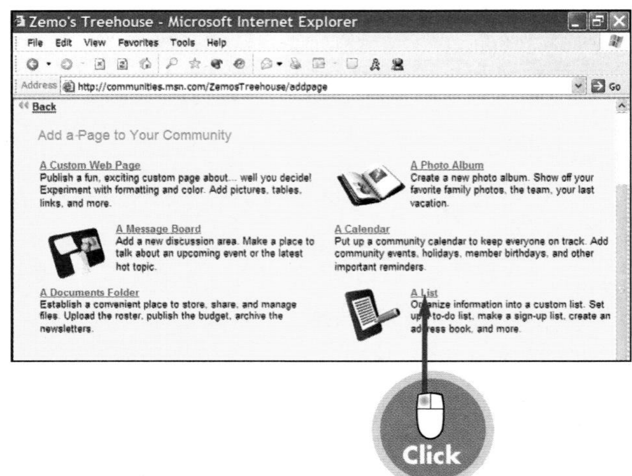

3 Customize the Page

To add a site list, scroll down the page and click the **Add a List of Web Links** hyperlink.

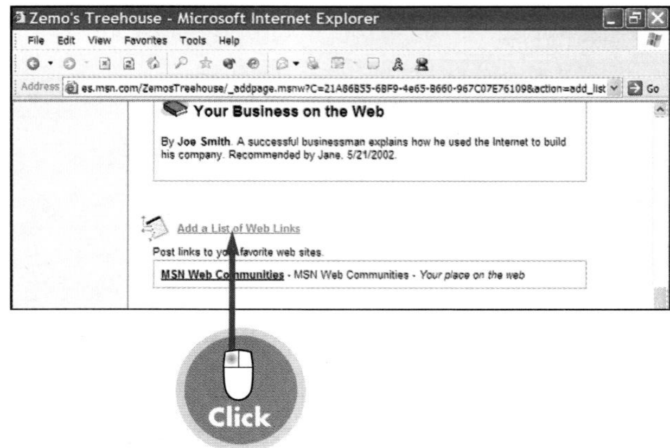

4 Name the Page

Every page you add to an MSN site must have a name. The name you give the page should be descriptive but brief—no longer than 15–20 characters. Type the name for your page in the **Type a name for your new list** box and click the **Create This List** button.

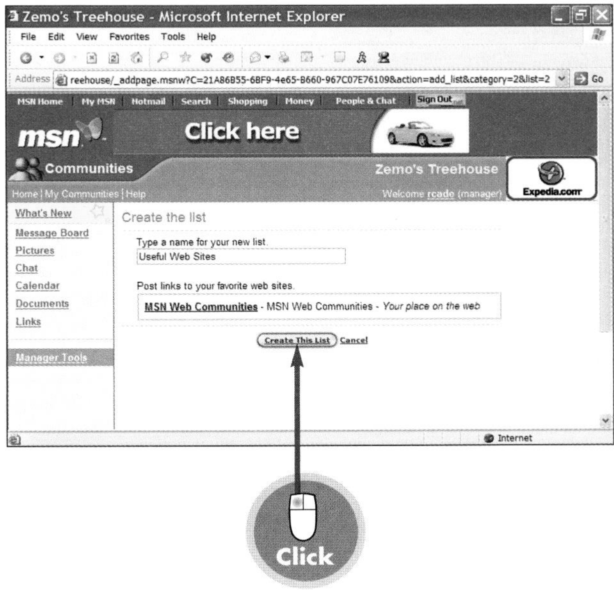

5 Work on the List

The list will be empty when the list page is added to your site. Click the **Add Link** hyperlink to begin filling the list with items.

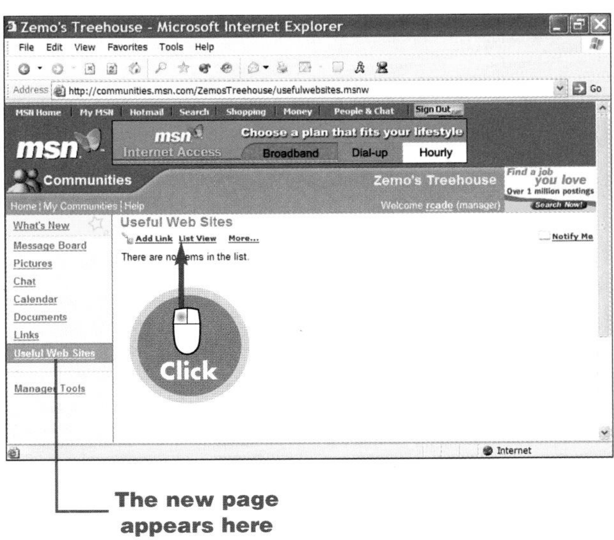

6 Add an Item to the List

If you want to create a list of Web sites (as shown in this example), type the site's address in the **Link** box and then type a succinct description of the site in the **Description** area. You can use formatting buttons to add bold, italics, fonts, and hyperlinks to the description. Click the **Add** button when you're finished.

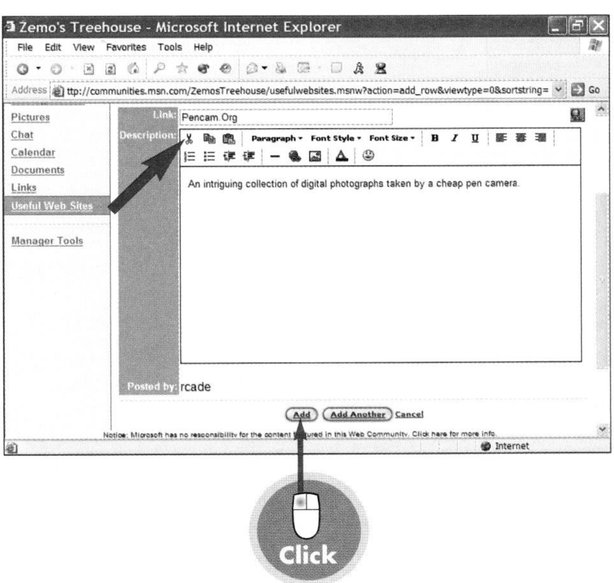

How to Hint: Adding Items to a List Quickly

If you have several items to add to a list, the easiest way to work on the list is to click the **Add Another** button instead of the **Add** button in Step 6. This button causes MSN to add the item and then redisplay a form for adding a new item to the list.

How to Make Your Site Invitation-Only

An MSN site can have one of three membership policies: **public**, **public restricted**, or **private**. Public sites are open for anyone to read or join. Public-restricted sites are open for anyone to read, but you must approve members before they can join. Private sites can be read only by people you have invited to join and approved as members. Private sites also are hidden from MSN's community search engine.

1 View Your Web Sites

To view the MSN sites you have created (and other MSN sites you visit), type the URL `http://communities.msn.com/MyWebSites` into your browser's **Address bar** and press **Enter**. You may need to sign in to your Microsoft Passport account.

2 Choose a Site

On the **Communities** page, click the hyperlink of the MSN community for which you want to change the membership policy. By default, the new communities you create on MSN have public access. In this task, you'll switch a site from public access to private access.

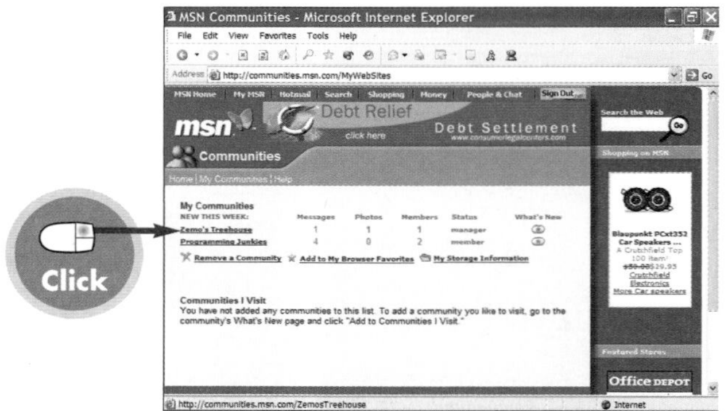

3 View Your Site Settings

Click the **Community Settings** link in the **Manager Tools** box. The **Community Settings** page opens in your browser.

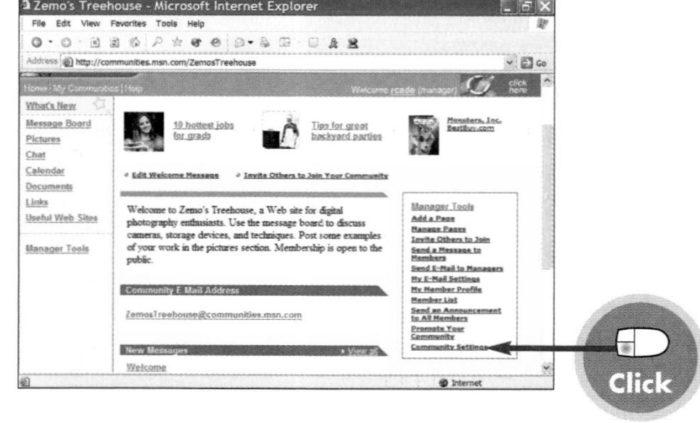

4 Change Your Policy

To change your site's membership policy, click the desired option in the **Membership Settings** list and click the **Save Changes** button.

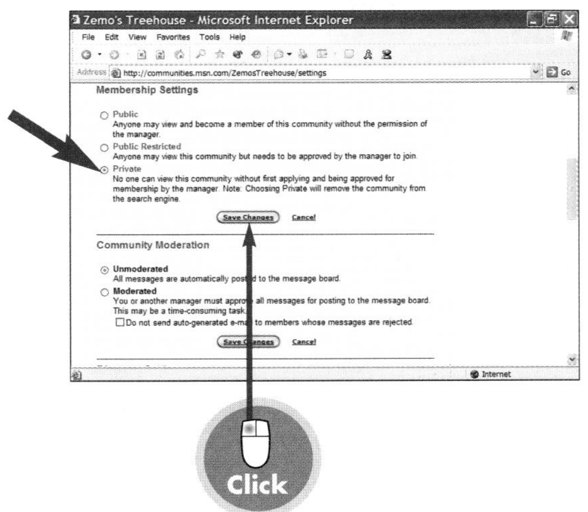

5 Invite Someone to Join

If you make your MSN site private, the only way for people to view your site is if you invite them to join. To do this, click the **Invite Others to Join** link in the **Manager Tools** box.

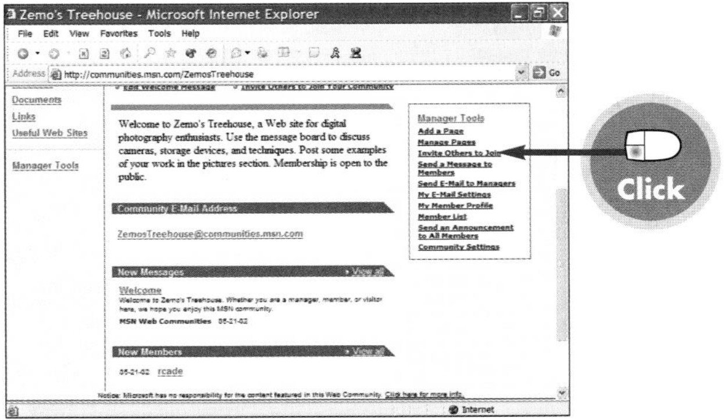

6 Send the Invitation

You can invite more than one person simultaneously: Type their email addresses in the top box separated by commas. You have the option of including a message with the invitation. Click the **Send Invitation** button when you're done.

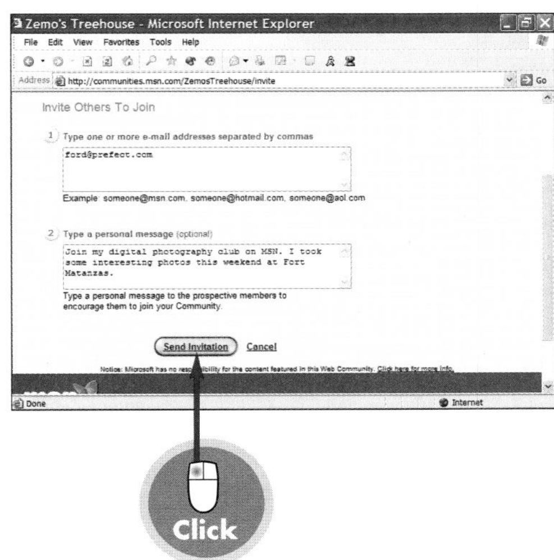

How to Hint

Banning Someone from Your Community

Even on a public site, you can kick a member out and prevent him or her from rejoining. To do so, click the **Member List** hyperlink in the **Manager Tools** box on your site's home page, then scroll through the **Role** drop-down list to the **Banned** option. Select it, and click the **Save** button. Your former member will still be able to read the contents of your site (if the site isn't private), but can't do anything that's limited to members (such as posting on a message board).

How to Create a Weblog

During the past two years, a new kind of personal Web site has become popular: the weblog. Weblogs vary in content, but the form is usually the same—a publisher adds 1–4 short items a day that link to things on the Web with commentary about them. One popular weblog is Joshua Marshall's Talking Points Memo at the URL **`http://www.talkingpointsmemo.com`**. More than 60,000 weblogs exist today because they are easy to create (and fun to read). This task covers how to start your own weblog in less than five minutes.

1 Visit Weblogger.com

Weblogger.com offers a free trial weblog for 30 days. If you decide to subscribe, the cost is $79.95 per year. To visit the site, type the URL **`http://www.weblogger.com`** in your browser's **Address bar** and press **Enter**.

2 Start a New Weblog

You can create a new weblog and begin working on it right away—and unlike with some free subscriptions on the Web, you aren't asked for a credit card or any other payment information. To begin, click the **Start Your Own Website!** graphic.

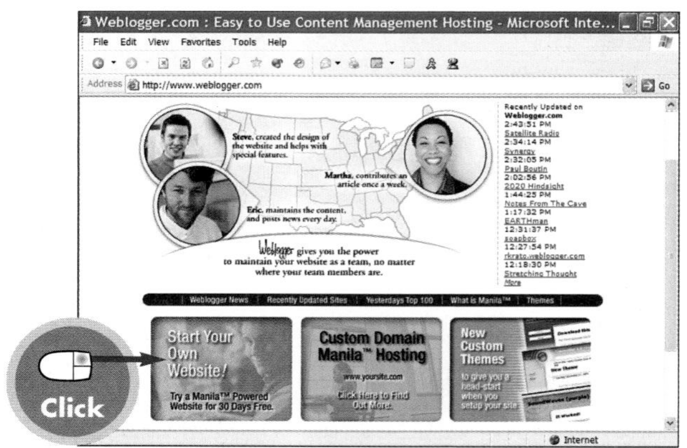

3 Review the Terms

Before you can create a weblog, you are presented with Weblogger.com's terms of use. If you agree to them, click the **Create a New Web Site** link at the bottom of the page.

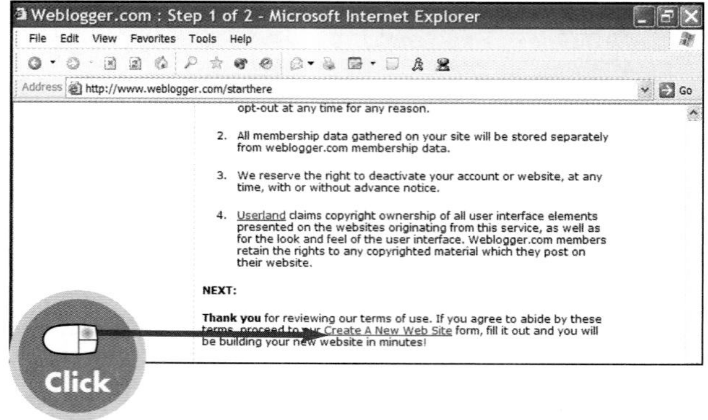

4 Name Your Weblog

Type a name for your weblog in the **http://** box and provide your sign-up information in the **Name** and **Email** boxes. Type the password you want to use for this account in the **Password** box and then click **Submit**. If the name you want is taken, you'll be asked to choose another.

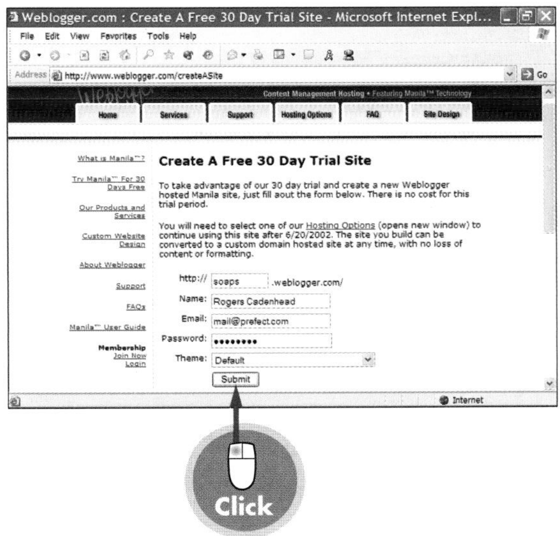

5 View Your Weblog

Weblogger.com creates your new weblog. Make a note of the URL in your browser's Address bar; this is your weblog's address. To begin working on your site, click the **log in** link.

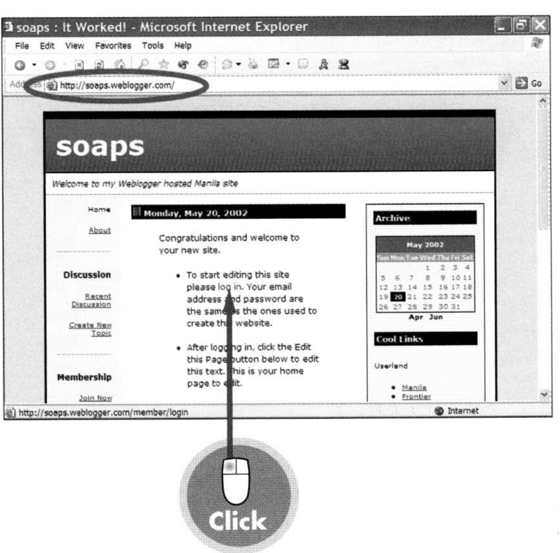

6 Sign In

You must be signed in to your weblog before you can make any changes to it. Type the e-mail address and password you used in Step 4 in the text boxes and click the **Login** button. For help editing your new weblog, proceed to the next task.

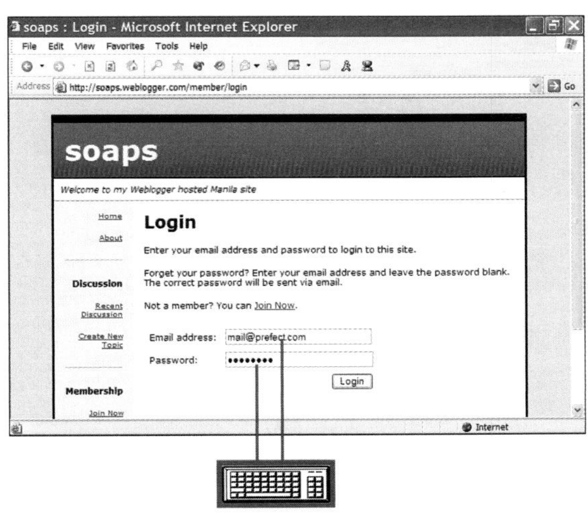

How to Hint: Viewing Other Weblogs

One of the best ways to learn about weblogs is to read several of them. Weblogger.com's home page links to several weblogs that have been updated by its customers recently. To visit one of these sites, type the URL `http://www.weblogger.com` in your browser's **Address bar** and press **Enter**, then click the name of the weblog you want to view.

Task 8

How to Edit Your Weblog

Weblogger.com uses weblog publishing software called Manila, which was developed by UserLand Software and is used on hundreds of different sites. You don't need to download special software to work on your Manila weblog at a service such as Weblogger.com. You can add things, delete things, and make changes using a Web browser such as Internet Explorer 6. Before proceeding with this task, start your own weblog by following the instructions in the preceding task, "How to Create a Weblog."

1 Visit Your Weblog

The address of your weblog begins with `http://` followed by the name you chose and `.weblogger.com` (for example, if **soaps** was the name you picked, your weblog would be at **http://soaps.weblogger.com**). To work on your site, type your weblog's URL in your browser's **Address bar** and press **Enter**.

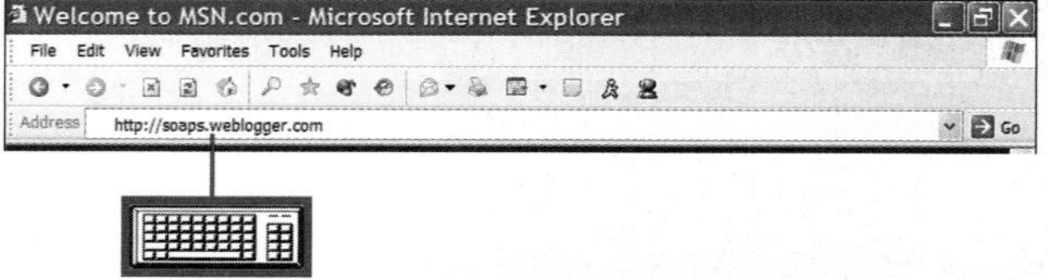

2 Check Your Status

You should see an Editors Only list of links at the top of the page. If not, click the **log in** link or the **Join Now** link farther down the page to sign in.

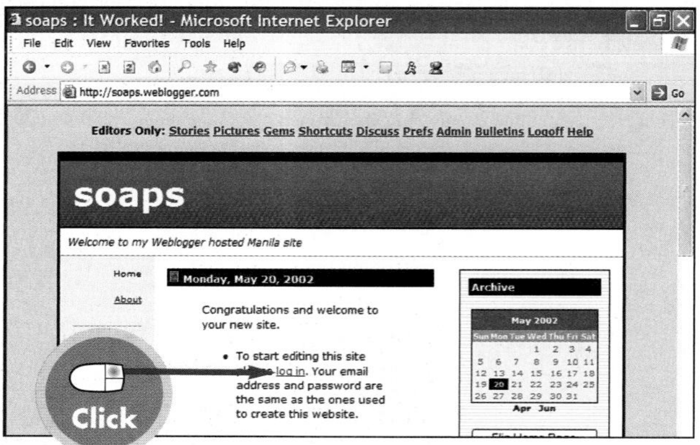

3 Edit Your Weblog

You can edit a feature of your weblog by clicking the **Edit** or **Edit this Page** buttons. To add a new link to your weblog, click the **Edit this Page** button.

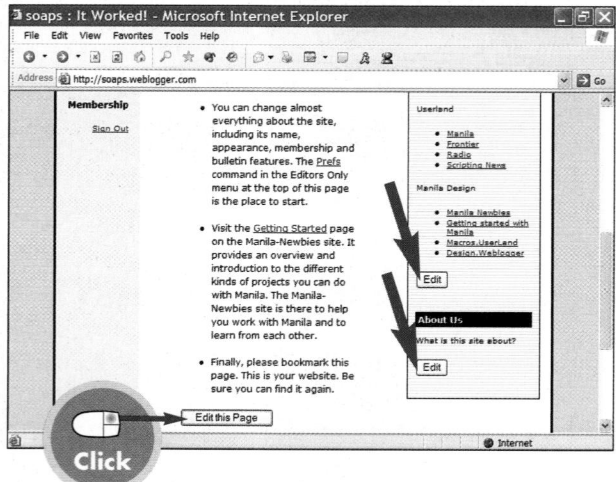

4 Edit the Text

Weblogger.com opens an editing page with **Title** and **Text** boxes loaded with the existing contents of the page. To make changes, click your mouse in either box and edit it with your keyboard.

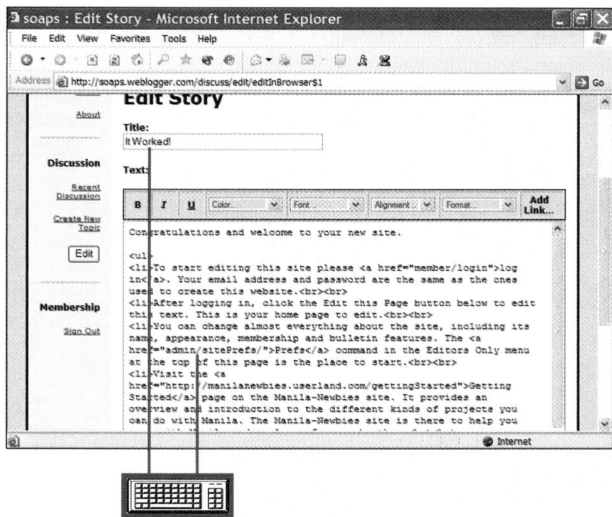

5 Write a New Item

For your first weblog item, you will probably want to delete all the existing text and start with something new. Type the text of a Web page you want to discuss in the **Text** box. Use the buttons atop the box to add bold, italics, and other formatting.

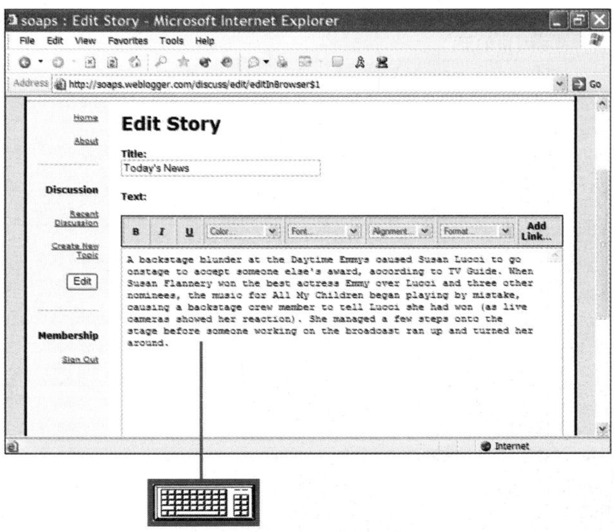

6 Add a Hyperlink

Most weblogs link to the page (or pages) being discussed. To add a link, drag your mouse over the text that should be linked and then click the **Add Link** button.

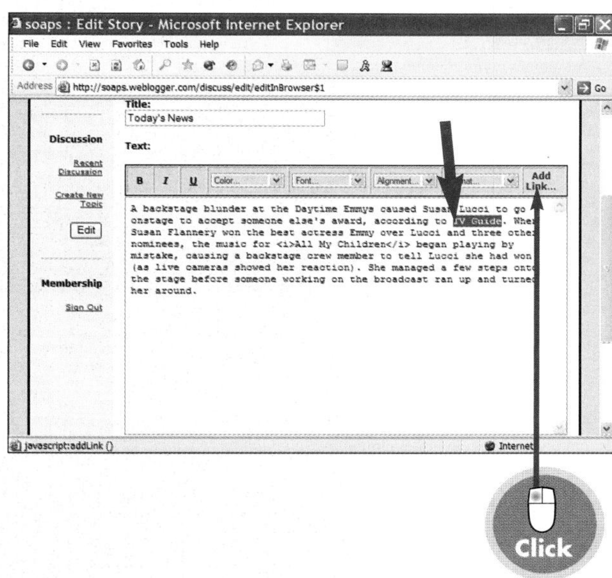

7 Enter the Link

The **Explorer User Prompt** dialog box opens. Type the hyperlink in the **URL** text box and click the **OK** button. HTML formatting will be added to the text you selected so that it links to the URL.

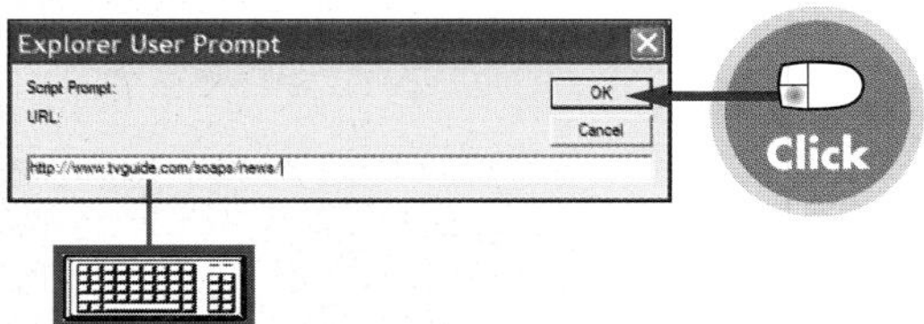

8 Publish the Page

When you're finished editing, click the **Post Changes** button. The page is published immediately, and your weblog opens so you can review your work.

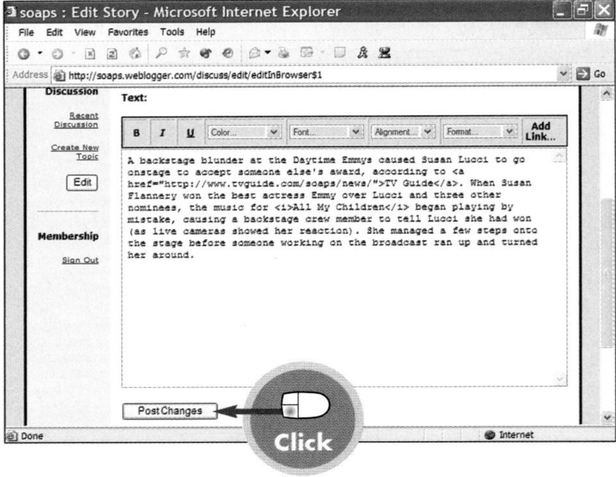

9 Add Something New

Your visitors can see the changes to your weblog the moment you publish them. To add something new to the page on the same day as the last item, click the **Edit this Page** button again.

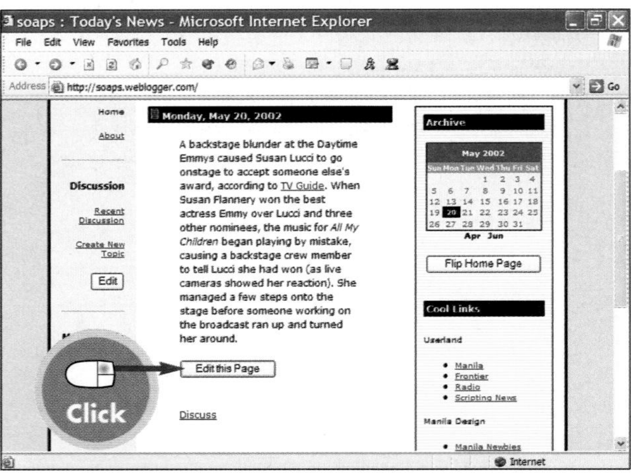

10 Modify the Text

To add a new item, click your cursor at the top of the text box so your new text is inserted above what's already there. Be sure to leave a blank line between each item. Click **Post Changes** when you're done.

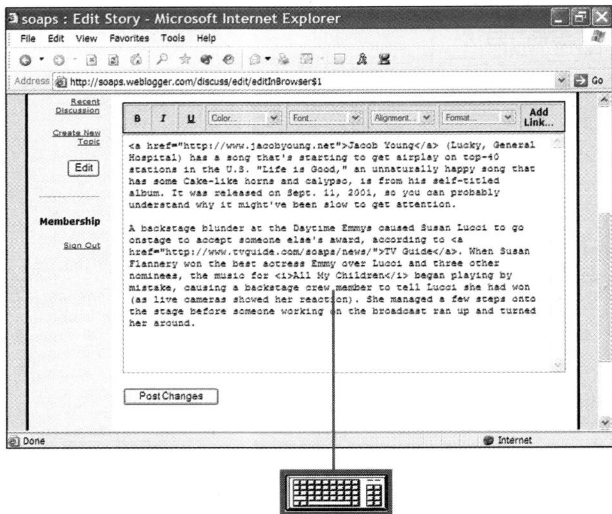

11 Start a New Day

Your weblog is organized so that each day gets its own page, which you can view using the links on the calendar. To create a new day page so you can add the first item of the day, click the **Flip Home Page** button.

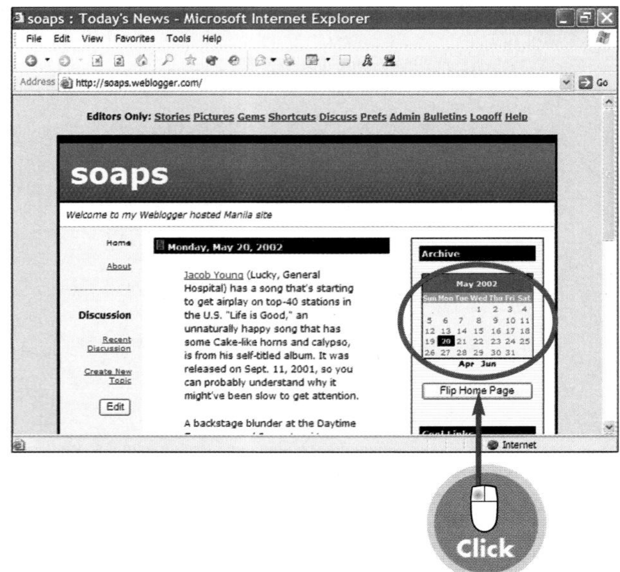

12 Confirm the Flip

Flipping the home page should be done only if you haven't yet added any items today. Click the **OK** button to confirm that you want to do this.

13 Add a New Item

After you flip the page, your current day has nothing on it. Click the **Edit this Page** button to open an editing page so you can add an item to it.

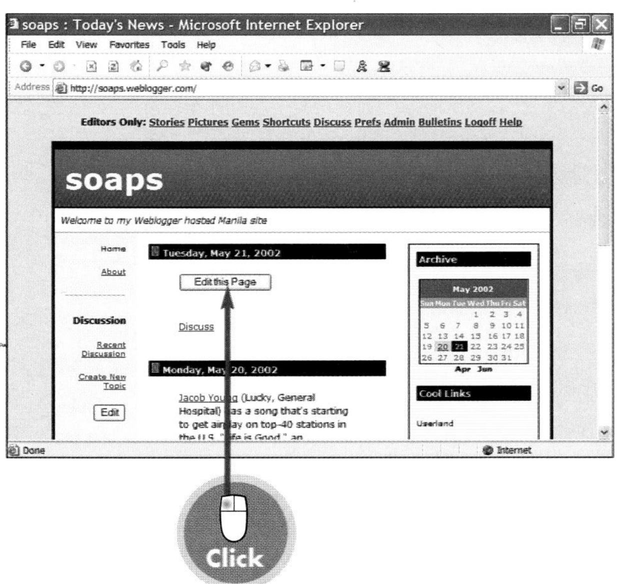

14 Update Your Weblog

The text box will be empty. Type the text of a new item in this box and click **Post Changes** to publish it.

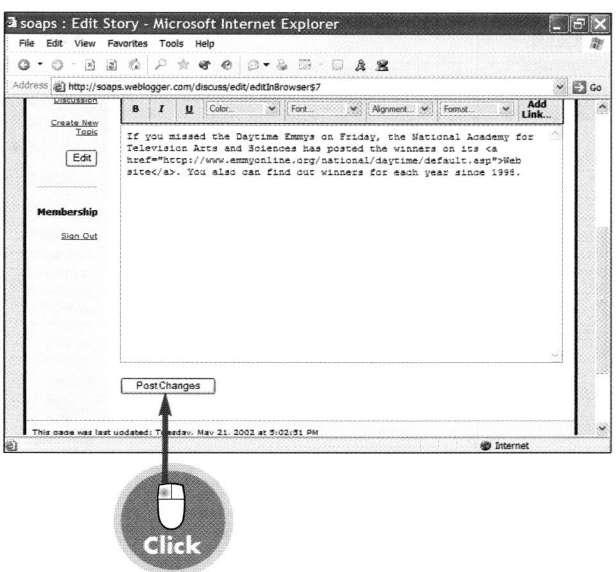

How to Hint

Describing Your New Weblog

Every new weblog created on Weblogger.com comes with an About page, where you can describe the purpose of the weblog (and yourself, if you're so inclined). To edit this page, click the **About** link along the left side of any page of the weblog. The **About** page loads with the default text "Who are you? What's this site about? How can people send you feedback?" Click the **Edit this Page** button to open the page in an editing window. After you make changes, click **Post Changes** to republish the page.

How to Change Your Weblog's Look

One of the perks of using Manila, the software that runs Weblogger.com, is that you can give your weblog a professional-looking design even if you aren't a Web designer. Weblogger.com offers more than 50 *themes*, ready-made site designs you can adopt simply by choosing one from a menu. Changing themes takes only a few minutes and does not alter any of the content of your site. If you don't like the new theme, you can return to the one that was used when the weblog was created.

1 Visit Your Weblog

The address of your weblog begins with **`http://`** followed by the name you chose and **`.weblogger.com`**. To work on your site, type your weblog's URL in your browser's **Address bar** and press **Enter**.

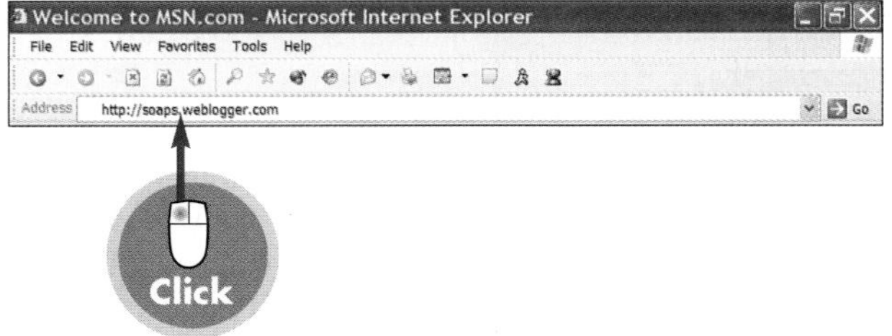

2 Edit Your Weblog

The **Editors Only** menu contains 10 links you can use to maintain your site. Click the **Prefs** hyperlink to load a page where you can customize your weblog.

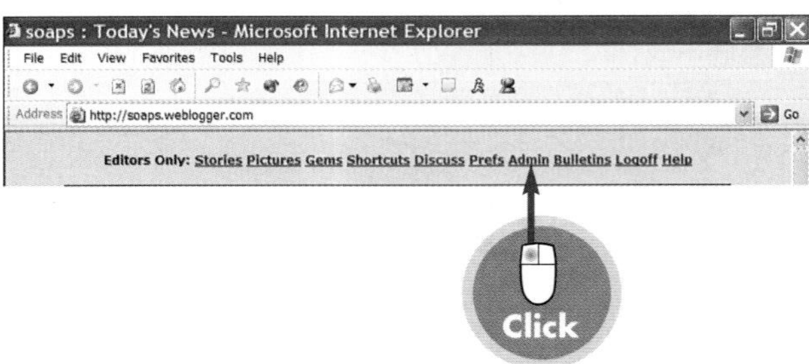

3 View the Themes

The preferences page has 15 links along the side of the page that can be used to change your membership policy and many other aspects of your weblog. Click the **Themes** link.

4 Preview a Theme

The **Themes** page lists more than 50 themes you can use on your Weblogger.com site. To see what a theme looks like, click its name.

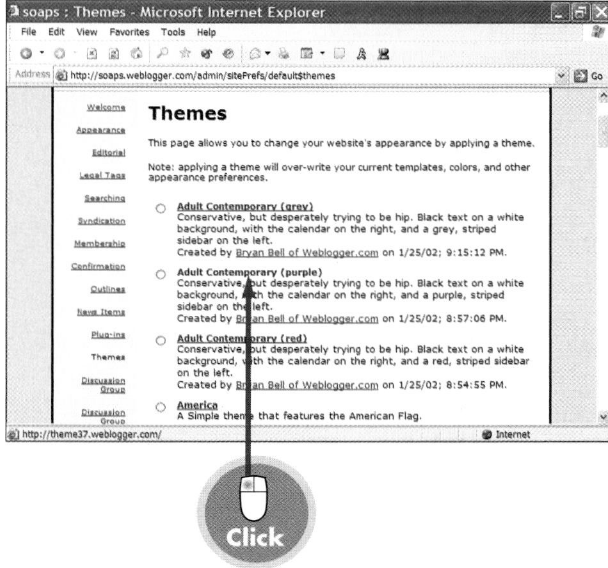

5 Return to the List

A demo weblog that uses the theme is displayed. To return to the list of themes, click the **Back** arrow on your browser. (Don't download the theme—that's an advanced feature for people who run a Web server.)

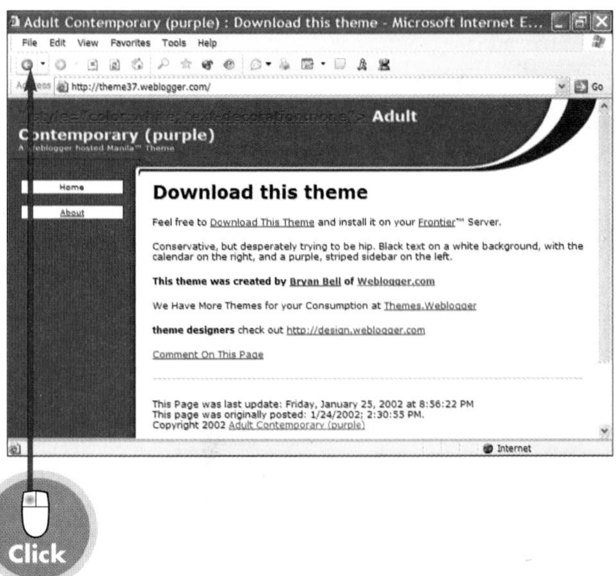

6 Choose a Theme

When you find a theme you like, click the radio button next to the theme's name, scroll to the bottom of the page, and click the **Apply Theme** button. A page opens asking to confirm your choice. Click **Yes**.

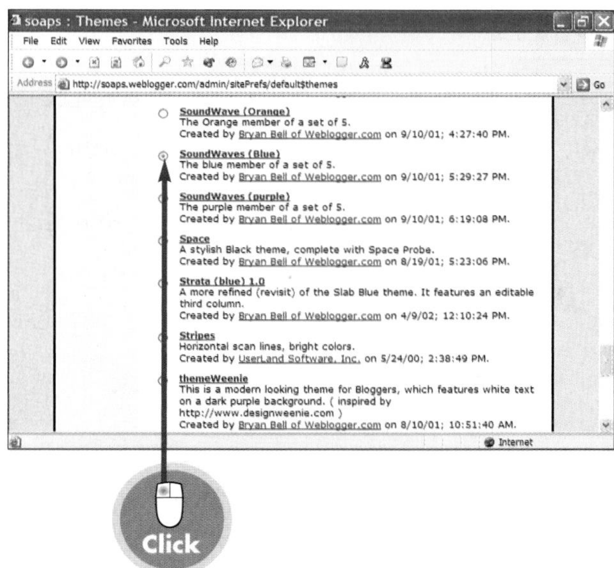

7 Return Home

All pages of your weblog are updated immediately with the new design. To return to your weblog's home page (and see how it looks), click the title of your weblog.

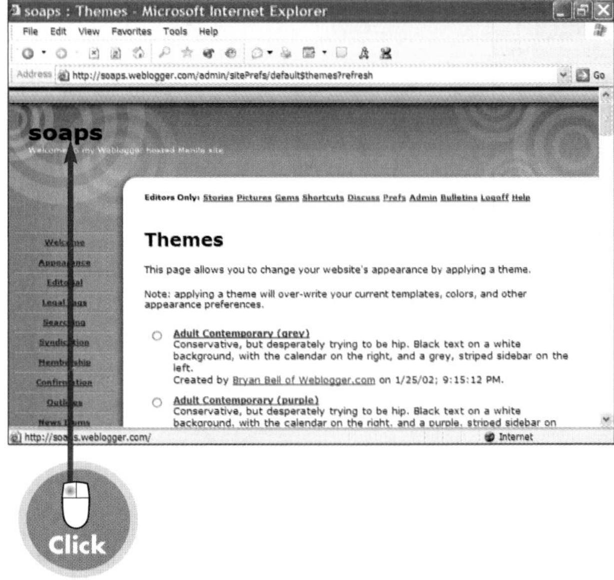

Glossary

A

access number The phone number your computer will dial to connect to the Internet. If this number is a long-distance call, you'll be running up long-distance charges every time you use the Internet, so you should choose the number carefully when setting up an account with an Internet service provider or America Online.

Address bar The text field along the top edge of a Web browser where you can type a Web page's URL and press **Enter** to load the page.

address book A personal database of your email correspondents that is created in Outlook Express. Most other email programs offer a similar feature, including Qualcomm Eudora and PocoMail.

Autosearch An Internet Explorer feature that enables search text to be typed in the browser's Address bar. Internet Explorer looks for the site (or sites) that best match the text.

B

bookmarks Shortcuts to your favorite Web sites, also called *favorites*. This feature is available in Netscape Navigator, Internet Explorer, Opera, and other Web browsers. You can save bookmarks to sites you visit often, making it easier to load them in your browser.

broadband connection A connection to the Internet that's at least 10–20 times faster than you can get using a dial-up modem. Most broadband connections are made using television cable or DSL telephone line technology and cost about $40 to $70 per month. Contact your local cable or telephone company to see whether it offers high-speed Internet connections. Broadband connections do not use your computer's modem. They require special hardware that may need to be set up by a professional such as a cable TV or phone installer.

browser *See* Web browser.

Buddy List A feature of America Online that enables you to keep track of friends, relatives, and other acquaintances who also use the service. The Buddy List lets you know when someone is connected to AOL or AOL Instant Messenger so that you can send the person an instant message.

C

cable connection *See* broadband connection.

chat *See* chat room.

chat room Also called simply a *chat*. The "place" in cyberspace where people gather to discuss a particular topic. In reality, people sit at their computers, separated by huge distances, and type questions, comments, and criticisms. Other users respond to those comments in real time. Although the discussion may be hampered by slow typing speeds, the effect is as if you are sitting in a coffee bar someplace talking over the events of the day with other people who share your interests. *See also* chat.

community *See* MSN Community.

cookie A special browser file stored on your system that a Web site can use to personalize your visit to the site. Web sites can read the cookie files they have created, which enables a site to recognize who you are when you visit. By design, browsers send cookies only to the site that created them.

D

dial-up connection A way of connecting to the Internet using a phone modem and an ordinary phone line. Your computer dials the number of an Internet service provider's modem and attempts to make a connection. No one else can use the phone line while you're connected to the Internet; as a result, many people add a second line that's strictly for use by a computer.

dialog box A small window that opens on your computer as a program is running, often to ask a single question that can be answered by clicking a button containing a label such as **Yes**, **No**, or **Cancel**.

download To copy a file from another computer to your system, using a network such as the Internet or another means of connecting computers. You can download data files, programs, and many other types of files from sites all over the Internet to your local server or hard drive. A word of caution: Downloaded files are a major source of computer viruses, so you should have up-to-date antivirus software on any computer to which you are actively downloading files. You also should download files only from sources you know and trust.

DSL connection *See* broadband connection.

E

eBay A popular Web site where members buy and sell items using auctions that usually last from 7 to 10 days. A unique bidding method keeps a prospective buyer's maximum bid secret until it is needed to outbid someone else. To visit the site, type the URL `http://www.ebay.com` into a Web browser's **Address** bar and press **Enter**.

email (electronic mail) An Internet service that lets you send and receive messages to and from anyone who has an Internet email address. These messages, which are almost always free to send and receive, usually arrive within minutes of being sent.

encryption A way to encode data so that it remains confidential. Some Web servers can encrypt Web pages and other data so that you can enter confidential information on a site, such as when you are buying a product online and want to transmit your credit-card information.

F

favorites *See* bookmarks.

feedback rating A numeric ranking that is listed with every eBay buyer or seller, so that you can evaluate whether or not you want to do business with that person. *See also* eBay.

file sharing The practice of downloading files from other people and making your own files available to others, which is most popular among people who are exchanging MP3 files. Millions of people use file-sharing programs such as WinMX or services such as AudioGalaxy and Gnutella, a source of ongoing controversy because these services do nothing to stop people from exchanging copyrighted music by popular musicians.

firewall *See* proxy server.

frames A way of dividing a single Web page into separate sections, each of which can have its own scrollbar and border. Clicking a hyperlink in one frame often causes a page to be opened in a different frame.

H

handle A screen name that identifies you to the Internet-using public. Comparable to a CB radio handle, an Internet handle can say something about your personality (Grumpy1), your career (BeanCount), or your hobbies (QuiltingB). Of course, it can also be an easy-to-remember moniker such as *FirstName.LastName*.

home page The first page your browser loads when you start up the browser. Your browser's home page is often a page on MSN or one hosted by your computer's manufacturer. There are many portals you may want to consider as candidates for your home page. You can specify the home page that loads when you start up the browser. Web sites also have home pages; these pages are the first page you see when you visit a Web site. *See also* portal.

host In the context of the World Wide Web, to make pages and other documents (a Web site) available to users of the Internet. Many Internet service providers offer a limited amount of free space on their servers for you to publish your Web pages; companies are also available that will host sites for free. The provider's server then becomes the host for your site.

hover To position the mouse pointer over an area without clicking the mouse button. Hovering the mouse pointer over a hyperlink on a Web page displays the filename or the URL of the page that will load if you click that hyperlink. Hovering over an area in a program window will frequently display a ScreenTip or a ToolTip.

HTML (HyperText Markup Language) The text formatting and presentation language used to create most Web pages.

hyperlink Text, graphics, or other elements of a Web page that you can click to load a new document into your Web browser. When you click a hyperlink, your browser loads the document to which the link refers; that document can be a Web page, a graphics file, or some other type of information. When you create your own Web page, you can include hyperlinks to any other file—whether that file is a graphics file on your local hard drive or a sound file on somebody else's Web site, for example.

hypertext Text on a Web page you can click to load a new document and jump to a particular location within that document.

I

ICQ The software that pioneered the instant-messaging style of communication. The program is named for the phrase *I Seek You*. An estimated 100 million people have downloaded ICQ's free software, making it one of the most popular instant-messaging services on the Internet.

instant messaging A style of chat in which you keep track of people you know who are using the same software. A server tells you when selected people are online and provides the same information about you to others. You can send private messages that are received instantly on another user's computer.

Internet service provider (ISP) A company that offers access to the Internet through your computer's modem. You can find local ISPs in your local Yellow Pages; national ISPs such as America Online, AT&T WorldNet, and EarthLink are also options. All ISPs offer assistance in setting up your computer to work with the Internet.

intranet A private network of computers that are connected together at a business, school, or another organization. If you are connecting to the Internet using a computer on an intranet, you may have to consult your network administrator for details on how to access the World Wide Web, email, and other services.

M

mailing list A group discussion that takes place entirely with email. People who are interested in a list's topic send an email message to a specific address to subscribe. If the list allows public participation (as many do), you can use a special email address to send a message to all list subscribers. Any message sent by another member to the list of subscribers appears in your Inbox.

Microsoft Passport A free account you can use on all Microsoft Web sites and more than 125 other sites, including 1-800-Flowers.com, Buy.com, eBay.com, RadioShack.com, and Starbucks.com. On Windows XP, you can associate a different Passport account with each person who uses your computer. To set up a Passport, you must have an email account.

MP3 (MPEG-1 Audio Layer 3) A popular format for presenting recorded sound on a computer. The format was developed with the goal of preserving sound quality while making files as small as possible.

MSN Previously known as the Microsoft Network, MSN is a free Web portal that includes news, email, travel and consumer information, instant messaging, and Web hosting. To visit the site, type the URL `http://www.msn.com` into your browser's **Address** bar and press **Enter**.

MSN Community Web sites created by MSN members that can include message boards, photo albums, a place for files, and other features. There's no cost to set up these sites, which require a Microsoft Passport.

MSN Messenger *See* Windows Messenger.

N

netiquette Commonly accepted standards for behavior on the Internet.

news In the context of Usenet, public messages contributed to the newsgroup.

news server An Internet site that can send and receive Usenet newsgroup messages.

newsgroups *See* Usenet.

NNTP A protocol used by servers that offer Usenet, a form of discussion on the Internet. When you subscribe to an Internet service provider, you may be given the name of an NNTP server. Use this name to set up newsgroups on Outlook Express or another program that offers access to Usenet.

O

offline viewing Looking at a Web document while not actually connected to the Internet. If your telephone and your computer share the same line, you can look at pages offline as you're talking on the phone—which you can't do if you're viewing online.

P

Passport *See* Microsoft Passport.

password A word, phrase, or combination of letters, numbers, and punctuation that you must use to gain access to a Web site, online store, Internet service provider, or another service on the Internet. It's a good idea to make your passwords impossible for others to guess; one way to do this is to make a password two unrelated words separated by a punctuation mark (such as **eve*school** or **ace!radar**). *See also username.*

phishing An attempt to steal a user's password or credit-card information. On America Online and other places where instant messages and chat are popular, a person might masquerade as a system administrator who needs your password or credit-card number because of a problem of some kind. This is always a hoax: No legitimate employee of an Internet provider asks for this information in email, instant messages, or a chat room.

pop-under window An extra browser window that opens as you are visiting a Web page but is immediately minimized and out of view. The window shows up on your taskbar with other browser windows that have been opened but are not currently visible. Like pop-up windows, these are used most often for advertising purposes.

pop-up window An extra browser window that opens as you are visiting a Web page, usually to display advertising. The name comes from the way they pop up on the screen in front of the page you're trying to view.

POP3 (Post Office Protocol version 3) A protocol used by servers that deliver email. When you set up an account with an Internet service provider, your provider will often give you the name of a POP3 server to use when receiving mail. Save this information; you need it to set up an email program such as Outlook Express.

portal A commercial Web site that functions as a gateway to the Internet. If you designate a portal as your browser's home page, you can start every online session on that page, giving some structure to your Internet experience.

presets Shortcuts to your favorite Web radio stations in Windows Media Player 7. Click a preset to begin listening to a particular station.

proxy server A server set up between your computer and the Internet (generally in an office or academic environment). To get to the Internet, you have to go through the proxy server, which performs security checks to make sure that outsiders cannot access your company's network illegally. Also called a *firewall.*

publish To upload files to a Web server to make those files available to users of the Internet. One way to design Web pages is to create them on your computer and then publish the pages to a Web server that has direct access to the Internet.

S

screen name *See* username.

ScreenTip A small pop-up box containing text that defines or describes a particular area of the screen. You can display a ScreenTip by hovering the mouse cursor over the area of the screen in question. Some applications call the ScreenTips that appear for toolbar buttons *ToolTips.*

search engines World Wide Web sites that use computers to catalog millions of Web pages, which you can use to search for specific text. Some of the most popular search engines are AltaVista (`http://www.altavista.com`), Google (`http://www.google.com`), and HotBot (`http://hotbot.lycos.com`).

secure Web server Most often used for online shopping. A secure server encrypts information (such as a credit-card number) that is sent to the server and received from it so that confidential information is hidden from anyone who might try to view it. These servers make use of Secure Sockets Layer (SSL), a protocol for protecting private information over the Internet.

security certificate A special browser window that vouches for the authenticity of a program's author. After you see the security certificate, you can decide whether you want to let the program run on your machine. A security certificate is required only when you're working with ActiveX technology; Java doesn't require this kind of direct action by the user.

server A computer that sends information to other computers, either in response to a request or through an automated schedule. A popular type of server on the Internet is a Web server.

signature file Text that is automatically appended to email, Usenet postings, and similar documents. These files often contain your name, email address, favorite quote, and other personal information.

SMTP (Simple Mail Transfer Protocol) Like POP3, a protocol used by email servers. When you sign up with an Internet service provider, your provider will often give you the name of an SMTP server to use when sending mail. You need this information to set up an email program such as Outlook Express.

spam A kind of unsolicited Internet marketing in which thousands of email messages are sent out to anyone with an email account. An electronic version of junk mail, spam often promotes unsavory businesses and is forged so that the sender's identity is hidden. Spam is a widely loathed practice that is illegal to send in a few jurisdictions. The name was inspired by a Monty Python comedy sketch and is unrelated to the Hormel spiced meat product of the same name.

SSL *See* secure Web server.

status area *See* system tray.

streaming audio Sound on the Internet that begins playing as soon as the file is selected rather than at the end of a complete download of the sound file. This format is especially well suited for concerts and live radio.

synchronization In Outlook Express, the process of receiving new messages in Usenet newsgroups to which you have subscribed.

system tray The part of your Windows taskbar that's next to the current time (usually in the lower-right corner of the display screen). This is also called the *status area*, and it may contain icons representing your Internet connection, speaker volume, antivirus software, and other programs that are running on your computer.

T

taskbar The strip along the bottom or side of your Windows display screen in which appear the Start button, the buttons for all active programs, the current system time, and the system tray.

ticker symbol A short, unique code assigned to a company by the stock exchange on which that company trades.

ToolTip *See* ScreenTip.

U

URL (uniform resource locator) A unique address that identifies a document on the World Wide Web. You can direct your browser to a particular Web page by typing the page's URL in an address field and pressing **Enter**. A site's address can take many forms, but most of the largest Web sites have similar-looking and simple URLs, such as `http://www.yahoo.com`, `http://www.quepublishing.com`, and `http://www.metafilter.com`.

Usenet A collection of public discussion groups covering a diverse range of topics. Usenet groups, which also are called *newsgroups*, are distributed by thousands of Internet sites around the world.

username A short version of your name, nickname, or handle that identifies you on a Web site or another service offered on the Internet. On America Online, a username is called a *screen name*. A username is usually paired with a password, and many Web sites such as Yahoo! require both of these when you are logging in to access the personalized features of the site.

V

virus A program that creates copies of itself, usually without permission, and may cause damage to files on your computer or reveal personal data to others. Viruses can be spread on floppy disks and by email, so you should protect yourself by installing an antivirus program on your computer. You also should not open any attached file you receive in email unless you know the sender (especially if the file is a program).

visualization In a sound player such as the Windows Media Player or WinAMP, an animated program that reacts to sound as it is being played.

W

Web browser The tool that lets you view pages on the World Wide Web. After you connect to the Internet, you load a browser; then you can see and interact with pages on the Web. Some of the most popular browsers are Microsoft Internet Explorer, Netscape Navigator, and Opera. Internet Explorer 6 is used in many of the tasks in this book.

Web directory World Wide Web sites that use human editors to categorize thousands of Web sites according to their content and make recommendations about the best sites. The main way to use these directories is to navigate to the categories you are interested in. Web directories include Yahoo! (`http://www.yahoo.com`), Lycos (`http://www.lycos.com`), and the Open Directory Project (`http://www.dmoz.org`).

Web server A server on the Internet that sends Web pages and other documents in response to requests by Web browsers. Everything you view on the World Wide Web is delivered by a Web server to your browser. *See also* server.

Web site A group of related Web pages. When you are creating related Web pages in a program such as FrontPage Express, you should make an effort to link all the pages together as a site.

weblog A Web site that's published as a series of diary-style entries, usually with the most recent entry listed first. Weblogs are often used to link to interesting Web sites and share personal details of the publisher's life. Two good examples: CamWorld at the URL `http://www.camworld.com` and MetaFilter at the URL `http://www.metafilter.com`.

Windows Messenger Instant-messaging software from Microsoft that has an estimated 25 million users. You can send and receive instant messages, keep a list of contacts you communicate with regularly, and send email when one of the contacts is not connected to Messenger.

wizard A program that divides a task into a series of simple questions, making it easier to complete the task. Most software developed by Microsoft includes an installation wizard that simplifies the process of setting up the program on your computer.

Index

A

B

C

D

E

F

G - H

J – K

L

M

N

O

P - Q

X – Z